THE ECONOMY OF DUBAI

The Economy of Dubai

Edited by
ABDULRAZAK AL FARIS
and
RAIMUNDO SOTO

OXFORD
UNIVERSITY PRESS

OXFORD
UNIVERSITY PRESS

Great Clarendon Street, Oxford, OX2 6DP,
United Kingdom

Oxford University Press is a department of the University of Oxford.
It furthers the University's objective of excellence in research, scholarship,
and education by publishing worldwide. Oxford is a registered trade mark of
Oxford University Press in the UK and in certain other countries

First Edition published in 2016

Published in the United States of America by Oxford University Press
198 Madison Avenue, New York, NY 10016, United States of America

British Library Cataloguing in Publication Data
Data available

Library of Congress Control Number: 2015944463

ISBN 978–0–19–875838–9

Acknowledgements

The editors of the book and the Secretary General of the Dubai Economic Council would like to express their gratitude to all the contributors to this fine piece of economic research, including authors, research assistants, and all government entities that helped make this volume possible. In particular, we would like to thank the directors and staff of the Dubai Statistics Center, the Dubai Land Department, the Dubai Department of Tourism and Commerce Marketing, the Dubai Ports and Free Zones Authority, Dubai Customs, the Dubai Knowledge and Human Development Authority, the Dubai Department of Economic Development, the Dubai Electricity and Water Authority, the Department of Finance, the Dubai Events and Promotions Establishment, Dubai Municipality, the Dubai Supreme Council of Energy, and the Dubai School of Government. The editors would also like to thank Hosam Ibrahim and Irfan Al Hasani for their relentless support and significant contributions throughout the publication process.

Contents

List of Figures

List of Tables

List of Contributors

Abdulrazak Al Faris works at present as chief economist counselor of Economic Policy and Research Center, the operational arm of the Secretariat-General of Dubai Economic Council. He obtained his PhD in economics, from the University of Oxford, in April 1990. He has held several academic and official positions, including professor of economics, UAE University, associate dean for Scientific Research, College of Business, UAE University, alternate executive director, IMF (1999–2001), visiting scholar at Oxford University, MIT, Dundee University, and OPEC. Prior to joining academia, he held several governmental positions in the UAE, including assistant under-secretary for Planning, Ministry of Education. In addition, he worked as a consultant to UNDP, Crown Prince Court (Abu Dhabi), Ministry of Economy, National Assembly, Dubai Municipality, Department of Economy (Dubai), and as an economic advisor to the Federation of Chamber of Commerce and Industry, and Tanmia. His research interests include the energy market, with special emphasis on oil and gas, the economics of labour markets, education and human resources, poverty and income distribution, and macroeconomic policies and public finance. He has published fourteen books, and numerous articles in international refereed journals in both English and Arabic, and attended more than 100 international and regional conferences, forums, and symposia.

Raimundo Soto is associate professor of economics, Pontificia Universidad Católica de Chile. He received his PhD in economics from Georgetown University. Professor Soto specializes in macroeconomic theory and econometrics and has published extensively in international journals on long-run growth, exchange rate misalignment, and monetary policy, as well as corruption, resource curse, institutions, and labour markets. He has been a visiting scholar in institutions in the US, Europe, Asia, and Latin America and international organizations such as the World Bank and the Federal Reserve Bank of Minneapolis. Professor Soto served as president of the Chilean Economic Association and, between 2010 and 2012, he was Director of International Development at the Dubai Economic Council.

Hessa Al Ameemi specializes in research and planning. She gained skills in project management at the Dubai Economic Council. Hessa has an MSc in Project Management from the British University in Dubai Associated with Manchester University and has a BSc in Integrated Communication from Zayed University. She has had training experience with Meydan, Azadea

Company-Virgin Megastore, The United Arab Emirates Ministry of State for Federal National Council Affairs, and has worked for the Arab-US Association for Communication Educators event organization Committee (AUSACE). She has been involved in Zayed University, Academic Excellence for several years.

Mahmoud Al Iriani is economic advisor at the Economic Policy Research Center (EPRC), Dubai Economic Council (DEC) in Dubai, UAE. He received his PhD in economics from Kansas State University (KSU) in 1998. He subsequently joined Sana'a University (SU), Yemen as an assistant professor of economics at the College of Commerce and Economics. In the year 2000, he left for the United Arab Emirates where he joined the United Arab Emirates University (UAEU) in Al Ain. Dr Mahmoud spent six years in the UAEU, where he taught courses and conducted research at the College of Business. In June 2006, Dr Mahmoud returned to Yemen where he rejoined Sana'a University as an associate professor of economics. After spending four years at Sana'a University, Dr Mahmoud was offered his current position at DEC in April 2010. During his professional career, Dr Mahmoud has been teaching college students, participating in community services, and doing scientific research, mostly in the area of economic policy. Dr Mahmoud has a number of published and unpublished research articles and working papers, and he has refereed research articles for a number of regional and international journals.

Eshrak Al Maamari worked as a research assistant at the Economic Policy and Research Center at the Dubai Economic Council. She graduated from the UAE University-College of Business & Economics and specialized in Economics. She has trained at the Dubai Electricity and Water Authority (DEWA), 'UAEU women's Debate Society' United Arab Emirates University, Al Ain 'Opportunities and challenges for Female Entrepreneurs in Times of Global Crisis workshop' UAEU, Al Ain, 'Stock Game Competition' Dubai Financial Market and is currently working for DEWA.

Ali Tawfik Al Sadik joined the Dubai Economic Council in 2007 as a senior economist/project manager. He worked at the Arab Monetary Fund for almost a quarter of a century where he held leading roles in research and management; the last was as director of the Economic Policy Institute. Dr Al Sadik has published over forty papers and edited nine books on various economic and finance topics, authored *Arab Economic Integration* and published more than 100 newspaper articles in *Alhayat* and *Alkhaleej* newspapers. Dr Al Sadik holds a PhD from North Carolina State University and an MSc from the American University of Beirut.

Ibrahim Elbadawi has been the director of the Macroeconomic and Forecasting Department of the Dubai Economic Council since March 2009. Until February 2009 he was lead economist at the Development Research Group of the World Bank, which he joined in 1989; and before that he was an associate professor of economics at the University of Gezira in Sudan. He has published widely on macroeconomic and development policy, democratic transitions, and the economics of civil wars and post-conflict transitions. He is (a non-resident) research fellow at the Center for Global Development and an associate editor of the *Middle East Development Journal.* He is the thematic leader for the Natural Resource Management and Economic Diversification theme at the Economic Research Forum and member of the Advisory Board of the Arab Planning Institute.

Dhuha Fadhel was, at the time of writing, senior economist at the Dubai Economic Council where she worked for more than six years. Dhuha holds a Bachelor in Economics from UAE University, an MSc in finance and banking from The British University in Dubai and an MSc in economics from Warwick University in the UK. Her research interests cover economic development and financial economics. Dhuha has a number of published and unpublished research papers. Prior to joining DEC, Dhuha worked as a sales and production planning analyst at Dubai Aluminum Company. She has also worked as a short-term consultant for the World Bank in the Kingdom of Saudi Arabia.

Michael Klein is Senior Adjunct Professor of International Economics at Johns Hopkins University. He recently served as vice president for financial and private sector development at the World Bank. In the past Professor Klein was visiting professor at Harvard University, chief economist of Royal Dutch Shell Group, and headed the Non-Member Country Unit in the Organization for Economic Co-operation and Development's Economics Department. His current research interests include infrastructure policy and regulation, business environment policy and regulations, and mobile banking regulation. Professor Klein received his PhD in economics from the University of Bonn in Germany.

Boaz Nandwa is an economist with the International Monetary Fund. Previously he served as senior economist at the Dubai Economic Council and as an assistant professor of economics at universities in the US and UAE. He has also served as a consultant at the United Nations University (UNU)/WIDER. Dr Nandwa holds a PhD in economics from Kansas State University and Post-doc from the Economic Growth Center, Yale University.

Yousif Rashid worked as an editor at the Economic Policy and Research Center, Dubai Economic Council. He graduated from Southern Methodist University (SMU)-Dallas, Texas with double major, Bachelor of Science in Economics with distinction and Bachelor of Arts in Philosophy. In 2010 he specialized in finance and marketing. After leaving the DEC, Mr Rashid worked primarily as a web programmer and analyst in the private sector in the USA.

Mohamed Trabelsi is a senior economist at the Dubai Economic Council and research associate of the Economic Research Forum (ERF). He holds a PhD in economics and was former professor of economics at Carthage University (Tunisia) and researcher at the Centre de Recherche et Developpement en Economique (University of Montreal). He is also a member of the Middle East Economic Association (MEEA) and the Société Canadienne de Science Economique (SCSE). He has written extensively on growth and financial reforms in developing countries and participated many times in international conferences. His main contributions include empirical investigations on the finance and growth nexus in the MENA region and has recently published his latest book *Growth Theory*. His current research focuses on capital account reforms in developing economies.

1

Introduction

Abdulrazak Al Faris and Raimundo Soto

Despite its small size, the Emirate of Dubai has garnered public attention and worldwide media coverage as a vibrant and dynamic economy. Numerous books and articles have been published on Dubai's history, social life, and modern architecture. Yet, a comprehensive study of the economy of Dubai, with a systematic analysis of its achievements and its failures, its strengths and weaknesses, is currently unavailable. Against this background, this book provides an economic and historical account of the evolution of Dubai since the foundation of the United Arab Emirates in 1971, focusing on its transformations and experiences over the years, and the roles played by government policies and private sector initiative. This book, therefore, aims at filling the gaps in our understanding of the trajectory of modern Dubai and, based on solid analysis, it provides a perspective and policy recommendations on the way forward in an intensely increasing competitive global economy.

A study of the economic structure and experience of Dubai is important for several reasons. First, its current development stance is the result of a long tradition of commitment of its government to liberal and open-economy policies. This book provides a systematic account of such policies and their effects both in the long and short run, placing emphasis on how Dubai rides the current globalization wave, a period where most economies in the world are embracing and benefiting from similar liberal policies. Since its foundation in the early 1830s by the Al Maktoum family, Dubai has cultivated an image of a business-friendly city. Its successive rulers consistently adhered to the open-door, pro-business philosophy and continuously supported international trade by reducing trade barriers and improving maritime port facilities (such as deepening the Dubai Creek, establishing Rashid port, and dredging Jebel Ali port to accommodate more and larger ships that could operate at lower costs). These initiatives created a healthy business environment and provided generous trade incentives that attracted merchants and businessmen from neighbouring countries. By the second half of the nineteenth century, Dubai was already reputed to be the main port connecting the Arabian Gulf with India and Africa. In the first half of the twentieth century Dubai consolidated its free-market economy, navigated through the turmoil of two world wars and the Big Depression, and re-asserted its vision of private initiative as the basis for sustained economic growth. It was not surprising then that during the oil rush of the 1970s and 1980s, when most Arab Gulf countries favoured a model based on a welfare state and a large public sector to absorb the national labour force, Dubai, on the contrary, adopted a strategy based on investing oil revenues on infrastructure and diverse industries, resisting the pressure to have a large, overstaffed public sector. Furthermore, it continued to maintain its free-market principle by declining OPEC's policies of fixing oil prices, preferring to sell its crude oil in the international spot market.

Second, perhaps one of the most remarkable achievements of Dubai is its success in diversifying its economic base away from hydrocarbons. Most likely, it is one of the few countries in recent economic history to be capable of engineering a complete turnaround in its economic base and, deservedly, has become the undisputed regional leader in terms of integration to the global business community, modernization of economic activities and government policies, as well as for its ability to developing its financial sector, trade, and tourism industries. With oil production peaking at about 500,000 bpd in the late 1970s and early 1980s, Dubai's government embarked on ambitious investment programmes aimed at modernizing the city infrastructure and building a multi-sector economy that depended less on the hydrocarbon sector. In the early 1980s the share of the oil sector in Dubai's GDP was 45 per cent; by 2010 it was reduced to less than 5 per cent. This achievement is the main outcome of three successive strategic plans (1996, 2003, and 2007) designed to prepare Dubai for the post-oil era. The plans envisaged the diversification of the economy as a response to the depleting oil reserves and aimed at concentrating efforts in the development of carefully selected sectors deemed to attain a sustainable high rate of economic growth, and emphasized the development of human resources through better health services, education, training, and talent attraction and retention.

Third, realizing its limited hydrocarbon resources, Dubai embarked on an purposeful plan of institutional reforms that allowed the economy to stay ahead of the curve in the region in terms of innovation, competitiveness, and legislation upgrading. As discussed extensively in the different chapters of this book, these modernizing institutional reforms have been decisive in allowing private sector initiatives to flourish and industries to be developed. Government efforts initiated the development and modernization of infrastructure. In 1980 the Jebel Ali port was transformed into an independently operated, multi-industry free zone which became the first of its kind in the region and, in time, one of the largest in the world. The success of the institutional framework of Jebel Ali later led to the subsequent establishment of several new free zones devoted to rising industries (such as technology and media, internet, healthcare, and commodities) and to areas that have been traditionally neglected in the region such as international finance. The government also took the initiative of fostering strategic industries by developing an institutional framework that allows public sector property of companies to be managed in an independent and autonomous manner using modern private-sector regulations and incentives. This scheme of development was applied first to Emirates Airlines and its success paved the way for its application—with varying degrees of accomplishment—to other industries such as the Dubai Metro and some heavy industrial projects in aluminium smelting (Dubal) and high-voltage cables (Ducab). Since the mid 1990s, the Dubai International Financial Center (DIFC) has offered a modern institutional, legal, and judiciary framework attracting large-size multinational companies and financial institutions to install or relocate their regional headquarters to Dubai.

Fourth, due to physical limitations, weather conditions, and a lack of more scenic and cultural attractions, most Arab Gulf countries were historically tourist senders and not receivers. Dubai has set a new model by investing in a luxury international tourism industry that emphasizes high-end tourism and related cluster services: shopping malls, transport, tour operation, recreations, beach facilities, restaurants, and cafes. This was supported by well-articulated activities: sports events, shopping festivals, exhibitions, and conferences. Within a short period of time Dubai has become the preferred destination for travellers and the second largest tourist recipient in the Arab world after Saudi Arabia. Growth of the tourism sector has in the recent past supported the growth of other sectors of the economy, in particular services, trade, and transport.

Despite its long-term successes, Dubai has exhibited some of the classical weaknesses inherent to small open economies. While its open-door policy has contributed immensely to high economic growth and general welfare improvements, this policy has, nevertheless, also exposed Dubai to adverse external shocks. It is not, therefore, a coincidence that the three major economic downturns of the economy of Dubai (in the 1930s, 1980s, and 2008–10) have been originated by external shocks. For instance, during the 1930s and early 1940s, Dubai suffered from a protracted recession brought about by the large drop in the global demand for natural pearls courtesy of two events: the discovery of synthetic pearls by Japan and the Great Depression of 1929–33. Similarly, in the 1980s, Dubai's economy experienced a relatively long period of stagnation caused by the collapse of oil prices and the prolonged Iraq–Iran war (1980–8). The international financial crisis of 2008–10 also wreaked havoc on the Dubai economy and exacerbated the property bubble and public debt problem.

As it is argued in many parts of this book, the negative consequences of external shocks can be ameliorated when countries are better diversified in their economic base, export mix and destinations, and sources of public revenues. Small open economies are more vulnerable when they rely heavily on one or two sectors, when exports comprise a relatively small set of products, when goods are exported to fewer destinations, and when countries do not have well-structured public finances. While Dubai has made big strides during the last two decades in reducing its reliance on the oil sector, the studies in this volume show that there is an urgent need to accelerate economic reforms in a direction that will allow the economy of Dubai to move away from labour-intensive, low-skill activities to high-value-added globally competitive industries. Moreover, it needs to capitalize on its excellent geographical location and modern infrastructure to broaden its foreign trade by relying less on re-export and reinvigorate its exports. Dubai urgently requires modern public finance management that sets the stage for a well-designed structure for budget revenues that replaces the old fashioned fees and charges with few taxes. In the long run, initiatives dealing with fiscal transparency and responsibility, human capital development, and regulatory environments are necessary ingredients for sustainable growth and competitiveness.

1.1 THE AGGREGATE PERSPECTIVE

The first part of this book is dedicated to understanding the evolution of the economy of Dubai from an aggregate or macroeconomic perspective. This ample perspective aims at three objectives. First, it provides a long-run overview of the development of the emirate that serves as a frame for the subsequent analysis of sectors and markets. Second, it reviews the stance of one of the main actors in the development of Dubai—the government—in terms of its ability to guide the economy on its long-term path and its capacity to finance its share of the process. Third, it reviews the evolution and contributions of the other main actor in development—the private sector—aiming at unveiling the determinants of investment and productivity gains. As is amply recognized by policymakers and experts, the engine of growth rests on ever-increasing productivity levels: without investment in physical capital, education, technology, and institutions, development is not attainable and welfare does not increase.

Chapter 2 of this book by Ali Tawfik Al Sadik offers a long-term perspective on the economic growth of Dubai since its foundation in the early nineteenth century. In a concise manner, it traces its development path from a small fishing port in the Arabian Gulf to its current modern economy status. Al Sadik provides evidence of a notable period of sustained economic growth between 1975 and 2011, which locates Dubai as one of the economies with the fastest pace of development in the world. Nevertheless, he also finds two important weaknesses in the sustainability of Dubai's development path.

First, there is evidence that the phenomenal growth of the economy was mainly induced by the expansion of production factors, labour and capital, and not by achieving ever higher productivity levels. In fact, labour productivity in Dubai (measured by output per working-age person) remained stagnant for a long period of time (1987–2004). Total factor productivity—a measure closely related to economic efficiency—has grown slower in Dubai than in other economies enjoying similar structural characteristics (small, open, natural-resource-limited economies) such as Hong Kong and Singapore: in the period 1975–2008, total productivity in Dubai grew 1.6 per cent per year while that of Hong Kong and Singapore was 2.1 per cent and 2.5 per cent, respectively. Most chapters in this book provide complementary perspectives on why productivity has not grown as fast as would have been expected in the dynamic economy of Dubai and unanimously conclude that sustainable development requires policy reforms aimed at making production less resource dependent and increasingly more efficient.

Second, the economy of Dubai also exhibits significant vulnerability to external shocks and production is volatile despite its limited dependence on the hydrocarbon sector. Volatility of the growth rate of GDP in Dubai is more than twice that of Singapore and Hong Kong and more than four times that of the world GDP. The economy has also been historically sensitive to global economic cycles, in particular to the global financial crisis of 2008–10. The latter revealed that economic growth in Dubai during the first decade of the twenty-first century was largely influenced by large real estate projects that were financed mainly by a massive increase in public debt (mainly from government-related entities operating in real estate projects). Once such public debt could not be serviced, austerity measures enacted by the government led to a severe economic contraction.

The slow growth of productivity is indisputable evidence of important weaknesses in the development path of Dubai and points to the urgent need to undertake corrective measures since most of the empirical evidence indicates that sustained growth in the long run is largely dependent upon significant improvements in factor productivity. Productivity-enhancing measures are, most of the time, of a sectorial and microeconomic nature and they deal with issues such as human capital formation, technology upgrading, and physical capital accumulation. These policies, which are thoroughly reviewed in the remaining chapters of the book, tend to take a long time to produce their effects but when successful the effects are significant and sustainable.

The vulnerability of economic development in Dubai is partly the result of the lack of automatic stabilizers in the economy, themselves the outcome of government policies at both the federal and local level. In most economies, the excessive liquidity that in Dubai helped finance speculative real estate transactions that drove asset prices to unsustainable levels would have been dealt with by currency appreciation, thus releasing to some extent the financial pressure. The fixed exchange rate of the UAE prevented such automatic stabilization and weakened the capacity of the financial sector to accommodate the negative external shock. Nevertheless, it is also the result of the absence of expenditure stabilizers as the tax system cannot perform its countercyclical role (since it is largely based on fixed fees and not *ad valorem* levies) and government expenditures tend to be pro-cyclical (the result of the lack of consolidated, multiannual budget procedures).

The economy of Dubai is largely shaped by the absence of monetary policy resulting from fixing the exchange rate to the US dollar. This effectively eliminates monetary and exchange rate policies, leaving the authorities with fiscal policy as their main policy instrument. But fiscal policy in Dubai is limited vis-à-vis most economies in the use of taxes and other forms of government revenues since income and value-added taxes are conspicuously absent. The government, in fact, exacts taxes mainly in the form of fees for services which complement other revenues arising from its numerous business endeavours in real estate and trading. In Chapter 3 Boaz Nandwa and Ali Tawfik Al Sadik analyse the perils of having such an unusual revenue structure for fiscal policy.

The limited capability of the fiscal policy in Dubai came prominently to the fore during the global crisis of 2008–10. The precarious debt stance of government-related entities (GREs) forced the government to intervene and reschedule payments, sending waves rippling through the financial sector and the more exposed sectors of the economy (particularly real estate and construction). Nandwa and Al Sadik study the evolution of this crisis and its resolution as well as the outlook for the immediate future which is largely shaped by Dubai's need to repay a weighty proportion of its foreign debts in the period 2014–19. Whenever countries face significant financial obligations, fiscal sustainability issues inevitably arise. The authors discuss the major determinants of this crisis and, while indicating the soundness of the current fiscal policy, warn us that additional efforts are needed to mitigate risks arising from the timing of payments, the amount of the debt, and the perception of risks arising from the opaqueness in the performance of several GREs.

This first part of the book closes with a look into the future of Dubai's economy and the challenges ahead particularly from an institutional viewpoint. Michael Klein's chapter takes a long-term view of the economic history of the emirate, compares it with the trajectory of other successful cities (such as Singapore or Hong Kong), and provides answers to the following crucial questions: how will the demand for services for a place like Dubai develop in the future? And, what can Dubai do to develop new competencies?

Klein first identifies the sectors that are most likely to be at the heart of the long-term development of the emirate: tourism, financial services, and foreign trade. These sectors were shocked by the global downturn of the period 2008–10 and, while they recovered and regained momentum with the normalization of the world economy, Klein warns us of the vulnerability of the economy and points out that the emergence of regional competitors is a threat that needs addressing in the form of improved policies and market regulations. He also foretells that a new industry—medical tourism—holds the potential to become a significant contributor to economic growth but has yet to start developing.

The main contribution of Chapter 4, however, is not in identifying current and potential engines of sustained growth but its careful analysis of what is needed for such engines to fully realize their potential. In particular, Klein calls for enhancing the 'freedom to fail'. His argument stems from the notion that the development of businesses in Dubai is not only about attracting investors under good conditions but also about setting rules of the game that are clear, transparent, and conducive to an environment where only the most productive businesses survive. Producers must be free to fail because what matters for development is not more business, but more productive businesses. Predicting which businesses will be best for Dubai is not a task for the government but it can help in preparing and levelling the ground and it can even facilitate the development of certain sectors: ultimately competition will reveal what works and what does not.

1.2 THE CONTRIBUTION OF ECONOMIC SECTORS

The second part of the book takes a long-run view on the evolution of the most important sectors in the economy of Dubai. Small open economies—as is the case of Dubai—cannot rely on domestic demand for sustained development and must turn to foreign markets. The latter provide sizeable demand for exported products which in turn allow domestic producers to reap scale economies, incentivize the adoption of better and advanced production techniques, and reward prudent investment and the creativity of exporters. Moreover, foreign trade disciplines firms by forcing them to operate in more competitive environments. Overall, this boosts the efficiency and productivity of domestic firms thereby enhancing their competitiveness in the global markets. In Chapter 5, Raimundo Soto and Boaz Nandwa provide an analysis of Dubai's foreign trade stance and use econometric models to determine its trade potential.

The authors document how Dubai has benefited from its strategic geographical location and from developing world-class transportation and logistics networks aimed at making the emirate a leading hub of international trade. Participation in international trade has enabled Dubai to diversify and grow. However, improving its competitive capacity, building a resilient economic base, and profiting from the opportunities provided by fast-changing global markets require comprehensive trade policies to address the issues inherent to Dubai's trade patterns. In particular, because the advantages in terms of location as a regional hub are not unique to Dubai: Qatar, Bahrain, and even the other emirates share a similar location and could become competitors for, essentially, the same trade routes and cargo.

Soto and Nandwa identify several pressing issues that need policy actions. First and foremost, there is ample space for Dubai to expand exporting and re-exporting activities. Most countries with a similar size to Dubai's economy tend to export substantially more: the city-state economies that Dubai would like to emulate in its role of regional trade hubs—such as Hong Kong or Singapore—export and re-export four or five times more than Dubai. Fostering exports and re-exports should be a priority for Dubai's trade policy. Second, Dubai's exports and re-exports appear to be dangerously concentrated both in terms of the product space and in partners. Over 50 per cent of exports and re-exports are concentrated in one good (gold and jewellery), putting Dubai in a risky position as changes in international gold prices are frequent and hard to anticipate. In addition, Dubai's exports and re-exports are also largely concentrated on two partners: India and Iran. While trade with India ought to increase in the future as the Indian subcontinent grows, trade with Iran is far riskier. While historically Iran has been an important trade partner, current trade volumes are largely the result of UN sanctions and they would certainly reduce significantly should the sanctions be relaxed or lifted altogether. Third, Dubai's export and re-exports are concentrated on goods with low technological content and with little linkage to the rest of the economy: gold and jewellery contain some processing but their elaboration is not very sophisticated and does not link significantly with other industries.

In recent years, several countries have given importance and policy support to the development of free-trade zones, aiming at enhancing their exports and economic growth. Free zones are special areas or enclaves isolated from domestic economies, primarily designed to attract foreign investment, boost exports, and create employment in the host economy. In many countries these free zones have been quite successful, while in others they have failed to entice the private sector. Irrespective of their success, it is generally believed that their contribution to economic activity and growth is not substantial for the simple reason of their disconnection with the rest of the economy, its minor contribution to government revenue, and their tendency to use unskilled labour. This important issue is discussed by Mahmoud Al Iriani, Ibrahim Elbadawi, and Dhuha Fadhel in Chapter 6, which provides an empirical analysis of the linkages between the industries in the free zones and the economic sectors of Main Dubai.

Realizing their potential, the government of Dubai has encouraged the establishment of a number of free zones. JAFZA, the first of such endeavours, has become one of the largest and fastest growing free zones in the world. This chapter examines their evolution and assesses their economic and social impact on the economy of Dubai. A detailed sample of 700 firms operating in both free zones and Main Dubai in 2010, allows the authors to study the determinants and quantify the importance of three types of linkages (downstream production chains, labour markets, and the financial sector) while controlling for firm-specific characteristics, sectorial specialization, and economic region.

The empirical analysis by Al Iriani, Elbadawi, and Fadhel provides a wealth of results concerning the behaviour of firms and entrepreneurs in the different sectors and according to the characteristics of firms. On the basis of such results, which are amply discussed in the chapter, the authors distil several conclusions and useful policy recommendations. In particular, they find that conditional on firm characteristics and sectorial specialization, JAZFA firms are more likely than their counterparts in Main Dubai to create backward linkages with the labour market as well as with the financial sector. However, JAFZA firms do not link to local providers of intermediate goods while firms in Main Dubai do so. The other major free zone found to have a significant impact is the DIFC—and only in labour markets—while the rest of the free zones perform in similar fashion as firms outside free zones in Main Dubai. This evidence allows the authors to suggest that the positive externality of free zones make them an ideal tool for enhancing Emirati employment. Therefore, incentive packages ought to be provided by the government to firms willing to hire nationals on engineering, financial, and other relatively high-paying non-managerial professions. As a medium- to longer-term strategy, a major re-alignment of the educational system toward professions that are in high demand by the Dubai private sector will be required to eventually create a critical mass of nationals with the required professional qualifications and skills. The evidence also seems to indicate a role for the government in fostering potential upstream industries that could supply manufacturing firms and, subsequently, provide the appropriate incentives for the private sector to invest in these industries. Finally, the authors propose enhancing the linkages of JAFZA with the local industry in Main Dubai, for example by allowing local firms supplying intermediate inputs to firms in JAFZA to recover the customs fees on their imported primary inputs.

While trading goods has been historically the most important activity of foreign markets, trading services at the international level is becoming a crucial sector for sustained economic growth, particularly for small economies. Among traded services, tourism is undoubtedly at the forefront and grows at a spectacular rate: while in 1990 the number of worldwide international tourist arrivals amounted to 420 million, in 2012 the same number had reached one billion. Dubai recognized the importance of tourism long ago and has been investing significant resources to develop its industry with the declared purpose of becoming a regional hub for travellers and the main tourist destination in the Gulf of Arabia.

In Chapter 7 Raimundo Soto evaluates the development strategy of the tourism industry. As a tourist destination Dubai is largely a man-made project. Worldwide, demand depends mostly on the existence of attractions that justify visiting a particular place, the tourist accommodation offer, and the physical infrastructure that determines the quality of the visit for a tourist. The lack of historical, natural, or heritage attractions forced Dubai to base its industry primarily on the development of the latter two elements, which have been supplemented by carefully selected events to lure the visitors (e.g. the World Horse Race Cup or Dubai's shopping festivals). This mix has been quite successful and, until the recent global crisis, it made tourism an engine for sustained growth in Dubai. The crisis forced a pause in the continued growth in tourist arrivals but the authorities remain confident of the potential of the industry. Moreover, in the aftermath of the global crisis the tourism industry recovered faster than other sectors.

Tourism in Dubai has become a key sector and makes a significant contribution to economic activity: the hotels and restaurants segment alone generated around US$3 billion in value added in 2010 (around 3.5 per cent of total GDP). This underestimates the true contribution of the industry as it excludes tourist shopping, entertainment, and transportation as well as the value added of travel agencies and other related services.

Despite its success, Soto indicates the need to reappraise the strategy of the tourism industry, in particular vis-à-vis the emergence of regional contenders (e.g. Qatar). The weaknesses evidenced by the industry during the recent crisis suggest that the business strategy of the sector might have grown to maturity and offers limited expansion in the future. Much of the tourism in Dubai is associated either with the luxury segment of the market (sensitive to income fluctuations) or to low-income travellers (sensitive to price fluctuations); the more stable middle-income segment has been largely neglected. This makes the tourism industry in Dubai riskier than that in better-diversified economies and susceptible to downturns. Furthermore, by focusing on the luxury segment, the industry loses potential visitors from fast-growing emerging economies (China, India, and Brazil). In addition to expanding the scope of visitors, there is a role for the government in reducing the administrative cost for visitors, in particular vis-à-vis entry visas. Visa issuing is a cumbersome, expensive, and arbitrary process by which citizens of some countries are exempt of any requirement or costs while others need to secure a sponsor and pay the exorbitant sum of US$180 for a single-entry, no reapplication visa. International competition in tourism is only likely to increase in the future and current positioning does not guarantee future competitiveness.

Competition in world markets not only depends on the ability of Emirati entrepreneurs to produce and place goods at an advantageous price–quality relationship or to attract tourism, but also on the support and contribution of other sectors. In particular, the financial sector plays a crucial role in providing working capital for producers and trade financing for both exporters and importers, in channelling resources for investment and lending, and allowing the economy to develop instruments to cover fluctuations and business risks. Mohamed Trabelsi and Dhuha Fadhel review Dubai's experience in the financial market in Chapter 8, with particular interest in the operation of domestic banks which serve the largest majority of Dubai firms that have very limited access to the international financial market operating at the Dubai International Financial Center (DIFC).

The analysis of the financial sector starts by reviewing the soundness of the banking sector (assessing capital adequacy ratios, asset quality, and liquidity and profitability indicators) and its conformity with the new Basel requirements. This is most appropriate and timely since the global financial crisis that started in 2008 has unveiled not only the perils of under-regulated and under-supervised financial sectors but also the high cost to be paid by society once such underperforming financial markets fall into distress. Dubai has not been immune to the crisis and the authors discuss the need to address issues pertaining to the existing debt overhang of government-related entities and its effects on the banking sector as well as the limited access of firms to bank financing in Dubai and the preference of the business sector to use internal resources to fund investment operations. If left unresolved, these issues will weigh heavily against the objective of the authorities of turning Dubai into a regional financial hub. Although the banking sector has been closely monitored by financial and monetary authorities in UAE since the unveiling of the global financial crisis in 2008, it seems that more is still needed to keep up the momentum of development steps and adjustments.

Trabelsi and Fadhel identify a set of policy recommendations to improve the working and projections of the financial sector. First, there is a pressing need to improve risk management practices in Dubai-based banks, including investing in data collection, reporting systems, and validation capacity. Banks need to strengthen the role of the chief risk officer, establish internal risk monitoring committees, revise collateral policies, as well as reduce the current high exposure to real estate and construction. Second, the supervisory role of the Central Bank ought to be enhanced by implementing more sophisticated instruments to deal with institutions that might increase systemic risks. Third, there is a pressing need to develop the domestic bonds segment of the market that would reduce instrument incompleteness, allow for banks' recapitalization, and avoid issuing foreign-currency-denominated sovereign bonds in international markets. Fourth, corporate governance standards in the banking sector are to be significantly improved, in particular to instil appropriate levels of accountability and enforce good practices in checks and balances. Finally, risk management frameworks must be implemented in government-related entities to avoid malpractices such as the uncontrolled borrowing that led to frequent demands for bailouts in the past.

In addition to the financial sector, other industries are closely linked to the perceived engines of sustained growth in Dubai, that is, foreign trade and tourism. Retail trade is one such sector and, perhaps, one of the most recognizable attractions of the emirate in the international arena. Boaz Nandwa and Hessa Al Ameemi's study of the retail sector in Chapter 9 is both an assessment of the strengths and weakness of the industry and an evaluation of the role of current regulations in fostering long-term investment and productivity gains. While selling at retail can be succinctly defined as the provision of goods and services to the end consumer, the retail cluster involves not only the producers, the consumers, and the sellers, but also comprises other linked activities that, in a complex and advanced economy such as Dubai, frequently interact with retailers to provide its characteristic shape to the business. In Dubai, retail is distinctively associated with large-sized thematic malls where shopping is provided along with entertainment, hostelling, supermarkets, and a large variety of customer services. Off-mall single shops and community shopping centres are less conspicuous.

Retail activities in the emirate have grown to maturity: its shopping malls are among the largest and most sophisticated in the world, luxury brands thrive, and the population benefits from access to a wide variety of goods and services in all qualities. The traditional form of retail—individual shops alongside the street—has also successfully consolidated and transformed in different areas of the city (from Deira to Bur Dubai), benefiting from their ability to sell in market niches such as textile, gold, and perfumes. Retailing activities have grown quite fast in the last decade and as of 2010 accounted for around 13 per cent of the total GDP of Dubai. In terms of value, the industry is about the same size as the financial sector, the real estate, or the construction sector.

As witnessed in the aftermath of the global economic crisis, activities in the retail cluster are quite sensitive to economic cycles. Casual evidence suggests that luxury and higher-end goods suffered the most, but mass grocery weathered the downturn better and their sales dissipated only slightly. The crisis unveiled some limitations that should be addressed by government policies. First, access to finance is one of the most problematic factors for doing business. Credit contracted with the unravelling of the economic crisis in 2008 and has remained tight afterwards. Second, one out of three companies in Dubai indicates that the labour force is the most problematic factor for doing business. Government regulations and arbitrary labour fees reduce the flexibility of the labour market and the ability of firms to adjust to economic fluctuations. For example, retailers cannot hire part-time workers to cope with seasonal fluctuations (such as Christmas). Third, public bureaucracy is also identified by the CEOs of retail companies as a main limitation when doing business. Bureaucracy, red tape, and the lack of consistency in government rules and regulations further exacerbates inefficiency. There is a perceived lack of transparency in the operation of both the retail sector (and its associate, the real estate sector) and the government. Dubai ranks low in retail and real estate transparency, far below Hong Kong and Singapore and other emerging economies. Transparency becomes a decisive issue when attracting foreign direct investment, improving the operation of the different segments of the markets, and fostering innovation and technological upgrades. To the extent that retail operates largely in an international context, partnership with foreign retail companies is the cornerstone to further development of the retail industry in Dubai.

1.3 THE FACTORS OF SUSTAINED DEVELOPMENT

The third part of the book focuses on the factors underlying economic development in Dubai. Beyond the acquisition and use of intermediate goods, production in modern economies largely depends on the quality and training of its labour force, the working of the labour market, the cost of energy, access to physical capital (particularly land) and, naturally, the efficiency and productivity in the use of such resources.

Chapter 10 by Raimundo Soto presents a thorough assessment of the current stance of education in Dubai. In less than thirty years, Dubai has completely transformed its education sector from a group of weak schools without even its own curriculum into a modern, dynamic education system. Access to primary and secondary education has been extended to the entire population regardless of their nationality, while enrolment in tertiary education has grown dramatically in the last decade. This is a remarkable achievement that speaks highly of the commitment on the part of the government to human capital formation.

Soto's analysis indicates, however, that the task is only half completed. Although access to education has increased markedly, the quality of such education has not progressed at a similar pace. While primary education is of average quality by international standards, secondary education is quite limited and does not match either the skills demanded by the labour market or the minimum abilities required at university level. The evidence indicates that the quality of education is also highly unequal, with private schools outperforming public sector schools by a substantial margin, and gender biased, whereby boys in public sector schools and universities perform worse than girls and drop out at a much higher rate.

A mediocre quality of education system is a serious limitation to long-run development. The government of Dubai recently started to implement measures to improve quality, yet these measures are timid and/or in their initial stages for them to be properly evaluated. The federal government has also started to address the serious limitations of public sector schools and national universities. Soto's main conclusion is that, to improve quality, the government ought to change the industrial organization of the education sector, modifying the incentives given to the different actors so that they operate under more efficient frameworks, implementing new policies where existing ones are insufficient or incomplete, and injecting accountability where none is currently in place.

The natural goal of the education and training system of any economy is to prepare its population to participate efficiently and fruitfully in the labour market. While some students might eventually choose to remain inactive, for most of the population the formation acquired over the years in the different educational entities is a lifelong investment in human capital. In fact, one can judge the quality of the education system by the fate of graduates in the labour market.

Chapter 11, by Raimundo Soto and Yousif Rashid, precisely focuses on the working of the labour market in Dubai. As is the case with other GCC countries, Dubai's workforce is largely shaped by two concurrent phenomena. On one hand, the sponsorship system (*Kafala* in Arabic) governing the participation of expatriates. On the other hand, the protection for nationals embedded in both the Emiratization programme and public sector employment policies.

The *Kafala* has been instrumental in bringing in massive amounts of low-skilled expatriate workers that enter the country under the sponsorship of an Emirati national or Emirati-controlled firm. Since workers cannot change sponsor unless they obtain written consent from its current sponsor, employers enjoy market power and collect sizeable economic rents. On the contrary, Emiratis are not subject to the sponsorship system and are increasingly protected by the rules and regulations emanating from the Emiratization programme. While these shelter them from openly competing with expatriates in the labour market, it reduces their employability (particularly that of young and inexperienced workers with high reservation wages). Since the private sector cannot afford the relatively more expensive national workers, they are mainly employed by the public sector (around 80 per cent are civil servants) and they tend to occupy high-level positions sometimes uncorrelated to their educational achievement.

The evidence collected by Soto and Rashid indicates that, beyond inducing unemployment among Emiratis, the dual labour market causes additional problems. By distorting incentives for effort among Emirati and expatriate workers, current labour market regulations reduce businesses' efficiency and technology adoption. Distortions disconnect efforts from salaries, induce non-accountability, and hamper human capital accumulation. Such distortions are further exacerbated by public employment policies that often use the labour market to distribute oil-based wealth among nationals.

Although the sponsorship system and the existing public sector employment policies are largely responsible for current labour market distortions, historical reasons justify its implementation in the early 1960s when the UAE had to overcome the shortage of native workers in order to develop the countries' physical and industrial infrastructure. Attracting large volumes of low-cost workers with little education may have been the optimal policy at that point. But Dubai can no longer be considered an economy at the take-off stage and, consequently, the *Kafala* system is no longer an efficient development instrument. In keeping the sponsorship system as a centrepiece of economic policy, the authorities might have been induced to believe that increases in labour costs would reduce the profitability of firms and, therefore, the incentives to invest in new, more efficient technologies. The empirical evidence indicates that this is incorrect: private sector profits and wealth have grown significantly since the 1990s and employment has expanded massively, but labour productivity has stagnated because keeping wages low has not given entrepreneurs an incentive to acquire more advanced technologies.

Manpower is, naturally, not the only significant production factor. In Dubai, as discussed by Mahmoud Al Iriani and Eshrak Al Maamari in Chapter 12, the availability of inexpensive energy shapes not only household consumption patterns but also the industrial development of the emirate. As elsewhere, the evolution of the energy sector is affected by five factors, the first three connected to energy supply and the last two linked to energy demand. First, conventional energy resources in Dubai are very limited making the emirate a net energy importer. Second, there are ample possibilities for importing energy resources from other emirates (mainly Abu Dhabi) and neighbouring countries in the Gulf (e.g. Qatar) at very low cost. However, these costs are steadily increasing. Third, while conventional energy resources are scarce, Dubai has great potential for developing alternative types of energy. Fourth, the demand for energy has expanded quite fast in the last decade as a result of the rapid growth in overall economic activity and is expected to continue to grow fast in the foreseeable future. Finally, Dubai's energy sector is also affected by the degree of efficiency in managing available energy resources. As a result of suboptimal government policies, energy efficiency in Dubai is relatively low and can be enhanced by proper policies. Energy efficiency is a key determinant of productivity gains as it demands from producers to enact cost-saving measures and better technologies.

This chapter provides policy recommendations to guide energy provision and use in Dubai along economically rational patterns. The authors indicate the need for expanding the supply chain to keep up with the increasing demand for energy of all types. This, in turn, requires large investments in building new power stations, power transmission lines, and fuel storage and supply facilities. As a result, there are mounting pressures on the public sector to provide such investments. But government provision in the past has not necessarily solved the issue in an efficient manner. In fact, scrutiny of the current supply structure reveals the overwhelming control of the public sector in the production and distribution of energy (electricity is produced and distributed solely by DEWA and other fuels for manufacturing and transportation are provided by a small number of publicly owned companies). Government control has led to prices that are not market-driven and to energy being heavily subsidized. As an alternative, Al Iriani and Al Maamari suggest two complementary policies. First, regarding the supply of energy infrastructure they call for allowing public–private partnership projects and a change in current regulations to increase the private sector's willingness to invest in energy projects. Evidence from other countries reveals that efficiency in energy provision improves when opportunities for the private sector are opened up. Second, for a more rational use of the available energy they call for a combination of demand-side management programmes (such as load management programmes, peak-clipping, and load-shifting in electricity) and economic incentives to reduce consumption (peak-load pricing, energy-saving rebates, etc.). Economic incentives have proved to be the most powerful tool for energy-saving in many countries but in Dubai they have not been used: with minor exceptions, nominal prices of all types of energy are largely fixed (implying that real prices are actually declining) and do not reflect the total cost of production plus the cost to the environment. A reform is, therefore, urgently needed.

In a rapidly expanding economy, the demand for land to locate new business can be overwhelming, particularly in the vicinity of major infrastructure projects such as highways, ports, and airports or financial and business centres. Dubai has been no exception and the unsustainable speculative episode of the late 2000s is an example of the costs and perils of mismanagement. Ibrahim Elbadawi undertakes a thorough evaluation of commercial land markets in Chapter 13. In most economies of the world, land availability is not an issue or deterrent to economic growth. In some economies, as in Europe, land is scarce but appropriate market regulations and well-defined property rights allow the price mechanism to allocate the available land to its most efficient or socially profitable use. Arguably, land markets in these economies can fall prey to speculation and housing price bubbles, thereby suggesting that monitoring is needed in addition to market regulations and property rights. In Dubai the commercial land market is significantly different in all three dimensions and this affects the efficient use of resources, productivity growth, and economic development.

The market for commercial land is based on allocating usage as opposed to rights: only Emirati individuals and companies can own land while expatriates can, at best, obtain a long-term right of usage even within the confines of free zones. While land ownership is widespread in the world, some countries have developed rental markets for land that are highly sophisticated when property changes are not allowed (e.g. central London). This, however, requires an institutional framework for rent leases capable of mimicking the positive outcomes of full property rights. Elbadawi's motivation for inquiring into the functioning of Dubai's land market is the empirical evidence that over 50 per cent of firms surveyed by the 2010 Enterprise Level Survey claimed that 'lack of access to land' is their major obstacle to their business operation. This chapter, therefore, asks two fundamental questions: what are the regulatory and institutional factors that hamper access to land? And, equally important, what are the consequences for economic development?

Elbadawi undertakes an econometric analysis of 709 companies in Dubai and its free zones and finds that, compared to their counterpart in the free zones, firms in Main Dubai are less likely to be constrained in their access to land. This, however, depends also on the ownership of the company: firms in Main Dubai that are foreign owned are more likely to have problems of access to land than their counterparts in free zones or firms in Main Dubai fully owned by Emirati entrepreneurs. With regards to the consequences of restrictions to access land, the author finds that lack of access to land has adverse effects on both physical and human capital investment: firms claiming that they lack access to land invest significantly less in physical capital and provide little or no training to their employees. This has clear negative implications for the industrial development of Dubai's industrial sector.

In the different chapters in this volume the authors have identified strengths and weaknesses in the operation of the different industries and markets. While there is substantial heterogeneity in experiences there is, nevertheless, one common thread emerging from virtually all analyses: the contrasting vigorous and sustained growth of the economy of Dubai with a lacklustre performance in terms of productivity growth. That is precisely the focus of Chapter 14 where Ibrahim Elbadawi studies the differences in productivity levels between firms located in free zones and those located in Main Dubai. The detailed database of 709 firms allows the author to quantify productivity levels and link such estimated values to the different sectors (light and heavy manufacturing, financial and non-financial services, trade, and construction) and the different locations in which they operate. This analysis, therefore, provides microeconomic evidence of the performance of firms and identifies reasons for the observed stagnation in productivity in some sectors of the economy.

The main results can be summarized as follows. First, firms located in the free zones outperform their counterparts in Main Dubai in terms of productivity in four out of five sectors: light manufacturing, heavy manufacturing, financial services, and non-financial services. Second, firms in free zones accumulate higher levels of physical capital, especially in heavy manufacturing and non-financial services, which contribute to their better performance in most sectors. Third, human capital accumulation had contributed more than physical capital to induce a superior performance of firms in free zones when compared to those in Main Dubai. Fourth, unlike physical and human capital, labour intensity has had no impact on the differences in value added observed between the two economic regions. Fifth, the differences in labour productivity observed are largely shaped by the combined effect of location—free zones vs Main Dubai—and total factor productivity (TFP). The positive externality of being located in the free zones provides the largest contribution to the differences in value added in favour of the free zone in all sectors, except for the trading sector. In addition, differences in TFP reinforce the location advantage of firms in free zones in three out of five sectors (light manufacturing, heavy manufacturing, and financial services). However, firms in Main Dubai outperform in terms of productivity those in free zones in trading and non-financial services.

The last chapter of this volume, by its editors, collects the main policy recommendations by the authors of each chapter and provides a comprehensive view of the reforms needed to foster and sustain economic growth in Dubai in the decades to come. There is now consensus among scholars and policymakers that sustained economic growth and successful development strategies depend much more on implementing adequate and timely economic policies than on being blessed with natural resources or being located alongside fast-growing economies. Dubai is, undoubtedly, an example of how an economy can overcome the exhaustion of its deposits of natural resources and diversify into other industries if policies anticipate events and react with promptness to internal and external shocks.

Although Dubai has made great advances in terms of economic development, the ever-changing conditions of economic activity, the presence of foreign shocks, and the development of the society of Dubai will require implementing new policies in the short and long run to secure those achievements. The concluding chapter identifies guidelines for the main reforms that ought to be implemented, sooner or later, to cope with the current and most pressing limitations of the development strategy.

2

Macroeconomic Overview

Ali Tawfik Al Sadik

2.1 HISTORICAL BACKGROUND

The foundation of modern Dubai can be traced to the settlement of the area by Al Bu Falasah (part of Bani Yas of Abu Dhabi) led by Sheikh Maktoum bin Butti (the head of Al Maktoum family) who moved from Abu Dhabi in 1833 and settled on the Shindagha Peninsula at the mouth of the Creek and declared the area an independent emirate. The newcomers brought with them a new spirit that transformed the city over time to growth, prosperity, and wealth. The 'open-door policy' engineered by the first ruler, Sheikh Maktoum bin Butti, attracted new economic activities such as pearling and trade and this in turn assisted the traditional sectors of agriculture and fishery. The local economy took a boost in the second half of the nineteenth century under the reign of Sheikh Hasher bin Maktoum who emerged as the most pro-business leader on the coast of Oman. During his era, Dubai's population doubled, and of the ninety large trading vessels serving on the coast of Oman, twenty belonged to Dubai's merchants. In 1887, a year after Sheikh Rashid bin Maktoum became the new ruler, a new wave of migrants from Iran and other Arab traders, escaping the use of the port of Lingeh due to the high taxes imposed by the Iranian authorities, settled in Dubai, revitalizing its economy and bringing with them vast wealth, experience, and global connections.

A more liberal trade policy in Dubai was reinforced with the assumption to the Sheikhdom of Maktoum bin Hashir in 1894, who in 1901 abolished or substantially reduced tariffs on trade and sent private envoys to the remaining Lingeh merchants to offer them generous incentives to relocate to Dubai. At that time, a British report stated that 'the 350 trading stalls in Deira Souq made it by far the biggest along the coast. During the first decade of the new century, a census counted nearly 7,000 men from Dubai who were directly or indirectly employed in the pearling industry, the highest figure on the coast' (Wilson, 2010: 38). However, Dubai's prosperity from trade was not to last for too long.

Dubai faced its first major economic shock in the late 1920s with the collapse of the pearl industry, caused by the discovery of the relatively cheaper Japanese cultured pearls, and the great depression of the 1930s which swept across the United States and Europe decreasing the demand for luxury commodities, among them pearls exported from Dubai. After a few years of relatively slow recovery in the late 1930s, Dubai's economy plunged again into recession during the Second World War which affected international trade and sea transport. Dubai is strategically located between Asia, Africa, and Europe. Therefore, the war disrupted the flow of traffic through Dubai, limiting opportunities for international trade. As with the rest of the world economies after the war, Dubai's economy stagnated in mid 1940s and early 1950s, until the first discovery of oil in mid 1960s in Dubai.

2.1.1 Rashid's Era

In 1958 Dubai was destined for new development with the accession of Sheikh Rashid bin Saeed Al Maktoum to the throne. He was no stranger to the emirate's affairs since he was in command of many critical issues delegated to him by his father, and had been the de facto ruler since 1939. With a vision of turning Dubai into a regional trade hub, he embarked on large-scale investment programmes to develop the essential infrastructure: ports, roads, electricity, and water, and during the first ten years of his reign, Dubai experienced tremendous economic activity. He marked his first year in office with the decision to deepen the shallow Dubai Creek to receive large vessels and took a loan from Kuwait to do the dredging. The project was completed in 1959 and around the same time the Dubai Electricity Company was established which launched its first power generator in Deira in 1961, and with it came completion of the first major water project to bring water from Al Awir to Ras Al Khor by a central pipeline to serve residential and industrial areas.

In 1960 Sheikh Rashid inaugurated Dubai International Airport and signed an agreement to start the construction works to build Al Maktoum Bridge to integrate the two parts of the city: Deira and Bur Dubai, a project that was opened for the public in 1962. In 1963 the first national commercial bank was established in Dubai; National Bank of Dubai (NBD), and by 1971 there were eight banks operating in Dubai. The fast development in the emirate and the need for a balanced growth necessitated a Master Town Plan which was drafted in 1965 and revised in 1971. With large vessels coming into Dubai from around the globe, and the inability of the Dubai Creek to cope with this traffic, a decision was taken in 1967 to construct Sheikh Rashid port which was inaugurated in October 1971 with sixteen berths, and thereafter increased to twenty berths in February 1976. From

1968 Sheik Rashid's attention shifted to political issues after the British government announced in January of that year its intention to pull out of the Arabian Gulf by the end of 1971. In less than two months (on 18 February 1968) Sheikh Zayed and Sheikh Rashid announced the formation of a federation between the two Emirates (Abu Dhabi and Dubai), opening the door for the rulers of other emirates to join the federation. The United Arab Emirates (UAE) was officially formed on 2 December 1971 bringing together six emirates; Abu Dhabi, Dubai, Sharjah, Umm Al Quwain, Fujairah, and Ajman. Ras Al Khaimah joined in February 1972.

The discovery of oil in Dubai in 1966 at the Fateh oil field marked a significant milestone in Dubai's economic development and added a new impetus to the local economy and though the first shipment in 1969 was small in quantity, production reached 300,000 bpd by 1973 (see Chapter 12 in this volume). The Arab–Israeli war of 1973 provided an opportunity for oil-producing countries to redraw a new contractual relationship between the oil-producing countries and the major oil companies. Consequently, oil prices more than quadrupled in a matter of months, and governments' shares in the barrel's revenue rose sharply. Unlike other Gulf states which rushed to extravagant public spending through subsidies, wage increases, and generous land and property compensation to their citizens, Dubai chose to invest in the future, and the bulk of the revenue was allocated to modernizing infrastructure. In 1972 the plan for Jebel Ali port was laid down, and in 1973 work was started to construct Dubai Drydocks which was in operation by 1979. The decade of the 1970s also witnessed the launching of some major industrial projects which included: Aluminium Smelter (later Dubal) and Dubai Natural Gas Company (Dugas) in 1975, and Dubai Cable Company (Ducab) in 1977. In 1985 Dubai's government announced the establishment of a free trade zone, Jebel Ali Free Trade Zone (JAFZA). Around that time two innovative projects appeared in Dubai which have had worldwide repercussions; the foundation of Dubai Islamic Bank in 1975, the first of its kind and which inspired a global resurgence in Islamic finance, and the establishment of Emirates Airlines in 1985 to become later on one of the most successful airlines in the world.

However, during the entire period of the 1980s, Dubai experienced some reverse in its fortunes. Early in the 1980s Sheikh Rashid suffered from a sudden decline in his health that forced him to cut short his public engagements, and his condition worsened by the middle of 1981. After the death of his wife Sheikha Latifa in May 1983, he withdrew from public life. That was coupled with a significant slowdown in economic activities caused by several factors, the most important are: the decline of oil prices since early 1982 and their collapse in 1986, the decline in global demand for oil, and the protracted Iraq–Iran war which started to spill over to the Gulf region after military attacks on commercial ships.

2.1.2 Sheikh Mohammed's Vision

In the mid 1990s Dubai began a renaissance in its modern economic history, with the appointment of Sheikh Mohammed bin Rashid as the Crown Prince of the emirate in January 1995, and after eleven years he became the new ruler in January 2006. A new vision was envisaged for Dubai to become the business hub of the region and the driving force for reform. Major initiatives were launched in the second half of the 1990s and the first half of the 2000s which included: 'Destination Dubai' which concentrated on tourism, 'Hub Dubai' that aimed to promote Dubai as a centre for global trade and transhipment, and 'e-Dubai' to develop the emirate to become a regional and probably a global capital for information technology and e-commerce.

Moreover, Dubai embarked on large-scale property development and overseas investments to accelerate the diversification of its economy. The scale of financing needed relative to the small local banking system induced Dubai's government-related enterprises (GREs) to borrow abroad in the form of syndicated loans, bonds, and Islamic *sukuks*. Thus, domestic credit expanded on average annually by 40 per cent during 2004–8. The credit surge went mainly to the suppliers of Dubai GREs and as personal loans for business purposes.

The surge in the inflation rate in the UAE during 2006–8 compared with the US inflation rate encouraged speculative bets on local currency (dirham) appreciation starting in mid 2007 in the form of US dollar inflows that were converted into dirham deposits in local banks. These inflows reversed abruptly in the second quarter of 2008 when it became clear that the authorities' commitment to the dollar peg was strong. By then, loan/deposit ratios had risen above 100 per cent.[1] The UAE deposit base is mainly composed of deposits from large corporations, as wage earners are primarily expatriates that remit earnings abroad.

The global financial crisis and the burst of the bubble in the local property market, coupled with the maturity mismatch between short-term liabilities and long-term cash flows, forced Dubai World (DW), one of the main GREs in Dubai, to restructure its debt. The DW debt restructuring led to an increase in Dubai sovereign debt, with ramifications for the banking sector and financial markets. Other Dubai GREs had to follow the DW-style debt-restructuring negotiations with banks. The recent and continued expansion and development of Dubai at the economic, social, and environmental levels raises the issue of sustainable development and the role Dubai wants to play at both regional and international level.

The rest of the chapter is organized as follows. Section 2.2 presents an overview of the performance of the economy of Dubai over the period

[1] UAE Central Bank regulations impose a ceiling of 100 per cent on the loan to stable resources ratio. Stable resources are defined as 85 per cent of deposits plus market funding above six months.

1975–2011 and analyses its sources of growth. Section 2.3 presents a structure of the economy and analyses the evolution of its main sectors. Section 2.4 outlines its macroeconomic policies.

2.2 OVERVIEW OF THE PERFORMANCE OF THE ECONOMY OF DUBAI

2.2.1 Economic Growth

The economy of Dubai witnessed extraordinary expansion in the period 1975–2012. Between 1975 and 2005, output, measured by gross domestic product (GDP), expanded by a factor of almost nine in real terms. However, between 2006 and 2011 output expanded only by a factor of 1.27. There is a break in the GDP series in 2006 because the newly established Dubai Statistics Center initiated a fresh start on the preparation of Dubai National Accounts resulting in a big jump of GDP in comparison with the value of 2005, as shown in Figure 2.1.[2]

The average annual growth rate in the period 1975–2005 is 7.5 per cent and 4.9 per cent during 2006–11. When neglecting the data break,[3] output expanded by 9 per cent in the entire period (1975–2011), which is among the highest in the world. However, economic growth has not been smooth, as evidenced by the high volatility of the growth rate of GDP which fluctuated between a high of 44 per cent in 1980 and a low of negative 15 per cent in 1986 (see Figure 2.2). Dubai's economy was also affected by the global economic and financial crisis triggered by the collapse of Lehman Brothers in September 2008. The direct impact of the financial and economic crisis was a contraction of Dubai's real GDP by 4.3 per cent.

In fact, the global economic crisis of the late 2000s exposed some weaknesses in Dubai's growth strategy. First, the growth rate of GDP exhibited high volatility of 9.7 per cent during 2000–10 despite its limited dependence on the hydrocarbon sector, indicating that the negative shock filtered through different channels (financial, trade, direct investment) in ways that had previously been seen as of secondary importance. Second, pre-crisis economic growth in Dubai had been generated by large real estate projects that were financed mainly by debt and that had to be postponed (and even cancelled) as foreign financing waned. This raised issues and concerns about the long-term sustainability of fiscal policy, most notably the public debt and that of

[2] We split the analysis into two intervals (before the break (1975–2005) and after the break (2006–11)). We also analysed the complete period (1975–2011) taking carefully into account the potential distortions emanating from the break in the data.

[3] In order to have a full sample series, we spliced together both periods using growth rates.

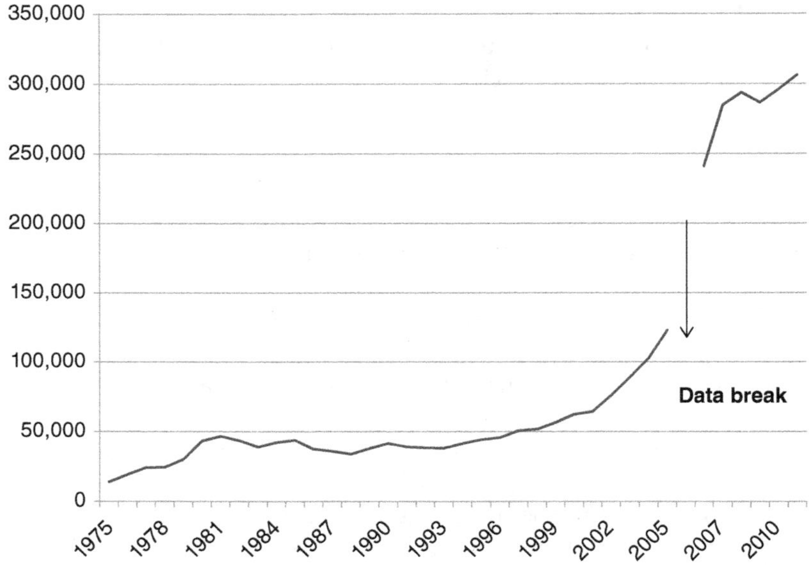

Figure 2.1. Dubai: Evolution of real GDP (million DH, 2000=100)

Source: Own elaboration based on data from Dubai Economic Council and Dubai Statistics Center

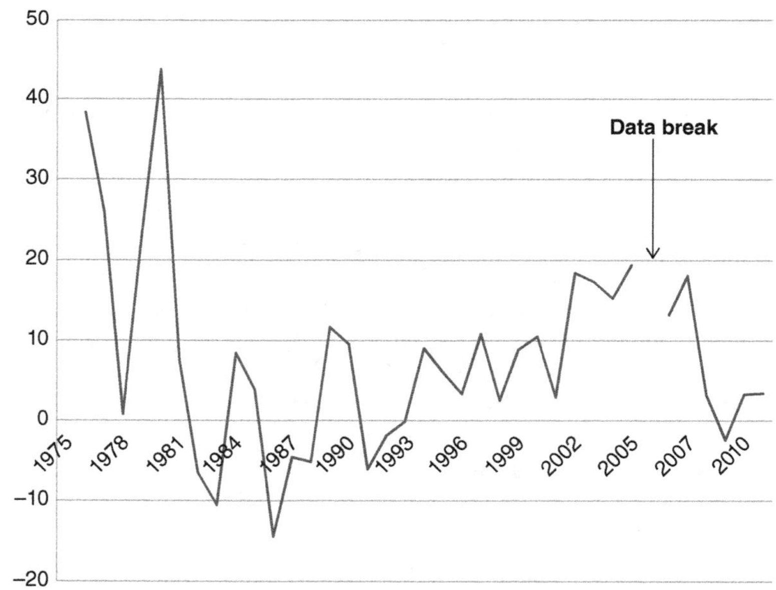

Figure 2.2. Dubai: Annual growth rate of real GDP (%)

Source: Own elaboration based on data from Dubai Economic Council and Dubai Statistics Center

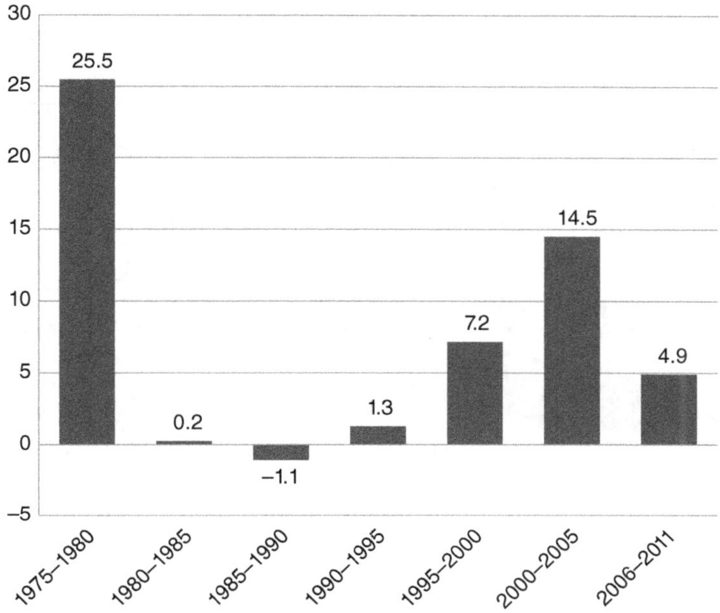

Figure 2.3. Dubai: Annual real GDP growth rates during five-year periods (%)
Source: Own elaboration based on data from Dubai Economic Council and Dubai Statistics Center

government-related entities (GREs).[4] Third, during the pre-crisis period excessive liquidity-financed real estate transactions drove the prices of assets to unsustainable levels. In addition to being inflationary, such growth cannot be sustained because the financial crisis induced a change in the global financial architecture (Dubai Economic Council, 2009).

Output growth was very fast during 1975–80 supported by increasing oil production and prices, followed by stagnant growth during 1980–5 and 1985–90 as a result of the collapse in oil prices in 1986, (Figure 2.3). Growth of the economy was negative during 1985–90, after which it traced a rising path which reached a peak during the period of boom of the early 2000s. The rising path of GDP growth was achieved through four strategic pillars: diversification of the economy to avoid its dependency on oil; expansion in the infrastructure that would transform Dubai and put it on a par with international standards; development of the financial sector and the establishment of Dubai Financial Market in 2000; and establishment of free zones to increase the attractiveness of the economy for multinational corporations (see Chapter 8 in this volume). The ascending growth path of Dubai GDP was interrupted by the global crisis and the bursting of the domestic real estate bubble.

[4] This issue is thoroughly assessed by Al Sadik and Nandwa in Chapter 3 of this volume.

Table 2.1. Annual growth rates of GDP (%)

	1980–1985	1985–1990	1990–1995	1995–2000	2000–2005	2006–2011	1980–2005	1980–2011	Standard deviation*
World	8.2	7.0	6.6	5.5	6.1	5.1	6.7	6.5	1.1
MENA	7.2	4.8	5.7	5.9	8.6	5.3	6.4	6.3	1.4
Dubai	0.2	–1.1	1.3	7.2	14.5	4.9	4.3	6.5	5.8
Hong Kong	11.2	11.2	7.8	4.4	6.6	5.5	8.2	7.9	2.9
Korea	14.7	14.0	10.5	7.0	7.2	5.5	10.6	9.7	3.9
Singapore	12.4	12.1	11.2	7.5	7.7	7.7	10.2	9.8	2.4

Note: (*) calculated for the periods (1980–5) and (2006–11).
Source: *World Economic Outlook* (IMF, 2013), Dubai Economic Council database and Dubai Statistics Center

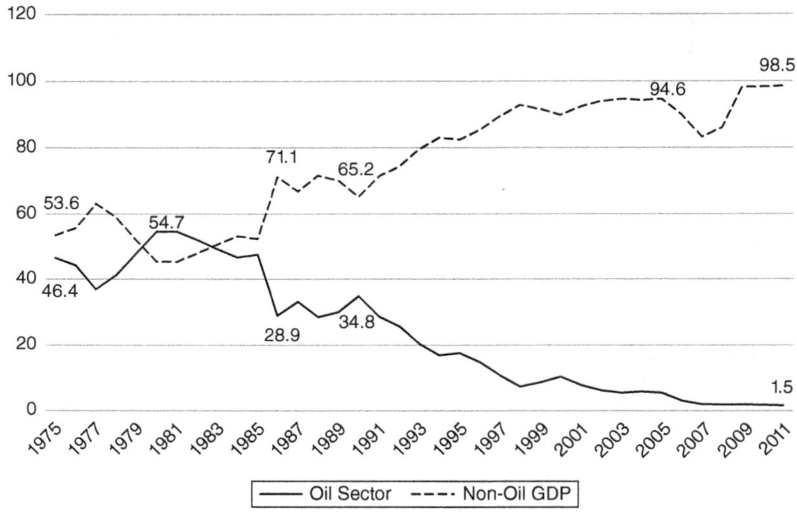

Figure 2.4. Dubai: Shares of oil and non-oil sectors in GDP (%)
Source: Own elaboration based on data from Dubai Economic Council and Dubai Statistics Center

The compound annual real growth rate of Dubai's GDP over the period 1980–2011 is the same as that of world GDP, but a little higher than that of the Middle East and North Africa (MENA) and lower than those of Hong Kong, Korea, and Singapore. However, the volatility of growth rate of Dubai's GDP is more than twice that of Singapore and Hong Kong and more than four times that of the global GDP (see Table 2.1).

The high volatility of the growth rate of Dubai's economy is connected with fluctuations in oil prices despite its declining dependence on the hydrocarbon sector as evidenced by its contribution to GDP. In fact, the share of the hydrocarbon sector in the GDP declined from a peak of 55 per cent in the 1980s to less than 2 per cent during 2007–11, as shown in Figure 2.4.

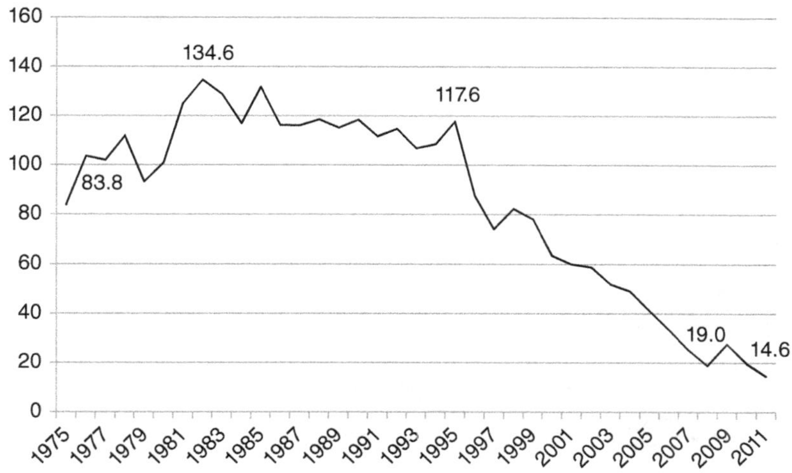

Figure 2.5. Dubai: Oil production (million barrels/year)

Source: Own elaboration based on data from Dubai Economic Council and Dubai Statistics Center
Note: Production is estimated as oil GDP divided by oil price.

The declining contribution of the hydrocarbon sector to Dubai's GDP is due to the contraction of oil production and the policies and measures the government adopted to diversify its economy as mentioned above (Figure 2.5).

Efforts to diversify the economy away from oil are reflected in the increasing role of the following six sectors: namely the wholesale and retail trade, real estate, manufacturing, construction, transport, storage and communication, and the financial sector. The share of these six sectors increased from a low of 40 per cent in the 1980s to 94 per cent in 2011 (Figure 2.4).

2.2.2 Sources of Economic Growth in Dubai

The aggregate growth of an economy as measured by changes in GDP can be disaggregated into the growth of factors of production, labour, and capital, and a residual that represents the growth rate of total factor productivity (TFP). Figure 2.6 shows the evolution of the capital stock, employment, and GDP in Dubai. These two factors of production evolved in tandem with GDP during most of the period with two exceptions, the early 1980s and the 2000s.

The expansion of the economy in Dubai is judged to be remarkable. However, output per working–age person has not followed suit. Output per working-age person is considered a measure of the average productivity of the working force in an economy. Empirical evidence indicates that average labour productivity in

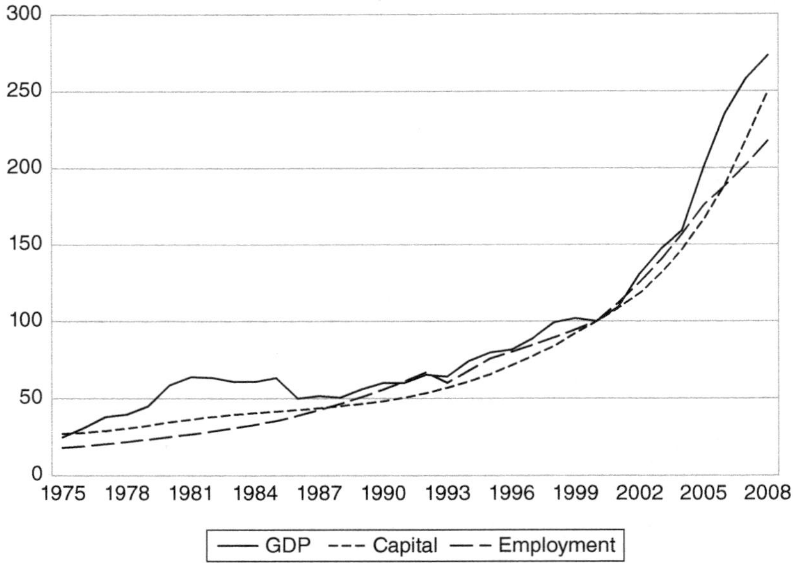

Figure 2.6. Dubai: GDP, capital stock, and employment (2000=100)
Source: Elbadawi and Soto (2012)

Dubai remained stagnant for a long period of time (1987–2004) after a substantial decline in the early 1980s. In contrast, productivity in Hong Kong and Singapore traced a rising path over the period 1975–2008, as shown in Figure 2.7.

Identifying the causes for the slow growth in average labour productivity in Dubai is an important issue for formulating policies to improve the performance of the economy. As outlined earlier, economic growth can be decomposed to growth of capital, labour, and TFP. The latter measures the efficiency of organizing the inputs and the factors of production to produce the output of the economy. To investigate the importance of TFP the standard Cobb–Douglas production function is utilized:

$$Y = AK^{\beta}L^{1-\beta} \tag{2.1}$$

where Y is GDP, A is TFP, K is Capital, L is labour, and β is the share of capital in GDP. The marginal productivity of capital, MPK, can be derived from equation (2.1) as:

$$MPK = A\ \beta\ k^{\beta-1} \tag{2.2}$$

where k is the capital–labour ratio. Equation (2.2) shows that for given k, MPK is positively related to A and β. In oil-rich Arab countries, production is very capital-intensive, and β is among the highest in the world at about 65 per cent (Zebregs, 1998).[5] Thus, one would expect to observe high MPK in these Arab

[5] The average for developing countries is 55 per cent and that of developed countries is 40 per cent.

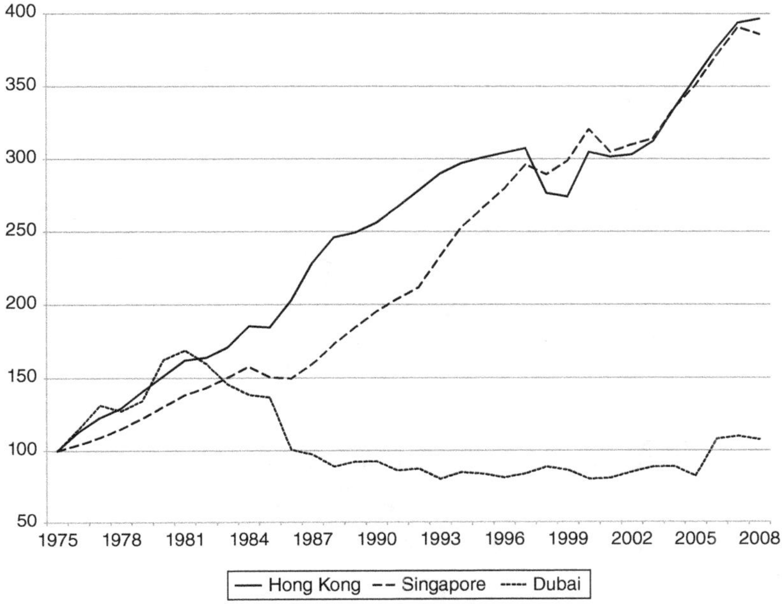

Figure 2.7. Average labour productivity in Dubai, Hong Kong, and Singapore (2000=100)
Source: Elbadawi and Soto (2012)

countries. On the contrary, due to their low productivity levels, the average MPK of oil-rich Arab countries is only 15 per cent compared to an MPK in excess of 25 per cent for developing countries (Sadik and Bolbol, 2001). A low TFP is an indication of an inefficient use of existing resources and inadequate investment and technological climate.

The effect of TFP on the growth of the economy can be examined by looking at TFP's behaviour over time. This is usually done by tracing the growth rate of GDP to the growth rates of K, L, and TFP as follows:

$$g = \beta k + (1-\beta)l + tfp \tag{2.3}$$

where g is growth rate of GDP, k is growth rate of K, l is growth rate of L and tfp is growth rate of TFP.

For MENA over the period 1975–2000 the estimates for the annual growth rate of the variables in equation (2.3) are: $g = 3.7$ per cent; $k = 3.8$ per cent; $l = 1.1$ per cent and $tfp = -1.2$ per cent (Sadik and Bolbol, 2001).[6] Hence, with a negative growth rate, TFP was subtracting from output instead of adding to it.

[6] Pritchett (1996) found that over the 1960–92 period, TFP regional growth averaged annually as follows: Middle East and North Africa, –1.3 per cent; sub-Saharan Africa, –0.6 per cent; South Asia, –0.9 per cent; Latin America and Caribbean, –0.1; East Asia, 1.2 per cent; and OECD, 1 per cent.

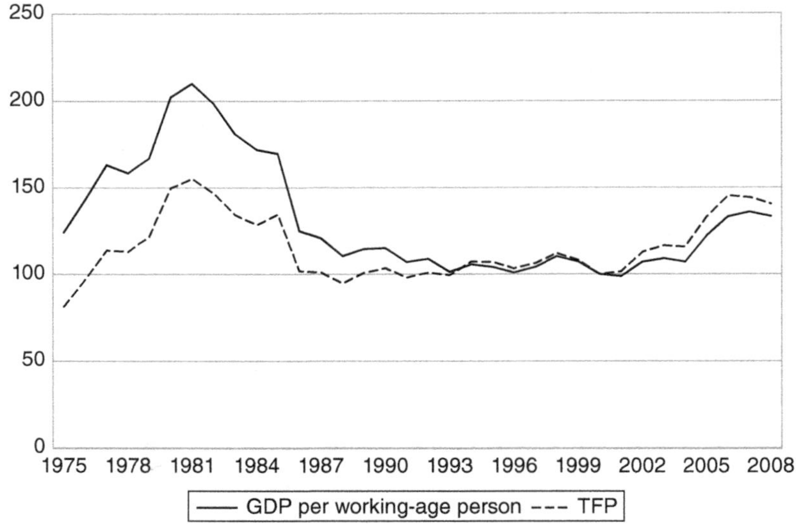

Figure 2.8. Dubai: GDP per working-age person and total factor productivity (2000=100)

Source: Elbadawi and Soto, 2012

For Dubai, Figure 2.8 plots the trajectories of TFP and GDP per working-age person over the period 1975–2008 as computed by Elbadawi and Soto (2012), extending equation (2.3) to consider improvements in the human capital of the labour force. It shows how closely the TFP data match those for GDP per working-age person, both in the level and the cyclical component. The correlation between the two variables is 0.98.

The implication of the high correlation between TFP and GDP per working-age person indicates that it is not the changes in factor inputs that were the main drivers for the evolution of GDP in Dubai, but rather the efficiency with which these factors were used. In addition to the impact of technological advances, productivity depends on the framework in which economic agents make decisions to work, invest, and consume. Consequently, TFP can be affected by the quality of macro- and microeconomic policies and transient phenomena, such as commodity booms or unemployment cycles (Elbadawi and Soto, 2012).

A comparison of the sources of real growth of GDP in Dubai over the period 1975–2008 with those of Hong Kong and Singapore reveals the following features: annual real GDP growth has been higher than that of Hong Kong and Singapore over the whole period 1975–2008 and the sub-period 1990–2008. However, both Hong Kong and Singapore performed better than Dubai during the period 1975–1990 (see Figure 2.9).

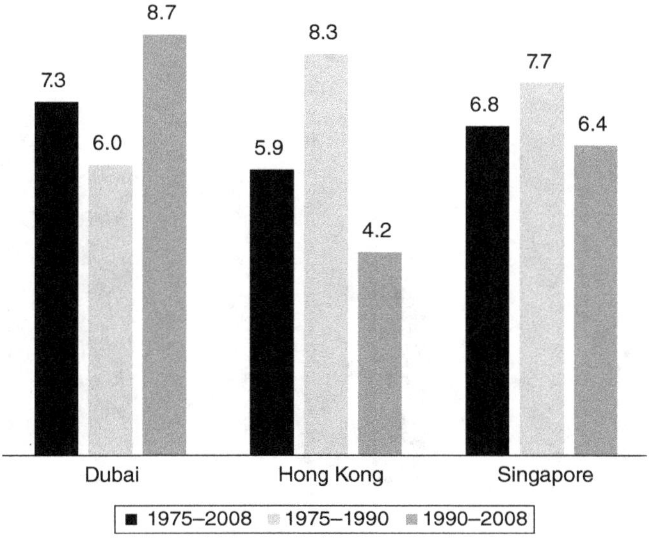

Figure 2.9. Annual real growth rate of GDP (%)
Source: Elbadawi and Soto, 2012

The decomposition of the sources of economic growth indicates important differences in the evolution of Dubai's economy vis-à-vis Hong Kong and Singapore. For capital accumulation, all three economies accumulated capital at the same rate. However, in Hong Kong and Singapore accumulation has been smoother than in Dubai, where accumulation was relatively slow in the period 1975–1990 and quite fast during the period 1990–2008 (Figure 2.10).

The second key difference between these economies lies in the use of the labour force. While in all countries immigration of foreign workers has been a significant source of inexpensive manpower, in Dubai the expansion in the labour force has been much higher than in Hong Kong and Singapore in the three periods, as shown in Figure 2.11.

A third difference among these economies is in the accumulation of human capital, which has been similar in the three economies during the whole period 1975–2008, but significantly higher in Hong Kong in the period 1975–1990 (Figure 2.12). The latter is the period of higher GDP growth in Hong Kong and Singapore indicating the importance of human capital in fostering economic development (see Figure 2.12). The weaknesses of human capital formation in Dubai are discussed in Chapter 10 of this volume.

The fourth important difference lies in total factor productivity. TFP growth in Dubai has been rather low in comparison to that of Hong Kong and Singapore: over the whole period, Dubai's TFP annual growth rate is 1.6 per cent while that of Hong Kong is 2.1 per cent and that of Singapore 2.5 per cent.

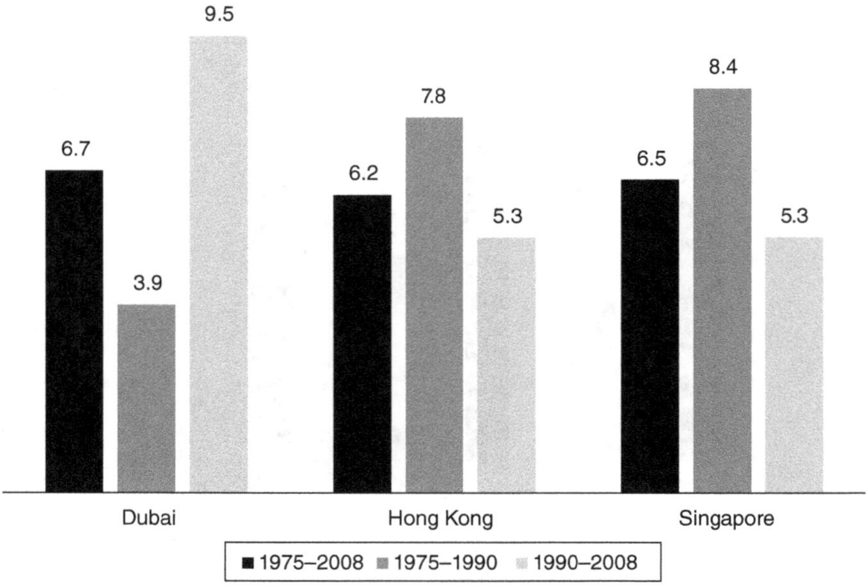

Figure 2.10. Annual growth rate of capital stock (%)
Source: Elbadawi and Soto, 2012

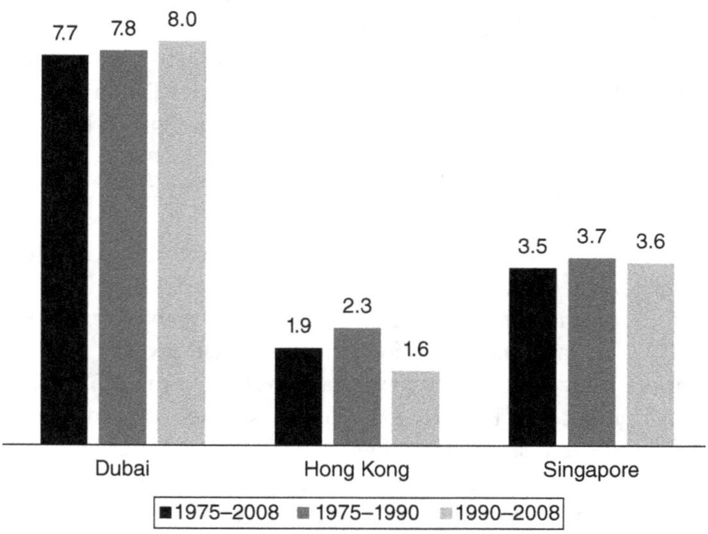

Figure 2.11. Annual growth rate of employment (%)
Source: Elbadawi and Soto, 2012

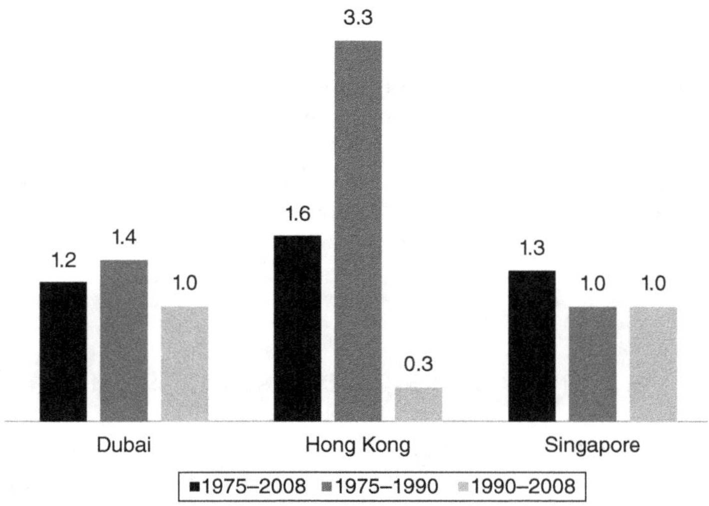

Figure 2.12. Annual growth rate of stock of human capital (%)
Source: Elbadawi and Soto, 2012

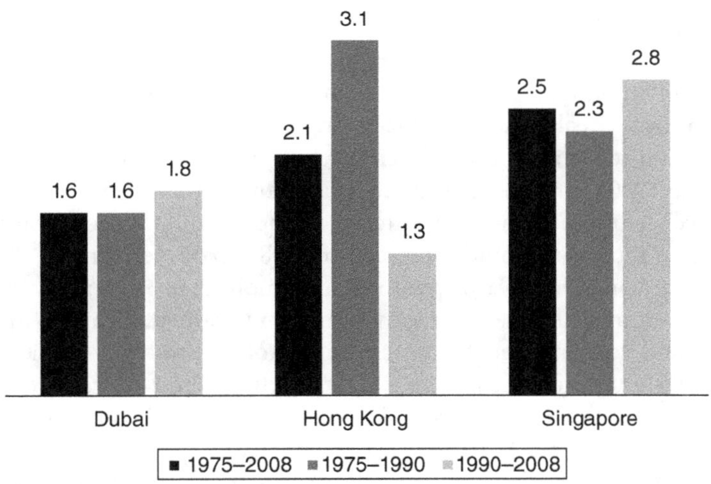

Figure 2.13. Annual growth rate of total factor productivity (%)
Source: Elbadawi and Soto, 2012

During the shorter period 1975–1990, annual rates of TFP reveal significant differences: 1.6 per cent for Dubai, 3.1 per cent for Hong Kong, and 2.3 per cent for Singapore (Figure 2.13). Low growth of Dubai's TFP is an advance warning to do something about it in light of the empirical evidence which indicates that sustained growth is largely dependent upon significant improvements in factor productivity.

As argued, and contrary to many other resource-rich economies, Dubai succeeded in diversifying away from the oil sector as evidenced by its insignificant contribution to GDP in 2012. As the contribution of the oil sector dwindled, the contributions of the other sectors advanced, reshaping economic activity and raising new and very different policy issues, as discussed in the next section.

2.3 STRUCTURE OF DUBAI ECONOMY

Oil discoveries and the swift oil price hike in the early 1970s sparked not only the formation of the Emirati nation but also a period of sustained development for Dubai. Oil revenues were channelled to finance ambitious public investment programmes—particularly in infrastructure—which, in turn, allowed the emergence of a thriving private sector. As shown in Figure 2.4, oil represented around 50 per cent of GDP in 1980. The dominance of the hydrocarbon sector in Dubai's GDP continued into the 1980s even if its share plunged from 48 per cent in 1985 to 29 per cent in 1986 as a result of the collapse of oil prices in international markets.[7] The share of six sectors, namely wholesale and retail trade; real estate; manufacturing; construction; transport, storage, and communication; and the financial sector, increased from a low of 40 per cent in the 1980s to 94 per cent in 2011, as seen before in Figure 2.4.

The six sectors took the lead in terms of their combined contributions to GDP which increased from 41 per cent in 1985 to 55 per cent in 1986 and continued tracing an upward trend reaching more than 94 per cent in 2011. Benefiting from a decade of massive public investment projects in roads, airports, and seaports and taking advantage of its strategic location along trade routes, the wholesale and retail trade sector (hereafter trade) expanded to dominate economic activities in Dubai: by 2011 trade had a share of more than 31 per cent of GDP, followed by manufacturing and transport sectors each contributing 14 per cent to GDP; real estate contributed 13 per cent, followed by the financial sector with a contribution of 12 per cent and construction 9 per cent (Figure 2.14). The structure and importance of trade activities is thoroughly discussed in Chapter 9 in this volume.

The expansion in trade took time to materialize after oil began to be pumped out of Dubai and exported. Its contribution to GDP experienced a swift decline

[7] Average oil price declined from US$26.5 in 1985 to US$14.64 in 1986 (historical crude oil prices: 1946–present, online information by Data Com accessed on 25 November 2012, based on data from BP 'Statistical Review of World Energy', June 2010, BP plc., London, UK).

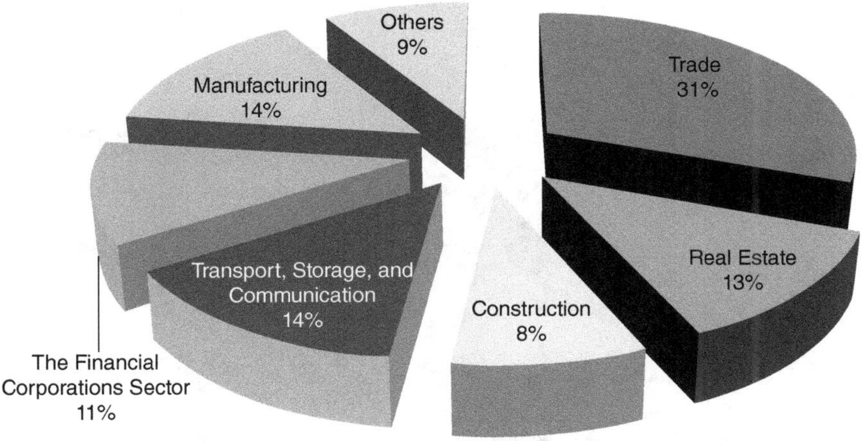

Figure 2.14. Dubai: Shares of main sectors in GDP in 2011 (%)

Source: Own elaboration based on data from the Dubai Statistics Center

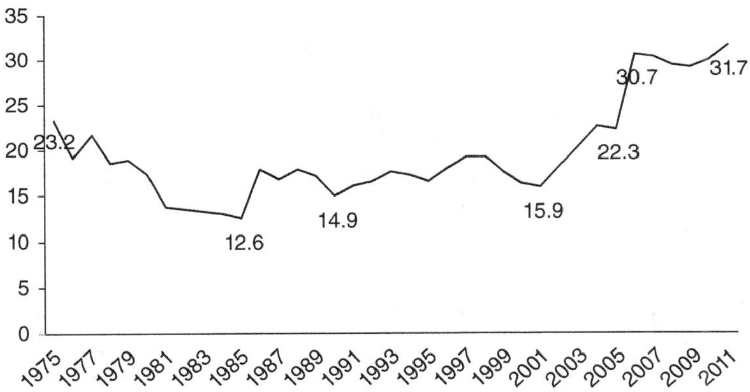

Figure 2.15. Dubai: Share of wholesale trade in GDP (%)

Source: Own elaboration based on data from the Dubai Statistics Center

between 1975 and 1985, as shown in Figure 2.15, when it contracted from 23 per cent to approximately 13 per cent. Between 1975 and 1980 trade began to expand steadily but its share in economic activities continued to decline because GDP was growing faster as a result of the surge of the hydrocarbons sector. Trade activities continued to expand thereafter at a slower rate than other sectors even when oil revenues began to decline, largely as a result of the development of other sectors in the economy such as transportation, financial services and, increasingly, real estate. However, in the late 1990s the trade sector began a process of fast and sustained development largely as a result of the

Figure 2.16. Evolution of manufacturing and the financial sector (% of GDP)
Source: Own elaboration based on data from the Dubai Statistics Center

expansion of internal and external tourism (see Chapter 6 in this volume) as well as retail activities closely related to regional tourism (see Chapter 9 in this volume). Over the period 1985–2011, the share of trade exhibited an upward trend from approximately 13 per cent of GDP to 32 per cent.

The financial and manufacturing sectors increased over the long term with small fluctuations. In fact, the share of the manufacturing sector jumped from less than 2 per cent of GDP in 1975 to more than 14 per cent in 2011 and that of the financial sector from 3.2 per cent to 11.6 per cent in 1975 and 2011, respectively (see Figure 2.16). Both are remarkable achievements considering that these sectors were almost non-existent in the 1970s.

The rapid expansion of the manufacturing and financial sectors was induced by a boom in construction and real estate which, in turn, were driven by the build-up of infrastructure by the government and the development of mega-projects in real estate and tourism by government-related entities (GRE) in response to the policy vision that these were the necessary pillars for making Dubai a tourist attraction and logistics hub (see Chapters 6 and 7 in this volume).

Similar to the other sectors, the real estate sector increased markedly from the early 1980s to the mid 1990s, followed by a flat path until the early 2000s and then experiencing a massive boom that was fed by the rapid growth of global liquidity, especially after 2003. By 2008 the boom was transformed to a bubble with accelerating real estate prices and real estate supply overshooting demand by a large margin. The impact of the global financial and economic crisis of

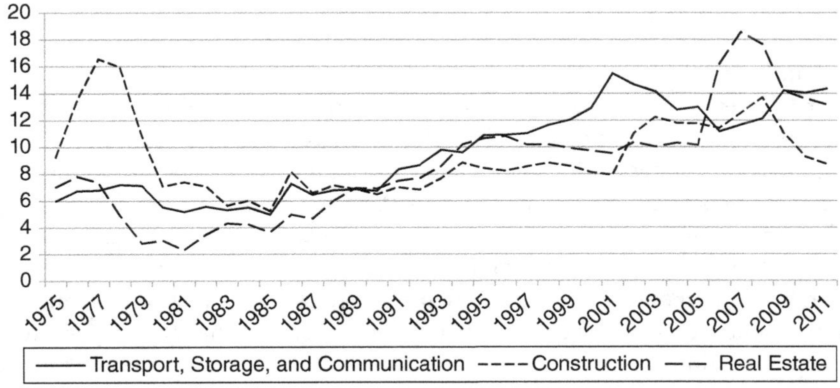

Figure 2.17. Evolution of construction, real estate, and transport sectors (% of GDP)
Source: Own elaboration based on data from the Dubai Statistics Center

2008–10 and local conditions induced the burst of the bubble in September 2008 at the time of the collapse of Lehman Brothers (for a detailed analysis of the real estate bubble see Renauld, 2012).

Unsurprisingly, the construction sector traced a similar path to that of the real estate sector. Transportation has been somewhat less prone to cyclical phenomena, as shown in Figure 2.17, as it experienced sustained development from the early 1980s and until 2001. The slight decline observed between 2001 and 2005 is not due to a contraction of the sector but is the result of the rapid expansion of other sectors—such as real estate, construction, and trade—which belittled the contribution of transport services. Note, nevertheless, the resilience of the transportation sector which seems to have gone unharmed during the downturn of the period 2008–10.

2.4 MACROECONOMIC POLICIES

Monetary and exchange rate policies are not specific to Dubai but are designed and implemented at the UAE federal level. As discussed below, the hard fixing of the currency to the US dollar virtually eliminates monetary management and exchange market interventions as policy tools, except for minor transitory policies linked to the provision of liquidity to the financial sector which, in any case, are not Dubai-specific. However, fiscal policy is mostly implemented at the emirate level. Inflation is also measured and considered at the emirate level, but it is affected by both monetary and exchange rate policies.

2.4.1 Inflation

The inflation rate in Dubai, as measured by the consumer price index (CPI), over the period 1980–2000 fluctuated between a negative rate (deflation) of 12.6 per cent in 1984 and a high rate of 12.1 per cent in 1987 (see Figure 2.18). Inflation was moderate during the first three years of the millennium ranging between 2.9 per cent and 3.5 per cent and traced a rising path reaching a peak of 11.3 per cent in 2007. The inflation rate declined a little to 10.7 in 2008 and dropped to 4 per cent in 2009 and less than 1 per cent in 2011.

In order to understand the underlying factors of inflation we investigate the components of CPI in Dubai. As of 2012, the weights of the main expenditure groups constituting the CPI are 43.7 per cent for the housing and related services category group, food 11.1 per cent, transport 9.1 per cent, and communication 6 per cent (see Table 2.2). In 2008, the last year of significant price hikes in the period, the annual inflation rate was highest in the restaurants and hotels group at 25 per cent, followed by the food group at more than 21 per cent, and 20 per cent for the clothing and footwear group, and 18 per cent for education.

Although inflation in the restaurant and hotels group was highest in 2008, its contribution to the overall inflation rate was not the highest at 1.4 per cent. In fact, the contribution of the housing group with an inflation rate of 5.6 per cent was the highest at 2.45 per cent due to its largest weight in the CPI. The food group with its 21 per cent inflation rate added 2.33 per cent to the overall inflation rate because its weight in the CPI was 11.08 per cent (Figure 2.19).

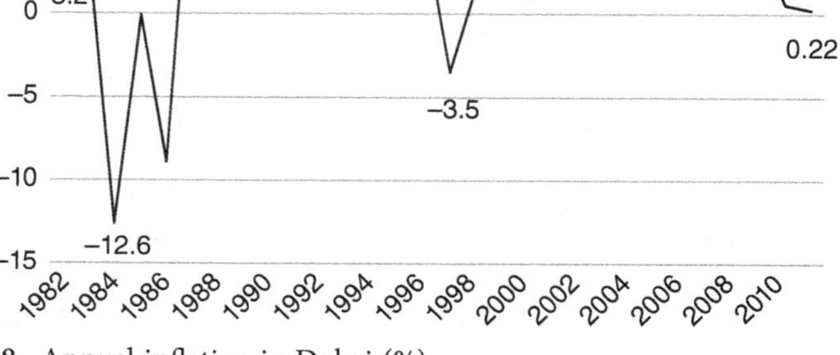

Figure 2.18. Annual inflation in Dubai (%)

Source: Own elaboration based on data from the Dubai Statistics Center

Table 2.2. Dubai: Inflation by main expenditure groups (%)

Main expenditure groups	*Weight in CPI index*	2008	2009	2010
Inflation rate	100.00	10.77	4.03	0.55
Food and non-alcoholic beverages	11.08	21.06	2.15	1.9
Alcoholic beverages and tobacco	0.24	5.65	5.61	0.33
Clothing and footwear	5.52	19.54	9.86	0.44
Housing, water, electricity, gas	43.70	5.60	2.41	-1.25
Furnishings and equipment	3.34	13.76	3.33	1.10
Health	1.08	6.66	5.31	3.43
Transport	9.08	8.95	4.36	6.64
Communication	6.00	1.71	-0.17	-10.59
Recreation and culture	4.24	18.45	2.55	0.53
Education	4.09	18.49	18.60	9.04
Restaurants and hotels	5.48	25.49	7.36	1.43
Miscellaneous goods and services	6.15	19.17	3.69	2.09

Source: Own elaboration based on data from the Dubai Statistics Center

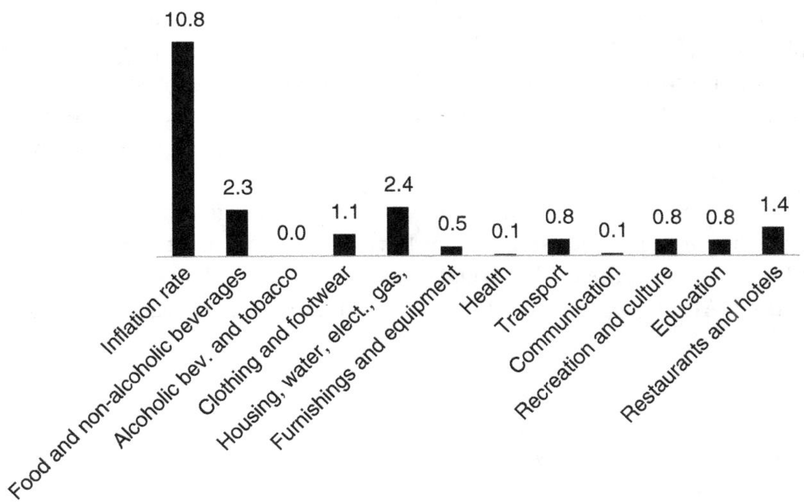

Figure 2.19. Contribution to the rate of inflation by main expenditure groups in 2008 (%)
Source: Own elaboration based on data from the Dubai Statistics Center

As an open economy, the inflation rate in Dubai is affected by both domestic and global developments. The surge in inflation during the period 2000–8 could therefore be explained by internal and external factors. Economic booms and expansions of demand in Dubai and Abu Dhabi due to rising oil prices and inflows of foreign direct investment and portfolio investment, in addition to large public investment projects, all pushed prices up as explained below (Dubai Economic Council, 2007). We review the importance of these factors in what follows.

Flourishing economy accompanied with high domestic demand: as mentioned above, the Dubai economy witnessed very high growth rates during 2000–10 which attracted investors and workers who fuelled the economy with demand for goods and services which led to pressure on the different sectors especially the housing, food, education, health, and the other expenditure groups in the CPI.

Price of oil and inflow of capital: the high growth is the result of a high rise in the price of oil, the inflow of foreign capital and large investment programmes, especially in infrastructure in both Dubai and Abu Dhabi. The growth rate of the money supply (M2) increased from an average of 19.9 per cent during 2000–5 to 41.1 per cent in 2007 when the inflation rate in Dubai peaked at 11.3 per cent. As the growth of the money supply eased, the inflation rate slowed too as shown in Figure 2.20.

Increase in the price of energy and other fees: the UAE government increased energy prices several times: 31.5 per cent in 2005 which raised the energy cost to almost twice that prevailing in other Gulf Cooperation Council members (GCC). This led to an increase in the consumers' expenditures on transport and an increase in the cost incurred by producers of goods and services which in turn fed into an increase in the prices of production of goods and services which were reflected in an increase in the CPI. In addition, fees collected by the federal and local governments contributed to the increase in the costs of production.

Imported inflation: severe fluctuations in the exchange rate of the US dollar against major currencies such as the Euro, Yen, and Pound sterling contributed to inflation in the UAE through the cost of imports. This is due to the fact that the UAE dirham is pegged to the US dollar and its exchange rate against

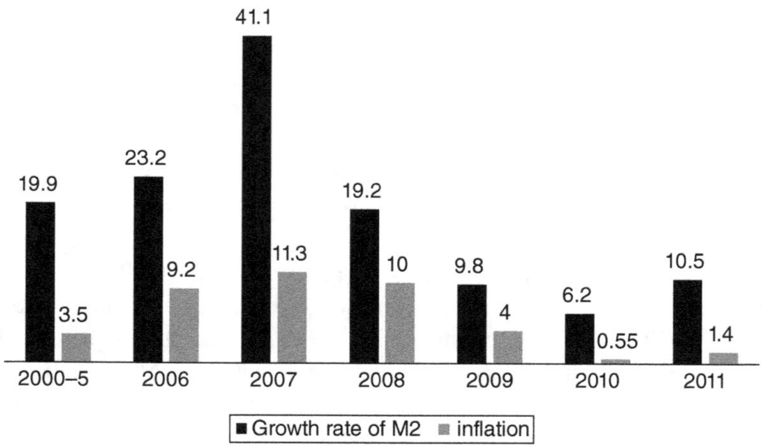

Figure 2.20. Annual growth rate of money supply and inflation (%)

Source: Own elaboration based on data from the Dubai Statistics Center and the UAE Central Bank

other major currencies moves in tandem with that of the US dollar. Thus, the decline in the value of the US dollar against the major currencies was reflected in a decline in the purchasing power of the dirham as it lost about 30 per cent of its value against the Euro and 8 per cent against the Yen. This led to a rise in the cost of non-dollar imports, which in turn contributed to the overall increase in the CPI and to the costs of production which pushed prices higher.

2.4.2 Monetary and Exchange Rate Policies

In 1978 the UAE dirham was officially pegged to the IMF's special drawing rights (SDRs), however, in 1997 the dirham was pegged to the US dollar at a rate of US$1=AED 3.67. Monetary and exchange rate policies in the UAE are conducted at the federal level and are therefore outside the purview of Dubai. In fact, since the dirham is pegged to the US dollar—de facto a fixed exchange rate—and the capital market is quite open, the UAE cannot conduct independent monetary policy: in fact, by virtue of the pegged exchange rate to the US dollar, the UAE monetary policy is closely tied to that of the US.[8] This policy choice served the UAE economy for a long time by providing an nominal anchor and financial stability, but it proved to be less than optimal during the build-up of the global crisis of 2008–9 when the UAE needed restricted liquidity to control the overheating of the economy at times when the US Federal Reserved embarked on an unprecedented monetary expansion.

Monetary policy in the UAE is constrained by three key factors (Maratheftis, 2009):

The US dollar (USD) peg: The hard peg dictates that interest rates in the UAE cannot deviate significantly from US rates. This implies that cyclicality of the US economy, for instance, lower interest rates, might not always be right for the UAE. In fact, the liquidity crunch following the global financial crisis is a result of economic excesses fuelled by the easing of US rates in 2008, when the UAE needed tighter policy. This led to significant distortions in the market and encouraged risk-taking behaviour, particularly in the housing market, which was perceived as the quickest way to make a profit. This in turn diverted investment from productive sectors of the economy and led to an unsustainable rally in property prices. In 2008, the pro-cyclical nature of monetary policy and low interest rates encouraged short-term profit-seeking activities over long-term strategic investment. The correction in the housing

[8] In small, open economies only two policies can be pursued from the following three: fixed exchange rate; independent monetary policy; and freedom of capital flow. This is the 'unholy' trinity.

market led to a rise in non-performing loans (NPLs) (see Dubai Economic Council, 2012).

Direct exposure to the real estate and construction sectors was as high as 37 per cent of total loans as of December 2008 for some local banks. In addition, 20–50 per cent of banks' personal loans may be exposed to the real estate sector. Loose monetary conditions led to an unsustainable rally in asset prices when the economy was booming. Given the banking sector's direct and indirect exposure to real estate, the asset price correction reduced banks' appetite to take on more risk at a time when NPLs increased from 2.5 per cent at the end of 2008 to 10.6 per cent in December 2011 in Dubai banks and from 1.7 per cent to 4.6 per cent in Abu Dhabi banks, Figure 2.21.

Debt restructuring and rescheduling deals have alleviated the pressure on government-related entities (GREs) and the banking sector temporarily, as a significant amount of Dubai debt will mature in the medium term, 2014–15 (IMF, June 2012).

Unsustainable credit growth funded by hot money: Throughout 2008 markets anticipated a revaluation of GCC currencies given the inconsistency between domestic needs (tighter policy was required to tighten liquidity and reduce inflation) and the monetary policy imported from the US as a result of the US dollar peg. As a result, the region received strong capital inflows, but these were largely speculative and short-term in nature. This created a problem of maturity mismatch, the bulk of these short-term deposits ended up being loaned out longer term. Banks aggressively increased lending during the boom times, and when the hot money inflows reversed and left the UAE, loans-to-deposit (L/D) ratios went above the 100 per cent ceiling set by the UAE Central Bank (Figure 2.22).

The excessive lending behaviour of 2008 created the tighter credit conditions that faced the economy later.[9] Banks that have breached the 100 per cent L/D ratio cap cannot lend even if they have access to liquidity, since this would cause their ratios to deteriorate further. The need to bring L/D ratios below 100 per cent has also led to fierce competition between banks to attract deposits, fuelling a sharp increase in deposit interest rates, which is then passed on to borrowers. This has led to the following paradox: banks were competing for deposits, but once they attracted them, they were unable to lend the funds out as long as their L/D ratios are in excess of 100 per cent. The only option they had is to place the funds on the interbank market. This is likely to push interbank rates (EIBOR)[10] lower, without improving credit conditions in practice.

[9] Claims on private non-banks jumped from AED 530 billion in 2007 to 777 billion in 2008, a growth rate of more than 46 per cent.

[10] EIBOR is the reference rate most commonly used by borrowers and lenders to conduct financial transactions in Dubai and the surrounding Emirates.

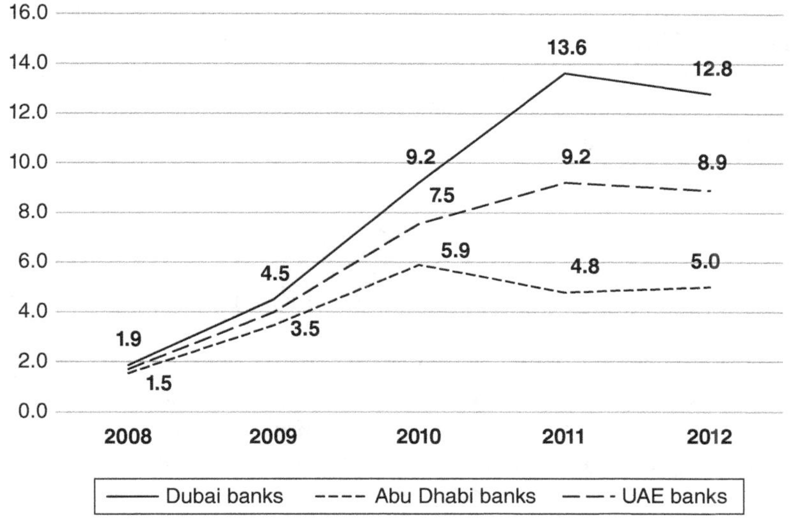

Figure 2.21. Ratio of NPLs to total gross loans

Source: Own elaboration based on data from the Dubai Economic Council

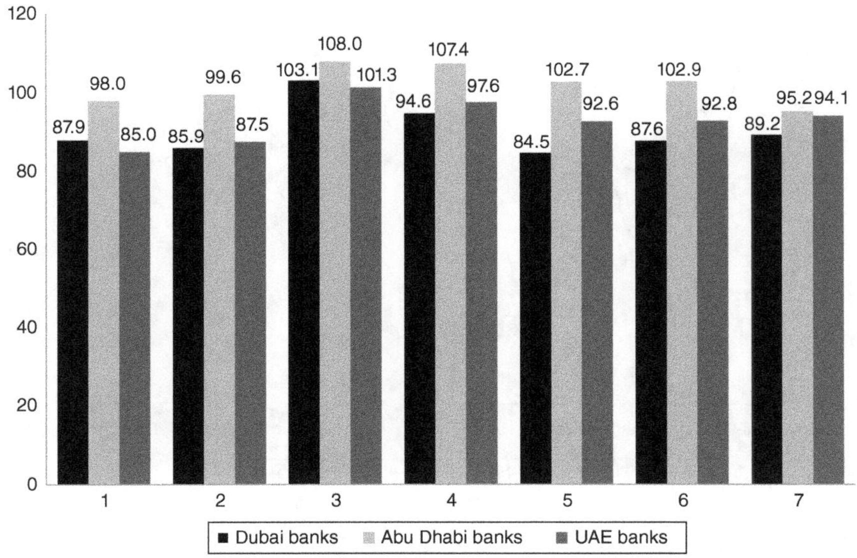

Figure 2.22. Loans to deposits ratio (%)

Source: Own elaboration based on data from the Dubai Economic Council

Broken transmission mechanism: The monetary policy transmission mechanism in the UAE is severely constrained and is not functioning properly. It is important to understand how the transmission mechanism usually works to appreciate this fact about monetary policy in the UAE. Central banks set the policy interest rate (in the UAE's case, the repurchase, or repo, rate), which is the rate at which banks can borrow funds from the central bank. Policy rates then affect market interest rates such as interbank rates, deposit rates, and lending rates. The change in market interest rates then begins to impact asset prices (and, in the case of freely floating currencies, the currency). The change in asset prices begins to affect expectations, which in turn affect inflation. In effect, when the central bank sets the policy rate, a chain of events begins that allows the monetary authorities to manage the economy more effectively. In the UAE, a change in the policy rate does not trigger this chain reaction. The monetary policy transmission mechanism is broken, and it is broken right from the beginning. It is interesting to compare and contrast the graphs in Figure 2.23.

The UAE Central Bank reduced the repo rate to 1 per cent in early 2009 without the desired effect on market rates, which remained high. On the contrary, when the Federal Reserve changes its policy rate US market rates move accordingly.

The monetary policy transmission mechanism in the UAE is not functioning properly because the policy rate is the repo rate, and the UAE banks do not use the repo window to a significant extent. This is due to the fact that the repo

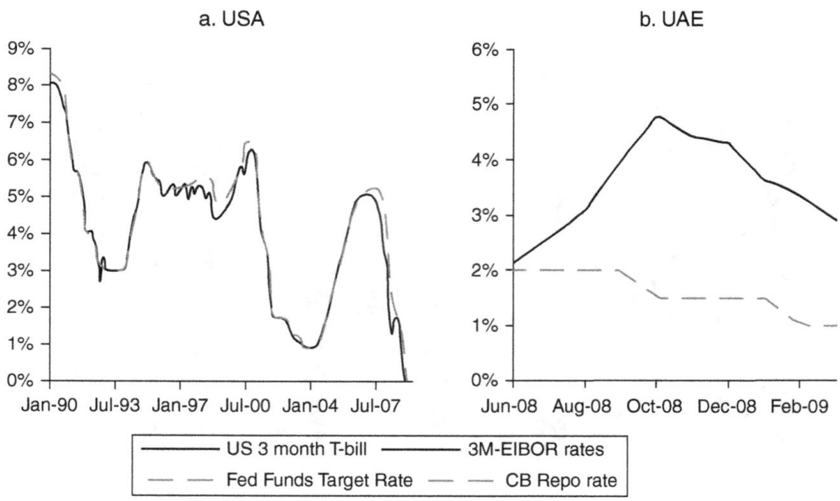

Figure 2.23. Monetary transmission mechanism

Source: Maratheftis, 2009

window is considered a temporary facility and there is uncertainty about the kinds of assets that could be used as collateral by banks.

2.4.3 Fiscal Policy

Except for matters that pertain to the federal government, fiscal policy in the UAE is highly decentralized. Each emirate has its own local government comprised of departments (authorities), thus able to retain and exercise political, judicial, financial, and economic autonomy. On this basis, each emirate manages its own budget on an independent basis, with no obligation to contribute to budgets of the other emirates. Fiscal policy, both at the federal and emirate levels, was pro-cyclical prior to the global financial and economic crisis that contributed to the collapse of the Lehman Brothers in September 2008. The Abu Dhabi and Dubai governments adopted counter-cyclical fiscal policies in 2009, with the support from accommodating monetary policy from the UAE Central Bank, and largely succeeded in containing the negative impact of the global financial crisis on the domestic economy. Both local and federal government budgets were increased in 2009 relative to 2008. In fact, the Dubai government expanded expenditures when both government revenues and growth of the economy contracted in 2009. This is reflected in the evolution of the government budget (Figure 2.24): the deficit increased

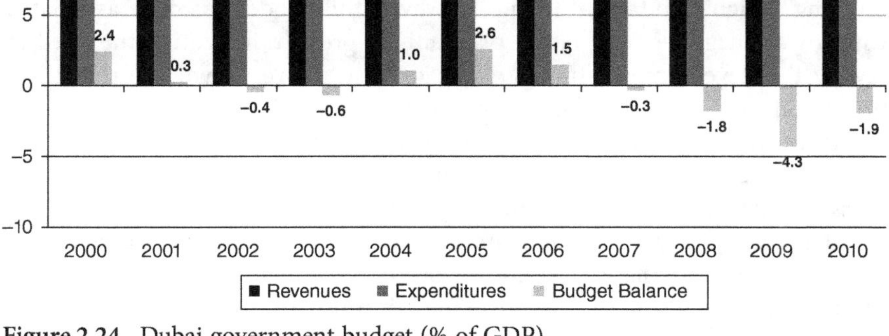

Figure 2.24. Dubai government budget (% of GDP)

Source: Own elaboration on the basis of data from the Department of Finance of Dubai

from less than 2 per cent of GDP in 2008 to more than 4 per cent in 2009 as a result of expanding expenditures by 9 per cent when revenues declined by 13 per cent between 2008 and 2009.

2.5 CONCLUSIONS AND OUTLOOK

Dubai is a small open economy that experienced very high and sustained economic growth over the period 1975–2011, outpacing the rest of the six emirates that form the United Arab Emirates, and turning the emirate into a pole of economic attraction in the Arab Gulf region. Such a remarkable growth record has been matched by only few countries in the world and, therefore, Dubai's economic strategy may serve as a potential model for other developing economies.

At the core of this period of sustained economic growth is Dubai's ability to implement macroeconomic and sectorial policies that have achieved a remarkable diversification away from hydrocarbons into services, particularly financial, trade, and tourism. Diversification supported the expansion of the economy despite dwindling oil reserves and production. In fact, economic policies were enacted in advance of the decline of the oil industry thereby avoiding a generalized economic decline and allowing for a relatively smooth restructuring of Dubai's economy.

In the past half of a century the economic development model in Dubai has relied heavily on a massive accumulation of production factors, primarily physical capital and unskilled migrant labour. The lack of an indigenous population largely explains the reliance on foreign workers, while physical capital accumulation was initially the result of public infrastructure projects which more recently have been overtaken by private investment. This model has served the economy of Dubai well in terms of high growth rates and building a high standard of living. However, this model has been associated with low-to-negative total factor productivity growth, indicating the need to review the development strategy so as to base future growth more on improved efficiency than on factor accumulation.

Short-term fluctuations in economic growth indicate both the vulnerability of Dubai's economy to international shocks as well as the impact of internal pressures brought on by Dubai's rapid pace of growth and the lack of counteracting policy instruments on the part of the authorities. Vulnerability to international fluctuations is not uncommon in small open economies that cannot hedge against risk by recourse to their internal markets. In the upswing of global economic cycles, these small economies benefit substantially. In the downswing, they tend to get hurt. This vulnerability, however, can be ameliorated by the cushioning effect of appreciations and depreciations of their currency. This mechanism is unavailable in Dubai as the currency is pegged by the UAE Central Bank to the US dollar. In the absence of this automatic stabilizer, there is a need to develop risk-hedging instruments to ameliorate the negative impact of foreign fluctuations.

On the internal front, short-term fluctuations are compounded by the lack of fiscal instruments available to the Dubai government. In most economies *ad valorem* taxes provide a cushioning effect against shocks: whenever demand is high, taxes are also high and reduce the build-up of unsustainable domestic pressures. Whenever demand is low, lower taxes fuel recovery. The tax system in Dubai does not provide such a mechanism as it largely focuses on fixed fees. Therefore, the government has to recourse to debt financing in order to provide some counter-cyclical policies, as exemplified during the global recession of the period 2008–9. Again this would indicate the need to develop more effective fiscal instruments for cyclical management.

The global financial and economic crisis of 2008 also revealed some weak structural features in the financing strategy of Dubai. Economic growth in Dubai has been highly leveraged, which raises the issue of the long-term sustainability of its fiscal policy, namely as a result of debt accumulation by government and the numerous quasi-public enterprises. In the few years leading to the global crisis, growth in Dubai was fuelled to a large extent by excessive liquidity and explosive appreciation of real estate prices. Such growth could not be sustained in the aftermath of the global crisis thus revealing the vulnerability of the economy to financial fluctuations. A long-term economic strategy for development in Dubai should include reform policies aimed at establishing a more balanced path where public and private activities are better coordinated.

REFERENCES

Dubai Economic Council, 2007. 'Inflation in the UAE and Dubai'. Dubai: Dubai Economic Council.

Dubai Economic Council, 2009. 'The Global Financial Crisis and its Fallouts: Toward an Actionable Strategy for Addressing the Consequences for Dubai and Anticipation of post-Crisis Transformations'. Dubai: Dubai Economic Council.

Dubai Economic Council, 2012. 'Dubai Economy Report'. Dubai: Dubai Economic Council.

Elbadawi, I. and Soto, R., 2012. 'Sources of Economic Growth and Development Strategy in Dubai'. In A. Sadik and I. Elbadawi (eds) *The Global Economic Crisis and Consequences for Development Strategy in Dubai.* New York: Palgrave Macmillan, pp. 121–53.

Maratheftis, M., 2009. 'Monetary Policy: Constraints and Measures'. Dubai Economic Council Working Paper No. 05, June.

Pritchett, L., 1996. 'Mind your P's and Q's: The Cost of Public Investment Is not the Value of Public Capital'. World Bank: Policy Research Working Paper No. 1660.

Renauld, B., 2012. 'Financial Crisis and Real Estate Bubbles: Dynamic and Policy Responses in Dubai'. In A. Sadik and I. Elbadawi (eds) *The Global Economic Crisis and Consequences for Development Strategy in Dubai.* New York: Palgrave Macmillan, pp. 87–119.

Sadik, A. and Bolbol, A., 2001. 'Mobilizing International Capital for Arab Economic Development: With Special Reference on the Role of FDI'. AMF Economic Papers No. 1, Arab Monetary Fund, Abu Dhabi.

Wilson, G., 2010. *Rashid's Legacy: The Genesis of the Maktoum Family and the History of Dubai*, Dubai: Media Prima.

Zebregs, H., 1998. 'Can the Neoclassical Model Explain the Distribution of FDI across Developing Countries?' IMF Working Paper WP/98/139, Washington, DC.

3

Public Debt Management and Fiscal Sustainability

Boaz Nandwa and Ali Tawfik Al Sadik

3.1 INTRODUCTION

In the aftermath of the global financial crisis, the role of fiscal policy in macroeconomic stabilization has become a prominent subject matter in policy discussions. This is particularly important for small, open, non-natural resource-based economies, such as Dubai, where the risks of exposure to both internal and external shocks are high and might lead to unsustainable debt levels. Generally, governments are not only required to build up the infrastructure, but also to provide quality education, housing, healthcare, and other services as well as social amenities to its citizenry. This presents the government with serious challenges in terms of how to mobilize sufficient resources in order to allocate them among competing needs. Dubai is part of the United Arab Emirates (UAE) federation, composed of seven emirates. The relationship between the federal government and the emirates allows for a relatively high degree of flexibility and autonomy in the exercise of local authority. Except for a few matters that pertain to the federal government, fiscal policy in the UAE is highly decentralized. Each emirate has its own local government comprised of departments (authorities), being able to retain and exercise political, judiciary, financial, and economic autonomy. On this basis, each emirate manages its own budget on an independent basis, with no obligation to contribute to the budgets of the other emirates. By virtue of their relatively well-endowed status, Abu Dhabi and Dubai are required to make a substantial contribution to the federal budget. The federal government in return provides a number of public goods and central services such as defence, immigration control, and coordinates national policies such as education and health with emirate-level authorities.

This chapter focuses on Dubai's revenue sources and expenditure allocation, underscoring the overall fiscal balance position of the government.[1] Further, we examine the structure and profile of the government's sovereign debt relative to the debt incurred by its quasi government enterprises (government-related entities, GREs). Since detailed information on the stock of public debt is not readily available, this chapter assesses the fiscal sustainability of Dubai based on revenue-to-GDP, expenditure-to-GDP, and overall budget deficit-GDP ratio indicators.[2] Policy recommendations are proposed to address issues regarding the long-term sustainability of the government's fiscal position. However, it should be noted that our evaluation is a gross approximation of the problem since a thorough analysis of the fiscal sustainability of the government of Dubai is limited by lack of reliable and timely data. Most of the data on fiscal operations and the stock of debt are not public. Similarly, information on the financial statements (assets and liabilities) and debt of the GREs is not available to the public. In turn, this reduces the confidence among investors and lenders regarding the fiscal soundness of the Dubai government and the solvency of the GREs.

Despite the data limitations, the study finds that the sovereign debt held by the government seems manageable over the long term. However, the financial difficulties experienced by the GREs, and the subsequent bailouts by the government, have undermined to some extent the fiscal sustainability of the government of Dubai. In addition, the large increase in government financing of the cost to rollover the debt after the global crisis has placed further strain on fiscal accounts increasing the risk of a negative spillover to the financial system. Finally, the successive build-up of maturities of the government and the GREs' debts have the potential of raising the short-term borrowing risk and increase the borrowing costs of the government and private sector in Dubai. If not comprehensively addressed, this could potentially undermine Dubai's macroeconomic stability and competitiveness as a regional financial and trading hub.

The rest of the chapter is structured as follows. In section 3.2, we examine the structure of the Dubai government's fiscal operations, exploring the management of Dubai's budget, sources of its revenues, expenditure allocations, and the debt profile of both the government and GREs. Section 3.3 analyses the fiscal sustainability of Dubai's debt followed by the conclusion and policy recommendations.

[1] Hereafter, the government corresponds to that of Dubai unless noted otherwise.

[2] This approach has been adopted in several studies, see, for example, Hakkio and Rush (1991), Buiter and Patel (1992), Cuddington (1997), and Gerson and Nellor (1997).

3.2 THE STRUCTURE OF DUBAI GOVERNMENT'S FISCAL OPERATIONS

Dubai's Supreme Fiscal Council (SFC) was established in 2007 to formulate fiscal policies and regulate its domestic and foreign borrowings. The Department of Finance (DOF) is the local ministry of finance and treasury (exchequer) and acts as the administrative unit for executing and monitoring the compliance of the various departments with the SFC decisions. In addition, the DOF is mandated with collecting all revenues and allocating funds to the various government departments. Investment Corporation of Dubai (ICD), Dubai World (DW), and Dubai International Financial Center Investments (DIFCI) are the principal investment entities of the government, otherwise known as Dubai Inc. These enterprises were formed as holding companies for a series of investments previously held by the DOF. Except for the period after the financial crisis, these entities are required to be self-financing operations, and from the profits generated, make contributions to the budget of the Dubai government.

The government budget commences in the second half of each calendar year and is prepared on a cash basis.[3] Generally, there are two major approaches used in preparing the budget: cash basis and accrual methods, with each method using different criteria to determine when to recognize and record revenue and expenses in the financial records. In the cash basis method, revenues are recognized and recorded when cash is received and deposited, and expenses recorded when bills are paid. On the other hand, in the accrual method, income is realized in the accounting period in which it is earned, regardless of when the cash from transactions is received. Similarly, expenses are recorded as they are owed, rather than when they are paid. The main advantage of using a cash-based approach is that it is much easier and cheaper to maintain, reducing bookkeeping expenses. However, accrual budgeting provides a better perspective on public resource management by comparing government's performance against private sector business performance since it matches income to expenses more accurately.[4]

[3] In 2009, the government began implementing a new pricing mechanism for government services aimed at measuring accurately their cost of provisions. As of 2013 no public study has evaluated whether this mechanism proved to be cost-effective or efficient.

[4] A basic illustration of this difference can be applied to credit cards. Suppose an individual buys an item using a credit card, which he/she does not instantaneously pay off from his/her personal checking account—this is a cash budgeting method. However, if he/she uses the credit card and then writes a check immediately to settle the credit card debt, regardless of the due date of the bill, then this is accrual-based budgeting. In this case, the accrual method imposes accountability, and also makes the individual aware of his/her spending limits.

3.2.1 Fiscal Performance of the Dubai Government

The budget comprises revenues, current expenditures, development expenditures, grants (domestic and foreign) and Dubai's contribution to the federal government.[5] The budget, as indicated, excludes GREs. In addition, the budget also includes financing items such as loan disbursements and repayments. The budget preparation is coordinated by DOF, which reviews and consolidates individual budgets of each of the major government departments.[6] The consolidated budgets are then submitted to the SFC, which reviews and approves the budgets in mid-December of each year. Prior to the global financial crisis of 2008–10, the government of Dubai maintained a fairly close match between its revenues and expenditure as illustrated in Figure 3.1.

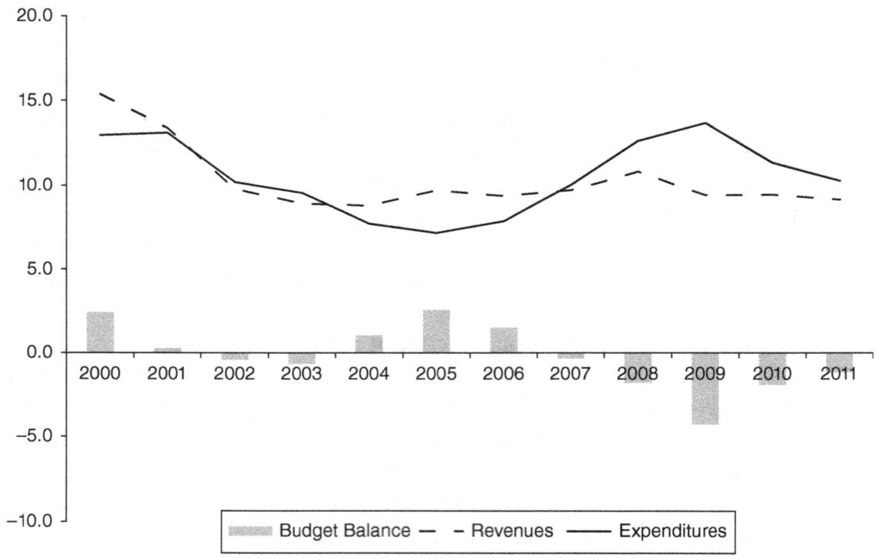

Figure 3.1. Fiscal performance of Dubai government (% GDP)

Source: Own elaboration based on data from Dubai's Department of Finance, Government of Dubai (2010), and IMF (2011)

[5] Fiscal analysis in Dubai is fraught with difficulties because of the often blurred delineation of the ad hoc financial activities of the government and the GREs. In addition, many transactions of the Dubai Water and Electricity Authority are not reflected in the consolidated budget, but rather settled in an off-budget account. This makes it hard to get a clear and accurate picture of the financial status of the government.

[6] These departments act as the main units of delegated authority, responsible for different administrative operations, e.g. Dubai Municipality, Department of Economic Development, Land Department.

Dubai exhibited a healthy fiscal balance during the period 2000–7. As seen in Figure 3.1 over the decade, except for the increased deficit of 4.3 per cent in 2009, the government was able to maintain its budget deficit within the internationally accepted standard of 3 per cent of its GDP (e.g. the Stability and Growth Pact of the eurozone and provisions in countries that have implemented fiscal policy rules). The rise in the budget deficit in the 2002–3 period coincided with an increase in government expenditure to finance the expansion of its infrastructure (e.g. expansion of Jebel Ali Port and Dubai International Airport) and further diversification of its economy through establishment of new GREs and foreign expansion of existing GREs (e.g. Dubai Ports). Over the period 2004–6, the government registered an impressive budget surplus due to an increase in non-tax revenues (mainly fees and charges), taxes (customs), and profits from its enterprises (GREs).

However, following the bursting of the real-estate bubble in early 2008 coupled with the global recession, Dubai experienced substantial budget deficits in the period 2008–10, which rose to 4.3 per cent in 2009, before being controlled by the authorities. This dramatic rise in the deficit was occasioned by the bailout of GREs: in 2009 the government borrowed heavily to establish the Dubai Financial Support Fund (DFSF) aimed at restructuring and providing financial support to GREs facing financial difficulties.[7] The revenues in 2012 are anticipated to be US$8.3 billion, slightly higher than US $8.1 billion in 2011, against expenditures of US$8.7 billion in 2012 which is markedly lower than US$9.1 billion in 2011. This represents a decline in budget deficit from 1.2 per cent of the GDP in 2011 to 0.6 per cent of the projected GDP in 2012.

The revenues collected by various Dubai government departments and agencies are credited to a single revenue account held by DOF. The revenue sources consist of two broad categories: tax and non-tax revenues as shown in Figure 3.2. The largest source of revenue is non-tax revenue which, in the period 2000–11, consistently generated over 70 per cent of the total revenue to the government. Dubai does not levy taxes on individuals' or businesses' incomes, therefore, it is not surprising that non-tax revenue is a significant share of Dubai's total revenue base.

Further, within these two broad revenue categories, there are various subcategories with varied contribution to Dubai's exchequer. Tax revenues are comprised of custom duty (levied at 5 per cent on imports from non-GCC countries), and income tax (levied at 20 per cent) on profits earned by foreign

[7] The DFSF was established in July 2009 with the objective of supporting GREs critical to Dubai's economy (specifically ICD, DW, and their subsidiaries). The DFSF was funded through proceeds of dollar-denominated securities issued by the government under a $20 billion 5-year unsecured programme ($10 billion from the UAE central bank and $10 billion from the Abu Dhabi government). The government entities are required to repay the loans, through the sale of assets and revenues among other sources, by March 2014.

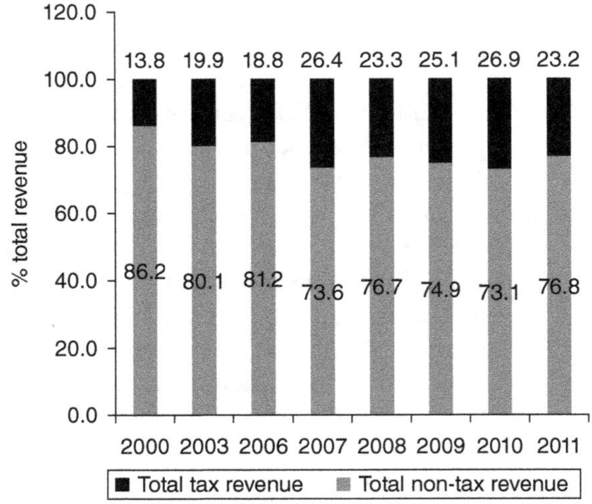

Figure 3.2. Dubai: Sources of government revenue (%)

Source: Own elaboration based on data from Dubai's Department of Finance

banks operating in Dubai, but not located in the free zone.[8] Of the tax sources in Figure 3.3, customs duty contributed the largest share of the revenues, especially with the surge in imports in Dubai and those destined for other emirates and neighbouring countries experienced since early 2000.

The launch of the Dubai International Financial Center (DIFC) in 2002, in addition to the establishment of other non-financial free zones, such as TECOM Business Parks, led to the attractiveness of Dubai as a dynamic financial hub in the region. This contributed to an increase in the number of foreign banks and other financial institutions opening their branches, with some of these banks setting their headquarters in Dubai as a platform to serve the region. In 2000, customs duty generated 12 per cent of total tax revenues while taxes on foreign banks contributed 1.5 per cent of the cumulative tax revenues. A decade later, there was an exponential increase in these shares, with customs registering over 63 per cent in revenue growth while tax revenue on banks' profits grew by over 100 per cent. Dubai (the UAE and GCC countries) does not levy taxes on individuals' or businesses' incomes.[9] Similarly, as is characteristic of the GCC countries, Dubai (and the UAE) does not

[8] Foreign banks are restricted to operating seven branches in the whole of the UAE. The branch expansion is not restricted geographically, that is, a foreign bank can have one branch in each of the seven emirates or a total of seven branches in one emirate. This explains the concentration of foreign banks' branches in Dubai.

[9] Deliberations are still ongoing regarding the feasibility of implementing VAT by the GCC countries, although there is no definite date when this will be done. Dubai will have less control over the VAT rate and its mechanism as this will be implemented at the regional (GCC) and federal (UAE) government levels.

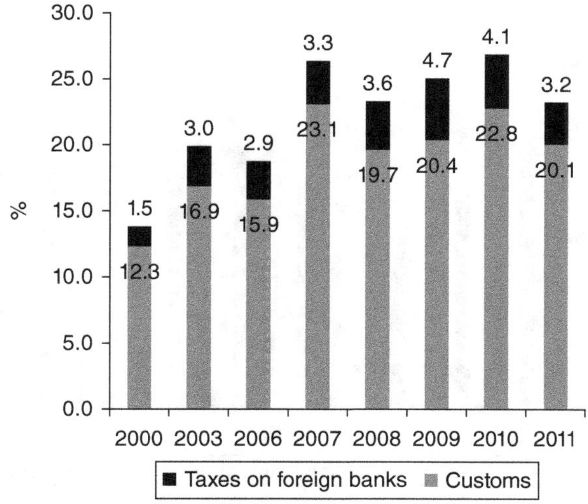

Figure 3.3. Dubai: Tax revenue sources (%)

Source: Own elaboration based on data from Dubai's Department of Finance, Government of Dubai (2010), and IMF (2011)

levy value-added taxes (VAT). The limitations of not being able to pursue this option have become more evident as governments in the GCC countries find themselves unable to generate enough revenues to fund increased demands for the improved welfare of its citizens and infrastructure development. In addition, these economies are unable to undertake efficient countercyclical policies—for lack of monetary policy instruments due to the US dollar peg. This renders them incapable of devising mechanisms (e.g. through automatic stabilizers provided by VAT) to escape the oil-price cycles that permeate to other domestic sources of revenues (see Elbadawi and Gelb, 2010).

The non-tax-based revenue sources are comprised of a range of fees and fines levied by various Dubai government departments. In addition, other non-tax revenue sources are: revenues from oil and gas (petroleum) and income from investments made by the Dubai government through its GREs; Investment Corporation of Dubai (ICD), Dubai World (DW), and Dubai International Financial Center Investments (DIFCI) enterprise profits, as presented in Figure 3.4.

The share of petroleum (oil and gas) revenues has declined precipitously over the years, reflecting diminishing reserves and importance in Dubai's economy (see Chapter 2). In 2000, revenues from oil accounted for over 50 per cent of the total non-tax revenues. However, in 2011, the share of oil and gas revenues declined to less than 10 per cent. Similar to oil-producing economies, oil and gas revenues in Dubai are pro-cyclical. The increase in revenues in 2000–8 was a direct result of increases in international oil prices, rather than an increase in actual output in the same period. As a corollary, the decline in oil and gas

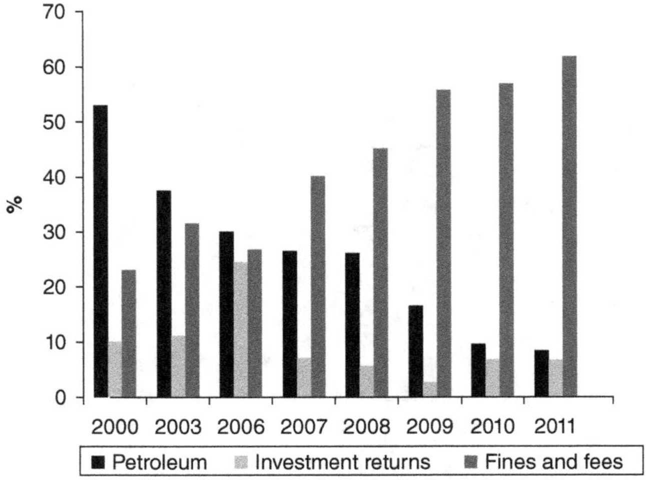

Figure 3.4. Dubai: Non-tax revenue sources (%)

Source: Own elaboration based on data from Dubai's Department of Finance, Government of Dubai (2010), and IMF (2011)

revenues in 2009 is attributed to a decline in international oil prices following the global recession precipitated by the financial crisis. Given the significant involvement of the GREs in Dubai's economy and investments abroad, revenues from these entities in the form of profits and dividends have also become quite important for the fiscal budget. However, these GREs have also become a major source of risk to Dubai's fiscal sustainability due to their accumulated debts and the refinancing risks they pose to its public debt in the short to medium term. In addition, revenues from these entities are pro-cyclical, especially in the period 2008–10 when returns declined precipitously due to the global financial crisis. Finally, over the years, fees levied by the government for services rendered have increased exponentially, reflecting their importance to Dubai as a major source of revenue. For instance, in 2010, revenue from these fees was about US$4.5 billion.[10] While this has become important revenue for the government, it is neither sustainable nor efficient over the long term for various reasons. First, fees and charges are pro-cyclical, therefore negatively impinging on government revenues during recessionary periods. Second, these fees and charges are regressive to SMEs since they are often applied as a flat rate regardless of the size of the firm. Third, revenues from fees and charges are not predictable, therefore making it difficult for the government to plan and budget effectively over the long term.

[10] Heavy reliance on fees has been criticized for not only being distortionary, but also inefficient and regressive since they penalize and introduce hidden costs to the SMEs. In addition, fees are pro-cyclical and unpredictable, exacerbating budget deficits during recessions.

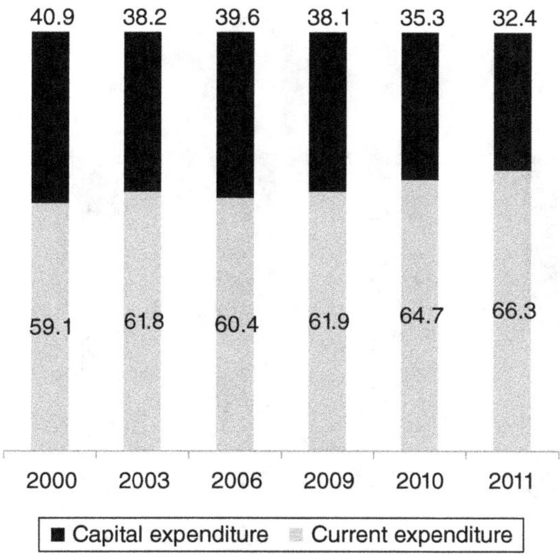

Figure 3.5. Dubai: Government expenditure allocations (%)

Source: Own elaboration based on data from Dubai's Department of Finance, Government of Dubai (2010), and IMF (2011)

The expenditures of each of the government's departments are monitored by DOF and reported periodically.[11] The government's expenditures are broadly categorized as current and development expenditures, as illustrated in Figure 3.5. Over the past decade, current expenditure[12] allocations consumed about 60 per cent of the total government expenditures, with capital (development) expenditure being allocated less than 40 per cent. In the 1990s and early 2000, capital expenditure allocations were much higher than in the past few years, largely due to a significant increase in infrastructure development, such as roads construction, expansion of the Jebel Ali port, Dubai Creek, and Dubai International Airport, among other major infrastructures.

In Figure 3.6, the government's current expenditures largely comprise of housing construction for Emiratis (over 40 per cent in the past four years), subsidies and transfers, salaries and wages paid to the civil service, and the direct cost of goods and services rendered by the various government departments. In the recent past, wages and salaries as a share of the current expenditures have

[11] The DOF prepares annual financial statements which are audited by the Emirates' Financial Audit Department (EFAD). However, these statements are not published. In addition, except for dividends from the GREs to DOF, the government does not consolidate the budgets of the GREs.

[12] Expenditures incurred by the government for water and electricity payments and Dubai Municipality expenditures, although substantial, are not reflected in the government budget, but rather in an off-budget account. This has the effect of understating the true fiscal position of the government.

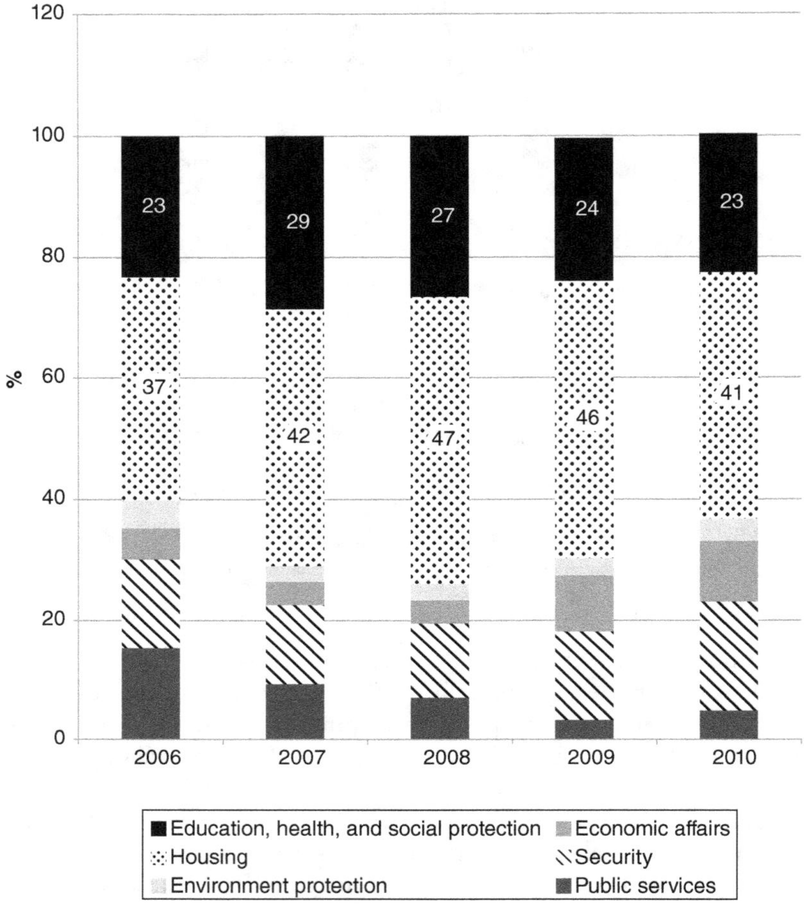

Figure 3.6. Sectoral expenditure allocations (%)

Source: Department of Finance, Government of Dubai

increased due to two main reasons. First, an increase in public sector employment favoured by Emiratis has raised the government wage bill. For the same level of education and experience, Emiratis attract relatively higher wages compared to expatriates.[13] Second, an increase in the cost of living fuelled by inflationary pressure from the housing bubble in the pre-2008 financial crisis, compelled the government to adjust its wages upwards. Due to wage rigidity and inflexibility in the labour market for Emiratis, it is unlikely that the

[13] This phenomenon has often led to the perception that government employment of Emiratis is a source of wealth transfer and redistribution mechanism, rather than an avenue of gainful employment.

government would impose a wage-cut or freeze on public sector employment. This is expected to have a cascading effect on future current expenditures, impinging on fiscal sustainability of Dubai (and the UAE).

Further, in Figure 3.6, to strengthen and enhance its regional position, the government has focused more of its expenditure allocation on the economic sector (comprising infrastructure, transportation, and other general development). In the period 2008–10, allocation to the economic sector increased by 150 per cent, reflecting the government's commitment to develop and increase its infrastructure in order to remain regionally competitive since other emirates (e.g. Abu Dhabi) and neighbouring countries (e.g. Qatar) have over the past five years heavily invested in developing their infrastructures in order to attract more FDI and spur economic growth.

3.3 DUBAI'S DEBT STRUCTURE AND PROFILE

Over the past two decades, Dubai has relied on external borrowing to finance its rapid expansion of infrastructure development to spur economic growth. Foreign borrowing was necessitated by the lack of developed domestic capital markets and the availability of cheap credit on the international capital markets. On this basis, both the government and the GREs turned to international capital markets for their lower cost of funding, leading to a build-up of huge foreign currency denominated debt (in addition to over-leveraged domestic borrowing from national banks). Until 2007, the government debt

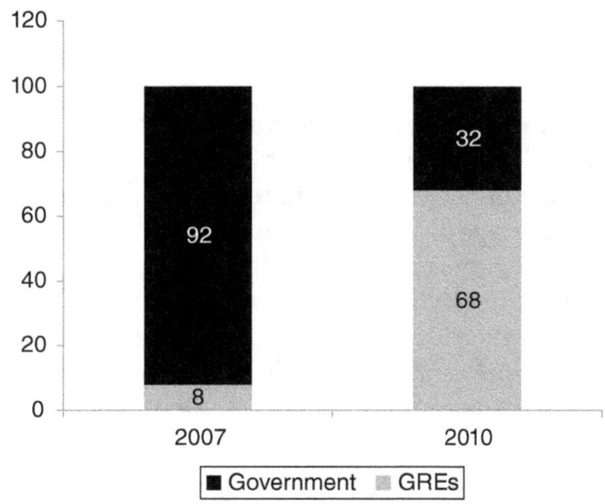

Figure 3.7. Dubai total debt stock (%)
Source: IMF (2011) and own elaborations

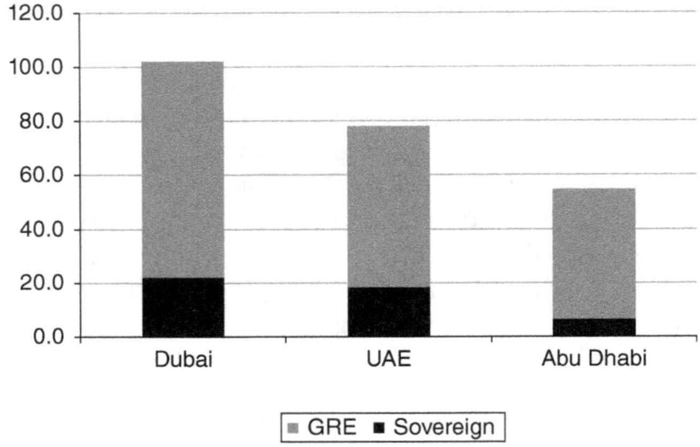

Figure 3.8. Total gross debt (% GDP), 2010
Source: IMF (2011)

mainly comprised the sovereign debt as shown in Figure 3.7, whereby the sovereign debt was 92 per cent of the Dubai's total debt stock and the GREs' share was only 8 per cent. However this changed significantly with the inception of GREs, which were formed in part as a way of diversifying Dubai's economy under the guidance of the government in strategic sectors of the economy, such as real estate, tourism, transport and logistics, and trading. The other principal reason leading to the formation of GREs was as a means of generating revenues for the government to build its infrastructure and provide for social and economic development of the emirate. As a result, however, Figure 3.7 shows that, in 2010 the share of GREs debt rose to 32 per cent, while the sovereign debt share had declined to 68 per cent.

Further, in Figure 3.8, while the share of the sovereign debt in Dubai as a percentage of GDP is similar to that of the UAE, the debt share of GREs in the total gross debt (combined sovereign debt and GREs debt) is almost twice for Dubai compared to the average for UAE or Abu Dhabi combined GREs debt.[14] In addition, the share of GREs in Dubai's total gross debt in 2010 was over 80 per cent, while the average debt of their counterparts in the UAE was about 60 per cent and only 48 per cent for those in Abu Dhabi. The sovereign debt showed a similar pattern: while for Abu Dhabi the debt was lower at 6 per cent of GDP, for Dubai and the UAE the share of sovereign debt in GDP was close to 20 per cent and 18 per cent, respectively. While the large size of the debt of Dubai (GREs and sovereign) presents a dim view of Dubai's debt stance, it is

[14] Dubai's publicly held sovereign debt does not include guarantees of the Dubai government to the Dubai Electricity and Water Authority (DEWA) and Road and Transport Authority (RTA). These would further increase the total debt. It is notable that a significant share of the UAE gross debt arose from Dubai.

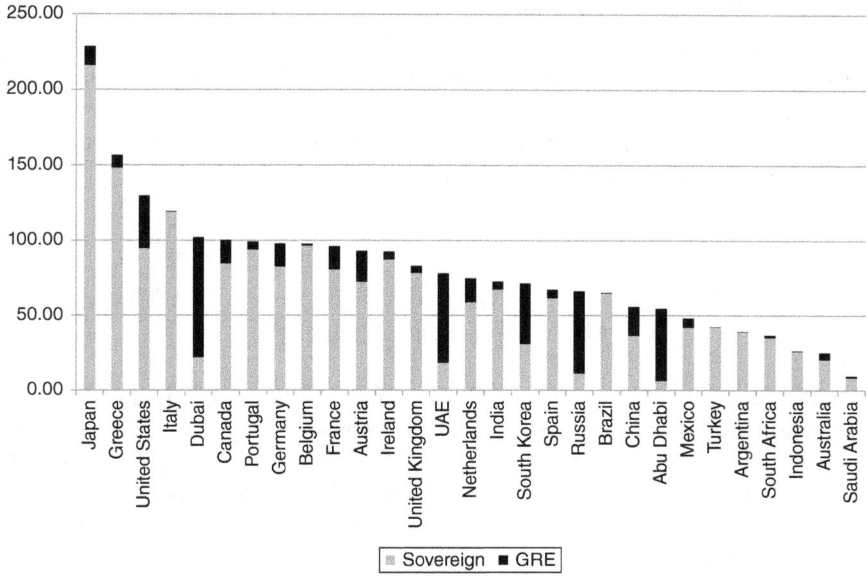

Figure 3.9. Comparative total gross debt (% GDP), 2010
Source: IMF (2011)

important to note that the government, the GREs and their affiliated subsidiaries hold significant foreign assets such that, in net terms, Dubai's foreign exposure is significantly lower. However, most of the foreign assets owned by the government and GREs are not liquid; rather, they are held in the form of acquisitions in foreign commercial entities, real estate, and other physical—and relatively illiquid—capital.

Figure 3.9 illustrates international comparisons of total gross debt, consisting of sovereign and GREs debt profiles, as a share of GDP. Incidentally, countries with substantial total gross debt, such as, Japan, the USA, and various European countries are also some of the high-income countries. For instance, Japan's total gross debt is over 200 per cent of its GDP yet it is the third largest economy in the world after the USA and China. In this context, it is not the total gross debt which might pose macroeconomic stability challenges, but rather, its composition. Sovereign debts are owed by governments, while GREs' debts are owed by corporations formed by governments, expected to operate and be financially independent. However, in some cases such as Dubai, the delineation between sovereign and GREs debt is often blurred. While the share of Dubai's sovereign debt is comparable and even lower than the majority of the developed economies, however, it is the share of the GREs debt that is worrisome. This can be attributed to the structure of Dubai economy which is dominated by large GREs formed by the government as holding companies used for investment purposes to generate revenue to fund Dubai's growth and also diversify its economy by investing in strategic sectors, for example, telecommunications, transportation, aviation, hospitality, electricity and power generation, oil and gas, heavy industries, and real estate development, among other ventures. Similar trends in large GREs debt relative to the sovereign debt can also be observed in Russia, Abu Dhabi, South Korea, and China, where GREs are also prevalent.

3.4 GLOBAL FINANCIAL CRISIS AND THE DUBAI GOVERNMENT'S DEBT

The unravelling of the global financial crisis in late 2008 had significant adverse implications for Dubai. In 2008, its external debt stood at US$115 billion, representing about 152 per cent of GDP.[15] During this period, over 60 per cent of the external debt (US$75 billion) was owed by its two major GREs (ICD and DW). In the aftermath of the financial crisis in 2009, the government recognized it had to restructure the sovereign debt of its largest GRE (DW, and its two real estate subsidiaries, Nakheel Properties and Limitless World). The Dubai government announced a standstill in repayment of its maturing debt of approximately US$60 billion between November 2009 and May 2010 to allow it time for orderly debt restructuring. In early 2011, the Dubai direct sovereign debt (i.e. excluding debt owed by its GREs) was estimated to be US$31.1 billion, which represented about 45 per cent of GDP. This is in addition to the financial contingencies and extended guarantees committed by the government during the restructuring.[16] About half of this debt was incurred by the government in setting up the Dubai Financial Support Fund (DFSF) in July 2009, with the aim of providing financial support to those struggling GREs of strategic and development importance to the economy.[17] The DFSF was capitalized through the proceeds of the government's US$20 billion, five-year unsecured borrowing issued by the central bank of the UAE and the government of Abu Dhabi. These unsecured bonds mature in March 2014, when the GREs are expected to have repaid the loans either from their own funds, profits, or sale of assets.

15 This is substantial compared, for example, to Singapore which in 2008 had an external debt of US$115 billion, but where this represented only 63 per cent of its GDP.

16 In 2010, these contingencies and guarantees were in relation to financial obligations of DEWA (US$3.6 billion), RTA with respect to Dubai Metro ($1.8 billion), and US$2.19 billion towards restructuring of DW.

17 The funds were conditional that the GREs have until March 2014 to repay the DFSF. The reason for this cut-off date is to enable the government to meet the $20 billion debt repayment in March 2014 when its borrowing to set up the DFSF matures. Information on the eligibility criteria and the list of GREs that received DFSF support and how much was allocated to the GREs have not been made public.

Limited information on Dubai's sovereign and GREs debt stock and profile, coupled with the opacity of government–GREs relationships, generated substantial uncertainty among investors and potential lenders, leading to a significant widening in the spread on Dubai credit default swaps (CDS).[18] For instance, prior to the crisis, the CDS spread between Dubai, Abu Dhabi, Qatar, and Saudi Arabia was fairly close. However, amid tightening credit on the international capital markets and financial difficulties experienced by Dubai in the period 2008–9, there was a substantial widening in the CDS spread in late 2008 from 800 basis points to a peak of 950 basis points in early 2009 before dissipating later that year, albeit remaining above Abu Dhabi, Qatar, and Saudi Arabia. This trend is expected to continue over the next five years when most of the rollover debts will be due. The capacity of Dubai to service these debts and pay off the maturing debts is going to be a critical factor in determining the widening or narrowing of the spread. In late 2009, Dubai's CDS tightened above 400 basis points as a result of publication of information on Dubai sovereign debt in the issuance of dollar-bonds under the Euro Medium Term Note (EMTN) programme[19] and the government restructuring of its GREs with the support of the UAE Central Bank and the Abu Dhabi government. Subsequently, in the period 2010–12, the CDS spread stagnated above 350 basis points, indicating that investors view the fiscal situation in Dubai as neither improved nor less opaque.

The widening CDS spread for Dubai in mid 2011 primarily reflected the uncertainty and risk associated with lack of accurate information on sovereign debt levels and concerns about the ability of Dubai to repay its debts (both sovereign and GREs). This is reflected in Figure 3.10 which shows cumulative probability default (CPD) of various countries in 2011. CPD is computed by CMA Datavision, an independent CDS pricing agency based on intraday price data collected by CMA's consortium. CPD quantifies the probability of a country being unable to honour its debt obligations over a given period of time, or probability of restructuring the debt. The top five countries; Greece, Portugal, Argentina, Ireland, and Italy are the countries which were hardest hit by the global financial crisis, and which are currently experiencing fiscal difficulties. In the post-crisis era, Greece, Portugal, Spain, and Ireland have at some point or

[18] Credit default swaps (CDS) are financial contracts intended to protect bondholders against default by the issuer. An increase in CDS spread signals deterioration in the credit quality of the issuer.

[19] The EMTN programme allows flexible placement of bonds in various currencies on the European bond market. Therefore, EMTNs make it easier for issuers to enter into foreign markets for capital. EMTNs are issued directly to the market with maturities of less than five years and are offered continuously rather than all at once like a bond issue. With EMTNs, the issuer maintains a standardized document (known as a programme) that can be transferred across all issues and has a great proportion of sales through a syndication of pre-selected buyers (e.g. investment and commercial banks, pension funds, insurance funds). The Dubai government used the proceeds from the bond issue for general budgetary purposes to supplement its internal revenue sources.

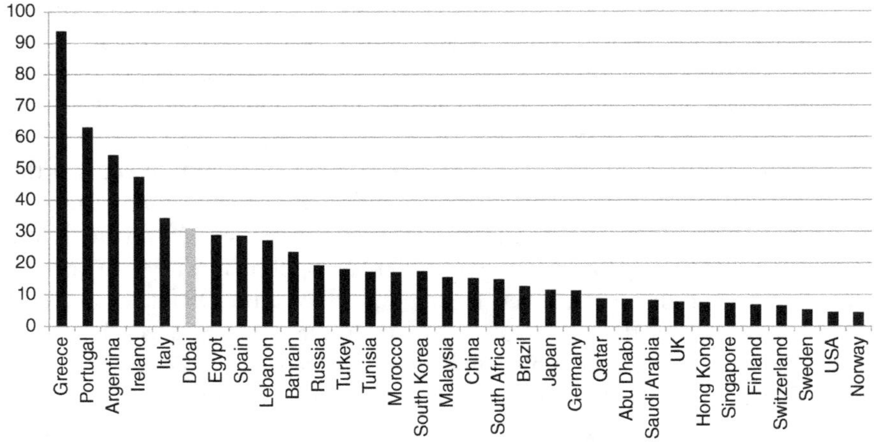

Figure 3.10. Cumulative probability default of sovereign debt (%), March 2011
Source: CMA Datavision and own elaborations

another defaulted on their foreign debt obligations.[20] For Greece, Portugal, and Ireland, the source of their fiscal difficulties can be traced to private debt incurred by their financial institutions, which necessitated government bailouts. For Spain, the origin can be traced to fiscal profligacy of its provincial governments. While the sovereign debts of these countries were manageable, it is their timing which contributed to their default. It is seen that, at 30.4 per cent, Dubai is ranked among the top 11 most likely economies to default (due to rescheduling of the GREs debts), while Singapore, Hong Kong, Switzerland, Abu Dhabi, and Saudi Arabia are among the top 10 economies with safe sovereign debt. This is an area of concern for Dubai which requires immediate attention. Similar to the top five countries at risk of default, it is the timing and size of the debt repayments which led to their default. Most of Dubai's debts mature in the period 2014–19. Given the limited revenue generating options for Dubai and expenditure inflexibility, this is expected to put a strain on Dubai's finances.

3.5 FISCAL SUSTAINABILITY

Unlike the capitalist (free market) economic development model pursued by developed and emerging economies, Dubai (and most of the GCC economies) has a unique economic development model, which overly emphasizes

[20] Coupled with austerity measures, bailouts from the European Community and IMF have temporarily forestalled Greek's debt default.

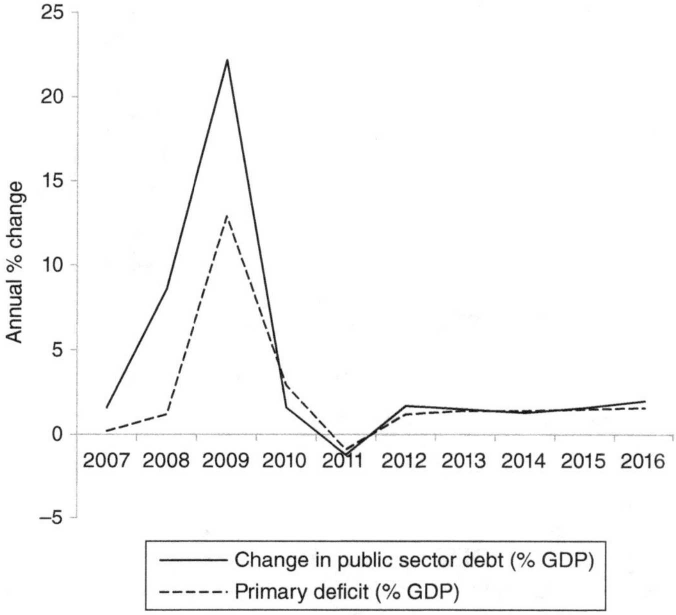

Figure 3.11. Dubai public debt and primary deficit (% GDP)
Source: IMF (2011) and own elaborations

government establishment of corporations (GREs) with a view to generating revenues in order to contribute to the budget and diversification of its economy. Often, as evidenced in the post-2008 financial crisis, there is a lack of a clear delineation between the government and GREs' operations and finances. While this model has served Dubai well in the past, in the aftermath of the global financial crisis, this opacity proved to have significant adverse implications on fiscal sustainability. In this section Dubai's fiscal sustainability can, therefore, be assessed on two levels: sovereign debt and debt held by GREs.[21]

Dubai's sovereign debt is manageable, even small by international standards (less than 2 per cent GDP in pre- and post-financial crisis) with primary deficit projected to be within 3 per cent of GDP. This is similar to the deficit–GDP threshold level adopted in the Stability and Growth Pact of the eurozone. In Figure 3.11, the public (sovereign) debt spiked in 2008–9 largely due to financial difficulties experienced by the government in the aftermath of the financial crisis when it could not sufficiently meet its obligations from domestic revenue sources, which necessitated the government borrowing in order to offset previous debts which were maturing and establishing the Dubai

[21] Appendix II outlines the structure and profile of Dubai's sovereign and GREs debt for 2012 and beyond.

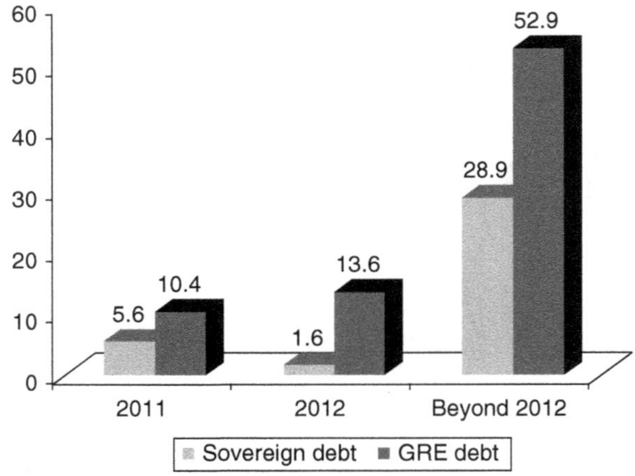

Figure 3.12. Dubai: Gross public and publicly held debt (US$ billion)
Source: IMF (2012) and own elaborations

Financial Support Fund (DFSF). However, the primary deficit (deficit without interest payments) in the post-crisis era declined significantly and it is projected to revert to its pre-crisis level, signalling sustainability of the public debt over the long-term horizon.

However, it is the GREs debt which is worrisome to Dubai's fiscal sustainability (Figure 3.12).

Figure 3.12 depicts the relative stock of Dubai public debt (sovereign and GREs). In 2012, the sovereign (government) debt declined by over 70 per cent from its peak in the post-financial crisis era through repayment of loans which matured in the first half of 2012, while GREs debt increased by over 30 per cent in the same period, largely due to rescheduling of previously issued loans. However, it is beyond the year 2012 that will prove to be challenging for Dubai, since all the debts (especially for GREs) will be due, as seen in Figure 3.13, which shows the maturity profile of the debt held by Dubai's GREs. It is evident that with most of the restructured and non-restructured debts maturing by 2017, this is expected to put a lot of strain on Dubai's finances in the short and medium term. This is the case even though about US $25 billion worth of debt due in 2012 was restructured in 2011 and payments postponed until 2018, with a significant share of the debt owed by the GREs (US$9.6 billion due to DW and US$12 billion to ICD). (See Figure 3.14.)

Due to the substantial debt owed by its GREs, Dubai is the top-ranked economy in the world in terms of GRE gross debt as a share of GDP, followed by Russia, a similar economy where GREs are an important element, especially in banking, telecommunications, and the oil and gas sectors. The share of GREs debt to GDP for economies which defaulted on their debt, Greece, Portugal, and Spain, is relatively small. Hence, for Dubai, future timing and the size of

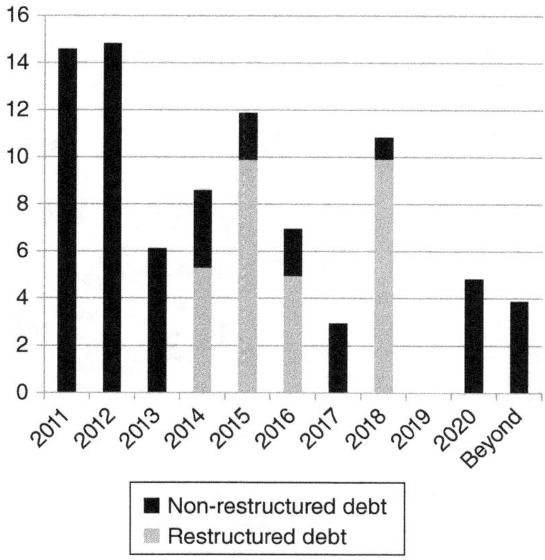

Figure 3.13. Maturity profile of Dubai GREs debt (US$ billion)
Source: IMF (2011)

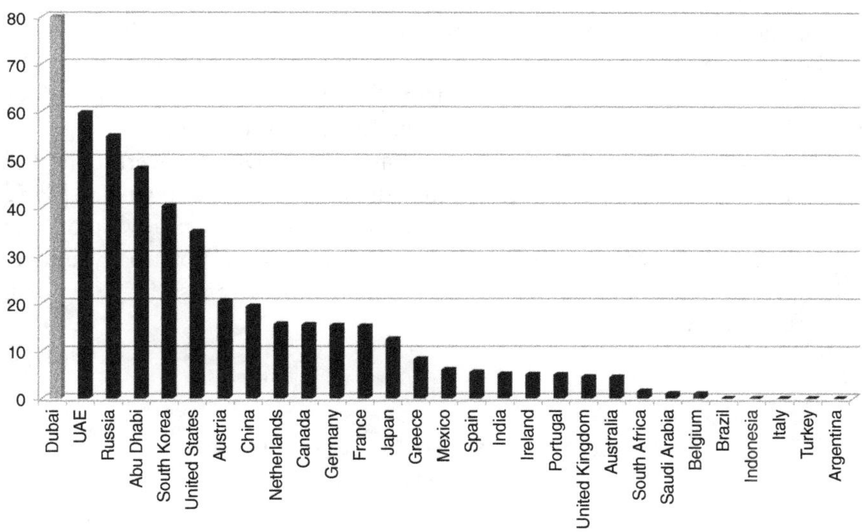

Figure 3.14. GRE gross debt (% GDP)
Source: IMF (2011)

the debt due for repayment are both expected to put its finances in a precarious position. From 2012 onwards, Dubai faces high short-term rollover risks on GRE debt. Table 3.1 shows the future external debt service of Dubai (only the principal debt due is shown since it is not clear how much interest Dubai will

Table 3.1. Dubai external debt service (US$ billion)

Year	o/w Syndicates (Loans)	o/w Bonds	Total external debt stock
2009	12.4	6.9	19.3
2010	7.3	2.8	10.1
2011	9.4	2.7	12.1
2012	11.6	3.6	15.2
2013	4.3	0.5	4.8
2014	0.8	1.0	1.7
2015	0.5	—	0.5
2016	0.6	1.0	1.6
2017	1.8	2.8	4.6
2019	0.6	—	0.6
2020	0.3	—	0.3
2022	1.8	—	1.8
2037	—	1.8	1.8
Total	**51.4**	**23.0**	**74.3**
% of Dubai GDP			**107%**

Note: These estimates are for Dubai as a whole including Dubai Inc. and the private sector. However, the estimates exclude the US$20 billion owed by the government to the UAE Central Bank and Abu Dhabi government.
Source: Deutsche Bank Global Market Research

pay on the loan repayments). The external debt excludes the US$20 billion owed by the government to the central bank of UAE and Abu Dhabi government. The period 2011–17 is, therefore, expected to be fiscally challenging for Dubai since over 70 per cent of the external debt will mature in this period alone.

Therefore, the successive build-up of maturities of Dubai government and GREs debts has the potential of raising the short-term borrowing risk and increase the borrowing costs of the government and the private sector (see Table 3.1). If not comprehensively addressed, this could potentially undermine Dubai's macroeconomic stability and competitiveness as a regional financial and trading hub.

3.6 CONCLUSIONS AND POLICY RECOMMENDATIONS

The role and size of the government, its expenditure and revenue mobilization strategies are at the core of the macroeconomic stabilization policy debate and sustainable economic growth. On this premise, the key to fiscal sustainability is a discipline in public debt management, in particular, keeping fiscal deficits to manageable levels. In their study, the IMF and World Bank (2001) identified three core principles of effective public debt management. These comprise the organizational framework, analytical framework, and operational framework of public debt management. The organizational framework entails ensuring that the government financing needs and its payment obligations are met at the lowest possible cost over the medium and long run and consistent with a prudent degree of risk. In addition, making available credible and verifiable information which adheres to international standards about the size, structure, and financing of government debt is imperative in effective public debt management as it enables constant monitoring and evaluation of debt incurred by investors (for example, following the methodological guidelines of the Public Sector Debt Statistics Database promoted by the IMF and the World Bank).[22] The analytical framework encompasses debt and risk management strategies. In this context, just like in the corporate business world, it is imperative for public debt management to conform to the best international business practices regarding risks associated with the size and structure of government debt. Finally the operational framework calls for development of an efficient government securities market to minimize risks and costs to the government, and in the process also help to develop a deep and liquid domestic capital market. These frameworks can be complemented by other fiscal consolidation measures, such as the adoption of fiscal rules which not only constrain discretionary government expenditures, but also confer credibility to the conduct of macroeconomic policy by the government.

For Dubai, the organizational and analytical frameworks are critical given the opacity of Dubai's public debt management. Specifically, the non-disclosure by the government of its sovereign and GREs debt compound international markets' suspicion of Dubai's fiscal capabilities. It is for this reason that of the aftermath of the financial crisis, international rating agencies declined to rate the government bonds. Similarly, lack of close monitoring of the GREs contributed to over-borrowing and imprudent investment decisions beyond their competencies.

In order to remain competitive and sustain its economic development trajectory, there is an urgent need for the Dubai government to undertake fiscal consolidation measures in order to enhance its revenue mobilization capabilities and align them with its expenditure requirements. The need to invest in infrastructure and social development programmes to spur higher economic growth is expected to put pressure on government expenditures because of the limited resource revenue base. While the government has in the recent past initiated fiscal policy consolidation measures to achieve manageable public debt levels, there are several issues that need to be further addressed by the government.

Foremost, lack of a clear delineation of the government–GREs relationship has put fiscal policy credibility into question to an extent that global rating

[22] The IMF and World Bank launched an online Public Sector Debt Statistics Database in December 2010 (see http://www.tffs.org/PSDStoc.htm). The database is aimed at facilitating timely, quarterly dissemination of contemporary debt data for the public sector, with countries participating voluntarily and encouraged to provide a detailed breakdown of debt information (e.g. by term, currency of denomination, and residency).

agencies declined to rate government-issued securities. This is compounded by the lack of information on the size and profile of government debts and the outstanding contingent liabilities of the GREs and their financial capabilities. In addition, weak corporate governance in the GREs and their inclination to over-extend or indulge in investment activities beyond areas of their investment competencies have overburdened the government and contributed to imbalances in the economy. The GREs should be operated according to the international best practices, with regular public reporting of their financial statements. Coherent and transparent strategies need to be put in place to manage the borrowing needs of the government and GREs, with a clear stipulation as to whether the GREs borrowings are guaranteed by the government or not. Information on the borrowings should be made publicly available. This is important to avoid a recurrence of a previous market assumption of implicit government guarantee of GREs debts.

Crucially, instead of relying on annual cash-based budgetary preparation, the Dubai government should move to initiate a medium-term expenditure framework (MTEF) to guide its multi-year fiscal operations to ensure long-term fiscal sustainability. The MTEF serves as a 'linking' framework that allows expenditures to be driven by policy priorities and disciplined by budget realities. Further, the MTEF is intended to facilitate a number of important outcomes: greater macroeconomic balance, improved inter- and intra-sectorial resource allocation, greater budgetary predictability for line (major) departments, and more efficient use of public finances. However, on its own, an MTEF cannot succeed in the presence of a weak budget management and execution system, key to which is information gathering and reporting in a transparent manner which conforms to international reporting standards. The inception of MTEF should be accompanied by fiscal rules as adopted in most developed and emerging economies to enhance the discipline and credibility of Dubai government fiscal policy.

To augment government revenue mobilization resources, establishing a capital market in Dubai that is geared towards government (and corporate) debt instruments denominated in local currencies (AED) will be integral in Dubai's fiscal consolidation efforts. This is because, trading in the government securities (bonds, T-Bills, etc.) denominated in the domestic currency will not only deepen financial markets in Dubai, thus enhancing Dubai's stature as a regional financial hub, but also provide the Dubai government with an avenue for raising funds at a lower cost and avert some of the refinancing risks associated with foreign currency denominated debt.

Fees and charges levied by the government represent a significant share of its total revenues. This mode of revenue generation is not only unpredictable and pro-cyclical, but also regressive as it imposes hidden costs on small and medium enterprises (SMEs). The government therefore needs to explore more broad-based avenues of raising revenue that will avoid the distortionary effects of the current fees and charges. Even though discussions on the implementation of value-added tax (VAT) are still ongoing, one consideration would be replacing the fees and charges with some form of taxes that are more predictable and transparent. While policy decisions and implementation of VAT will be done at the regional (GCC) and federal (UAE) levels, with minimal government influence, the prospects of introducing VAT will be a major fiscal policy reform effort, with significant impact on government administration, the business community, and the public in Dubai.

Experience in various countries suggests that several prerequisites are needed in successfully designing and implementing VAT. For Dubai, this will entail advance preparations in setting up the institutions and manpower capacity, adequate investment in tax administration, an extensive public education programme to gain support from consumers and the business community, and the need for initial visible offsets to the perceived adverse distributional effects of the VAT on low-income earners and SMEs. To this end, the government should initially start with multiple VAT rates and higher thresholds, and gradually move toward a single VAT rate and lower thresholds. However, the government needs to be cognizant of the trade-offs inherent in any taxation system. With regard to VAT, setting a low threshold will be administratively costly and have regressive effect on SMEs. On the other hand, setting a high threshold will enlist fewer firms and might lead to lower revenue collection, although the administrative costs will be lower. Therefore, setting an optimal level of threshold for firms is imperative if the government wishes to increase the compliance, efficiency, and competitiveness of businesses. Further, to accommodate SMEs which dominate the wholesale and retail segment in Dubai's economy, the government can permit SMEs to file a tax return annually rather than quarterly or monthly, subject them to taxation under special schemes, or it can tax the SMEs, but allow them to retain a percentage of the tax collected to compensate them for their substantial higher compliance costs.

Finally, while there are many variations of the VAT structure and how it is implemented, for Dubai, the final base of the tax should be on consumption. This is because with such a VAT, which requires tax on capital goods to be credited, it will not distort the prices that producers face in buying and selling from one another, and, accordingly, has the desirable feature of preserving production efficiency and productivity. Similarly, given that VAT is levied at each stage of production, ensuring that the VAT falls only on consumption allows for both full crediting of the tax already paid on inputs and the absence of breaks in the VAT chain. This calls for minimizing the number and categories of zero-rated and exempted goods and services. To enhance compliance and minimize administrative costs, a single rate invoice credit VAT method should be used. This is because, by explicitly linking single rather than multiple tax credits on the purchaser's inputs to the tax remitted by the supplier of those inputs, it discourages fraudulent undervaluation of intermediate sales.

APPENDIX I: DUBAI INC.

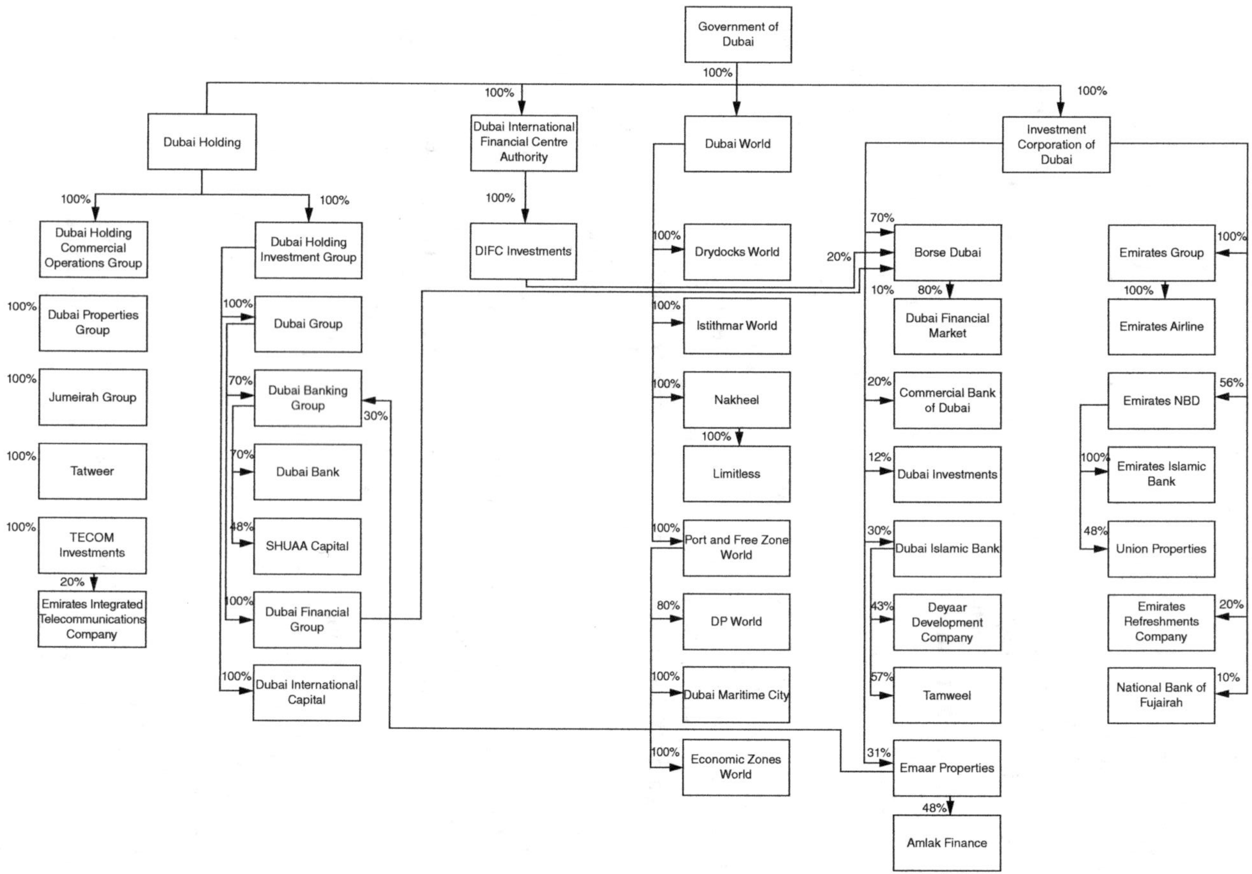

Figure 3A.1. Dubai Inc.

Source: IMF (2011)

APPENDIX II: DUBAI DEBT PROFILE

Table 3A.1. Dubai debt profile

	Maturing Bonds and Syndicated Loans[1,2] (US$ millions)					
Debt type	2012	2013	2014	2015	Beyond	Total
Dubai World and subsidiaries						
Bonds	2,043	—	350	3,200	3,600	9,193
Loans	3,000	546	409	6,662	12,937	23,554
Total	5,043	546	759	9,862	16,537	32,747
Dubai Holding and subsidiaries						
Bonds	—	93	995	—	977	2,065
Loans	—	—	3,645	705	5,220	9,570
Total	—	93	4,640	705	6,197	11,635
Investment Corporation of Dubai and subsidiaries						
Bonds	1,678	1,288	67	—	4,374	7,407
Loans	2,282	2,080	93	510	9,473	11,438
Total	3,960	3,368	160	510	10,847	18,845
Other Dubai Inc.[3]						
Bonds	1,250	871	—	1,000	2,000	5,121
Loans	2,639	1,100	3,090	—	2,289	9,118
Totals	3,889	1,971	3,090	1,000	4,289	14,239
Total Dubai Inc.	12,891	12,891	5,978	8,469	12,077	37,871
Other Dubai Inc.[4]						
Bonds	750	599	—	—	520	1,869
Loans	1,000	1,100	1,149	—	1,676	4,925
Total	1,750	1,699	1,149	—	2,196	6,794
Government of Dubai						
Bonds	—	1,770	21,211	500	2,250	25,731
Loans foreign	—	—	—	—	1,011	1,011
Loans domestic	—					18,026
Total	—	1,770	21,211	500	3,261	44,767
Total Dubai debt	14,641	9,447	31,008	12,577	43,327	129,027
In per cent of Dubai and NE 2011 GDP	11	7	22	9	31	92
Memorandum items:						
Restructured debt	—	—	5,400	10,005	15,100	30,505
Government guaranteed[5]	648	2,734	748	748	3,414	8,292
Total GD including Guarantees	648	4,503	21,959	1,248	6,675	53,059

[1] Excluding bilateral bank loans and accounts payable, except for bilateral domestic loans.
[2] Regardless or residency of debt holders.
[3] Includes DEWA, DIFC, DAE, Bourse Dubai, and others.
[4] Dubai GREs with government ownership below 50% (Emaar, DIB, CBD).
[5] Mainly ICD holding level and DEWA debt, in addition to the governments'.
Source: IMF (2011)

REFERENCES

Buiter, W. H. and Patel, U., 1992. 'Debt, Deficits and Inflation: An Application to the Public Finances of India'. *Journal of Public Economics,* 47: 171–205.

Cuddington, J., 1997. 'Analyzing the Sustainability of Fiscal Deficits in Developing Countries'. *World Bank Working Paper Series,* No. 1784.

Elbadawi, I. and Gelb, A., 2010. *Oil, Economic Diversification, and Development in the Arab World,* Cairo: Economic Research Forum.

Gerson, P. and Nellor, D., 1997. 'Philippine Fiscal Policy: Sustainability, Growth and Savings'. In J. Hicklin, D. Robinson, and A. Singh (eds) *Macroeconomic Issues Facing ASEAN Countries.* Washington, DC: International Monetary Fund, pp. 91–129.

Government of Dubai, 2010. *Dubai Strategic Vision 2015,* Dubai: Government of Dubai.

Hakkio, C. S. and Rush, M., 1991. 'Is the Budget Deficit Too Large? *Economic Inquiry,* 29: 429–45.

IMF, 2011. *IMF Country Report No. 11/12: United Arab Emirates: Selected Issues and Statistical Appendix,* Washington, DC: International Monetary Fund.

IMF, 2012. *IMF Country Report No 12/136: United Arab Emirates: Selected Issues and Statistical Appendix,* Washington, DC: International Monetary Fund.

IMF and World Bank, 2001. *Guidelines to Public Debt Management,* Washington, DC: International Monetary Fund and The World Bank.

4

Strategic Axes for the Development of Productive Business

Michael Klein

> My grandfather rode a camel, my father rode a camel, I drive a Mercedes, my son drives a Land Rover, his son will drive a Land Rover, but his son will ride a camel.

The quote is much cited and typically attributed to HH Sheikh Rashid bin Saeed Al Maktoum, Dubai's ruler from 1958 to 1990, who managed the city-state's transition into today's world. It vividly sets out the long-term challenge for Dubai's rulers. The city rose to riches on the back of oil and gas discoveries in the region and the state itself. Yet, the reign of oil will be ephemeral. In Dubai itself, it has already lost most of its importance. In the wider region it may sustain wealth for decades. Yet, the challenges to the region's stronghold on oil and gas are subtly rising. For example, most of the very large reserves of so called non-conventional sources of oil and natural gas, such as shale oil and gas are located outside the Middle East, mostly in the Western Hemisphere, China, and Russia. By 2020 already the Western Hemisphere may no longer be a net importer of hydrocarbons.[1]

It is not just the future of oil which matters for Dubai and similar states. Growth so far has been spectacular. The very success has given rise to new interests, to habits, and to predicaments that could complicate future development and the ability to respond to new challenges. The recent financial and real estate crisis has served as a reminder of the fragility of development. It may yet lead to a good outcome as questions are being asked that go to the heart of the city's long-term development challenge.

The Dubai Economic Council has embarked on a programme of investigation that promises to shed light on the relevant questions that matter for the

[1] For one such scenario see 'Oil's New World Order' by Daniel Yergin, *Washington Post*, 28 October, 2011.

business environment and hence for the development of productive businesses—what some people like to call 'the competitiveness' of an economy. This chapter discusses key questions for such an endeavour and for the direction of potential reforms.

4.1 DUBAI'S STORY

Dubai rose from a regional trading post to a fledgling metropolis within the span of just four decades since the formation of the United Arab Emirates and the discovery of oil in Dubai in 1971. The population grew from just 59,000 at the time of the first census in 1968 to about 2 million in November 2011.[2] Income per capita grew to some US$45,000 in 2009.[3] That makes Dubai one of the richest economies in the World with an income level per person similar to that of the United States, Hong Kong, or Switzerland.

All the while growing rapidly, Dubai underwent dramatic structural shifts in its economy. In the first half of the twentieth century Dubai was already a thriving commercial centre in the Gulf region. After the Great Depression the economy was hit by reduced demand for pearls, one of Dubai's main exports at the time. The discovery of oil in 1966 changed all this, boosting growth until the economy relied on oil for close to 60 per cent of value added in the early 1980s. Then followed a massive shift to trading, finance, and tourism with a boom in construction—altogether accounting for some 90 per cent of GDP by 2009. Today, less than 2 per cent of value added derives from oil[4] and hotel guests of 2.2 million outnumbered residents in 2011.

Only a few other cities in the world exhibit similar dynamism and structural features. Shenzhen, a small fishing town near Hong Kong, rose from just 350,000 inhabitants in 1982 to over 10 million today. Per capita income increased from less than 200 dollars to over US$14 thousand by 2010.[5] Hong Kong itself went from 500,000 inhabitants in 1945 to over 7 million today relying on trade and finance. There is the rise of Singapore since independence in 1965 relying on trade, finance, and manufacturing, and now also recreation and entertainment. There are other cities in the region, like Riyadh, the capital of Saudi Arabia, or Doha in Qatar with similar rapid development strongly driven by discoveries of oil or natural gas. And then there is the story of Las Vegas, growing from 8,000 inhabitants in 1940 to almost 600,000 today, based mostly on entertainment. Finally, so as not to forget how unusual the shape of success can be, there is Iceland, a remote,

[2] According to the 'population clock' on the website of the Dubai Statistics Center.

[3] Dubai Statistics Center. [4] Dubai Statistics Center.

[5] Shenzhen Municipal Statistics Bureau.

inhospitable island in the Atlantic. It is one of the great success stories of development during the twentieth century. Population quadrupled from 1900 to about 318,000 people in 2010. Income per person reached a similar level to that of Dubai just before the financial crisis hit in 2008 knocking both economies back a bit.

4.1.1 Dubai's Performance

As of 2012, Dubai has several legs to stand on. It is not like Las Vegas dependent on tourism only. Between trade, tourism, and finance it has successfully diversified away from oil. As analysed in a study by the Dubai Economic Council (Elbadawi and Soto, 2012), productivity in Dubai's leading sectors—manufacturing, trade, transport and communications, real estate, construction, hotels, and finance is broadly at par with that of Singapore.

The success has benefited from the global economy. Best practices have been imported from abroad in all sectors, whether by sending locals to study overseas, employing expatriates, or allowing foreign companies to invest and operate in Dubai. At the same time massive numbers of largely male workers, mostly from the Indian sub-continent, the Philippines, and Indonesia have provided cheap labour to respond to the demand from investment and daily operations. As a result only about 15 per cent of the population are UAE nationals, the rest foreigners of one type or another. For every female there are about 3.5 males living in Dubai.

There are also underperforming sectors in the economy—a smattering of agriculture, oil, utilities, and government services. Together these sectors account for barely over 10 per cent of GDP. However, they drag down the productivity of the economy as a whole, clearly below that of Singapore. Intriguingly, employment in these sectors has risen, while productivity has not. Nationals dominate among the employees. Some 90 per cent of nationals are employed in government services. For them unemployment has also risen to 14 per cent from just 6 per cent in 1995. At the same time nationals command a wage premium over foreign labour (Elbadawi and Vazquez-Alvarez, 2011).

The impression is thus one of 'jobs for the boys' funded by rapid growth and solid productivity in the rest of the economy. Given the opportunities open to nationals they tend to have a high 'reservation wage' making them reluctant to take lower paying jobs with salaries commensurate to productivity. The tendency to support nationals by allowing them relatively well-paid jobs is, of course, entirely understandable. Yet, it also contains seeds of potential problems. Slowly imbalances are building up. Economic potential is not being reached. Nationals are not fully showing what they can do and in the future it may not be possible to fulfil their expectations.

Then came the financial crisis of 2008. The real estate market weakened. Major defaults occurred, notably that of the real estate empire of Dubai World. GDP at market rates dropped from about 94 billion dollars in 2008 to 80 billion a year later. The country experienced a banking crisis—the first in the Middle East actually. As depicted in recent IMF reports the crisis brought into the limelight the system of government-related enterprises (GRE). These are financial institutions, investment vehicles, and commercial ventures that dominate most sectors of the economy. The government of Dubai either directly or indirectly owns most of their shares. In early 2011 just the debt of the GREs amounted to some US$89 billion—over 100 per cent of Dubai's GDP. A shadow economy was thus allowed to grow off the visible public balance sheet. As in so many other countries and firms, off-balance-sheet liabilities can pose major dangers, precisely because they are so conveniently hidden.

As is well known, in the end the oil-rich government of Abu Dhabi had to step in to prevent a financial meltdown. The image of Dubai got some serious dents. As a result the economic recovery in the whole of the UAE after the crisis has been slower than in the rest of the GCC states (IMF, 2011). Major debt problems persist, albeit backed by a credible oil-rich state.

Had it not been for oil, where would Dubai be now? Structurally, its location in an oil-rich region provides demand for its services. The crisis was contained only due to oil resources. Was the Emir Sheikh Rashid bin Saeed Al Maktoum right, when he painted a gloomy picture of post-oil Dubai? Has the development of Dubai really laid strong foundations that may outlast the age of oil? Is Dubai after all nothing more than a regional Las Vegas at the mercy of economic developments in the surrounding region?

4.1.2 Competing Visions of the Future

The recent crisis raises the question of the future of Dubai with renewed vigour. Yes, Dubai is a success story, but its success is limited compared to the most successful cities in this world. First, one needs to note that Dubai has roughly 3.5 times more men than women. In other economies the relationship is, of course, typically around 1 to 1. If Dubai had as many women as men, there would have been a population of roughly 2.8 rather than 1.8 million in 2009 for a total GDP of roughly US$80 billion. If all women were carrying out unremunerated household work, recorded income per person would have been just US$29,000. If the extra women had been working per capita income would have been somewhere in between US$29,000 and 45,000, maybe around US$35,000. This is still a very high income somewhere between Greece and Germany.

As a city-state Dubai has a high income per person compared to other nations, but when one looks at the income of just cities and not nations, Dubai's per capita income looks a little less impressive. Maybe it should not surprise that some oil-rich cities had higher per capita income, like Doha at over US$80,000 or Oslo at US$75,000. Yet, other cities were able to reach higher levels of income without help from natural resources: Singapore, US $57,000 by relying on trade, manufacturing, finance, and tourism; Luxembourg, US$90,000 based on finance. Bermuda, US$69,000, and Jersey, US $57,000, reached success with specialized financial and corporate services.[6] Macau made it to US$60,000 based mostly on tourism. San Jose in Silicon Valley comes in at US$90,000 based on innovation in modern technology.

The story of other successful cities suggests that there are several conceivable avenues for Dubai to raise income substantially. How will demand for services for a place like Dubai develop in the future? And what can Dubai do to develop new competencies?

First, the prospects for tourism look structurally good. As the world gets richer people have more leisure time and more discretionary income (Fogel, 2000). In the special case of Dubai, the city offers entertainment that is not easily available in the surrounding region, except traditionally in Beirut. The troubles of Lebanon thus tend to benefit Dubai. Furthermore, border security measures in rich OECD countries make it relatively more attractive to stay in the region than travel further afield. At the same time Dubai is concerned about retaining legitimacy in the cultural context of the region by limiting the 'raciness' of entertainment; hence, for example, restrictions on gambling—contrary to the trend in Singapore.

Second, financial services will surely also be needed. Here Dubai faces multiple competitors globally and regionally, including Bahrain, Saudi Arabia, and Qatar. Financial centres can differentiate themselves by the type of service they deliver. For example, the city could emphasize the quality of the legal and contractual environment offering highly efficient services to firms and financial institutions in a region where weaknesses in legal systems continue to exist and relationships and positions of political power may matter relatively more than in places like London, Singapore, or New York. The city could also try to be a safe haven for wealth from neighbouring countries and further afield. This would require the city to have a credible way not to be drawn into potential strife in its volatile region.

Third, trade will, in principle, remain a good business as long as the wealth of the region continues. Here again competitors exist. Yet, as long as Dubai continues to develop efficient trading practices, it can stay ahead. The key is openness to innovation in the field. An efficient financial system can

[6] The per capita income of Bermuda and Guernsey is expressed on a PPP basis (Central Intelligence Agency, 2011).

complement trade, particularly trade-specific financing. As in the case of finance, a secure and efficient legal and contractual environment helps.

Fourth, there are new areas of activity that Dubai might develop. Potential areas include medical facilities that cater not only to locals but also export services to foreigners, the so-called medical tourism. While there is surely demand for some level of medical services, Dubai may not be a low-cost player and may have trouble competing with places like Thailand or India. Hence, as elsewhere, there is the popularity of promoting knowledge-based innovation, the stuff that made Silicon Valley one of the richest urban areas in the world. Dubai is trying to promote the bases for it, for example, through initiatives like Internet City. Yet, the fascination with high-end knowledge-based areas such as information technology, nanotechnology, or biotechnology can lead into treacherous waters. Radically new innovation is a high-risk gamble. Much solid progress is typically possible by improving—step by step—on the current strengths of an economy. In the case of Dubai that might mean innovations in logistics, in construction, or in the hospitality business. This in turn might generate new ancillary businesses that produce inputs necessary to support such innovations.

4.2 THE POTENTIAL ROLE OF BUSINESS ENVIRONMENT REFORMS

4.2.1 Neighbourhood Effects

Possibilities abound. The challenge is to realize them. To some degree that depends on the 'neighbourhood' of Dubai and to some degree on its own efforts. Possible neighbourhood effects come in various forms. In the long run oil may lose its current importance in the region. If the region failed to adjust successfully to an age after oil, that would affect the demand for services and would put a premium on providing those that appeal to a clientele beyond the region. Yet, this is not likely to happen for some decades.

In the near term there are potentially significant political and geo-political challenges. It remains unclear where the 'Arab Spring' will lead. For example, will it lead to more liberal or more conservative social systems? Will it affect countries not yet shaken significantly? Will it dampen economic growth for a sustained period of time in the non-oil economies of the Middle East? Will it shift the geo-political realities of the region? The region exhibits major fault lines as it is. These may further shift and come under greater stress with or without the effect of the Arab Spring. For a non-oil economy at the heart of the region, like Dubai, this enhances the interest in maintaining cultural and political legitimacy in the eyes of those around it. It also raises the question of who will protect it, should sharper conflict materialize. All these factors entail that it might be helpful to develop a truly distinct service offering that is not easy to find in the region and that creates an interest among surrounding states to keep Dubai intact, even in the midst of conflict. In some sense this is the kind of role that Switzerland played even in the worst of times in Europe. Tourism alone is hardly likely to be that offering, but the ability to do deals, including trade and finance, reliably and efficiently, might. All this points to the desirability of providing easy and efficient ways of establishing businesses, arranging contracts, and settling disputes.

4.2.2 A General Take on the Current Business Environment

Developing a business environment that can take advantage of the possibilities and help deal with the neighbourhood effects is a task for Dubai itself and the UAE. A first cut at assessing the quality of Dubai's business environment compared to other countries can be obtained by looking at international benchmarking exercises. Typically Dubai is not ranked, but the UAE is. The World Economic Forum (WEF) places the UAE 27th among 142 nations. The World Bank's Doing Business (DB) indicators have it 33rd among 183 economies and Transparency International's Corruption Perception Index (CPI) places the UAE at 28 out of 178 countries.

Within the neighbourhood the toughest rivals to the UAE are Saudi Arabia ranked 11 by DB, 17 by WEF, and 50 by the CPI. Qatar comes in at 14 in the WEF rankings, 19 in the CPI, and 50 in DB. Globally, the UAE are placed in respectable company—close to China and South Korea in WEF, close to Chile and Slovenia in DB and not far from Slovenia and Spain in the CPI. While much has been achieved, the distance to the best rankings in the world remains significant. That should not be seen as a problem, but as scope to improve and enhance performance even further. The UAE and Dubai clearly have a further upside. If made use of, it would seem plausible that economic performance can be ratcheted up yet again.

More insights may be gained by looking at the detailed data behind the rankings. In some areas Dubai already ranks at the top globally. Dubai boasts great infrastructure. It has opened the economy for trade and immigration thus creating access to a large market for products and factors of production that is not available at home. The monetary and exchange rate regime is providing exemplary stability. The system of taxes and the trade regime are highly competitive. The sophistication of UAE businesses is well judged in the WEF exercise. This combines with a fairly good reputation for the government's fairness towards business and the best ranking on the Corruption Perception Index in the wider region next to Qatar.

These very good ratings co-exist with some more problematic areas. The weaknesses revealed by the recent financial crisis have already been mentioned. Excessive investment in real estate, consequent non-performing assets in the financial sector, and a rather high level of quasi-fiscal debt have dragged down the standing of Dubai and the UAE as evidenced in some backsliding on the WEF scales. Beyond these macro-financial issues there appear to be potential weaknesses in some aspects of the education system and in the extent of actual innovative technological activity. The education system has already greatly improved in quality. What remains underdeveloped are enrolment rates. As for innovative activity, actual R&D activity and its output measured by utility models or patents remains mediocre. Here UAE ranks just 50th of 142 countries in the WEF's report on competitiveness.

One area with scope for improvement sticks out from the DB exercise and is also reflected in the judgements expressed in the WEF's investor surveys: formal legal and contractual protections could be stronger and more efficient. When it comes to creditor rights, shareholder protection, and the enforcement system for commercial claims, the UAE ranks far below the global average. DB places the system of creditor rights at 78, shareholder rights at 122, the bankruptcy system at 151, and the enforcement system at 134 out of 183 countries. It may, of course, be that the rules in Dubai are a little better than in the UAE, but the pattern is worth noting. Perceptions on the independence of the judiciary and the effectiveness of the legal framework in settling disputes or challenging regulations are among the weaker ones in the WEF competitiveness index. A plausible interpretation is that the system of law and contract remains heavily dependent on the exercise of discretion by the administration.

So far, as recorded by the Competitiveness Report of the World Economic Forum, the perception of business seems to be that discretion has generally been well exercised. At the same time the build-up of problems in the real estate and finance sector gives cause for worry. Likewise, the noted rigidities in employment within the government and for nationals more generally may turn out to be impediments in the future. When a time comes where the interest of dynamic new businesses is at odds with that of entrenched old ones, pressures to bend the rules in favour of the incumbents may be strong. Also, if Dubai wishes to establish itself as a place where everyone can fully trust the rules, it may be wise to anchor the rules more directly in law and regulation and reduce discretion on the part of the authorities while strengthening the judicial system. In that regard, as measured by the DB report, the UAE has recently made less efforts than other countries in its league; hence some lowering of its ranking in DB.

The rankings and the underlying judgements presented so far are, of course, not perfect. They give rise to questions and further debate and investigation. This is why the research programme of the Dubai Economic Council (DEC) holds particular promise.

4.2.3 Does Reform of the Business Environment Matter?

Having said all this, one can argue that the business environment issues discussed above are not all that important. For example, why are China and India growing so fast with highly incomplete reforms? Why do better-ranked countries not grow faster? Should one not look at other matters, for example, government promotion of special sectors and the like?

Arguing like this risks falling prey to a basic misunderstanding. The countries best ranked tend to have the highest productivity and, therefore, income levels. A good business environment is part of what made it possible. Singapore's success is not independent of the fact that it has the most efficient business environment in the world as measured by DB. Yet, the most advanced countries do not grow as fast as countries catching up with world best practice, because raising productivity 'at the global frontier' requires genuine innovation. Adopting and adapting what others have already invented, be it technology, management practices, or ways of running public administrations is easier. The fastest growth tends to happen in countries coming from behind, countries that are improving their business environment in the process. In fact, those systematically improving their business environment seem to have the best chances to grow. China and India are actually examples of this.

Both countries have steadily improved their business environment over the years, China more so than India. As measured by DB, China is one of the most relentless reformers in the world. Reform comes step by step and sometimes at a slow pace, but it happens. Yes, but why did business activity in both China and India take off before some of the bigger reforms of the business environment (Rodrik and Subramanian, 2004)? What matters are the expectations of businesses. If businesses confidently expect the government to move in a certain direction they will move and invest. If they have serious doubts, they hold back.

Businesses do not just sit back and wait to make decisions until all laws are in place. Businesses take risks. They may move before reforms are made to be the first benefiting from what they expect the business environment to be. Chinese firms started behaving as if they owned property privately long before the government amended the constitution to make private property legal. But businesses could observe the process of legislation that started in 1993, years before the actual constitutional amendment passed in 2007. So far, the expectations of business have been validated. Similarly in India. Minor reforms to the domestic business environment started in the mid 1980s. Arguably, Indian businesses saw this tentative opening as signs of a clear departure from the previous belief in economic command and control by government. The economy started growing faster in the 1980s. When more significant reforms followed in 1991, they validated the expectations of many businesses. Today, investors are getting wary as reform efforts in India have slowed and the future stance of policy appears more uncertain.

Each economy is, of course, a little different. Sometimes major reforms are needed. Sometimes smaller steps can do. Importantly, the credibility of policymaking shapes business expectations and, therefore, investment. In some countries credibility can be established by a break with the past. In others, disruptive reforms are widely expected to be reversed again by future governments. Each economy needs to solve on its own how to move ahead with reforms, while enhancing credibility of the overall direction. Of course, opponents of reform will argue that is preferable to go slow and warn of disruptive steps. They may cite cases like India or China to undermine progress. This risks entrenching old practices and enhancing rigidities in the economy. In the case of Dubai what seems to matter are credible steps to deal with the legacy of the real estate bust and to enhance reform efforts of the business environment more broadly so as to counteract the reality and perceptions revealed in the financial crisis and the backsliding relative to other economies. How to do so is the art of policymaking that requires local knowledge informed by analysis such as that underway at DEC.

4.3 LONG-TERM PERSPECTIVES ON BUSINESS ENVIRONMENT REFORM

Any reform effort needs to face reality and deal with a myriad of little rules and regulations, with institutional reforms and adjustment processes. In the daily battles it is easy to lose sight of the broader principles that may usefully govern reform. Two 'big ticket' items are worth highlighting. One is the value of the rule of law; the other the value of openness to experiment and failure.

4.3.1 The Advantage of Rule-based Systems

It is a commonplace by now that a place making its living off finance and trade needs credible, efficient, and impartial rules. It was not always so. China's Kang Hsi Emperor (1661–1722) saw the matter like this: 'Lawsuits would increase to a frightful amount if people were not afraid of tribunals and if they felt confident of always finding in them ready and perfect justice . . . I desire, therefore, that those who have recourse to the tribunals should be treated without any pity and in such a manner that they should be disgusted with law and tremble to appear before a magistrate' (Kinkley, 2000). Thanks to such experiments in history we now know that this approach does not work so well.

History has provided a resounding verdict in favour of rule-based systems. Economic and geo-political success is found in systems that do not depend on the good luck of having a wise ruler or ruling elite to sort out the trade-offs and conflicts confronted by people. Having said this, to get to a decent result relies precisely on the traditional elite. Changing the nature of the exercise of power requires enlightened rulers. It also takes time and needs to progress within the context of a particular country. As stated before, the direction taken is what matters.

4.3.2 Openness to Experiment and Failure

Good rules are not enough for a country to progress economically. Intriguingly, history's biggest experiment exemplifying this comes from the rule of Genghis Khan:

> Genghis Khan . . . organized . . . history's largest free-trade zone . . . He lowered taxes for everyone, and abolished them altogether for doctors, teachers, priests and educational institutions . . . He established a regular census and created the first international postal system . . . He created an international law . . . [he] insisted on laws holding rulers as equally accountable as the lowliest herder . . . He insisted on the rule of law and abolished torture.

Yet, 'The Mongols made no technological breakthroughs . . . their own craftsmen could not weave cloth, cast metal, make pottery or even bake bread' (Ratchnevsky, 1991).

As mentioned already, in a world where somewhere someone has come up with useful innovations, it is possible to adopt and adapt these and progress. This is the essence of what Dubai has very successfully done relying heavily on foreigners. It is another thing to create significant innovation oneself.

Innovation is by nature uncertain. One can never know what will work or not, what avenues for research are fruitful and which ones not. Even mastering existing technologies is hard. Consider the experience of Hyundai with the production of its first automobile. It took fourteen months of trials before creating the first prototype, then eleven more prototypes before one survived the test, then 2,888 engine design changes, then ninety-seven test engines, then more than 200 test transmissions and 150 test vehicles before the first car was launched in 1992. Even a proven complex technology is hard to master. Malaysia's attempts at car production show that it may fail. Inventing completely new products or services is still more fraught with the risk of failure.

To create new and productive businesses, there needs to be an openness to allow new ideas to be tried. As the Hyundai example shows, this applies also to 'just' adopting and adapting known technology. In business terms, that means new entrants have to be able to establish themselves in a market. They then try out their ideas. When successful it is important that these companies find a business environment that enables them to grow—secure property rights, access to finance, trading opportunities, and so on. Importantly, the companies that do not succeed need to be free to fail. If substandard companies are propped up in the market, they block the entry of new firms. Barriers to exit are barriers to entry. They drag down overall productivity and with it personal incomes.

Well before true innovation becomes an issue, one needs to consider the most important typical fact that links business performance to economy-wide productivity. In all countries at any one time, there are several firms active in most sectors. Some may perform close to world class, others significantly less so. By far the biggest initial boost to growth in most countries can be obtained by bringing average productivity in any sector closer to best-in-class performance (Harberger, 1998). For example, for India Banerjee and Duflo have estimated that bringing average practice to the level of best practice would raise India's productivity close to that of the United States (Banerjee and Duflo, 2005). For this underperforming firms have to go out of business in some fashion, via closure, liquidation, restructuring, or merger. The mechanism that achieves this is an environment of open competition with easy entry, easy exit, and the opportunity for successful companies to grow.

That sort of competition is also part of what is needed for true innovation. Any account of the success of Silicon Valley is replete with observations that many people try often and fail often. Failure is not seen as a shameful experience, but an opportunity to grow. Venture capitalists are more comfortable with someone who has tried hard and learnt lessons than someone who never tried and failed.

If Dubai wants to go the route of the knowledge economy it needs to create some such environment. Dubai already has one requisite strength—it is a city. Cities are the place where innovation happens. They facilitate the flow of ideas and make adjustments easier for firms and people due to the proximity with others. As the quip on Silicon Valley has it 'people can change jobs here without changing car pools' (Saxenian, 1996). In the United States 45 per cent of all product innovation comes from just four urban areas: New York, Los Angeles, San Francisco, and Boston (Glaeser, 1998). Cities are the biggest and most successful 'clusters' or 'incubators'. They help create new ideas and firms that implement them.

What is needed in Dubai is an environment that allows experiment and failure—including for nationals of the country who will otherwise either not participate in the process of learning and innovation or block promising businesses. That is why the rigidities revealed by the financial crisis and the drag of old businesses are such worrying signs for the future of Dubai. An environment of competition has to be complemented, as is already underway, with efforts to create world-class institutions of learning and research. Creating 'science parks' and the like can help, if the environment is right, but one cannot engineer a new Silicon Valley. It has to emerge from the freedom of people to learn, experiment, and fail.

4.4 CONCLUSION

Any future 'beyond oil' depends on the development of businesses in Dubai. It is not just about attracting businesses with good conditions. Yes, businesses should feel enticed to establish in Dubai. Whether domestic or foreign, they should feel that the rules of the game are clear and the environment is conducive to working and living. But they should also face competition that ensures only the most productive businesses survive. They must be free to fail. What matters is not more business, but more and more productive businesses. Only then will incomes stay high and rise. One cannot predict which businesses will be best for Dubai. Governments can help prepare the ground, can even facilitate development of certain sectors, but ultimately competition will reveal what works.

Dubai has had remarkable success so far in a very short time span. The recent crisis has revealed some weaknesses of the current model. A closer look also shows that significant parts of the economy are underperforming. The big challenge for the future is to maintain the flexibility and dynamism that made Dubai great. The danger is that, as in many countries, the beneficiaries of the initial success become a drag on development in the future.

Thus the basic directions for Dubai presumably encompass:

- the search for a system of law and regulations that are strongly anchored in sound institutions and not too reliant on the wisdom of individuals, and
- the search for a system of competition that enables the country to benefit, first of all from existing best practices and second, prepares the country for a potential future as an innovative knowledge economy.

As for sectorial emphasis, the economy is already relatively well diversified given its location in an oil-rich region. The development of new businesses will be necessary to provide a basis for development 'beyond oil'. While dreams of high-tech industries are tempting, the biggest chance for success may lie in building steadily on existing strengths. Productivity improvements and innovation in and around the core sectors that drive Dubai's current success, such as logistics, construction, and hospitality may hold the key to sustained progress. Government can help facilitate such development. This means paying attention to the legitimate concerns of business, providing an education and research system that responds to industry needs, and ensuring freedom to fail so that the competition can do its work of selecting the real winners.

REFERENCES

Banerjee, A. and Duflo, E., 2005. 'Growth Theory through the Lens of Development Economics'. In P. Aghion and S. Durlauf (eds) *Handbook of Economic Growth*, vol. 1A. North Holland: Elsevier, ch. 7.

Central Intelligence Agency, 2011. *World Fact Book*, Washington, DC: CIA.

Elbadawi, I. and Soto, R., 2012. 'Sources of Economic Growth and Development Strategy in Dubai'. In: *The Global Economic Crisis and Consequences for Development Strategy in Dubai*, ed. A. Sadik and I. Elbadawi. New York: Palgrave Macmillan, pp. 121–53.

Elbadawi, I. and Vazquez-Alvarez, R., 2011. *Migration, Labour Markets and a Long-term Development Strategy for the UAE*, Dubai: Dubai Economic Council.

Fogel, R., 2000. *The Fourth Great Awakening*, Chicago: University of Chicago Press.

Glaeser, E., 1998. 'Are Cities Dying?' *Journal of Economic Perspectives*, 12(2): 139–60.

IMF, 2011. *IMF Country Report No. 11/12: United Arab Emirates: Selected Issues and Statistical Appendix*, Washington, DC: International Monetary Fund.

Kinkley, J. C., 2000. *Chinese Justice, the Fiction: Law and Literature in Modern China*, Redwood City, CA: Stanford University Press.

Ratchnevsky, P., 1991. *Genghis Khan: His Life and Legacy*, Oxford: Blackwell Publishing.

Rodrik, D. and Subramanian, A., 2004. 'From "Hindu Growth" to Productivity Surge: The Mystery of the Indian Growth Transition'. *IMF Working Paper WP/04/77*.

Saxenian, A. L., 1996. *Regional Advantage: Culture and Competition in Silicon Valley and Route 128*. Cambridge, MA: Harvard University Press.

5

International Trade: Potential and Policies

Boaz Nandwa and Raimundo Soto

5.1 INTRODUCTION

Small open economies largely depend on foreign trade for their economic development. Foreign markets provide demand for exported products which in turn allow domestic producers to reap scale economies, incentivize the adoption of better and advanced production techniques, and reward prudent investment and the creativity of firms that export. Further, foreign trade disciplines firms by forcing them to operate in more competitive environments. Overall, this boosts the efficiency and productivity of domestic firms thereby enhancing their competitiveness in the global markets.

Understanding foreign trade structures and their determinants is important for policy and development reasons. Economists have devoted substantial efforts to produce trade theories of a sufficiently general nature to explain and predict the trends and particularities of observed export and import flows. Classical theories explain foreign trade on the basis of the advantages provided by the endowment of resources, either natural or acquired (such as the availability of workers). Alternative theories based on the preferences of consumers for variety have been postulated to explain why economies producing similar products will trade with each other (e.g. Germany and USA exporting and importing automobiles).

None of these trade theories, however, perform very satisfactorily from an empirical viewpoint, usually failing when modelling or forecasting the determinants of aggregate trade volumes. More success has been achieved, however, when understanding the role of foreign trade in fostering economic development. Virtually every major research study on long-term sustained growth indicates that opening up to foreign trade and competition fosters economic growth (Rodriguez and Rodrik, 2000). The transmission channels through which trade induces sustained growth in economic activities and incomes are less clear. Falvey, Foster, and Greenaway (2004) classify these channels into four groups. First, a country can import better intermediate goods which enhance domestic productivity. Second, countries suffering from low productivity levels (i.e. inside the technological frontier) may imitate the products of advanced, efficient countries (frontier economies). Third, trade can encourage more efficient employment of resources through learning. Finally, international contacts can stimulate new indigenous technologies and improve entrepreneurial and managerial skills.

For Dubai and the UAE in general, foreign trade inevitably will continue to be a major source of income and development. Being a small economy, it cannot depend on internal markets to develop. Its vast oil resources, furthermore, guarantee a preeminent role to international trade in the foreseeable future. Moreover, the government of Dubai has stated that it envisions the emirate to be a leading financial and trade hub for the region and the world.[1] While there have been substantial advances on the path to becoming such a regional hub, there are several issues that need addressing. Among them, the needed diversification of the export and re-export base, the required increase in the efficiency of exporters to remain competitive at international levels, and the increase in sophistication of exported goods. These areas have the potential to generate risks to the development of Dubai.

5.2 STYLIZED FACTS OF FOREIGN TRADE IN DUBAI AND THE UAE

In economic terms, the UAE, and Dubai in particular, are no different from other small, open economies for which foreign trade has been the backbone of economic development since the 1850s. Historically, Emirati nationals have been traders operating between the Arabian Gulf and India. Naturally, with the discovery and exploitation of oil in the 1970s, foreign trade changed dramatically in both export and import volumes as well as in the composition of traded goods.

Figure 5.1 presents aggregate data on exports in the period 1981–2010 expressed in constant US dollars of 2005. Because price indices for exports in the UAE are not available, we have deflated the nominal values of exports (in current US$) by the World Consumer Price Index of the World Bank (2011). Note that the UAE has had a fixed exchange rate to the US dollar since

[1] See Government of Dubai (2010).

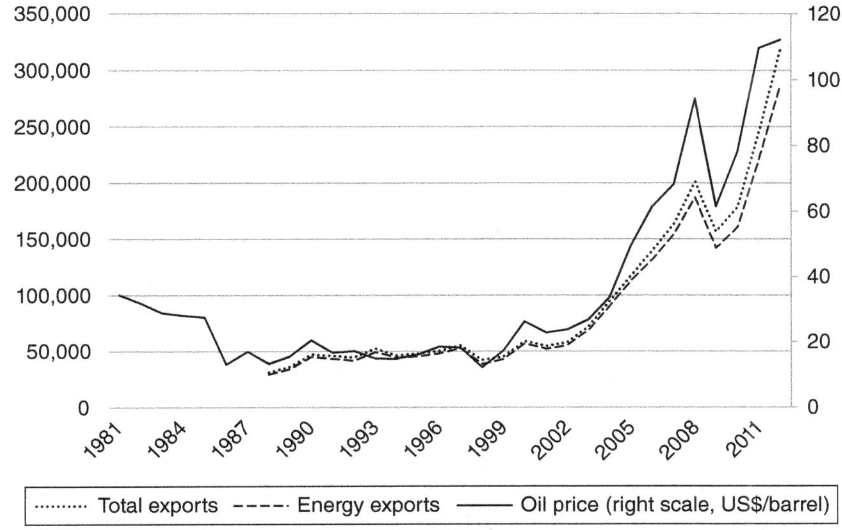

Figure 5.1. Total exports and energy exports (in US$ millions of 2005)
Source: Own elaboration based on data from UAE National Bureau of Statistics and World Bank

1971, so that real trade values are not distorted by nominal exchange rate movements (such as an abrupt devaluation).

Three features can be appraised from Figure 5.1. First, and not surprisingly for a GCC economy, exports of hydrocarbons (i.e. oil, oil condensates, and gas) are the main component of the total exports of the UAE. In the period 1988–2010 exports of hydrocarbons have steadily represented around 94 per cent of total exports.

Second, export values follow closely the evolution of oil prices: changes in physical production and exporting of hydrocarbons have not been the major sources of changes in export values. While it is true that there was an increase in production in the 1990s and 2000s, a significant fraction of it has been used indirectly to satisfy the expansion of domestic consumption of fuels.

Third, following the oil-price cycle, UAE exports underwent two different phases. In the first one, from 1980 to 2000, exports grew relatively slowly at around 4 per cent per year. In the second phase, between 2001 and 2010, exports grew at an impressive annual rate of 8.8 per cent. The global crisis of 2008–10 put an abrupt halt to the expansion in exports which contracted by around 22 per cent in 2009. The slow recovery of the world economy after the crisis has not given a boost to UAE exports, despite the recovery in oil prices. This presents a major trade policy challenge for both the UAE and Dubai.

When analysing the foreign trade of oil-exporting countries it is useful to isolate non-energy from energy exports. Energy exporting does not necessarily

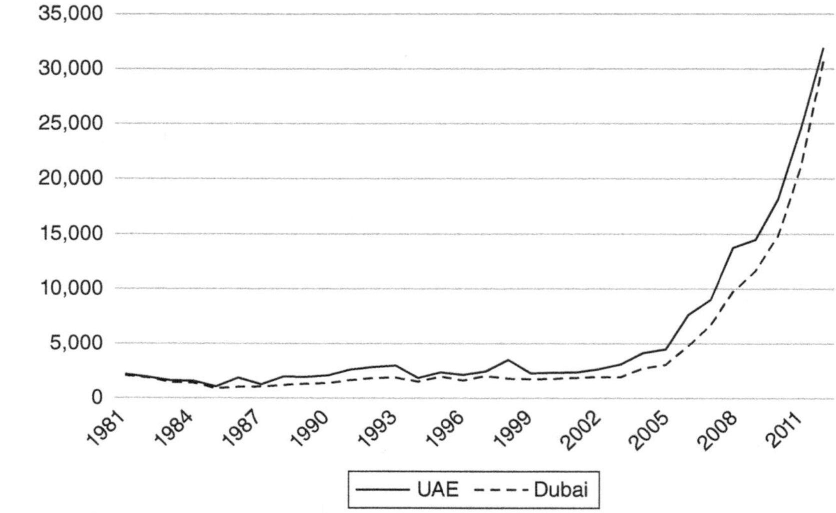

Figure 5.2. Non-energy exports (in US$ millions of 2005)

Source: Own elaboration based on data from UAE National Bureau of Statistics and World Bank

conform to standard trade patterns for several reasons, including the fact that it is primarily sold in commodity markets, the presence of the OPEC cartel, and the recurrent political interference in oil markets. Furthermore, oil exports are not of interest to us because the focus of this chapter is on Dubai, which is a non-oil-exporting emirate.

Figure 5.2 presents the evolution of non-oil exports in the UAE and Dubai. Real values are obtained by deflating nominal values in US dollars by the world CPI. It can be seen that the majority of non-oil exports actually correspond to exports from Dubai: in the period 1980–2010 they represented around 70 per cent of the total. One has to be careful, however, with these figures as they may overestimate the true export levels of Dubai since other emirates channel part of their foreign trade via Dubai ports and airports. Again, the evolution of non-energy exports presents two very distinctive phases. The first is one of very slow growth in real terms despite significant economic growth: between 1980 and 2000 total non-energy exports grew at only 0.4 per cent per year in the UAE and actually decreased slightly in Dubai (–0.5 per cent). Real GDP in the same period, on the contrary, grew annually by 2 per cent in UAE and almost 3 per cent in Dubai. This indicates that foreign trade in the 1980s and 1990s had not been the major engine for economic growth. The second period is one of substantial expansion, far above what normal economic growth would suggest. Between 2000 and 2010, non-energy exports increased by around 25 per cent per year in Dubai while GDP only expanded by 10.5 per cent in real terms. In this period, foreign trade has undoubtedly been an important force behind the substantial growth of the economy of Dubai.

While the evolution of exports is quite dynamic, one has to acknowledge that the level of exports in Dubai is still low in comparative terms. In 2010, exports totalled around US$18 billion, according to the Customs Authority. If, according to the Dubai Statistics Center, GDP in Dubai was around US$82 billion in 2010, this would indicate a ratio of exports to GDP of 22 per cent. Countries with income levels in the range of US$70 to 90 billion tend to export around 50 per cent of GDP (World Bank, 2011). Consequently, and to the extent that the experience of the majority of countries in the world is of any indication to Dubai, there is substantial space to expand exports.

Dubai is not only the main non-energy exporter in the UAE but it also accounts for most of the re-exporting activities. In 2010, Dubai re-exports reached around US$40 billion or 77 per cent of total re-exports (see Figure 5.3). These activities largely comprise manufacturing and transhipment of cargo performed at Jebel Ali free zone and the Dubai Airport. More than 200 factories operate at the Jebel Ali complex, which includes a deep-water port and a free-trade zone for manufacturing, distribution, and transhipment. A major power plant with associated water desalination units, an aluminium smelter, and a steel fabrication unit are prominent facilities in the complex.

Re-export activities are largely concentrated in two major partners: India and Iran. Dubai's re-exports to India reached US$14 billion in 2010, accounting for 35.7 per cent of the emirate's total re-exports. Furthermore, they increased almost fivefold between 2006 and 2010 so that India has surpassed

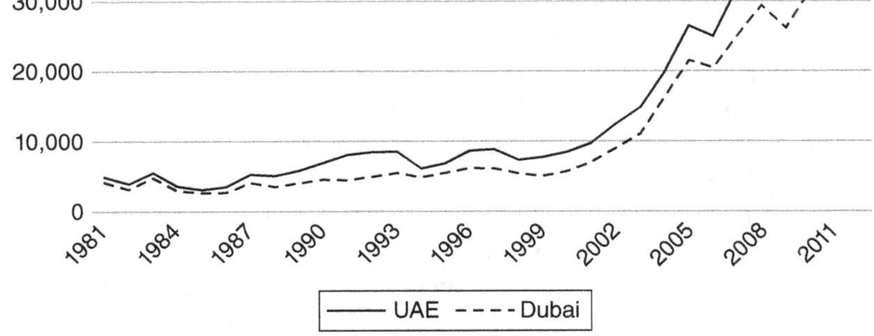

Figure 5.3. Re-exports (in US$ millions of 2005)

Source: Own elaboration based on data from UAE National Bureau of Statistics and World Bank

Iran as Dubai's top re-exports destination. The diamond trade is the major reason behind such phenomenal growth, reaching about US$12 billion in 2010 and representing more than 85 per cent of the emirate's re-exports to India. Gold is another major re-export item from Dubai to India. Competing against Switzerland and South Africa, Dubai has long been a leading source of India's gold imports. Reciprocally, in recent years Dubai has quickly turned into an export destination of India's gold, particularly polished gold, given the very strong local demand and emerging gold trading activities in Dubai.

Re-exporting from Dubai is a very successful activity from an international perspective. Countries with comparative levels of development or economic size tend to re-export substantially less than Dubai (on average, around US$2 billion). However, city states like Singapore and Hong Kong that share with Dubai an advantageous location and a trading tradition, re-export significantly more: US$234 billion in Hong Kong and US$201 billion in Singapore (excluding oil). That is, these two cities re-export around five times the level of Dubai; to the extent that Dubai can replicate the conditions in these Asian states, there is substantial space to expand re-exports.

Iran is the second largest re-export market for Dubai. In 2010, Dubai's re-exports to Iran increased by 12.6 per cent to US$6.5 billion, accounting for 12.7 per cent of the emirate's total re-exports. More than 10 per cent of Iran's imports come through Dubai. In contrast to re-exports to India, Dubai's re-exports to Iran are far more diverse: jewellery and gold are the most important re-export items, but they combine to account for less than 10 per cent of Dubai's total re-exports to the country. Dubai has long been an important trade link between Iran and the rest of the world, thanks to the strong UAE-based trade community of Iranian expatriates. Since 2006, trade has intensified as a result of a series of UN sanctions imposed against Iran for its refusal to halt its uranium enrichment activities. Sanction measures, including inspection of cargo suspected of carrying prohibited goods, banning all trade and supply of so-called dual-use items, tighter monitoring of financial institutions, and extension of travel bans and asset freezes, apparently have had limited impact on Dubai's trade with Iran.

Figure 5.4 presents the volume of real imports of the UAE and Dubai. Again, we deflated nominal values by the world CPI. It can be seen that most of the imports into the UAE actually correspond to Dubai's demand for foreign goods (around 75 per cent in the period 2005–10). This fraction is substantially larger than the share of Dubai's GDP in total non-oil GDP in the UAE (around 55 per cent in 2008) and could be the result of two elements. First, income per capita in Dubai is larger than in other emirates (except Abu Dhabi), allowing Dubai families to spend comparatively more on imports. Second, and probably more important in quantitative terms, recorded imports by Dubai may include those of other emirates which channel their foreign trade via Dubai's highly efficient ports. The evidence in Figure 5.4 also

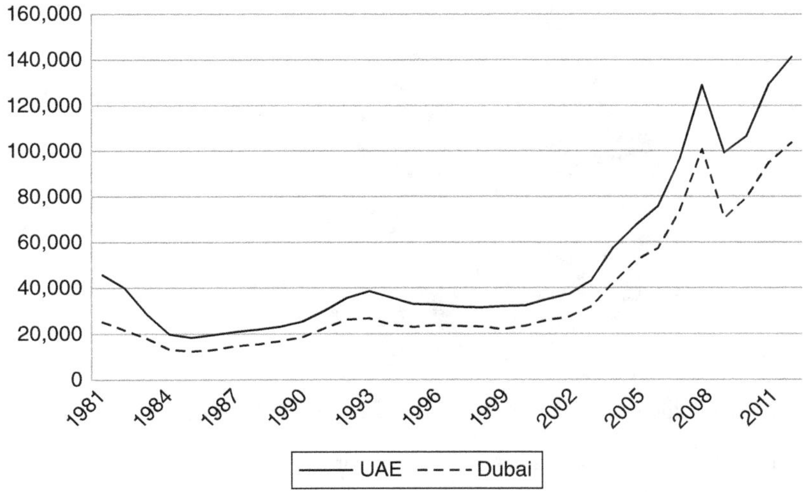

Figure 5.4. Imports (in US$ millions of 2005)

Source: Own elaboration based on data from UAE National Bureau of Statistics and World Bank

indicates that the two-phase phenomenon described for exports replicates likewise in imports. While in the last two decades of the twentieth century real imports stagnated (growth rate of 0.1 per cent per year), between 2001 and 2010, real imports grew by around 12 per cent per year in Dubai and the UAE.

A direct comparison of total import and export levels in the decade of the 2000s indicates that Dubai ran trade deficits in the last five years of around US $40 billion on average (in real US$2005). The deficit peaked in 2008 at US$62 billion but it later declined to the tune of US$33 billion. These are very sizeable deficits when compared to the GDP of Dubai of around US$82 billion: internationally, trade deficits are 6 per cent of GDP on average, while Dubai's is around 40 per cent.

Naturally, exports of services—which are not included in the UAE trade statistics—could help reduce such significant imbalance. Dubai is a significant net exporter of services from the financial sector, logistics, tourism, and so on. Nevertheless, even if one factors in services, the trade imbalance is likely to remain substantial as evidenced in the significant increase in Dubai's external debt during the period 2000–10.

5.2.1 Product Space

Dubai exports are concentrated on a few products. As shown in Figure 5.5, exports are dominated by precious stones which accounted for 63 per cent of total exports in 2010. Base metal products, prepared foodstuffs, and plastic

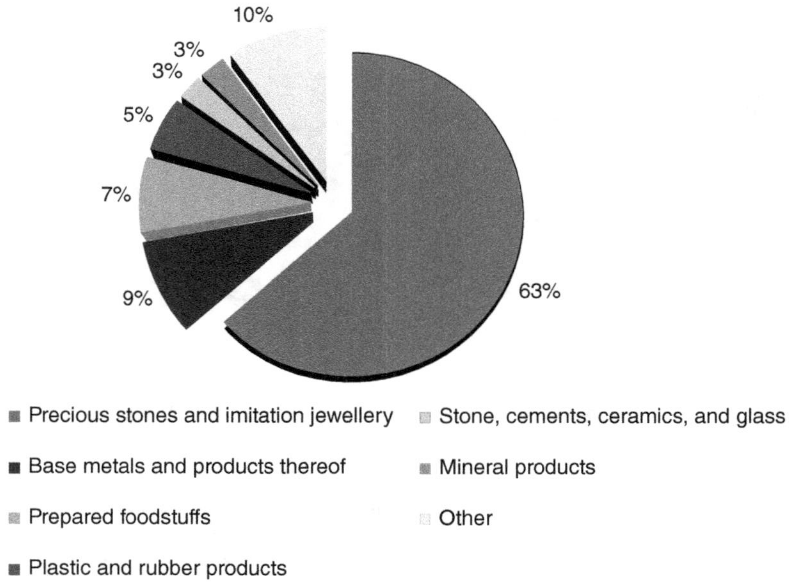

Figure 5.5. Dubai exports by type of good in 2010 (% of total exports)
Source: Own elaboration based on data from Dubai Customs Authority

and rubber products accounted for an additional 25 per cent of exports. The dominance of precious stones in exports is a new phenomenon: in 2004 these exports were around only US$500 million but by 2010 they have surpassed the US$12 billion mark. To a large extent, exports of imitation jewellery are sent to the Indian subcontinent. A salient feature of Dubai's main exports items is its dynamism: rubber and plastic products have grown at over 30 per cent per year in real terms in the previous five years, while the other main categories expanded at around 15 per cent annually.

The very fast growth rates of the main export items of Dubai attest to the entrepreneurship and competitiveness of Dubai firms and reflect their resilience to the global economic downturn of 2008–10. However, three issues deserve cautious analysis. First, the high concentration of exports in a few goods increases the risks of external cyclicality vis-à-vis more diversified economies. For example, any change in India's import policies regarding gold and jewellery could have a significant impact on Dubai producers. Second, the main export goods are relatively simple to produce and unlikely to generate additional exports to boost foreign trade. Third, the construction of Abu Dhabi's Port Khalifa will progressively increase competition for Dubai's Jebel Ali port. While this might divert some trade away from Dubai, it might also provide space for additional regional business, increased competition, and a benchmark for efficiency in Jebel Ali.

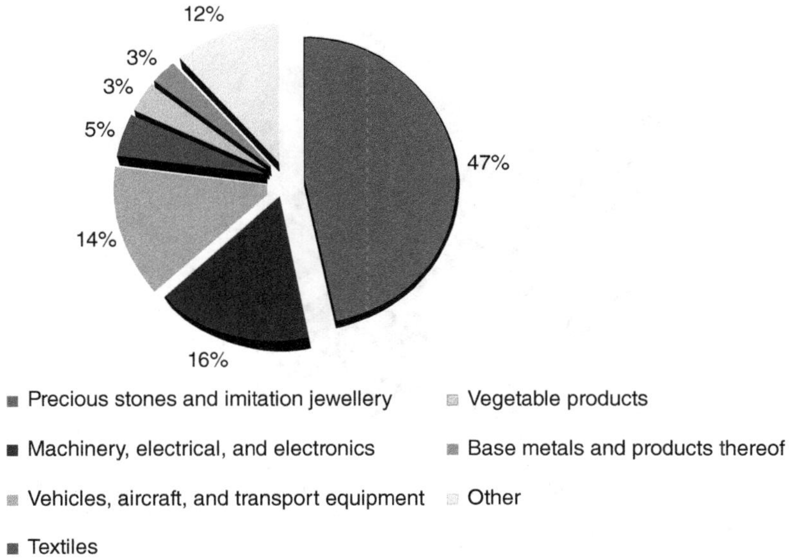

Figure 5.6. Dubai re-exports by type of good in 2010 (% of total re-exports)
Source: Own elaboration based on data from Dubai Customs Authority

As in the case of exports, precious stones also dominate the re-exports of Dubai but to a lesser degree. As can be seen in Figure 5.6, precious and semi-precious stones and imitation jewellery accounted for 47 per cent of total re-exports. However, in terms of value re-exports at US$18 billion in 2010 were around 55 per cent larger than direct exports. Combined, exports and re-exports of these types of good comprise over one-half of the total outbound trade of Dubai.

In spite of the importance of imitation jewellery and precious stones, re-exports in Dubai have a very different structure than exports. Exports of 'machinery, electrical, and electronics' and 'vehicle, aircraft, and transport equipment' were negligible in 2010, but re-exports were very significant with volumes of sales above US$5 billion in each grouping. Combined they represent 30 per cent of total re-exports. To a large extent, these types of goods are directed to regional economies, in particular to Iran which accounts for over 30 per cent of the total shipments. Undoubtedly, Dubai's privileged location justifies its concentration on servicing Iran, but the effects of the UN sanctions are not to be dismissed. An eventual lifting of the restrictions on Iran trade could have an adverse impact on Dubai's re-exporting firms.

One worrisome aspect of the re-exports of 'machinery, electrical, and electronics' is that in real terms they have stagnated since 2005. Other re-export categories of some economic significance (i.e. textiles, vegetable products, base metals and products thereof, plastics and rubber products, and

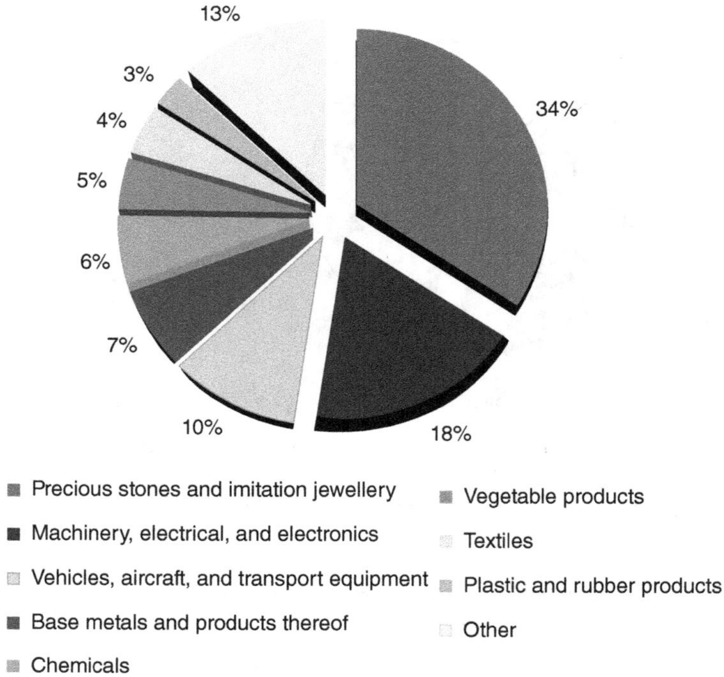

Figure 5.7. Dubai imports by type of good in 2010 (% of total imports)
Source: Own elaboration based on data from Dubai Customs Authority

chemicals which accounted for 27 per cent of the total in 2010) have also remained stagnant which, simultaneously, reflects the resilience of these industries to the foreign downturn and the concern of their inability to grow at par with world trade. An alternative explanation could be that Dubai is facing increased competition in these products from other markets or there is market saturation of the products, thereby leaving Dubai unable to expand market share of these products.

Finally, and not surprisingly, Dubai's imports mirror the pattern of exports and re-exports. The three major import items of the UAE and Dubai are precious stones, machinery, and vehicles which accounted for 62 per cent of the total in 2010 (see Figure 5.7). However, and contrary to exports, imports have taken a significant toll after the global recession: in 2008, total imports amounted to US$120 billion but by 2010 they had reduced to US$100 billion. While some of this reduction is explained by the lower levels of consumption of UAE families, the most significant contractions have been in areas that provide intermediate products to local producers (base metals and products thereof; machinery, electrical, and electronics equipment; vehicles, aircraft, and transport equipment). Notably, imports of precious stones rebounded very strongly after the global crisis and by 2010 were almost 10 per cent above the 2008 level in real terms.

5.2.2 Trade Partners

The concentration of exports and re-exports on a few categories of goods is replicated in terms of Dubai's foreign trade partners. As shown in Figure 5.8, India is the leading export destination country, accounting for over 50 per cent of Dubai's exports in 2010. Second to India was Switzerland which accounted for over 25 per cent of the export trade of Dubai. Arab Gulf countries (e.g. Saudi Arabia, Iran, Iraq, Kuwait, Egypt, and Bahrain) occupy a relatively minor position. To some extent, this is surprising because one would have expected Dubai to be able to supply a variety of goods to its oil-rich neighbours with high incomes and long-standing cultural and economic ties with the emirate.

Re-exports are also largely concentrated in India, albeit with slightly less market share in 2010 (48 per cent) as shown in Figure 5.9. However, and as expected when considering proximity and relative development levels, re-exports are significantly focused on the regional markets. Iran, Iraq, Saudi

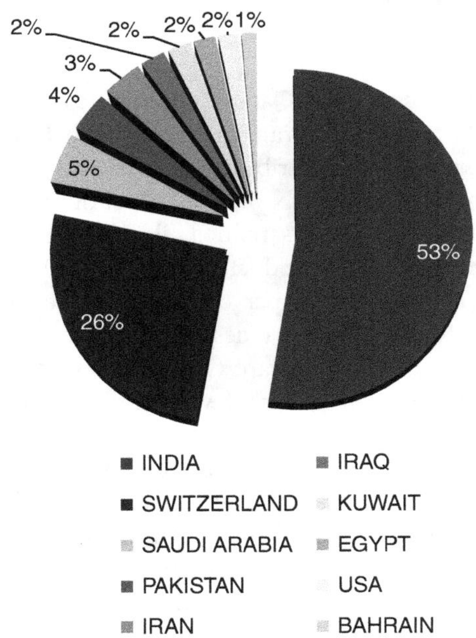

Figure 5.8. Exports by partners in 2010 (% of total exports)
Source: Dubai Statistics Center

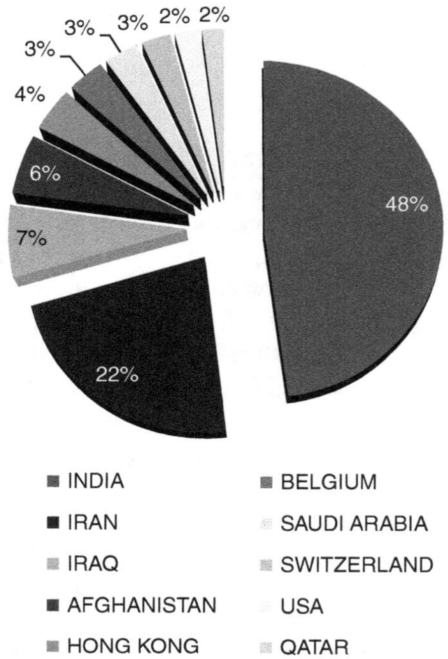

Figure 5.9. Re-exports by partners in 2010 (% of total re-exports)
Source: Dubai Statistics Center

Arabia, Afghanistan, Bahrain, and Qatar account for close to 40 per cent of the re-export market share of Dubai. Iran, as mentioned before, accounted for 22 per cent of the re-exports; this is attributed to both historical trade links as well as the sanctions imposed by the UN on Iran. Most of this trade is machinery and equipment, prepared foodstuffs, refined oil, vehicle, aircraft, and transport equipment, and manufactured products. Iraq is the third largest re-export market for Dubai with around 7 per cent of the re-exported volume and Afghanistan is the fourth re-export destination with 6 per cent. Notably, Kuwait does not appear as a significant trade partner of Dubai in spite of its proximity and relatively high income levels, while the USA, Belgium, and Switzerland barely reach the 3 per cent mark.

Imports, on the other hand, bear no resemblance to the rest of foreign trade in Dubai. Among the top ten originating countries, 50 per cent of total imports in 2010 came from OECD countries (see Figure 5.10). These countries are a major source of machinery and heavy equipment, electrical and electronics, and vehicle, aircraft, and transport equipment. In the UAE, refined oil products are very significant among imports, originating mainly from Japan. Unsurprisingly, China also accounts for a significant share of imports as is the case of most economies in the world. On the other hand, India is the most

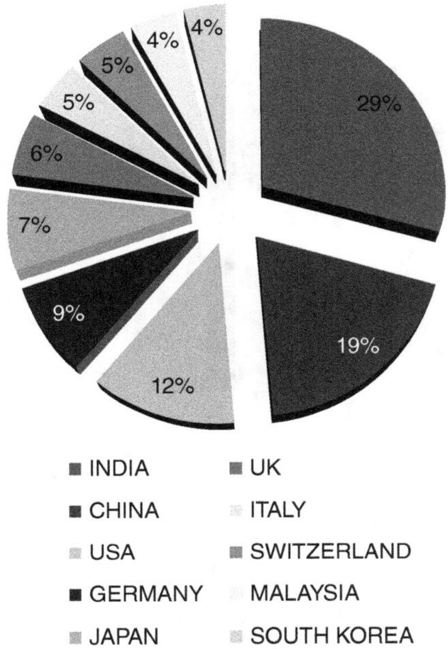

Figure 5.10. Imports by partners in 2010 (% of total imports)

Source: Dubai Statistics Center

significant origin country for imports (with around 30 per cent of trade) which, as discussed above, comprises gold and jewellery but a myriad of other goods that are increasingly being demanded by the Dubai population.

5.2.3 Regional Trade

As mentioned, regional trade is significant only for the re-exports of Dubai. In terms of direct exports and imports, regional markets play a minor role. Considering the production structure of most countries in the GCC this is hardly surprising: Saudi Arabia, Bahrain, Qatar, and Kuwait are leading producers of hydrocarbons and almost uniquely concentrated on exporting (oil and gas). Importing non-energy goods from these countries is not an option; importing energy unnecessary. Oman is the only country in the region that diverges from this pattern even if an oil exporter: as of 2010 Oman accounted for a significant share of Dubai's imports, mainly in the form of food and vegetables and live animals.

It can be seen that Saudi Arabia accounts for over 50 per cent of such trade (see Figure 5.11). The re-export trade to Saudi Arabia is the largest source of market for Dubai, worth over US$7 million in 2009 (constant real terms). This

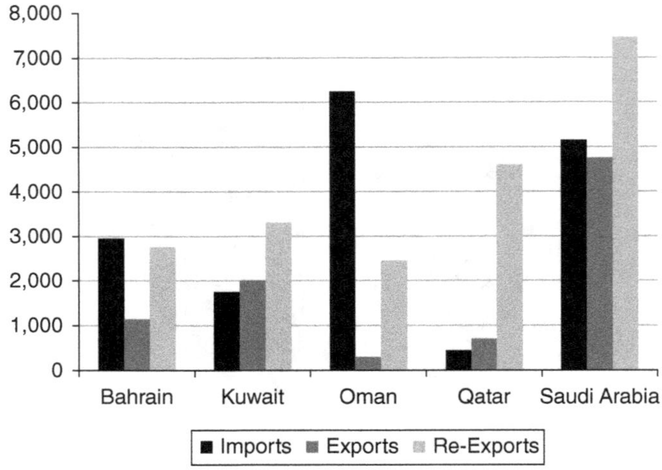

Figure 5.11. Dubai foreign trade with GCC countries, 2009
Source: Dubai Statistics Center

trade comprises of prepared foodstuffs, machinery, electrical, and electronics equipment, and vehicle, aircraft, and transport equipment. Similar products are re-exported to the rest of the GCC countries, albeit in much smaller volumes. Imports from Oman to Dubai account for the highest share in the whole of the GCC region. Dubai (and the UAE for that matter) mainly imports fresh fruit and vegetables, live animals, and confectionaries from Oman. This can be explained by the close proximity of Oman to Dubai which makes transportation by road to Dubai much cheaper. However, compared to more high-income countries in the GCC region, exports and re-exports to Oman are minimal.

5.3 POTENTIAL TRADE

In this section we analyse whether current trade volumes in Dubai correspond to the maximum trade achievable (potential trade) and if there is space for growth. Current levels of foreign trade in Dubai are determined by several elements. Naturally, the size of Dubai's economy determines the magnitude of its imports. Likewise its industrial base and the degree of economic development determine the capacity of the emirate to export the goods it produces. But other factors also intervene. For example, the distance to exporting markets largely determines the transportation costs and, evidently, the price at which such goods can be placed in the target markets. In addition, trade agreements—such as the GCC—potentially facilitate the ability of Dubai to penetrate foreign markets and determine exports and re-exports.

Nevertheless, beyond these factors a key determinant of foreign trade is the country's own efficiency and productivity levels. More efficient industries in a country are able to place their products at an advantage in international markets. Likewise, more efficient domestic industries capable of competing with foreign firms limit the need for imports. Determining the ability of a country to export and import, that is, determining the trade levels a country could potentially achieve, requires comparing the performance of such a country vis-à-vis other countries in the world.

Gravity models have become the workhorse of the empirical literature on the determinants of international trade.[2] The basic intuition behind a gravity model is that trade between two countries resembles the gravitational interaction between planets: the attraction force (equivalently, bilateral trade) is determined positively by their relative masses (i.e. economic size or trade potential) and negatively by the distance which separate them (i.e. the transportation cost). In addition to this basic framework, other variables are introduced to acknowledge the effects of bilateral trade arrangements: colonial and cultural ties, dissimilar factor endowments, and political factors. A vast empirical literature has examined bilateral flows between city pairs or regions, motivated by the observation that much economic interaction is concentrated at very short distances.

Using econometric procedures, we estimate 'gravity models' for the foreign trade of Dubai and the United Arab Emirates (UAE). As discussed above, the main component of foreign trade in the UAE is oil and gas with over 90 per cent of the total. Dubai, on the other hand, does not export energy in any form but its exports comprise the majority of non-energy exports of the UAE. These observations suggest separating energy from non-energy exports when estimating econometric models. The former would most likely represent the trade of the UAE, while the latter would adequately represent the case of Dubai. Likewise, a model for re-exports would represent almost exclusively the case of Dubai. Finally, the import structure of Dubai is available directly for modelling.

A generic gravity model for the trade flow at time t ($T_{ijt} =$ exports, imports, or re-exports) between two countries would be of the form:

$$\log T_{ijt} = k + \beta_1 \log Y_{it} + \beta_2 \log Y_{jt} - \beta_3 \log D_{ij} + \Sigma_n \beta_n \log F^n_{ijt} \qquad (5.1)$$

where the sub-index i represents the reporter country and the sub-index j corresponds to the partner country. Variables Y_{it} and Y_{jt} represent the trade potential of each economy, respectively, and D_{ij} is the distance that separates them. The variable F_{ijt} is a n-dimensional set of idiosyncratic factors thought

[2] See Anderson (2011) for an exhaustive account of their analytical development and Cardamone (2007) for a survey of empirical applications.

to have an important effect in determining trade volumes between two countries. Typical factors included in augmented gravity models are the level of economic development, membership in preferential trade areas (bilateral or multilateral arrangements), cultural affinity, vicinity (countries sharing a common border), and geographical particularities such as a reporter or a partner being an island or landlocked. In general, these factors are seen as inducing or reducing trade frictions and are signed a priori accordingly. Parameters $\beta_1, \beta_2, \beta_3,$ and β_n are unknowns to be determined empirically and k is a constant related to country-specific characteristics.

The gravity model predicts that countries have positive trade in both directions, even if this predicted trade may be small. Scrutiny of bilateral trade flows nevertheless indicates that recorded trade flows are sometimes zero or missing. According to gravity theories as conventionally specified, zero trade would only occur if the GDP of one or both countries equals zero which is obviously untrue. One way to rationalize zero trade is to modify the demand specification to allow for 'choke prices' above which all demand is choked off (Novy, 2010). Alternatively, zeroes could be the result of the presence of fixed export-costs inhibiting foreign trade by firms operating in monopolistic competitive markets (Elhanan et al., 2008). Naturally, at the empirical levels zeroes may correspond not only to actual inactivity (a true zero) but they may also reflect that no recording is made if shipments fall below a certain positive threshold (e.g. as imposed when compiling the statistics).

The presence of zero-trade flows complicates the estimation of the statistical models. Eliminating these data would entail biasing the results. We use a Tobit procedure that adequately estimates the models without eliminating any observations.[3] In the econometric estimation we exclude UAE from the analysis. Otherwise, using the model to forecast UAE and Dubai's foreign trade would be improper. Likewise, we exclude the developed economies as reporters (since the determinants of trade for advanced economies are too different from those of emerging countries) but not as partners (so that we can model trade with them). Finally, the models use the most updated sample of data available to estimate the parameters of the gravity equations and averages over the period 2005–9 to eliminate the influence of singular events (such as the economic downturn of the late 2000s).

Table 5.1 collects the econometric results when estimating gravity models for total exports, imports, energy exports, and re-exports. It can be seen that the elasticity of total exports with respect to distance is negative while it is positive for the economic size of the reporter and the partner. The results suggest that more developed economies tend to trade less with developing and emerging economies (recall that we excluded developed economies from the

[3] Other studies also use Tobit models to estimate the gravity equation with zero flows (e.g. Rose (2004) and Soloaga and Winters (2001)).

Table 5.1. Basic gravity models for different export groups and imports, 2005–9 dependent variables in US$ of 2005

	Total exports	Non-energy exports	Energy exports	Re-exports	Total imports
Distance	−1.77***	−1.72***	−5.26***	−3.41***	−1.47***
GDP reporter	1.79***	1.94***	2.94***	1.76***	1.55***
GDP partner	1.35***	1.30***	2.47***	1.27***	1.47***
Development reporter	−0.22***	−0.28***	0.23***	2.84***	−0.24***
Development partner	−0.18***	−0.22***	−0.34***	0.77***	0.05
Area reporter	−0.18***	−0.26***	−0.05	−1.91***	−0.21***
Area partner	−0.08***	−0.08***	−0.13***	0.36**	0.03
Border	0.38*	0.53**	−0.29	−2.92*	0.86***
Landlocked	−0.08	0.07	−1.40***	−16.53***	−0.21**
Common language	0.64***	0.67***	1.46***	−2.59***	0.86***
Island reporter	0.99***	1.22***	0.08	−1.74***	0.36***
Island partner	0.51***	0.34***	2.62***	1.47***	0.23***
Andean Pact	0.95	1.07	0.83	12.24**	0.62
ASEAN	−0.01	−0.35	1.00	−8.68**	1.02*
CACM	2.10*	2.50*	1.04	—	2.05*
CARICOM	4.42***	3.88***	9.22***	20.19***	2.73***
ECOWAS	3.53***	3.04***	7.50***	—	2.53***
Gulf Coop. Council	−0.62	−0.28	−1.48	15.62***	−0.26
LAFTA	0.26	0.32	2.15*	6.57***	0.59
Lome Convention	−0.25	−0.65***	1.78***	1.18	0.23
NAFTA	−0.78	−0.43	−1.62	—	−1.95
UDEAC	4.29***	4.32***	7.27***	—	2.38**
Constant	−40.44***	−40.92***	−80.23***	−70.09***	−42.97***
Observations	12,075	12,075	12,075	12,075	12,075
Censored (zeros)	509	554	5,575	10,393	536
Not censored	11,566	11,521	6,500	1,682	11,539
Likelihood function	−30,967	−30,890	−26,591	−9,209	−30,822
Std. error regression	3.27	3.27	8.52	14.64	3.25
Pseudo R^2	0.745	0.748	0.748	0.747	0.763

Note: *, **, *** = statistically significant at 90%, 95%, and 99%, respectively.

reporters). Likewise, large-area economies tend to trade less, most likely on the account that they have more access to natural resources and need less foreign partners. As expected, neighbouring countries tend to trade more as shown in the positive parameters for the border dummy. Being landlocked seems to have no significant negative effects in the countries in this sample, but islands trade more than continental economies. Cultural proximity—proxied here by common language—seems to enhance trade between countries. With regards to multilateral trade agreements, it can be seen that few of them seem to have had a positive effect on trade. The rest, largely the result of political motivations, have been unsuccessful in fostering economic integration or expanding trade (see Hachette, 2011). Notably, and to some extent not surprisingly, the GCC dummy is statistically insignificant: countries in the Gulf area are primarily oil-and-gas exporters and, consequently, one should not expect a trade union to be able to have a significant impact on total exports.

It can also be seen that the estimated parameters for non-energy exports do not differ quantitatively and qualitatively from those of the model for total exports. On the contrary, the estimated model for energy is quite different in terms of the parameters and the precision of the model. The estimated equation has a significantly larger number of zeroes (over 5,000), which is expected as most of the countries in the sample do not export oil or gas. The parameters for distance and economic mass in the energy equation are much larger in absolute terms, some parameters are now statistically insignificant (e.g. the reporter size and sharing borders) and a few of them become very significant (e.g. the economy being landlocked or the partner being an island). This indicates that the econometric model is unsatisfactory. This is expected as trading in commodities is conducted to a significant extent in centralized exchange markets (e.g. the London Exchange) where buyers and sellers do not operate on a bilateral basis but in a globalized market.

The econometric model for re-exports provides interesting and intuitive results. First, note that the estimated parameter of distance is twice that of the total exports equation while those for economic masses remain largely unchanged. This suggests, as one should expect, that location is a significant determinant of re-export (or transhipment) activities. Re-exports are usually tailored to the proximity to customers. In addition, we found that the more developed is the economy, the larger become the re-exporting activities and that as economies are smaller they tend to increase re-exporting activities. In fact, most of the largest transhipment facilities in the world are located in small size economies serving larger adjacent markets, including Hong Kong, Singapore, the Netherlands, and Belgium.

Finally, before turning to the forecasts and counterfactual-scenario analysis, we estimate gravity models for total imports. Using imports as the dependent variable potentially biases the results because imports are recorded using c.i.f. prices (including transport and insurance costs), likely to be correlated with distance (the variable proxying for transport costs). However, the inconsistency does not necessarily affect the parameters of the other variables since the correlation of distance with all other explanatory variables is very low. It can be seen in Table 5.1 that the estimated parameters for other variables are very similar to those of the total export regressions.

5.3.1 Potential Trade

We use the estimated gravity models in Table 5.1 to forecast the trade structure of the UAE and Dubai. These forecasts would indicate the 'normal' trade structure that an economy with the characteristics of Dubai and the UAE should have, if it were to act like the rest of the economies in the world. Naturally, the actual trade structure might differ from what is forecast to be 'normal' for a variety of reasons. Market forces, however, would tend to lead the economy into the normal path because such forces call for the best and most efficient use of resources. Hence, from the comparison of normal to actual export and import levels we can learn about the most likely evolution of foreign trade in the UAE and Dubai.

In Table 5.2 we present the actual and predicted normal foreign trade volumes by regions of the world for the period 2005–9. The data correspond to the per cent share of each region in actual trade flows as compared to what the models in Table 5.1 would predict. We eliminate energy exports because, as shown in the econometric results, the quality of the estimated models is quite disappointing. This, as mentioned before, it not surprising because oil trade does not conform to the standard determinants of bilateral trade as it is done primarily in centralized commodity exchanges where buyers and sellers engage in spot operations, futures trading, and derivatives.

Table 5.2. Actual and predicted foreign trade of the UAE with regional blocks, 2005–9 (in % of each trade flow)

	Non-energy exports		Re-exports		Imports	
	Actual	Predicted	Actual	Predicted	Actual	Predicted
MENA	35.4	39.0	51.8	100.0	10.8	23.6
Latin America	0.4	0.9	0.1	—	1.4	0.9
Africa	8.9	0.7	11.6	—	1.5	0.2
South & East Asia	30.9	28.2	22.8	—	44.6	26.6
Europe	19.2	22.4	8.2	—	31.8	22.7
USA and Canada	3.8	8.2	1.4	—	9.3	25.8
Transition	1.3	0.6	4.2	—	0.6	0.1
Total	100.0	100.0	100.0	100.0	100.0	100.0

The results in Table 5.2 indicate that, in terms of non-energy exports, Dubai conforms largely to the 'normal' pattern with only minor deviations. Trade with MENA countries and South and East Asian economies is around the values forecast to be adequate for the emirate: nearly 66 per cent of Dubai's exports go to both areas in line with the forecasted value of 67 per cent. Trade with Latin America and the Transition economies—both relatively distant and with low income levels—is in fact as low as predicted by the 'normal trade pattern' embedded in the econometric model. Current trade with Europe is within the ranges of variation of the forecast values. The only significant differences in the current trade pattern of Dubai is its relatively low penetration in the North American markets of 3.8 per cent vis-à-vis a 'normal' level of over 8 per cent and the higher participation of African economies (8.9 per cent) than what is suggested by the econometric estimates of 0.7 per cent. Trade with countries such as Djibouti, Mali, and Ethiopia far exceed the model predictions.

The model for re-exports produces a unique and singular prediction: in a 'normal' context, all re-exports should be concentrated in MENA economies. Furthermore, for a 'normal' economy the level of re-exports should be a minuscule fraction of Dubai's current levels (between 5 per cent and 10 per cent): as discussed, the majority of countries in the world do not re-export and only a few countries can benefit from the conditions for becoming a hub, that is, the combination of an adequate location, an affluent target region for re-export, and adequate infrastructure to undertake transhipment of cargo and processing. This extreme econometric prediction is primarily due to the high sensitivity of re-exports to transportation costs.

Finally, the model for imports indicates that in a normal situation Dubai ought to be trading substantially more with MENA and the US and significantly less with European economies and East and South Asian countries. Higher imports from MENA countries result from proximity—an aspect that the econometric model considers—but in reality this is limited by the fact that MENA countries have a very similar industrial base to the UAE and a large concentration on energy exports. This latter aspect is quite imperfectly captured by the econometric model. Trading with the US or Europe does not suffer from this problem and the findings—a significantly lower-than-predicted trade level with the US as well as a higher level with Europe—would indicate that to some extent, there may have been currency valuations effects in operation. Because the AED is pegged to the US dollar, the period of a strong dollar prior to the global crisis could have made imports from Europe more attractive.

Discussing the forecast of trade flows with individual trade partners is complicated because econometric models tend to be less able to single out countries with similar characteristics. For example, for Dubai's exports, countries like Sweden and Norway may be indistinguishable in the econometric terms of equation (5.1): both are located at roughly the same distance, both

Table 5.3. Actual and predicted trade of the UAE with individual countries, 2005–9 (in millions of US$ of 2005)

	Non-energy exports			Imports	
	Actual	Predicted		Actual	Predicted
India	3,036	1,860	China	12,893	5,982
Oman	2,203	738	India	12,703	4,063
Benelux	1,037	83	USA	9,008	26,178
S. Arabia	1,030	3,664	Germany	6,841	6,883
Qatar	985	1,145	Japan	6,827	14,970
Iran	866	371	UK	5,409	4,208
USA	743	1,581	Italy	4,328	3,314
Hong Kong	728	62	S. Arabia	4,177	16,797
UK	552	677	France	3,658	3,621
Pakistan	514	189	S. Korea	3,244	773
Kuwait	511	402	Turkey	2,746	1,157

have similar income levels, population, and potential economic size and other characteristics. Thus, forecasting at the regional level (Northern Europe) would be more precise than at the individual country level.

Despite its limitations, Table 5.3 produces interesting results concerning Dubai's trade with the different countries. It can be seen that the model predicts much higher volumes of exports to Saudi Arabia, considering its proximity and economic size, and much lower levels of exports to India. The latter gap could be explained by the extraordinary conditions in the gold market imposed by Indian regulations that has increased trade volumes beyond expectations. In addition, note that while forecasts are accurate for some countries' exports, for three of them there are substantial departures from expected exports: trade with Oman and Iran is much larger than predicted while that with the US is much lower.

In terms of imports, the main conclusions in Table 5.3 indicate that trade with the US and Japan is much lower than predicted while that with China and India is much larger. The latter is a widespread phenomenon: Indian and Chinese exports have penetrated most countries and Dubai is no exception. For the rest of the top 10 import partners, forecasts are pretty close to actual levels which is not surprising considering the traditional absence of trade restrictions of the UAE economy.

5.4 TRADE DEVELOPMENT AND TRADE POLICIES

Dubai has benefited immensely from its strategic geographical location. It has also developed a world-class transportation and logistics network aimed at promoting Dubai as a leading hub of international trade. Effective participation in international trade has enabled the economy of Dubai to diversify and grow. However, improving its competitive capacity, building a resilient strong economic base, and profiting from the opportunities provided by fast-changing global markets require a comprehensive trade policy to address some of the issues inherent in its trade structure and patterns.

First and foremost, there is ample space for Dubai to expand exporting and re-exporting activities. From a comparative point of view, most countries in the world with the size of Dubai's economy tend to export substantially more. Furthermore, city-state economies that Dubai would like to emulate—such as Hong Kong or Singapore—in its role of regional trade hub, rely significantly more on foreign trade to develop and, in terms of value, they export and re-export four or five times more than Dubai. Fostering exports and re-exports should be a priority for Dubai's trade policy.

Second, Dubai's exports and re-exports appear to be dangerously concentrated, both in terms of product space and partners. Over 50 per cent of exports and re-exports are concentrated in one good (gold and jewellery). Low export diversification puts Dubai in a risky position. Changes in international gold prices are frequent and can affect substantially the profitability of exporting and re-exporting activities. Indirectly, they affect the general level of economic activity in Dubai, even if the linkages of gold industries with the rest of the economy are small, as a result of perceived changes in wealth. The volatility of commodity prices is a well-known phenomenon; in particular, prices are high because gold is being used as a reserve of value in this current period of economic instability. However, a normalization of economic activity in Europe and North America would certainly make gold less attractive and prices would drop.

Beyond being concentrated in one good, Dubai's exports and re-exports are also largely concentrated on two partners: India and Iran. As mentioned, India imports the majority of Dubai's gold and is also the major provider of gold to Dubai. This might be the result of production specialization and the development of profitable market niches; in this case, there would be just the usual business risk. But it might also be the product of India's regulations on gold trading: any change in such regulations would affect adversely Dubai. Trade with Iran, on the other hand, is far riskier: while historically Iran has been a trade partner, the current levels of trade are largely the result of UN sanctions. Re-exports to Iran would certainly reduce significantly should the UN sanctions be relaxed or lifted altogether.

Furthermore, Dubai's export and re-exports are concentrated on goods with low technological content and with little linkages with the rest of the economy. The latter is particularly the case of re-exports that are processed in free zones and disconnected from other industries in Main Dubai. Goods that are transhipped and re-exported, by definition, do not link with other sectors of the economy beyond logistics, packaging, and transport activities within the free zone. Exporting firms from Main Dubai are also isolated by the nature of the goods they produce: gold and jewellery contain some processing, as well as base metal products, prepared foodstuffs, and plastic and rubber products. But their elaboration is not very sophisticated and does not link significantly with other industries.

An obvious drawback of producing unsophisticated export goods is that a relatively disconnected foreign trade sector does not provide a boost to the rest of the domestic economy in the upswing of the world business cycle. A more subtle aspect is that foreign trade in sophisticated export goods induces faster and more aggressive technological changes in production, fosters higher productivity gains, and improves human capital by the continuous demand of a better-educated manpower. Sectors producing non-traded goods tend to update and upgrade faster as a result of more demanding export industries. Singapore and Hong Kong made the transition from exporting low-quality, non-technological goods in the 1960s and 1970s to highly sophisticated, technology-rich products including electronics, chemicals, biotechnology, pharmaceutics, and precision engineering. Firms in these countries gradually shifted away from labour-intensive to knowledge-intensive activities by deepening their technology base and strengthening knowledge-based services.

The need to foster the export base of Dubai is pressing for, at least, three reasons. The most important is the imminent opening of Port Khalifa in Abu Dhabi and other transhipment facilities in the UAE. New ports and airports in Abu Dhabi or the northern emirates will increase the supply of re-exporting facilities and, potentially, might drive some businesses away from Dubai ports and airports. Evidently, Dubai ports and airports have the advantage of being already in place and competitive for international standards. However, such advantages may be eroded. Likewise, firms in Dubai's free-trade zones and other exporters have invested heavily in their businesses and sunk costs will prevent them from moving quickly to other locations even if such locations have lower production costs. But new business may not materialize in Dubai.

An additional issue is that Dubai's advantages in terms of location as a regional hub are not unique to Dubai: Qatar, Bahrain, and even the other emirates share a similar location and could become competitors for, essentially, the same trade routes and cargo. While Dubai has a significant advantage in terms of infrastructure and reputation vis-à-vis all other locations in the Gulf of Arabia, infrastructure is being built in most of these places which, eventually, can challenge Dubai's position of pre-eminence.

A third issue is that Dubai requires the trade sector to become instrumental in its dream of becoming a knowledge-based economy. So far, Dubai's development model has been based on accumulating capital and importing expatriate workers. While that strategy has paid well, it is deemed limited and not sustainable, calling for a gradual shift towards the production of knowledge-intensive goods in high-value-added industries. Considering the small size of the Dubai and UAE markets, such a dream will have to rely on foreign markets to provide incentives for such industries to develop. Regional markets are not big enough, so Dubai's trading firms will have to deal at the international level.

Competition in world markets requires changes in trade policies in Dubai. More important, it requires fundamental changes to other policies that support export and re-export activities. Among the latter, there is an urgent need to improve the 'soft infrastructure', that is, to enact world class market regulations (including competition protection and intellectual property laws), increase transparency, cater for a predictable trade and business environment, simplify customs procedures, and inject dynamism into the banking industry so that it can play a vital role in facilitating the financing of foreign trade.

REFERENCES

Anderson, J. E., 2011. 'The Gravity Model'. *Annual Review of Economics*, 3: 133–60.

Cardamone, P., 2007. 'A Survey of the Assessments of the Effectiveness of Preferential Trade Agreements Using Gravity Models'. *Economia Internazionale/International Economics*, 60(4): 421–73.

Elhanan, H., Melitz, M., and Rubinstein, Y., 2008. 'Estimating Trade Flows: Trading Partners and Trading Volume'. *Quarterly Journal of Economics*, 123(2): 441–87.

Falvey, R., Foster, N., and Greenaway, D., 2004. 'Imports, Exports, Knowledge Spillovers and Growth'. *Economics Letters*, 85(2004): 209–13.

Government of Dubai, 2010. *Dubai Strategic Vision 2015*, Dubai: Government of Dubai.

Hachette, D., 2011. *Latinoamérica en el siglo XX: crecimiento, comercio y pensamiento económico*, Santiago, Chile: Ediciones UC.

Novy, D., 2010. 'International Trade and Monopolistic Competition without CES: Estimating Translog Gravity'. Unpublished MS, Warwick University.

Rodriguez, F. and Rodrik, D., 2000. 'Trade Policy and Economic Growth: A Skeptic's Guide to the Cross-National Evidence'. *NBER Macroeconomics Annual 2000*. Cambridge, MA: MIT Press.

Rose, A. K., 2004. 'Do We really Know that the WTO Increases Trade?' *American Economic Review*, 94: 98–114.

Soloaga, I. and Winters, A. L., 2001. 'Regionalism in the Nineties: What Effect on Trade?' *North American Journal of Economics and Finance*, 12: 2–29.

World Bank, 2011. *World Development Indicators 2011*. Washington, DC: World Bank.

6

Economic Linkages between Free Zones and Main Dubai

Mahmoud Al Iriani, Ibrahim Elbadawi, and Dhuha Fadhel

6.1 INTRODUCTION

Free zones have been common initiatives by many countries aiming at enhancing their exports and economic growth in general. Terms such as Export Processing Zones, Free Trade Zones, Special Economic Zones, and Export Processing Factories refer to almost similar concepts with some variations to cater for the specific policy objectives behind establishing these special areas within the territory of the country (Madani, 1999). However, export processing zones and free trade zones are the most commonly used terms. Throughout this paper, we use the term free zones (FZ) to mean any of the above definitions, and DFZ to mean Dubai Free Zones.

FZ are special areas or enclaves that are isolated from domestic economies because they are subjected to different rules and regulations from the rest of the economy (they may be either fenced or non-fenced). They are primarily designed to attract foreign investment, boost exports, and create employment in the host economy. In order to attract foreign firms, a number of policy incentives are usually introduced. Common incentive packages include: tax exemptions or holidays, duty-free status, developed infrastructure and facilities, simplified administrative procedures, and liberalized systems (Ge, 1999). In return, FZ are expected to benefit host economies through technology and managerial skills transfer, job creation, promoting exports and foreign exchange earnings, and through their forward and backward linkages with the domestic economy.

It is generally believed that the extent of linkages between FZ and the main economy can provide a key indicator to the potential domestic economy gains from allowing for these enclaves to be established within the territory of the country and freely operate without government intervention in most cases. The more extensive and profound these linkages are, the more likely it is that FZ can generate long-term benefits for the main economy (Din, 1994; Tahir, 1998). Although the literature on FZ linkages with the main economy classifies these linkages into two main categories (i.e. backward and forward linkages), more recognition is generally given to the backward linkages since the FZ are export-oriented by definition. It is also believed that the purchases of domestically produced intermediate inputs by firms located in the FZ can be vital for stimulating the production of these inputs in the domestic economy, and therefore leading to a boost in the level of income and national welfare systems (Ge, 1993).

Realizing the potential of FZ in attracting foreign direct investment (FDI) and contributing to the local economy, and in its quest to adopt a diversified growth strategy to restructure the economy from direct oil-dependency, the government of Dubai has adopted a policy of encouraging free trade by establishing a number of free zones. The largest of its free zones, Jebel Ali Free Zone Authority (JAFZA), was established on 9 February 1985 as the pioneer in Dubai's free zones economy. Since then, the proliferation of DFZ has transformed its economic scenario in a short span of twenty-five years, bringing about tremendous change in the development scene of the emirate.

DFZ have been empowered with complete authority within their territory. This authority includes the right to master planning and zoning, management, setting rules and regulations for companies, registration and licensing, infrastructure and facility development, provision of services, leasing and sale of facilities, provision of human resources, and imposing appropriate fees. DFZ have been a success story, as reflected by their large share in the emirate's total foreign trade, which amounted to more than 35 per cent in 2012.

Given the current economic significance of DFZ in the emirate's economy and their phenomenal expansion, assessing their linkages to the rest of the economy outside the free zone (hereafter Main Dubai, or MD) is an important policy issue. In this context, this chapter examines the evolution of the FZ in Dubai and attempts to assess their impacts on its economy. Based on the evidence gleaned from the analysis, the chapter draws some policy recommendations for further enhancing the economic linkages and contribution of DFZ to the overall economy of Dubai.

Section 6.2 provides an overview of the typology of DFZ authorities and compares the main characteristics of the firms located in the free zones to those in the rest of the emirate's economy. Section 6.3 compares firms in DFZ and MD using data from a firm-level survey conducted in 2010 by the Dubai Economic Council (DEC) and covering more than 700 enterprises. This analysis contrasts firms in the two sub-economies (DFZ and MD) and across sectors in terms of their main characteristics, most notably including purchases of local inputs—a key indicator of backward linkages. Section 6.4

estimates the contribution of DFZ to the rest of the economy through the creation of linkages by the utilization of labour, local inputs, and demand for capital from local financial institutions. Section 6.5 summarizes the main findings and offers some policy recommendations.

6.2 DUBAI FREE ZONES

At the time when JAFZA was established, the free zones concept was new to the UAE and even to the Middle East region. Today, JAFZA is the largest FZ in the area. It has fifteen kilometres of quays which makes it the largest artificial port in the world. It also has the world's largest dry dock (Nowicki, 2007). JAFZA has become one of the strongest brands in the region and the name 'JAFZA' has acquired publicity and attention on the global scene. As a major regional distribution and logistics hub, it has become an important benchmark model of regulations and incentives. Its success has inspired other emirates and other countries in the region to set up their own FZ. But JAFZA has preserved its leading position as it is still the largest, most developed, and successful FZ in the region. In 2012, JAFZA was home for more than 7,000 companies, over 120 of which are branches or subsidiaries of Fortune's 'Top 500 Companies'. And even though JAFZA was originally established as a distribution/logistics hub, it has a steadily increasing service and manufacturing base.

The successful performance of JAFZA has encouraged the government to set up a number of other general and industry-specific FZ including single-commodity and single-activity zones, and a large-scale financial services zone. A total of twenty-three free zones are now operating in Dubai and additional FZ are being planned or are under construction (Table 6.1).

Despite the widely held perception that publicly owned FZ are generally less successful than those owned by the private sector (see for example World Bank, 2008), evidence suggests that the primarily government-owned DFZ might be an exception. The DFZ have been instrumental in attracting FDI and providing a source of foreign exchange to the emirate. As we show in this chapter, there appears to be concrete evidence that JAFZA has also contributed to Dubai's economy through both backward and forward linkages. Many factors have been responsible for the pronounced success of DFZ. The main and most important factor has been the continuous support of the government of Dubai in the form of land provision, initial infrastructure, and superstructure subsidies. The initial government support has greatly assisted new DFZ to gain commercial credibility and to become self-supporting. In addition, a set of common incentives across different DFZ were created to attract prospective customers (Box 6.1).

Table 6.1. Dubai free zones (2012)

	Zone	Date established	Owner
1	Jebel Ali Free Zone (JAFZA)	1985	Dubai World
2	Multi Commodities Centre (DMCC)	2002	Dubai World
3	Outsource Zone (DOZ)	2004	Dubai Holding
4	Car and Automotive Zone (DUCAMZ)	2000	Dubai World
5	The Gold & Diamond Park (DGDP)	2001	EMAAR
6	Flower Centre (DFC)	2004	Dubai Holding
7	Textile City (DTC)	2007	Dubai World
8	Internet City (DIC)	2000	Dubai Holding
9	Media City (DMC)	2001	Dubai Holding
10	Studio City (DSC)	2005	Dubai Holding
11	International Media Production Zone (IMPZ)	2003	Dubai Holding
12	Silicon Oasis (DSO)	2004	Emirates Group
13	Health Care City (DHCC)	2002	Dubai Holding
14	Knowledge Village (DKV)	2003	Dubai Holding
18	International Academic City (DIAC)	2007	Dubai Holding
15	International Financial Centre (DIFC)	2004	Gov. of Dubai
16	Biotechnology & Research Park (DuBiotech)	2005	Dubai Holding
17	Energy Park (DENPARK)	2006	Dubai Holding
19	International Humanitarian City (DIHC)	2007	Gov. of Dubai
20	Airport Free Zone [DAFZA]	1996	Emirates Group
21	Dubai World Central (DWC)	2007	Emirates Group
22	Logistics City (DLC)	2007	Emirates Group
23	Maritime City	2007	Dubai World

Source: http://uaefreezones.com and JAFZA

Box 6.1. **Common set of incentives in DFZ**

No customs duties
No trade, investment, or labour quotas
No foreign exchange controls
No restrictions on capital and profit repatriation
Long-term corporate and personal tax holidays
Streamlined labour procedures
100 per cent foreign ownership possible
Simple procedures and minimal legislation, low bureaucracy
Competitive land rates with long-term renewable leases

6.3 CHARACTERISTICS OF DUBAI FIRMS IN AND OUTSIDE THE FREE ZONES

The discussion in this chapter is based on the first Business Enterprise-Level Survey (ELS), conducted with managers of 709 enterprises located in Dubai. The survey draws on research done by the World Bank and was undertaken

Table 6.2. ELS sample characteristics

Industries	Area	Number of firms	% of firms in each size class 5–19 workers	20–99 workers	100+ workers
Light manufacturing	MD	89	71.9	18.0	10.1
	DFZ	4	0.0	50.0	50.0
Heavy manufacturing	MD	70	64.3	25.7	10.0
	DFZ	15	13.3	66.7	20.0
Trading	MD	43	74.4	20.9	4.7
	DFZ	42	66.7	26.2	7.1
Services	MD	163	65.6	31.3	3.1
	DFZ	42	61.9	31.0	7.1
Construction	MD	106	28.3	54.7	17.0
Financial services	DFZ	80	50.0	36.2	13.8
Total	MD	471	57.7	32.8	9.4
	DFZ	183	54.4	35.0	10.7

Source: First ELS, Dubai Economic Council, 2010

between January and June 2010. It aimed at promoting scientifically based research to understand how firms and policymakers should make optimal decisions with regards to competitiveness, employment, exports, and investments in infrastructure. The survey was designed to cover a representative sample based on six industrial sectors (light manufacturing, heavy manufacturing, construction, retail and wholesale (trading hereafter), services, and financial service sectors), and two economic regions (MD and DFZ areas).

Some fifty-five firms were eliminated from the sample because they did not report the percentage of intermediate inputs purchased from the domestic market, which is the key variable used in our analysis to measure the strength of backward linkages with the host economy. Table 6.2 shows the distribution of firms in the sample by industry, location, and size. Table 6.3 shows average characteristics of the sample firms by investment, capital intensity, age, and percentage of national ownership and local sales. It shows that, on average, firms located in the DFZ were attracting more investments than those in MD, are older, and have a lower share of national ownership.[1] Generally, share of local sales by firms in the MD economy tend to be higher compared to FZ firms, a result to be expected given the nature of DFZ firms which are export-oriented by nature.

On average, the 654 firms in the sample bought around 89.4 per cent of all intermediate inputs used in production from the Dubai local economy during 2009. The propensity of industry groups to purchase domestic intermediate

[1] Current rules and regulations restrict the foreign ownership in MD to 49 per cent as opposed to a 100 per cent ownership in DFZ.

Table 6.3. Average characteristics of sample firms by industry group and economic zone

	Investment (AED 000s)		Capital intensity (AED 000s/ worker)		Age (years)		National ownership (%)		Local sales (%)	
Industries	MD	DFZ	MD	DFZ	MD	DFZ	MD	DFZ	MD	DFZ
Light manufacturing	934	1,674	19	12	16	12	62	13	96	54
Heavy manufacturing	2,964	7,407	137	131	15	11	50	19	96	68
Construction	3,158	na	45	na	13	na	57	na	99	na
Trading	389	4,883	19	54	14	10	49	20	85	57
Services	2,122	4,961	73	73	14	8	50	19	98	94
Financial services	na	2,446	na	31	na	18	na	59	na	97
All industries	2,157	5,222	57	72	14	13.2	54	37	96	85

Source: First ELS, Dubai Economic Council, 2010

inputs and raw materials varied from less than 58 per cent in JAFZA to a full procurement from the local economy by firms in DIFC (Figure 6.1). Firms in Al Sofouh FZ area (i.e. Media City, Internet City, and Knowledge Village) had the second highest procurement of domestic intermediate inputs which constituted almost 96 per cent of their total inputs purchases. While with 92.4 per cent of local intermediate inputs, firms located in the local economy were the third highest procurers from that economy. Other DFZs and the airport free zone were the least dependent on purchases of local intermediate inputs which accounted for nearly 83 per cent and 70 per cent of their total purchases in 2009, respectively.

6.3.1 The Use of Intermediate Inputs

At the industry level, financial services (namely DIFC) were the most dependent on local sources of intermediate inputs with an average percentage of local purchases accounting for about 99.5 per cent of total purchases. Services had the second highest percentage of procurement from local sources (97.3 per cent) followed by light manufacturing (92.4 per cent) and construction (89.8 per cent), while the trading sector and heavy manufacturing had the lowest proportions of local intermediate inputs (75.8 per cent and 70.9 per cent, respectively) (see Figure 6.2). In terms of firm size, small firms (5–19 workers) had the highest share of local intermediate inputs (92.26 per cent), followed by medium-sized firms (87.99 per cent), while large firms were the least dependent on local sources for procuring intermediate inputs (77.7 per cent) (see Figure 6.3).

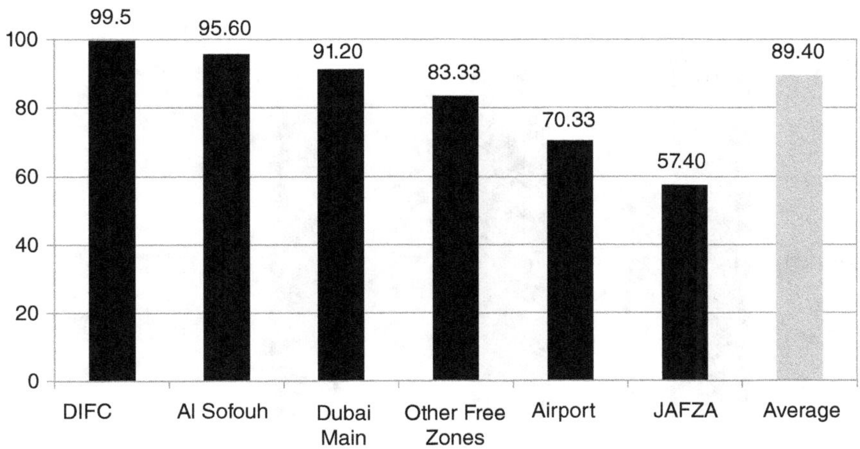

Figure 6.1. Average purchases of local intermediate inputs by location (% of total purchases)

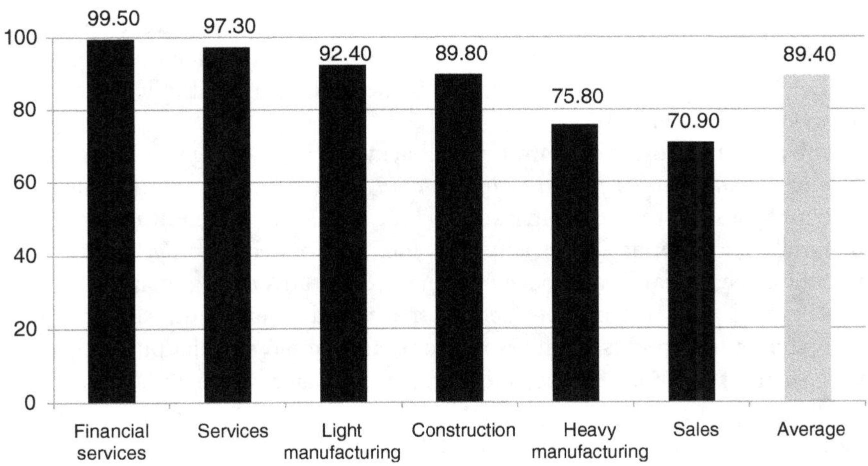

Figure 6.2. Average purchases of local intermediate inputs by industry (% of total purchases)

6.4 ESTIMATING DUBAI FZ BACKWARD LINKAGES

To assess the extent to which DFZ contribute to the local economy of Dubai, we use the ELS data to analyse the determinants of three channels of backward linkages created by firms in different industries, and operating in different economic zones. We consider five industries (heavy manufacturing, light manufacturing, construction, trading, and financial and non-financial

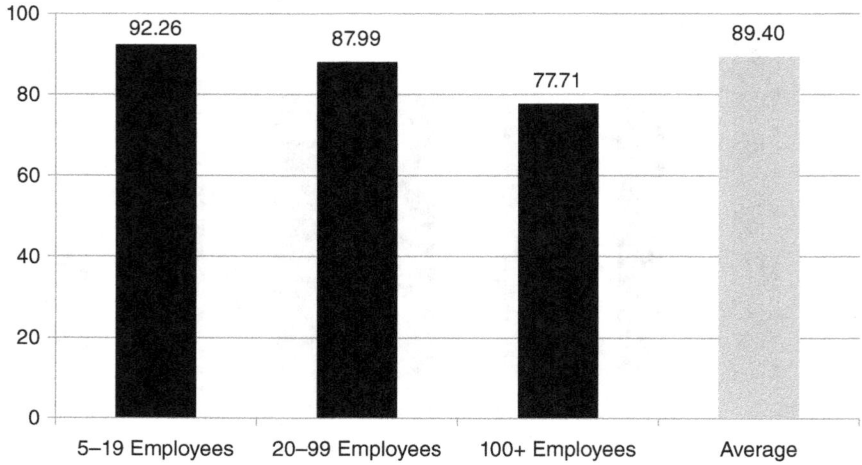

Figure 6.3. Average purchases of local intermediate inputs by firm size (% of total purchases)

services) and seven economic zones comprising Main Dubai and six free zones (Jebel Ali Free Zone Authority, Dubai Airport, Dubai International Financial Center,[2] free-zone businesses in the Al Soufouh area, and all other free zones lumped into one group).

The first and most important type of backward linkage is given by the *share of intermediate inputs procured by firms in the local economy*. Purchases of intermediates in the local market include domestic expenditures on raw materials and supplies, electricity and fuel, personnel training, repairs and maintenance, research and development (R&D), advertising, consulting and professional fees, leasing of factory space and equipment, subscriptions and payments to professional associations, and employee relations and activities (Jenkins, 2005).[3] The second backward linkage is the *total number of workers employed by firms*. Ideally we should assess the backward linkages in terms of the share of national to total labour but we do not have such a breakdown of labour force data at the firm level. Finally, the third backward linkage refers to *the extent of involvement of firms in the domestic banking sector* as users of loan finance from banks located in Dubai/UAE.

[2] Note that since the sample does not include financial firms in MD the DIFC Free Zone represents both an FZ location as well as the financial services sector.

[3] These items are included in the calculation of intermediate consumption following the recommendations of the United Nations System of National Accounts (1993). Also following those recommendations, local intermediate consumption does not include expenditure on wages and fringe benefits, relocation of employees, interest and depreciation, indirect taxes, donations and contributions, discounts on sales, amortization of pre-operating expenses, and expenses originated from sales of assets, inventory obsolescence, uncollected receivables, and exchange rate differentials.

6.4.1 The Econometric Model

First, we collect the core set of the explanatory variables in the following vector:

$$\begin{aligned} X_{ijl} = \{ & DumFZjafza,\ DumFZdifc,\ DumFZairport,\ DumFZsoufouh, \\ & DumFZothers,\ DumHM,\ DumLM,\ DumConst,\ DumTrade, \\ & CapInt_{ijl},\ NatInv_{ijl},\ Age_{ijl},\ Tinv_{ijl},\ LocSales_{ijl}\} \end{aligned} \quad (6.1)$$

Where *DumFZjafza, DumFZdifc, DumFZairport, DumFZsoufouh, DumFZothers* are dummy variables for free zones at JAFZA, DIFC, Airport, Soufouh, and other Dubai free zones, respectively. In addition, *DumHM, DumLM, DumConst, DumTrade,* are sectoral dummies for heavy manufacturing, light manufacturing, construction, and the trading sector, respectively. *CapInt* is capital intensity, *NatInv* is investment in the firm by nationals, *Age* is firm age, *Tinv* is total investment, and *LocSales* is sales in the local market.

Note that the MD dummy is excluded because it acts as a reference for the location effect, while the financial and non-financial services sector dummy is also excluded because it is used as a reference for sectors. Therefore, the marginal impact of any given DFZ location is estimated relative to that of MD and any given marginal sector effect is also estimated relative to that of the financial and non-financial services sector.

Second, we posit the following three regressions for each of three channels of linkages:

Intermediate input channel:

$$IntShare_{ijl} = A'X_{ijl} + \epsilon_{ijl} \text{ (OLS)} \quad (6.2)$$

Labour market channel:

$$Laborijl = B'X_{ijl} + \epsilon_{ijl} \text{ (OLS)} \quad (6.3)$$

Business finance channel:

$$\begin{aligned} DumLoan_{ijl} = & F(C1'X_{ijl} + C2\,Cost_{ijl} + C3\,IntFin_{ijl} \\ & + C4\,BankFin_{ijl}) + \epsilon_{ijl} \text{ (probit)} \end{aligned} \quad (6.4)$$

where *IntShare* is the share of intermediate inputs purchased from the local market, *Labour* is the total number of workers employed by the firm as in 2010, and *Dumloan* is a dummy variable that takes the value 1 if the firm applied for a bank loan or a line of credit from a local bank in 2010, 0 otherwise. Note that for the probit model (6.4) we also account for three more variables of high relevance to the analysis of the demand for bank finance. These are the cost of production at the firm level (*Cost*), given by the total firm's expenditure on machinery, vehicles, equipment, land and building; the proportion of a firm's working capital financed from returned profits and other internal funds (*IntFin*); and the share of a firm's working capital borrowed from banks (*BankFin*), which indicates the extent of a firm's exposure. While the first factor is expected to be positively associated with a firms' demand for bank loans, the latter two are likely to have negative effects (Trabelsi and Fadhel, 2011). In addition, X_{ijl} in the probit model includes other explanatory variables like a firm's profit (*Profit*) and a dummy for small and medium enterprises (DumSME) that take the value of 1 if the labour in the firm is between 5 and 100, and 0 otherwise.

The dependent variable (Y) in the probit model is binary (i.e. can only take two values, 0 or 1). The model is assumed to take the form:

$$\Pr(Y = 1|X) = \Phi(X'\beta) \tag{6.5}$$

where X is a vector of regressors, which are assumed to influence the outcome Y, Pr denotes probability, and Φ is the Cumulative Distribution Function (CDF) of the standard normal distribution. The parameters β are typically estimated by maximum likelihood.

6.4.1.1 Explanatory Variables

Zone-specific effects: As the analysis of sections 6.2 and 6.3 suggests, the creation of economic linkages at the firm level are likely to be influenced by the type of free zone in which it is located. For example, linkages with the domestic economy may depend on whether the DFZ firm is located inside industrial estates, such as JAFZA or in what is called an 'open' free zone, such Al Soufouh FZ. The latter resembles the model adopted by Mauritius, for example; while the former is prevalent in the FZ models of the Republic of Korea, Taiwan, and India. Given the wide diversity across free zones in Dubai, the zone-specific location is likely to be an important determinant. We account for this effect using zone-specific dummies taking value 1 if the firm is located in a particular free zone and 0 otherwise.

Sector-specific effects: Since industries differ with respect to their usage of intermediates in production, the extent of labour intensity of their operations, or their need for external finance, it is expected that backward linkages will vary across different industries. We account for this effect using sector-specific dummy variables taking value 1 if the firm is in a particular sector and 0 otherwise.

Firm-specific factors: Naturally there are many firm-specific factors at work affecting its capacity to generate backward economic linkages with the non-free-zone domestic economy.

The first firm-level explanatory variable we consider is its *capital intensity*, measured as the total investment of a firm divided by the total number of managerial and production workers actually employed. In particular, it can be argued that relatively capital-intensive operations demand more supplies and intermediates such as electricity and water, as well as specialized professional and maintenance in services, all of which are likely to be supplied by enterprises located in the domestic economy. In fact, whether these intermediates are available at a particular location may influence the multinational firm's decision to locate an affiliate there in the first place. Regarding demand for labour, more capital-intensive firms are likely to demand less labour; hence we expect a significant and negative effect for this factor on the use of labour. Finally, the impact of capital intensity on the demand for loans is likely to be positive because firms with high capital intensity are likely to be large and have high collateral and hence have better access to bank finance.

The second firm-specific explanatory variable considered is *the share of national ownership of the firm*. The received evidence from earlier experiences with free zones suggests that companies with higher foreign ownership are inclined to purchase a smaller proportion of their inputs in the host nation. For example, foreign firms in Ireland tended to buy less locally than domestically owned firms after controlling for age and other factors (McAleese and McDonald, 1978). It was also found that locally owned, export-oriented firms in the Republic of Korea tended to purchase more inputs locally than foreign firms producing the same commodity (Cohen, 1973). However, it is not clear if the type of ownership should affect labour use or demand for loans; hence we do not expect a statistically significant effect for national ownership on the latter two variables. We proxy national ownership by the share of local investors in the firm.

The third firm-level explanatory variable is *the age of the firm*, simply defined as the number of years that the firm has been operating. Several earlier studies (summarized in Jenkins, 2005) find this variable to be positively and robustly associated with a firm's demand for intermediate inputs. This result is supported, for example, by Halbach (1989) who argues that autonomous market forces lead to growing inter-firm linkages over time, and Ge (1993) who claims that the longer the free zone exists, the tighter the linkages become. Also, though we do not have received evidence from earlier studies on the impact of this variable on the linkages through the labour market, we expect older firms to be more labour-intensive, hence the age effect should have a positive and significant marginal effect on labour use. Finally, it is not clear a priori whether older firms are more or less likely to rely on bank finance. On one hand, other things being equal, they should have name recognition, track record, and, hence, better access to finance. However, because they might have higher retained savings, they are likely to be less inclined to demand bank finance.

The *overall size of the firm*—measured by total investment—is the fourth firm-specific characteristic that should influence a firm's capacity to generate linkages through labour and finance. While we conjecture the effect of firm size to be positive with regard to the latter two channels, the effect for intermediate inputs was found to be negative by earlier studies. In explaining this finding it was argued that 'larger enterprises may have more access to, knowledge of, or leverage with overseas suppliers of intermediates than small ones' (Smith and Barkley, 1991).

Finally, the fifth firm-specific factor considered is *the share of local sales*, which is expected to have a positive impact on the use of local intermediate inputs, as a firm's market orientation towards the domestic economy is likely to increase its propensity to source local inputs domestically. Also, it was found that import-substitution investments require less time to develop a network of inter-firm linkages than export-oriented ones (Halbach, 1989). There is ample evidence in support of this view, as documented by various studies (e.g. Smith and Barkley, 1991; Blomström and Kokko, 1997). However, it is not ex-ante clear what effect, if any, local sales might have on the other two channels of linkages, namely, labour and bank finance.

6.4.2 Empirical Results

We are now ready to discuss the main empirical results of the statistical analysis on backward linkage formation through different channels.

6.4.2.1 The Local Intermediate Inputs Channel

We start with backward linkages as measured by the propensity of these firms to purchase intermediate inputs in the local market. The results in Table 6.4 suggest that the only free-zone authority with a significant effect is JAFZA, with an estimated negative coefficient of around 0.18. Therefore, firms in JAFZA of identical characteristics to those in MD or other DFZ authorities have less use for local intermediate inputs, while firms with identical characteristics located in other DFZ or in MD have the same use of local intermediate inputs. As the estimates of regressions 1–3 suggest, the share of local intermediate input used by a JAFZA firm will be equal to 0.82 of the share of an identical firm located in MD or other DFZ outside JAFZA. This finding could be explained by the fact that the cost for firms located in JAFZA of sourcing local inputs might be higher due to its being located in a fenced and geographically distant economic zone from the core zones of economic activities in MD. Instead, the port and other logistic facilities available to JAFZA firms might promote the option of sourcing foreign inputs. Another plausible factor could be the limited range of locally produced intermediate inputs suitable for JAFZA firms.

The second set of determinants pertains to the industry effect. We find that relative to the (excluded) financial and non-financial services sector, firms in all other sectors tend to use less local input content. For example, the shares of local intermediate input sourced by firms specialized in light manufacturing, heavy manufacturing, construction, and the trading sector will, respectively,

Table 6.4. The demand for local intermediate inputs

	Pooled regressions [1]		Pooled regressions [2]		Pooled regressions [3]	
Variable	Coefficient	t-stat	Coefficient	t-stat	Coefficient	t-stat
DumFZjafza	−0.176	**−4.66**	−0.179	**−4.82**	−0.178	**−4.95**
DumFZairport	−0.068	−0.98	−0.075	−1.10	—	—
DumFZsoufouh	0.019	0.36	—	—	—	—
DumFZdifc	0.015	0.53	—	—	—	—
DumFZothers	−0.002	−0.03	—	—	—	—
DumLM	−0.074	**−2.71**	−0.077	**−3.02**	−0.075	**−2.94**
DumHM	−0.165	**−5.88**	−0.170	**−6.38**	−0.170	**−6.41**
DumConst	−0.085	**−3.33**	−0.092	**−3.88**	−0.090	**−3.83**
DumTrade	−0.168	**−5.46**	−0.171	**−5.73**	−0.179	**−6.13**
CapInt	−7.7e-08	**−2.84**	−7.8e-08	**−2.90**	−7.6e-08	**−2.82**
NatInv	0.022	0.95	0.024	1.06	—	—
Age	0.008	0.63	—	—	—	—
Log(Tinv)	−0.017	**−3.99**	−0.017	**−3.92**	−0.017	**−3.95**
LocSale	0.129	**3.15**	0.130	**3.23**	0.143	**3.63**
Constant	1.045	**14.10**	1.063	**15.47**	1.064	**15.69**
Observations	594		594		594	
R-Squared	0.3095		0.3085		0.3058	
Adj R-Squared	0.2928		0.2967		0.2963	
F	18.54		26.02		32.22	

be equal to about 0.93, 0.83, 0.91, and 0.82 of the share due to a financial or non-financial services firm with similar characteristics (regression 3). In general the received literature suggests that manufacturing firms tend to generate fewer backward linkages in the host economy due to the nature of the products they produced (e.g. Jenkins, 2005). For example, for the case of textile and electronics the separation of the assembly-type operations from the rest of the manufacturing process in these two sectors tends to be relatively less costly. Hence, in relatively low-wage economies assembly-type operations tend to dominate, while raw materials and other intermediates are manufactured or procured more frequently from overseas locations. Moreover, for the case of Dubai/UAE, most inputs for the construction sector, food processing, and pharmaceutical industries are not produced locally and have to be imported. Finally, firms operating in the trading sector are not likely to forge backward linkages because these firms are mainly engaged in the distribution of goods and therefore consume only a very small amount of local intermediates (mostly packing materials) from domestic suppliers.

Conditional on location and industry, we finally analyse the results for firm-specific characteristics. We find that age and national ownership do not have any significant impact on local input use, as detected by their statistically insignificant coefficients. In addition, large firms (as measured by total investment) were found to use less local input as a share of total, while capital-intensive production technology is found not to have a significant impact on local input use, as reflected by the very small coefficient. The finding on large firms is consistent with the international evidence from the received literature, in that larger firms tend to purchase a smaller proportion of their intermediates domestically. This finding corroborates the view that larger firms have 'better access and perhaps more leverage with overseas suppliers, or are part of a multinational system and therefore import more of their intermediates than a stand-alone entity' (Jenkins, 2005). Our results also suggest that export orientation matters and is statistically significant and negatively associated with the use of local inputs. For example, an increase of 10 per cent in the share of a firm's exports would reduce the share of the local intermediate inputs used in its production processes by 1.4 per cent. Naturally, this finding is expected, as firms selling a high share of their products to the local markets are likely to find it in their best interest to develop links with domestic suppliers.

6.4.3 The Labour Market Channel

Results for backward linkages through the labour market are presented in Table 6.5. As the results indicate, the DIFC and JAFZA location effects were found to have positive and significant labour effects. That is, compared to MD

Table 6.5. The demand for labour

	Pooled regressions [1]		Pooled regressions [2]		Pooled regressions [3]	
Variable	Coefficient	t-stat	Coefficient	t-stat	Coefficient	t-stat
DumFZjafz	0.283	**1.60**	0.299	**1.78**	0.254	**1.61**
DumFZairport	−0.167	−0.52	—	—	—	—
DumFZsoufouh	0.001	0.01	—	—	—	—
DumFZdifc	0.263	**1.97**	0.252	**1.99**	0.253	**2.00**
DumFZothers	−0.052	−0.12	—	—	—	—
DumLM	0.184	1.44	0.172	1.43	0.172	1.43
DumHM	0.063	0.48	—	—	—	—
DumConst	0.789	**6.60**	0.777	**6.97**	0.784	**7.07**
DumTrade	−0.129	−0.89	−0.167	-1.25	−0.120	-1.57
CapInt	-7.8e-07	**-6.12**	-7.7e-07	**-6.12**	-7.7e-07	**-6.09**
NatInv	0.052	0.48	—	—	—	—
Age	0.197	**3.12**	0.206	**3.34**	0.208	**3.39**
Log(Tinv)	0.384	**18.88**	0.384	**19.02**	0.383	**19.02**
LocSale	0.118	0.62	0.144	0.78	—	—
Constant	-2.472	**-7.11**	-2.477	**-7.32**	-2.332	**-8.23**
Observations	594		594		594	
R-Squared	0.477		0.477		0.476	
Adj R-Squared	0.465		0.469		0.469	
F	37.74		59.05		66.40	

Note: The distribution of labour demand was normalized using the logarithm of data.

and other FZ authorities, firm located in these two FZ authorities tend to be more labour-intensive than other firms with similar characteristics. Given the almost identical estimated coefficients it can be stated that, other things being equal, the size of labour employed by a firm located in DIFC or JAFZA will equal 1.29 times the size of a similar firm located in MD or any other DFZ location. The finding that the FZ location effect on labour use was overall similar to that of MD and was better for the cases of DIFC and JAFZA is an important finding. It would suggest that the DFZ, especially the two premier FZ authorities, could provide job opportunities for Emirati nationals, provided that their reservation wages and professional qualifications are competitive from the perspective of the FZ firms.

The evidence on the marginal effect due to industry is dominated by the construction sector, which as expected has a highly significant and positive effect on labour use, with an estimated coefficient of 0.79. This suggests that the size of labour employed by a construction firm will be equal to 2.18 times the size of labour force for a firm with identical characteristics producing in any other sector. The construction sector, however, mainly retains unskilled labour and operates like an enclave within MD. As expected, light manufacturing has a positive marginal impact on labour use but the estimated effect is not highly significant. On the other, also as expected, the trading sector marginal effect is negative but not significant as well.

Finally, controlling for location and industry, the results for firm characteristics are consistent with prior expectations. We find that age is positively associated with higher labour use. This finding might be explained by the fact that older firms are likely to use less sophisticated technology and to rely less on highly skilled workers. On the other hand, results indicate that use of labour is likely to increase with the firm size (with higher total investment). In addition, the coefficient that represents the effect of capital intensity is very small despite being statistically significant. The remaining two firm's characteristics (local sales and local ownership) were found to be insignificant.

6.4.4 The Business Finance Channel

The demand for business finance by firms located in the FZ and sourced from the Dubai-based banking sector is another form of backward linkage. We estimated a probit model for analysing the determinants of the probability that a Dubai firm had applied for a bank loan during 2010.[4] As stated in the

[4] A probit model is a type of regression where the dependent variable (Y) is binary (i.e. can only take two values, such as if a bank applied to a bank loan: Y=1; 0 otherwise), where the model is assumed to take the form: Pr $(Y = 1|X) = \Phi(X'\beta)$, where X is a vector of regressors, which are assumed to influence the outcome *Y*, Pr denotes probability, and Φ is the Cumulative

Table 6.6. The demand for bank loans

	Probit [1]		Probit [2]		Probit [3]	
Variable	Coefficient	z-stat	Coefficient	z-stat	Coefficient	z-stat
Cost	0.142	**1.60**	0.184	**3.10**	0.175	**3.01**
IntFin	-0.024	-3.80	-0.024	**-4.54**	-0.021	**-5.41**
BankFin	-0.004	-0.45	-0.007	-1.11	-	—
DumSme	0.297	0.31	—	—	—	—
DumFZjafz	0.971	1.91	0.862	**2.04**	0.856	**2.10**
DumFZdifc	-0.488	-1.25	-0.251	-0.81	—	—
DumLM	-1.045	**-2.02**	-0.561	-1.34	—	—
DumHM	-0.580	-1.40	-0.341	-0.96	—	—
DumConst	-1.105	**-2.79**	-0.844	**-2.62**	-0.641	**-2.16**
DumTrade	-0.135	-0.32	—	—	—	—
CapInt	-0.000	-1.46	—	—	—	—
NatInv	1.448	**3.48**	1.177	**3.40**	1.153	**3.40**
Age	-0.094	-0.48	—	—	—	—
Log(Tinv)	0.102	1.01	—	—	—	—
Log (profit)	0.040	0.57	—	—	—	—
Constant	-2.619	-1.55	-1.081	-1.28	-1.483	-1.89
Observations	168		188		188	
LR statistic	58.16		54.52		50.83	
Value	0.00		0.00		0.00	
Log Likelihood	-74.86		-90.47		−92.31	

specification of the model, in addition to the set of the location, industry, and firm-specific explanatory variables used for the estimation of the intermediate inputs and labour use channels, we also consider other variables of high relevance to the analysis of the demand for bank finance. The results of the analysis are presented in Table 6.6.

Controlling for all these factors in an encompassing probit model, only five factors were found to be significantly and robustly associated with demand for bank loans. First, other things being equal, the probability that a firm located in JAFZA had applied for a loan is 2.4 times the probability for any identical firms located in MD or any other FZ authority. Therefore, the marginal JAFZA linkage effect is quite positive and powerful for the banking sector in Dubai. Second, compared to all sectors, construction firms tend to create the least linkages with the banking sector, where the probability that a typical firm in this sector had applied for a bank loan is about 0.53 of any other identical firm from other industries. Third, as expected, firms with high costs of production are likely to apply for bank loans, while those with a high level of internal finance available relative to working capital are less likely to need bank loans. However, our results suggest that a firm's exposure to bank loans

Distribution Function (CDF) of the standard normal distribution. The parameters β are typically estimated by maximum likelihood.

does not seem to affect the likelihood of a demand for loans, as the share of working capital borrowed from banks was not found to be significant. Fourth, the positive and highly significant age coefficient is consistent with our expectations that the older age of a firm is associated with a higher probability of a demand for bank loans. This is because an older firm must have built a good reputation with the financial sector and is also likely to have adequate collateral.

6.5 CONCLUSIONS AND POLICY RECOMMENDATIONS

This chapter analyses the capacity of firms located in the Dubai free zones (DFZ) to create backward linkages with the rest of the economy of Dubai outside the free zone (MD). Using firm-level data based on a representative sample of more than 700 MD and DFZ firms generated by the Dubai Economic Council in 2010, we estimate the determinants of three indicators of backward linkages at the firm level. These include the linkages to the upstream production chain,[5] as measured by the share of local to total intermediate inputs; the labour market linkages, given by the size of the firm's labour force; and the linkage to the financial sector, accounted for by the incidence of a firm's holding a loan from Dubai/UAE banks. The regression models account for three types of determinants: the firm-specific characteristics; the marginal impact due to the sectorial specialization of the firm; and the marginal impact of the economic regions, including MD and the various free zones in Dubai.

A summary of the main findings are reported in Tables 6.7 to 6.9. In terms of the firm-specific determinants, we find that, controlling for other factors, older firms or those with large investments tend to have larger labour forces (Table 6.7). Moreover, large investment firms also tend to source smaller shares of local intermediate goods, while those with high shares of local sales tend to source larger shares of local inputs. Finally, the backward linkages to the financial sector were significantly impacted by only one of the above standard firm-specific characteristics, where we find that firms with high shares of national ownership are more likely to be holding loans provided by banks located in Dubai/UAE. Moreover, of the three additional firm characteristics that are specific to firms' demand for bank loans, two were found to be significant determinants. Firms facing high costs of production tend to have a high demand for bank loans, while those with high levels of

[5] Upstream production refers to those industries that provide intermediate products and services to producers in the (downstream) free zone.

Table 6.7. Summary of firm-specific backward linkages effects

Firm characteristics	Channels of linkages		
	Share of intermediate inputs	Size of labour inputs	Incidence of demand for bank loans
Capital intensity	NS	NS	NS
Share of national Ownership	NS	NS	+
Age (years in operation)	NS	+	NS
Firm size (total investment)	–	+	NS
Share of local sales	+	NS	NS
Cost of production	NA	NA	+
Share of internal finance	NA	NA	–
Share of bank finance	NA	NA	NS

Note: NS = not significant; NA = not applicable; + = positive and statistically significant effect; – = negative and significant effect.

Table 6.8. Backward linkages: marginal impact of sectors relative to financial and non-financial services

Free zone sectors	Channels of linkages (multiples of financial and non-financial sector's score)		
	Share of intermediate inputs	Size of labour inputs	Incidence of demand for bank loans
Light manufacturing	0.93	1	1
Heavy manufacturing	0.84	1	1
Construction	0.92	2.18	0.53
Trading	0.83	1	1

Note: 1 = the same marginal impact as that of the reference variable (financial and non-financial services sector).

retained internal savings are less likely to depend on bank finance. However, we do not find high debt exposure to be statistically significant as a determinant of backward financial linkages.

Conditional on firm characteristics and location effects, we assess the marginal impact of the sectorial specialization of firms relative to the reference sector of financial and non-financial services (Table 6.8). We find that all sectors have had lower marginal impact, especially trading and heavy manufacturing. As discussed in the main text, the mainstay of the trading sector is distribution and promotion activities, which are very low input-using activities; while heavy, and to a lesser extent light, manufacturing sectors are based

Table 6.9. Backward linkages: free zone marginal impact relative to Main Dubai

Free zone area	Channels of linkages (multiples of the MD's score)		
	Share of intermediate inputs	Size of labour inputs	Incidence of demand for bank loans
JAFZA	0.82	1.29	2.35
DIFC	1	1.29	1
Airport	1	1	1
Soufouh	1	1	1
All other free zones	1	1	1

Note: 1 = the same marginal impact as that of MD.

on assembly operations (e.g. textile, consumer electronics) that source parts from foreign markets, or use raw inputs that are not available in the local markets, e.g. agricultural inputs). Finally, except for construction, all sectors have similar marginal impacts on labour market and financial backward linkages as the reference sector. As expected, construction firms tend to have significantly higher backward linkages to the labour market. However, these firms tend to have much smaller linkages to the financial sector.

Finally, conditional on firm characteristics and sectorial specialization and relative to the reference location of MD, we find JAZFA, the premier DFZ authority, to have significant marginal impact on backward linkages (Table 6.9). JAFZA firms are more likely to create more backward linkages with the labour market as well as the financial sector. However, the marginal impact of JAFZA on sourcing local intermediate inputs was negative. In the main text we suggest that the latter finding might be linked to the higher transaction and logistic costs of sourcing local inputs due to JAFZA being a fenced DFZ. The other major free-zone authority found to have a significant marginal impact was the DIFC, where firms located in this DFZ are found to have generated larger linkages to the labour market at par with JAFZA firms. Also DIFC has had similar marginal backward linkages impact as MD for the case of local inputs and finance. Moreover, all other DFZ were found to have similar marginal impacts as MD on all three types of backward linkages.

Our results suggest that DFZ have done well in terms of linkages to the main economy of Dubai, in that, except for the case of JAFZA with regard to sourcing of local inputs, firms located in DFZ have similar or better linkages capabilities than their counterparts in MD. Moreover, the two positive JAFZA backward linkages effects are likely to be quite substantial, we would argue, especially the one associated with the labour market. The general equilibrium effects associated with the presence of a large labour force in the economy of Dubai is probably one of the key factors that the impact of JAFZA at the macroeconomic level of the economy was assessed to be quite substantial.

Admittedly, the above conclusions should be regarded as tentative, given the one-shot database underlying our findings; nevertheless, they are sufficiently robust to merit the following three policy implications.

First, the high positive externality of the JAFZA and DIFC effect on labour use suggests that the two premier FZ entities could be targeted for enhancing Emirati employment, as part of a public sector strategy, as has been recently hinted in the context of the ongoing Dubai 2015 Strategic Plan. Such a programme might consider two strategic initiatives:

- In the short-run the Dubai Government might consider providing an incentive package to firms willing to hire Emiratis in engineering, financial, and other relatively high paying non-managerial professions.
- As a medium- to longer-term strategy, a major realignment of the educational system toward professions that are in high demand by the private sector will be required to eventually create a critical mass of nationals with the required professional qualifications and skills.

Second, the tendency of manufacturing firms to source lower shares of local inputs might be related to the absence of upstream industries or to regulatory constraints. This would require a further and more specialized study but as a first approximation, public policy is likely to have a positive role by identifying potential upstream industries that could supply manufacturing firms and, subsequently, providing the appropriate incentives for the private sector to invest in these industries.

Third, similarly the findings on the relatively limited use of local inputs by JAFZA firms might merit public policy intervention to incentivize these firms to source a higher share of local inputs and hence further enhance their backward linkages capability to the upstream local industry in MD. For example, allowing local firms supplying intermediate inputs to firms located in JAFZA and other FZ to recover the customs fees on their imported primary inputs would generate an incentive for higher backward linkage capabilities of the free zones.

REFERENCES

Blomström, M. and Kokko, A., 1997. 'How Foreign Investment Affects Host Countries'. Policy Research Working Paper No. 1745, World Bank.

Cohen, B. I. 1973. 'Comparative Behavior of Foreign and Domestic Export Firms in a Developing Economy'. *Review of Economics and Statistics*, 55: 190–7.

Din, M.-U., 1994. 'Export Processing Zones and Backward Linkages'. *Journal of Development Economics*, 43: 369–85.

Dubai Economic Council 2010. *Enterprise Level Survey 2010*, Dubai: Dubai Economic Council.

Ge, W., 1993. 'Export-processing Zones, Multinational Firms, and Economic System Transformation'. Dissertation available from ProQuest. Paper AAI9413834.

Ge, W., 1999. 'The Dynamics of Export-processing Zones'. UNCTAD discussion paper No. OSG/DP/144.

Halbach, A., 1989. 'Multinational Enterprises and Subcontracting in the Third World: A Study of Inter-Industrial Linkages'. ILO Multinational Enterprises Program Working Paper No. 58, 1989.

Jenkins, M., 2005. 'Economic and Social Effects of Export Processing Zones in Costa Rica'. International Labour Office Working Paper No. 97.

McAleese, D. and McDonald, D., 1978. 'Employment Growth and the Development of Linkages in Foreign-owned and Domestic Manufacturing Enterprises'. *Oxford Bulletin of Economics and Statistics*, 40: 321–39.

Madani, D., 1999. 'A Review of the Role and Impact of Export Processing Zones'. World Bank Policy Research Working Paper, Issue WPS 2238.

Nowicki, L., 2007. 'Investment and Entrepreneurship in Arab and Muslim-Majority Countries: The Case of Free Zones'. International Trade and Finance Association Working Paper No. 5, 2007.

Tahir, J., 1998. 'An Assessment of the Free Economic Zones (FEZs) in Arab Countries: Performance and Main Features'. Presented at the 'Conference on Economic Developments and Their Impact on Arab Economies', Tunis, 3–5 June 1998.

Trabelsi, M. and Fadhel, D., 2011. 'The Demand for Bank Finance in Dubai'. Working Paper, Dubai Economic Council.

World Bank, 2008. 'Special Economic Zones: Performance, Lessons Learned, and Implications for Zone Development'. Advisory service of the World Bank.

7

Competitiveness and Sustainability of Tourism

Raimundo Soto

7.1 HISTORICAL BACKGROUND

In recent decades tourism has become a strategic sector with a significant impact on economic growth and welfare in both developed and developing economies. In 1990 the number of worldwide international tourist arrivals amounted to 420 million whereas in 2012 they surpassed one billion. Worldwide tourism has thus increased at a cumulative average rate of 4 per cent per year. In the same period, worldwide revenues from tourism increased from US $280 billion to US$1,300 billion at constant prices, that is, an average real increase of 6.2 per cent per year (UNWTO, 2013). This places tourism as one of the most dynamic industries in the world, surpassing manufacturing and services that grew at annual real rates of 2.7 per cent in the period 1990–2012 (World Bank, 2013).

Dubai is among those economies for which tourism has become a key economic sector and, alongside foreign trade, is expected to be a cornerstone for sustained development in the future. In a matter of two decades, Dubai has positioned itself as a worldwide destination for high-income travellers and businessmen, within and beyond the Arab Gulf. Although detailed tourism statistics are not available, it is estimated that the sub-sector of 'Hotels and Restaurants' alone generated around US$3 billion in value added in 2012 (Dubai Statistics Center, 2013). This figure would likely increase more than twofold if we could add the contribution of other tourism components, such as entertainment, transportation, complimentary services, and tourist shopping in the world famous malls of Dubai.

As a tourist destination Dubai is largely a man-made project. Worldwide, the demand for tourism depends mostly on three elements (Mak, 2004). First, the existence of attractions that justify visiting a particular place (e.g. the

Pyramids in Giza for Cairo). Second, the offering of an attractive ratio of price to quality for tourist accommodation (hotel, hotel-apartments, camping facilities, etc.). Third, the supply of physical infrastructure that determines the quality of life of tourists during the visit to a particular place. As discussed later in this chapter, the lack of historical, natural, or heritage attractions forced Dubai to base its tourism industry primarily on the development of the latter two elements, which have been supplemented by carefully selected events to lure the visitors (e.g. the World Horse Race Cup or Dubai's shopping festivals). Good infrastructure and an ample offer of high-quality hotels, restaurants, and shopping malls are the trademarks of Dubai.

This mix has been successful and, notwithstanding the global crisis of 2008–10, it makes tourism an engine for sustained growth in Dubai. At the regional level, the emirate has certainly become a hub for tourism and, particularly, for the international businessman operating between Asia and the Middle East. Despite its success, there are several elements that indicate the need to reappraise the evolution of the tourism industry in Dubai in particular vis-à-vis the future development of tourism worldwide and the emergence of regional contenders (e.g. Qatar). In addition, after two decades of sustained growth, the business strategy of the sector might have grown into maturity which suggests limited future expansion.

The global economic crisis put an abrupt halt to the growth of the tourism industry in Dubai and in 2008 hotel occupancy rates, room rates, and revenues all declined significantly. Although the recovery of the world economy was not vigorous, international tourism regained momentum quickly and the UNWTO estimated that by 2010 the worldwide number of tourist arrivals had surpassed the pre-crisis peak levels by 2.5 per cent (UNWTO, 2013). Inbound tourism in Dubai recovered by mid 2011 in the number of visitors but less so in terms of rates, revenues, and occupancy. The gap between improvements in tourist arrivals and in expenditures observed in Dubai is typical in periods of recovery when, following major shocks, volume (arrivals) tends to recover faster than income, as competition toughens and suppliers make serious efforts to contain prices, with tourists also tending to travel closer to home and for shorter periods of time (ESCAP, 2011).

Despite this setback, the authorities in Dubai have assigned tourism a major role as a strategic sector for the economic development of the emirate, as it has been explicitly recognized in the 2015 Dubai Strategic Plan. It is in such a context that the present chapter aims to evaluate the tourism industry in Dubai and identify the key issues that would need addressing by policymakers. Our aim is to understand better how demand, supply, and the institutional setting interact to determine the performance of tourism activities in Dubai, in particular vis-à-vis other competitors in the region (including competition within the UAE), and to identify possible development strategies that help Dubai to strengthen its tourism industry.

7.2 RECENT TRENDS IN TOURISM IN DUBAI

Tourism in Dubai has become a key sector making a significant contribution to economic growth and employment. Detailed statistics on the value added of tourism are not available, so we are forced to use the sub-sector 'Hotels and Restaurants' (hereafter H&R) of Dubai's national accounts as a measure of activity. According to the Dubai Statistics Center (2013) H&R generated around US$3.5 billion in value added in 2011, equivalent to around 4 per cent of the total GDP of Dubai (the contribution of H&R to GDP has been very stable in the range of 3 per cent to 4 per cent of GDP since 2006). This figure underestimates the true contribution of tourism as it excludes tourist shopping, entertainment, and transportation as well as the value added of travel agencies and other related services. As a point of reference, in the UK the H&R activities comprised around 35 per cent of total tourism expenditures in 2009, while in Singapore they reached 31 per cent in 2010.[1] If, as expected, economic activities in those economies are a good indication of the contribution of tourism in Dubai, one could conjecture that tourism activities in the emirate might have generated around US$9.5 billion in 2011.

Despite the limitations in measurement, the importance of tourism is significant not only for Dubai but also for the UAE. In fact, Dubai contributed one half of the total revenue of US$6.1 billion generated by H&R in the UAE in 2011. These estimates are biased downward as they follow a period of economic downturn resulting from the global financial crisis. Worldwide, tourism is highly pro-cyclical and quite sensitive to the international business cycle. The recent global crisis hit Dubai hard and tourism stagnated in 2008. After vigorous growth of around 4 per cent in value added in the pre-crisis years, in 2008 the H&R sector value added grew by a meagre 0.5 per cent. In 2009 it recovered by 4.5 per cent and it is estimated to have grown similarly in 2010. Figure 7.1, however, shows that in the aftermath of the crisis Dubai's tourism industry has recovered faster than other sectors in the economy.

Recovery in tourism in Dubai after the recent crisis is not only the result of the recovery of worldwide tourism: local operators and authorities also reacted in view of the magnitude of the cyclical downturn. In what follows we review the recent developments in the (inbound) demand for tourism services, the changes in the supply of hotels and other facilities, and the main institutional aspects that affect tourism.

[1] See Singapore Tourism Board (2010) and VisitBritain (2010).

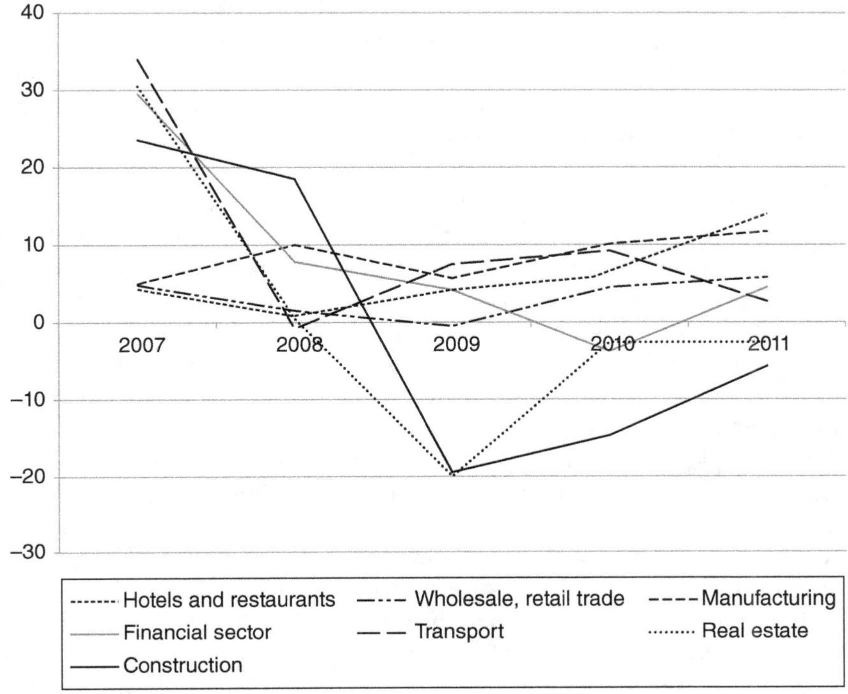

Figure 7.1. Rate of growth of value added in Dubai's tourism and other sectors

7.3 DEMAND FOR TOURISM IN DUBAI

Dubai has two key characteristics that define its comparative advantage as a potential tourism destination: location and climate. On one hand, proximity to Europe, Africa, and South and East Asia makes Dubai an attractive alternative for business travellers, an ideal place to develop transportation hubs, and a welcome stop-over for passengers on long-duration flights. On the other hand, the pleasant climate during the winter months of the northern hemisphere becomes a key advantage for Dubai as a getaway for tourists from Europe, East Asia, and North America.

However, and despite their importance, the development of the tourism industry cannot rest on climate and location alone. Clearly other emirates in the UAE and other economies in the Gulf of Arabia (e.g. Qatar, Bahrain, Oman, Saudi Arabia, or Kuwait) enjoy the same strategic location and an almost identical climate. Yet, their tourism sectors are not as developed as in Dubai. Indeed, the demand for tourism depends on more substantial issues such as the existence of attractions that justify visiting a particular place, the offer and quality of accommodation, and the supply of physical infrastructure that determines the quality of life of tourists during visits. In the past the private sector and the Emirati authorities have been able to provide high-quality infrastructure and an ample supply of hotels and shopping centres to meet the demands of tourists and, in view of the lack of natural attractions, they have created a number of high-visibility events to bolster the appeal of Dubai as a tourist destination.

As a result, Dubai has successfully developed a supply of services that can cater for a heterogeneous clientele throughout the year irrespective of the weather conditions. A number of outdoor activities are developed during the pleasant winter months for worldwide tourists, while large shopping malls attract GCC tourists during the hottest months of the Arabian summer (July and August). Tourism services also supply the resident expatriate population with entertainment similar to what could be found in their countries of origin, thus generating a local demand basis to justify investing in tourism infrastructure.

From a regional perspective, Dubai is undoubtedly the leading destination in the Arab Gulf. According to the World Tourism Organization (UNWTO, 2013), the UAE (and Dubai at the forefront) accounted for 22 per cent of international tourism receipts in the Middle East in 2012. These revenues were generated by 8.9 million international visitors to the country. In contrast, Saudi Arabia—which benefits from obvious historical, heritage, and religious attractions—generated about 15.8 per cent of all international tourism-based receipts in the Middle East from a total of 13.7 million visitors. Egypt, another leader in tourism among MENA countries is not very far from the UAE with 21 per cent of total revenues but an inflow of 11.1 million visitors (see detailed discussion in Section 7.5). Thus, although Dubai lacks specific attractions (e.g. Mecca in Saudi Arabia or Petra in Jordan), it has successfully marketed itself as an attractive tourism destination in the Middle East.

7.3.1 Evolution in Guests

According to the Department of Commerce, Tourism and Marketing (DTCM, 2013), in 2012 Dubai received 9.9 million visitors measured by passengers staying in hotels (7.8 million) or in hotel apartments (2.1 million). These figures have three limitations which render them not directly comparable to that of the WTO. First, since 87 per cent of the population are expatriates, possibly a significant number of visitors do not stay in hotels but with friends and relatives. Lack of adequate surveys (e.g. surveys at the point of arrival or departure) implies that non hotel-based tourism is not directly measured. Second, hotel passengers are registered according to nationality and not by place of residence. Consequently, passengers that are expatriates residing in the UAE or Dubai are treated as 'international visitors'. Arguably, this group could be of limited size. Third, official data in Dubai includes all passengers as

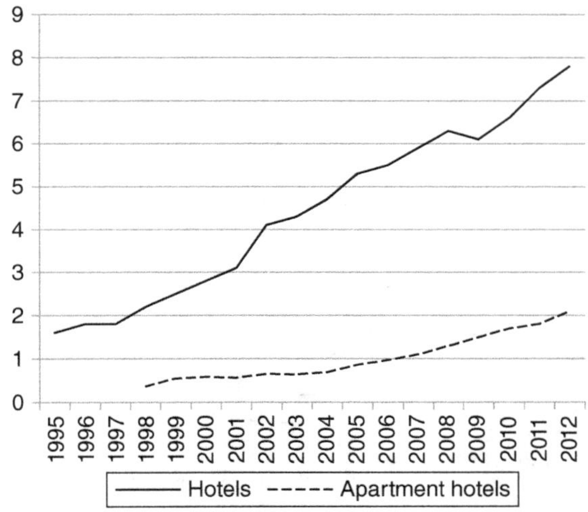

Figure 7.2. Guests in hotels and hotel apartments in Dubai (millions, per year)

visitors even if they are transit passengers and stay overnight as a result of flight connections; as Dubai is a travel hub the number of this type of passengers could be sizeable.[2]

Dubai has become a hub for international tourism and for visitors from other emirates in the UAE. Figure 7.2 shows the number of guests in the two types of accommodation. It can be seen that relative to 1995, the number of hotel guests has increased fourfold whereas relative to 1998 (first survey of hotel apartments) the number of guests staying in hotel apartments expanded by a factor of five. This is a very fast rate of growth and puts Dubai as one of the most dynamic tourism markets in the world. It is, nevertheless, important to mention that hotels are predominant: around 84 per cent of all visitors in Dubai demand hotel accommodation (6.1 million in 2010). Apartment hotel accommodation is a relatively new and still minor phenomenon: despite servicing only 16 per cent of the demand for accommodation in Dubai, apartment hotels have seen an explosive growth in the last decade. In 2001, around 0.5 million guests stayed in apartment hotels; by 2010, this figure had more than tripled to reach 1.7 million. These trends also show the transitory yet perceptible adverse effects of the 2008 global crisis, with the number of guests declining in hotels by around 5 per cent between 2008 and 2009. However, in 2010 visitors picked up again and returned to their historical trend suggesting that the reversal was transitory.

In terms of the nationalities of the guests, the demand (aggregating the two choices of hotel accommodation) has been dominated by two groups:

[2] For example, in Singapore—another world-class travel hub—around 22 per cent of visitors spent one day or less in the city (Singstat, 2011).

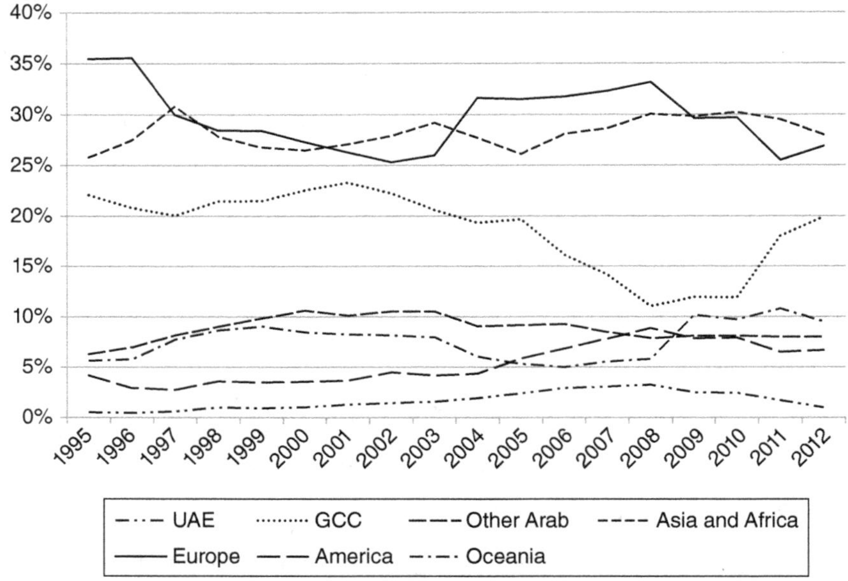

Figure 7.3. Passengers in Dubai hotels and hotel apartments (share by nationality)

European nationals from the eurozone and Asian visitors. Since 1995 Europeans have accounted for about 30 per cent of all incoming visitors, although the recession in the mid 1990s (due to spiking oil prices, the aftermath of the Gulf War, and the Asian financial crisis) had adverse effects on the number of visitors of European origin. This is an example of how sensitive the tourist industry is to geo-political and economic turns. On the other hand, the inflow of Asian visitors (mostly Iranians and Indians) has steadily grown to account for 30 per cent of all hotel-based tourism in 2012. Figure 7.3 also shows that, compared to other nationalities, the share of visitors from neighbouring GCC economies dropped considerably over time until the global crisis and then recovered abruptly in 2011/12. In 1995 they accounted for 22 per cent of all visitors whereas in 2010 they represented only 12 per cent. One reason for the progressive decline in GCC visitors is that these economies have mimicked Dubai and developed their own tourism facilities. As a result, nowadays other cities in the region (e.g. Doha, Kuwait City, or Muscat) are in a position to offer tourist attractions and entertainment events comparable to those offered in Dubai. Another reason is that during the boom of the early 2000s tourism became extremely expensive in Dubai thus inhibiting GCC travellers; the subsequent decline in hotel rates and travel tickets allowed for the return of Gulf-based tourists.

Figure 7.3 also shows that other groups of tourists (such as non-GCC Arabs, Americans, and guests from Oceania) have a much smaller share of the demand. Non-GCC Arab visitors come mostly from the less-developed MENA countries, whose citizens have limited disposable income and cannot afford the relatively high cost of tourism in Dubai. In contrast, tourists from America and Oceania have the spending capacity to afford Dubai prices but have to face the relatively high-cost of transportation over great distances to reach the emirate. Nationals from Oceania (mainly Australia and New Zealand) have represented a steady 2 per cent of Dubai's tourism throughout most of the 2000s. American visitors, on the other hand, have gradually increased relative to other nationalities to reach around 8 per cent of visitors in 2010.

Last but not least, the proportion of UAE guests—that is, Emirati nationals from the other emirates of the federation—remained fairly stable until 2008, representing on average 7 per cent of all guests in hotels or hotel apartments. The demand increased significantly after 2008, possibly as a consequence of the global crisis, by which the perception of loss in wealth of the Emirati population might have induced them to substitute international tourism for tourism in Dubai. The fact that Dubai has been able to become a substitute for international tourism for UAE residents from other emirates is an indication of the potential of Dubai as a strong competitor in the international market for tourism.

7.3.2 The Length of Stay

Tourism in Dubai is characterized by a relatively short stay by passengers. In 2012 the average number of days per visitor in hotels or hotel apartments was about 3.5 days; hotel visitors stayed on average 3.0 nights, whereas visitors in hotel apartments spent on average 5.0 nights. In the period 1995–2010, the average length of stay increased by less than 0.5 day in the case of hotels and slightly more in hotel apartments. As a point of reference, the average stay of visitors in UK hotels was 6.9 days in 2012 (VisitBritain, 2012) while in Singapore it was 5.1 days in 2010 (Singstat, 2011).

Because the large majority of visitors stay for less than around three nights in Dubai, one should conclude that a substantial fraction of tourism in Dubai corresponds to business trips, conference participation, and weekend getaways. However, the difference of two days between the two categories of accommodation is quite significant and suggests the existence of two different types of visitors: in addition to short-stay visitors as described above, there seems to be a type of passenger that stays longer—from one week to months—typically in establishments with fewer features but with a more convenient price/quality ratio, that is, furnished apartments that can accommodate families or provide for working accommodation in flats with more than one bedroom.

According to Figure 7.4, the length of stay in hotels by nationality is quite stable and has not varied over time in the last two decades: except for Europeans, all other foreigners stay between two and three days, including visitors

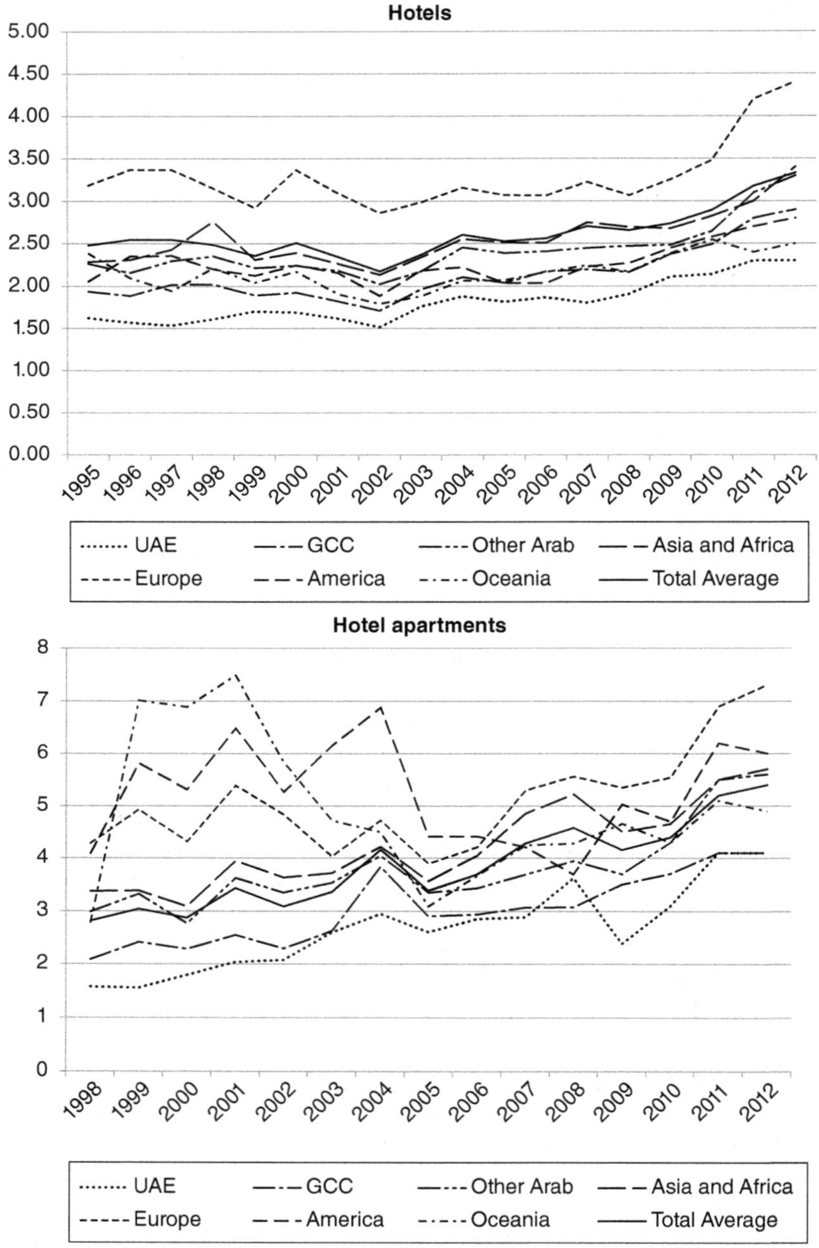

Figure 7.4. Guests by length of stay, nationality, and type of hotel

from faraway origins such as the Americas or Oceania. Europeans stay on average an extra night. The shortest stay corresponds to citizens of the UAE (between one and two nights). This pattern is to some extent puzzling as there is systematic evidence that the length of stay does vary and moreover it depends on variables such as nationality, education, and income (see Barros and Machado, 2010). The homogeneity observed in Dubai is not easy to explain.

On the other hand, visitors in hotel apartments tend to stay for much longer periods, although there have been significant variations over time, most likely associated with the emergence and subsequent consolidation of this segment of the market. Note that by 2012 the length of stay by nationality in apartment hotels resembles that in hotels in that visitors from regions further away (Europe, America, and Oceania) have longer stays than visitors from regions nearby (UAE, GCC, or other Arabs countries). European, American, and Oceania visitors staying in hotel apartments stayed an average of five nights in Dubai whereas UAE, GCC, and non-GCC MENA Arabs staying in the same type of accommodation stayed on average up to four nights.

7.3.3 The Seasonality of Demand

As mentioned, climate is an important factor determining the demand for tourism in Dubai. But climate varies significantly throughout the year giving rise to marked seasonal patterns. In the period 2005–10, the seasonality in demand is revealed in a systematic reduction in the number of hotel passengers in the months of May (–5 per cent on average), June (–12 per cent), and July (–2 per cent) vis-à-vis the average for the rest of the year. These estimates are a dampened measure of the true seasonal effects because, as mentioned, Dubai has implemented events and promotions designed to cope with the adverse effects of seasonality (e.g. Dubai Summer Surprises). This highlights the importance of persevering in marketing Dubai as a tourist destination and also calls for coordination among the different entities in the industry (private sector and authorities). A second significant seasonal pattern emerges as a result of Ramadan (the Muslim holy month) and its mandatory period of fasting. Data indicates that in 2010, Ramadan accounted for a decline of around 10 per cent in expenditures in H&R.

Not only do guest levels change markedly as a result of seasonal effects but also the composition of the visitors by country of origin is affected as shown in Figure 7.5. During the summer months, the share of Europeans in the market drops by around 10 per cent in both hotels and apartment hotels. On the contrary, the share of visitors from other GCC economies expands by 8 per cent in hotels—and a noteworthy 15 per cent in apartment hotels—most likely associated with school and work holidays. Finally, Figure 7.5 also suggests that seasonality is not important for other nationality groups.

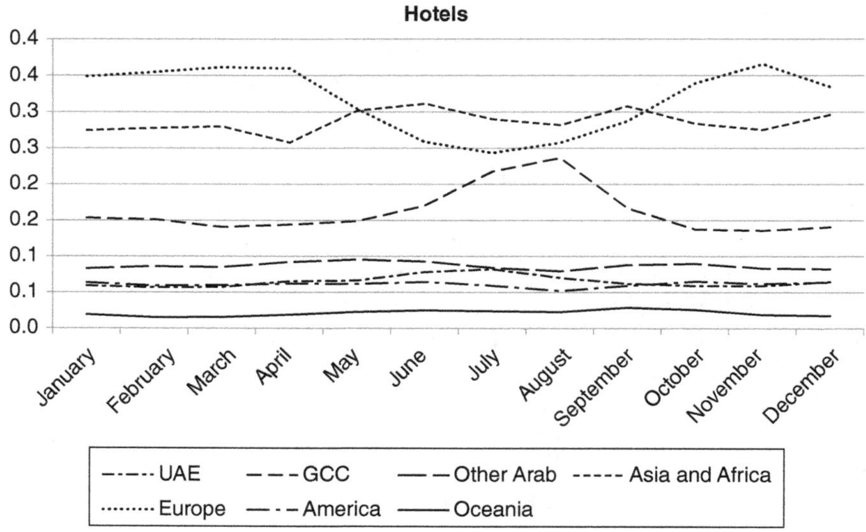

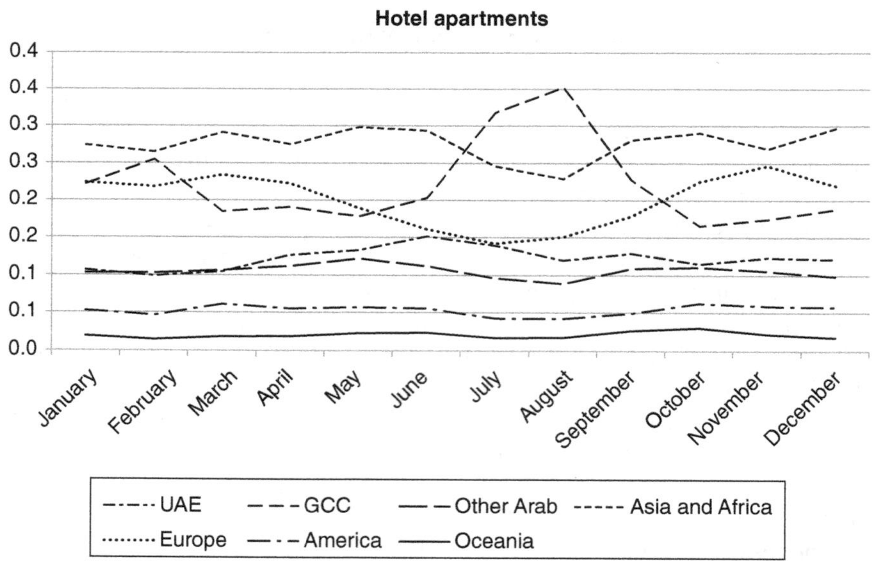

Figure 7.5. Guests by nationality and type of hotel (average 2005–12)

7.4 SUPPLY OF TOURISM IN DUBAI

As mentioned, tourism is typically affected by the supply of three elements (attractions, accommodation, and physical infrastructure) but it is also influenced by economic variables (such as room rates, the cost structure, and overall efficiency) that determine the profitability of the industry. In this section we provide an overview of the three types of 'supply' for Dubai and the role of economic variables.

7.4.1 Attractions Offer in Dubai

The lack of natural and historical attractions in Dubai has already been mentioned. The response of the authorities has been to cleverly articulate a sequence of international events such as conferences, festivals, culture gatherings, and sports competitions to attract tourists. Saidi, Scacciavillani, and Ali (2008) identify this as a main comparative advantage of Dubai in this industry. In 2011, Dubai hosted eighty-nine major international events of which fifty-three were conferences and exhibitions, eleven were cultural festivals and nineteen were international sports events. The relative importance of sports is staggering: the United Kingdom hosted only twenty-seven international sport events in the same year, that is, only eight more than Dubai (VisitBritain, 2012).

7.4.2 Public Infrastructure Offer

Dubai has made the provision of world-class infrastructure a policy priority and a trademark of its development. Physical infrastructure significantly affects the quality of a visit and, therefore, is a key determinant in attracting tourism. Infrastructure for tourism relates mainly to transportation (including roads, ports, and airports), utilities and telecommunications, and physical and real estate development.

The physical development of Dubai is, as opposed to most cities in the world, mainly the result of planning by the government. An urban planning committee (including the Municipality, Road and Transport Authority, the Electricity and Water department and public holdings) approves projects that often includes major attractions to make up for the lack of historical heritage. Among the latter, the artificial islands of Palm Jumeirah and Palm Jebel Ali, Burj Al Arab (the only officially rated 7-star hotel in the world), and Burj Khalifa (the tallest building in the world) have become city landmarks. Other developments that have been marketed as landmarks defining the identity of Dubai are the shopping malls, in particular the Dubai Mall (the fifth biggest shopping mall in the world).

Communications and transportation infrastructure in Dubai are among the best in the world, although road construction seems to be in a permanent state of flux, as a tour throughout the major landmarks of Dubai amply demonstrates. Among the key successes is Dubai's International Airport. In less than fifteen years it transformed from a regional airport serving the Arab Gulf to an international airport linking the East and the West of the world, catering for 57.6 million passengers in 2012 (ranked second worldwide) and harbouring the biggest travel retailer of the world, the Dubai Duty Free with sales above US$1.6 billion in 2012. Significant investment on roads and the construction of the Metro provide easy and expedite access to around 95 per cent of the metropolitan area.

7.4.3 Accommodation Offer

The accommodation on offer in Dubai is substantial and has grown significantly over the past fifteen years. As shown in Table 7.1, the number of hotels grew from 262 in 2001 to 399 in 2012. The global crisis did not have any significant impact on the opening of new hotels and hotel apartments in recent years, most likely because gestation lags in construction are significant. The most noteworthy expansion was in four- and five-star hotels, revealing a deliberate strategy on the part of the authorities to position Dubai as a destination for luxury tourism. While in 2001 Dubai had fifty-three four- and five-star hotels, by 2012 they had increased to 152, equivalent to 38 per cent of the total. Low-quality hotels (1-star and listed) remained virtually stagnant. Not only has the number of hotels increased markedly, but new hotels are also of bigger size. For example, four-star hotels built before 2001 had 136 rooms on average, while those built in the last decade averaged 215 rooms. The number of total rooms in hotels more than doubled in the decade, growing from 21,428 in 2001 to 57,345 in 2012. Again, the lion share of the expansion was in four- and five-star hotels which increased their share to 68 per cent of all rooms.

Table 7.1. Hotel accommodation and rooms in Dubai by type of hotel

	Number of establishments		Number of room/flats	
	2001	2012	2001	2012
Total hotels	262	399	22,203	57,345
5 stars	27	71	8,286	23,706
4 stars	26	81	3,523	15,319
3 stars	32	64	3,656	8,714
2 stars	43	46	2,573	4,690
1 star and listed	136	137	4,165	4,916
Total apartment hotels	68	200	7,418	23,069
Deluxe	16	58	2,445	8,896
Standard and listed	52	142	4,973	14,173

Source: Dubai Statistics Center

Apartment hotels have not followed these trends. Although the number of apartment hotels has increased much faster than that of hotels, there has been no tendency towards concentration in the upper-end of the market: the share of rooms in deluxe apartment hotels had remained constant at around 30 per cent of the total. Nor has there been an increase in the size of establishments: in fact, new apartment hotels in the luxury segment are of similar size to those built before 2001.

As a reference for the degree of concentration of Dubai into the luxury market, it is useful to look at the case of London, which we use as an example of a mature hostelling market (Milburn, 2011). According to the English Tourist Board, London had 580 hotels operating in 2011 of which 70 were classified as five-star and offered 12,934 rooms. The number of visitors to London in 2010 was around 30 million (Eurostat, 2011). It can be concluded that there are many fewer luxury hotels as a proportion of visitors in London (one every half-million visitors) than in Dubai (one every 150,000) and relative to all hotels (12 per cent in London vs. 39 per cent in Dubai), and that hotels are of much smaller size (185 rooms on average in London vis-à-vis 350 in Dubai). On the other hand, 41 per cent of all hotels in London were two-star or below while in Dubai the same segment represented 68 per cent of all hotels.

This indicates that the segment of middle-income hotels is far less developed in Dubai than in London. This is, most likely, the result of the deliberate policy of targeting the luxury segment of the market. However, the lack of middle-income hotels could be a weakness of the industry as this market segment tends to be less sensitive to business fluctuations and, consequently, allows for better hedging of occupancy risks. The hotel industry is considered a high-risk business by lenders and mortgage investors (Elgonemy, 2002). Hotels typically have high operating expenses in comparison to other types of property and fixed costs are significant: revenue lost when demand weakens only trims a fraction of expenses (Mammoser, 2009). As such, during a recession, a decline in revenues could seriously impact the solvency of hotel properties that incurred large amount of debt.

7.4.4 Hostelling Performance

The best measure of performance is the profitability of tourism investments (e.g. return on investment). In Dubai, cost estimates are unfortunately not available forcing us to concentrate on revenues, which come from three sources: revenue associated with lodging, other revenues collected within lodging premises (restaurants, bars, and other in-house services), and revenues from activities outside the lodging premises (e.g. shopping, events, intra-city transportation, and other services mostly associated with retail

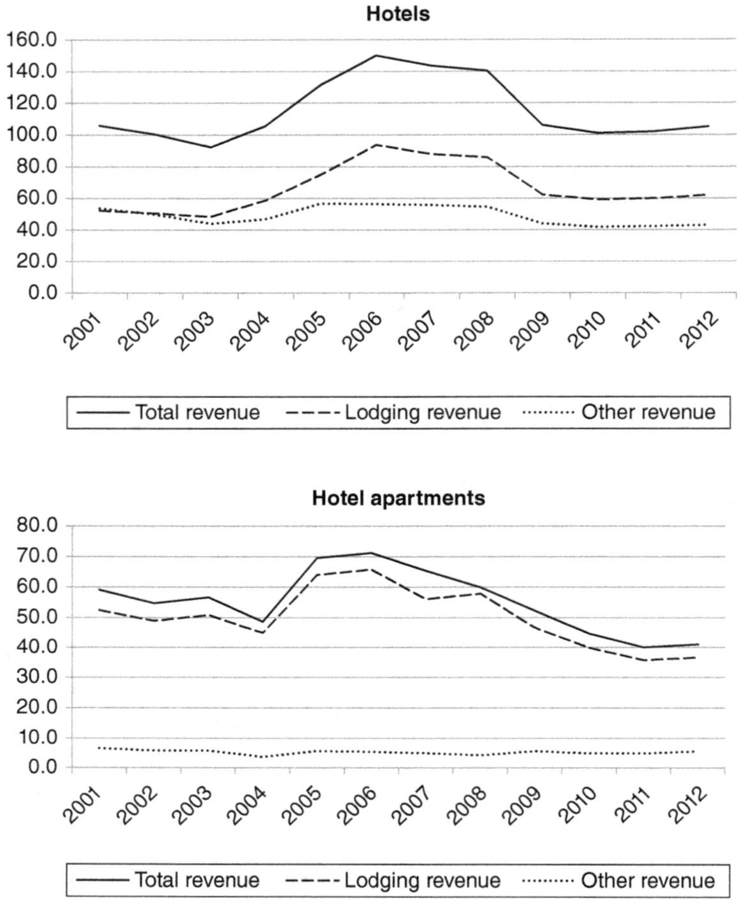

Figure 7.6. Real revenues per visitor per night, by type of revenue (in US$ of 2001)

trade). The DTCM collects monthly data on the first two categories: lodging revenues and a more diffuse grouping labelled 'other revenues'. The latter may include services that complement lodging (hotel restaurants, bars, and other services) as well as other services sold by hotels to non-passengers such as events, weddings, conference rooms, and so on. As mentioned, no institution surveys the third category and there is no information about expenditures by tourists in shopping, entertainment, transportation, and the like.

Figure 7.6 shows the evolution of real revenues (at constant 2001 prices) per visitor/night for hotels and hotel apartments. Several conclusions can be obtained. First, total revenues per passenger/night are significantly higher in hotels than in hotel apartments. On average total revenues per guest/night were US$115 in hotels and US$55 in apartment hotels in the period 2000–12.

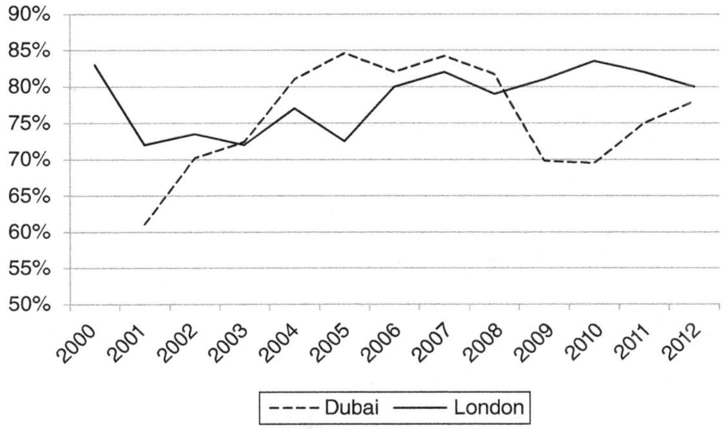

Figure 7.7. Hotel occupancy rates in Dubai and London

This would confirm the notion that they cater for different types of consumers. Second, total revenues in hotel apartments are far more stable than in hotels: the latter experienced a quite significant bubble in the period 2005–9 emanating from lodging revenues, likely to be associated with the overheating and posterior crisis of the economy. However, hotels are quite heterogeneous in quality, services, and price strategies, as detailed below, so that the bubble seems to have affected only the top-end of the market. Third, hotels derive significantly more revenues from non-lodging sources than apartment hotels. Thus, whereas lodging revenue for hotel apartments represented about 90 per cent of all revenues in the period 2001–10, in the case of hotels, it only accounted for 57 per cent. The fact that apartment hotels collect a relatively insignificant volume of revenues from non-lodging services indicates that possibly they offer a smaller range of services and a more homogenous product to a better-targeted clientele.

Lodging revenues are a combination of two factors: room rates and occupancy rates. The latter is the number of rooms at any point in time being actually occupied by passengers. This indicator combines both the demand and supply sides of the market. For any given capacity, an increase in demand translates into higher occupancy. For any given number of tourists, an increase in hotel infrastructure translates into a lower occupancy rate. Hotels usually adjust room rates to keep occupancy above a certain threshold so as to pay the fixed costs of running the operation. For that reason a higher occupancy rate indicates that hotels are more profitable.

Figure 7.7 shows the evolution of the occupancy rate in hotel and hotel apartments in Dubai and London. In Dubai, occupancy rates of hotels are quite similar to that of apartment hotels, so we grouped them together. It can be seen that average occupancy improved from a relatively low level of

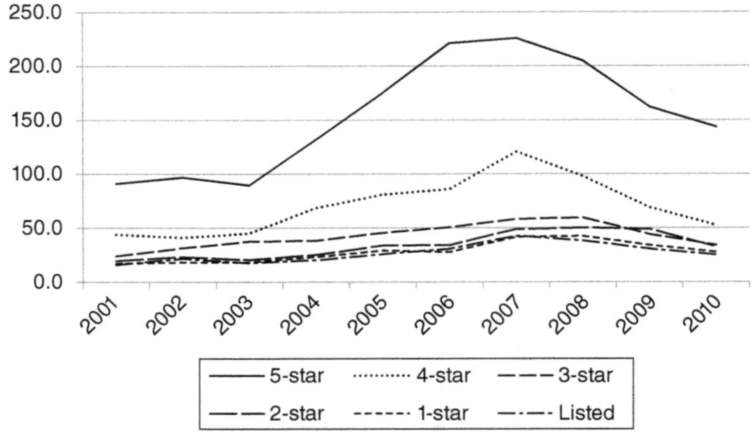

Figure 7.8. Average room rate in Dubai ($ per night)

65 per cent in 2001 to a high level of 80 per cent in 2005 and remained there until the unveiling of the global crisis in 2009. Note that occupancy rates in London also peaked in the three years prior to the crisis which indicates that international tourism boomed at the time and that Emirati hoteliers took advantage and profited from the world tourism cycle. Note also that prior to the boom, London hotels operated with occupancy rates in the range of 70 per cent for most of the period 2000–5. Using eleven years of occupancy data from Smith Travel Research (De Roos, 1999), found a natural occupancy rate of 62.9 per cent for US hotels.

After the booming years of 2003–8, tourism in Dubai was severely hit by the global crisis. In 2009 the occupancy rate declined some fifteen percentage points to the neighbourhood of 70 per cent and remained stagnant throughout 2010 and most of 2011 to recover slightly in 2012. The decline in occupancy rates was accompanied by a significant reduction in room rates, particularly among four- and five-star hotels (see Figure 7.8). Consequently, there was a compounding effect: lower room rates reduced revenue per passenger and the lower number of guests reduced total revenue. Causality between these two events goes from hotels reducing tariffs to induce occupancy. The fact that occupancy did decline after the crisis indicates that either price reductions were not aggressive enough or that the magnitude of the demand shrinkage was too large to be counteracted by room prices. By 2011 occupancy rates returned to pre-crisis levels but room rates remain substantially below those of 2007.

The different dynamics of revenues suggests the existence of different adjustment patterns for hotels and apartment hotels when facing the economic cycle. It can be seen that revenues per visitor/night in hotels increased significantly during the period 2003–7, but declined also significantly

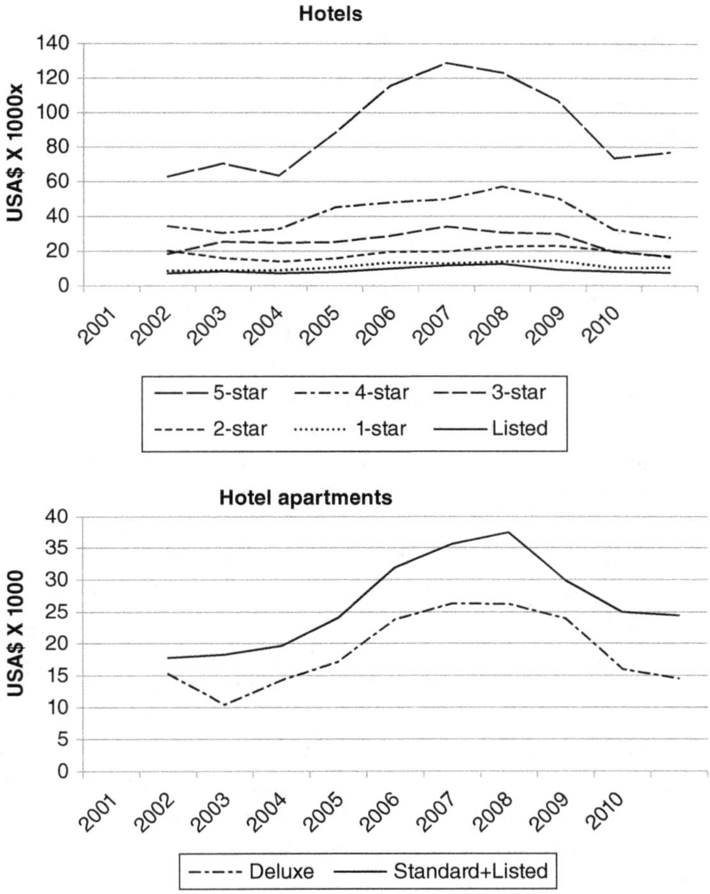

Figure 7.9. Real revenues per visitor per night, by type of hotel

afterwards, especially during the period leading up to and after the global crisis. In 2010, revenues per visitor/night had returned to similar levels as those prevailing at the beginning of the decade. Apartment hotels benefited less from the upswing but also suffered less during the downswing. The decline in lodging revenues has been more pronounced for hotels than for hotel apartments: this indicates that hotels have undergone a more significant price adjustment than apartment hotels. The reasons for such asymmetric adjustment are discussed below, but it is worth mentioning that for a segment of the hotels this is in part due to the growing competition from hotel apartments which nowadays offer services of comparable quality at virtually the same tariffs as that of hotels.

In order to understand better the structure of the hostelling industry it is useful to split revenues by type of hotel (see Figure 7.9). Hotels are classified in ascending levels of quality between one and five stars. Hotel apartments, on the other hand, are described as deluxe and standard. Figure 7.9 shows that most of the dynamics in total real revenues actually reflects the evolution in four- and five-star hotels. In fact, hotels ranked between one and three stars resemble very closely apartment hotels, both in terms of total revenue per passenger and in their evolution in time.

Hotels in the upper-income segment of the market—particularly, five-star hotels—present a very different trajectory. Prior to the crisis, revenues per passenger increased very fast: between 2001 and 2007 they nearly doubled. However, concurrent with the global crisis they declined significantly and had not recovered as of 2011. Three effects are behind this phenomenon. First, the significant decline in revenues was in part due to the worldwide contraction in the demand for tourism as a result of the crisis. However, as explained above, this could only partially be an explanation since the number of visitors did not fall significantly and the length of stay remained constant. Second, the increase in competition particularly among 5-star hotels, brought about by the entry of a number of new hotels of larger capacity. In 1995 there were twenty-seven five-star hotels in Dubai; by 2006 the number had expanded to forty and then to fifty-six in 2010. Third, the switch in the demand from high-income European travellers toward less affluent visitors from other countries. An increase in the supply of hotels coupled with a decline in the demand for luxury hotels easily explains the inverted U-shape in revenues of five-star hotels in Figure 7.7. The same argument applies to four-star hotels. However, the less pronounced decline in revenues in the latter suggests that four-star hotels might have served as substitutes to five-star hotels during the crisis.

Seasonality in visitors is also mirrored in revenues, as shown in Figure 7.10. Luxury hotels experienced significant seasonality in revenues per visitor/night in 2010 while lower quality hotels and apartment hotels did not face significant changes in month-to-month revenues. One reason for the asymmetric dynamics in revenues is that adjustment in four- and five-star hotels require significant access to financial resources in order to hedge between periods of high and low demand. In periods of high demand, luxury hotels can impose a significant surcharge to tariffs as luxury travellers have low sensitivity to prices. In periods of low demand—such as in the summer months when luxury travellers are not willing to come to such a hot place—luxury hotels are willing to reduce prices significantly to lure aspirational middle-income travellers and maintain a high occupation rate. Smaller size hotels cannot afford a strategy with highly variable cash flows. The fact that lodging prices in hotel-apartments are less elastic than in hotels suggests again that hotels and hotel apartments in Dubai cannot be considered substitutes for each other.

So far the analysis has focused on seasonal and cyclical changes in the demand for tourism in Dubai. Long-run trends, however, cannot be explained on the basis of short-term fluctuations. One key determinant of the long-run

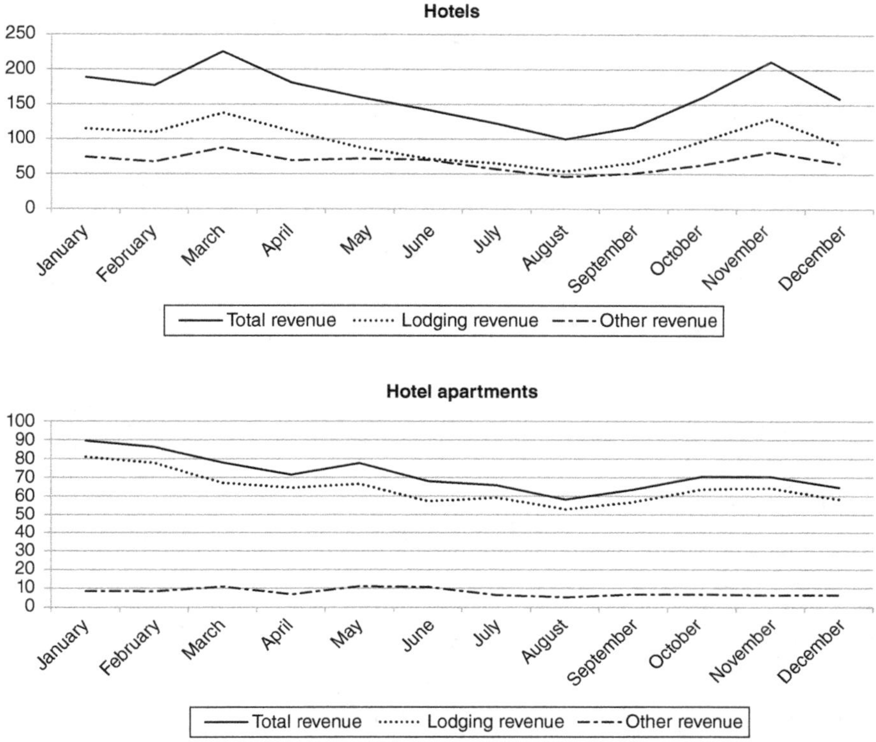

Figure 7.10. Seasonality and real revenues per visitor per night, by type of hotel

demand for tourism is the purchasing power of tourists. Figure 7.11 plots the (log) of number of visitors in Dubai between January 2007 and December 2010 from four regions (Europe, Americas, Oceania, and the Indian subcontinent) against the value of their currencies relative to the US dollar, that is, relative to the purchasing value of the Emirati dirham. The trends in each panel of Figure 7.11 suggest that as the corresponding currency of visitors to Dubai appreciates (relative to the value of the dollar, therefore, the dirham) the number of inbound visitors to Dubai increases. Thus, the purchasing power of incoming visitors affects the demand for tourism.

7.4.5 Competitiveness

The World Economic Forum issues annually the *Travel and Tourism Competitiveness Report* which ranks the UAE vis-à-vis around 140 countries. The UAE ranked 28th in the world in 2013 and, unsurprisingly, first in the MENA

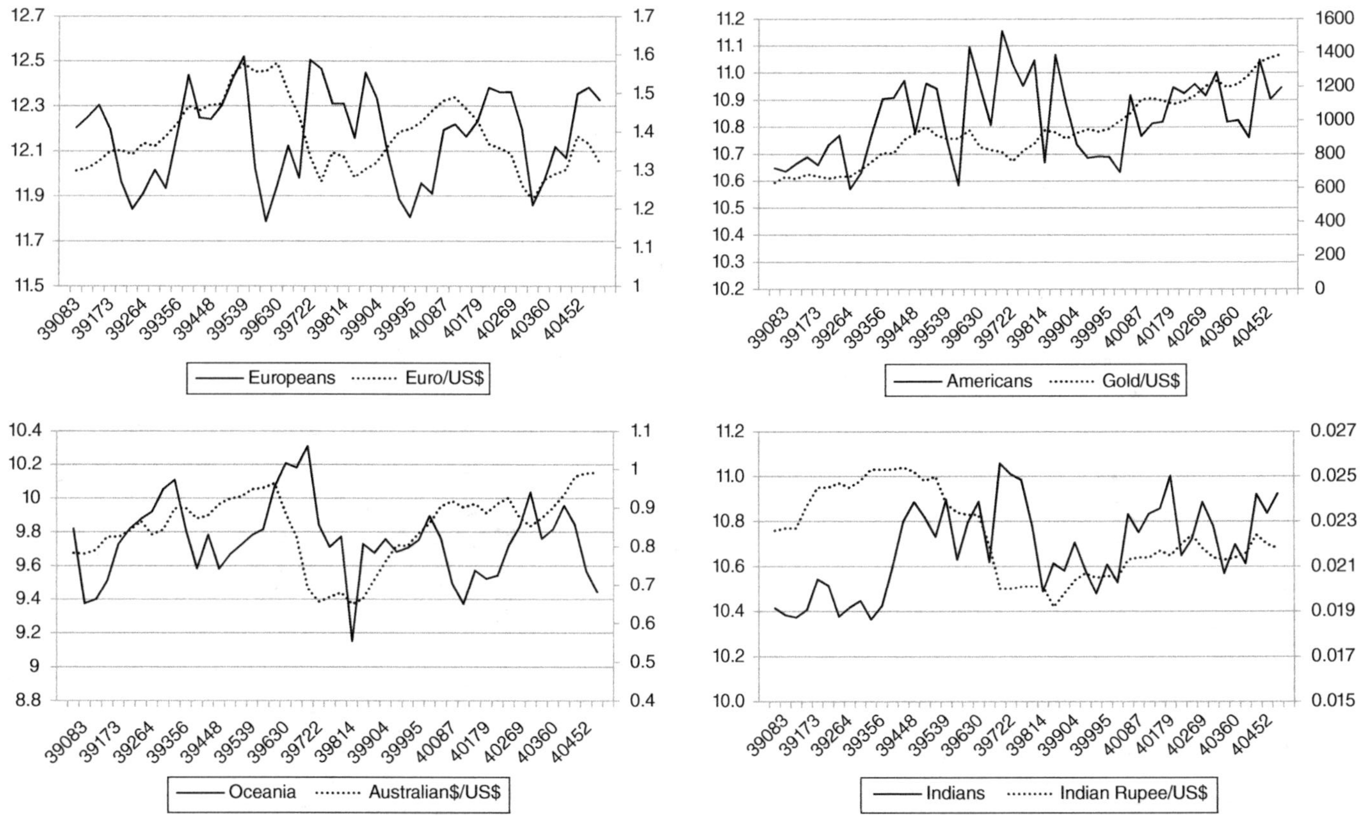

Figure 7.11. Inbound visitors to Dubai compared to value of currency at origin

region (WEF, 2013).[3] This indicates, naturally, that the UAE enjoys high levels of competitiveness in tourism, in the league of countries such as Greece or Mexico. While competitive, however, the UAE was below the levels of other tourism and business hubs, such as Singapore (which ranks 10th worldwide) or Hong Kong (15th). These countries provide insights and benchmarks on the policies needed to foster competitiveness in Dubai.

The WEF classification is based on individual rankings covering different aspects of the tourism industry, which are combined to produce the final ranking. Individual rankings indicate that the strongest asset of the industry in the UAE is business environment and infrastructure (9th in the world), which largely compensates for the weaknesses in terms of human, cultural, and natural resources (35th) and regulatory framework (45th). Note that in terms of cultural and natural resources, Hong Kong or Singapore rank as low as the UAE, which is not surprising considering the size and geographic characteristics of these city-states. Likewise, there is not much difference in terms of infrastructure and business environment, where the UAE and its benchmark rank among the top ten countries in the world. The main difference between Dubai and Hong Kong or Singapore lies precisely in the quality of regulation, where the UAE ranks comparatively low.

A more detailed analysis of the regulatory weaknesses of the UAE tourism sector unveils some noticeable similarities with Hong Kong or Singapore. First, no country is blessed with rich natural resources to lure tourists and their cultural resources are mediocre at best. Second, all countries excel in tourism infrastructure, ICT, and transportation services (air transport in the UAE and land and sea transport in the other two). Third, price competitiveness in the three countries is rather low, that is, tourism services are comparatively very expensive. This could be the outcome of a deliberate policy of focusing on the high-income niche of the tourism market but most likely is the result of the high-income level of the host country since in the WEF rankings the most expensive tourism destinations are invariably in the OECD economies. Fourth, and a matter of concern for policymakers, all countries rank quite low in terms of the environmental sustainability of the tourism industry: the UAE, in particular, ranks 91st among 139 economies indicating the urgent need for significant policy reforms.

Nevertheless, there is one key difference between the UAE and Hong Kong and Singapore: the latter two countries rank among the top three economies in the world in terms of policies and market regulations, while the UAE is in a mediocre position: in 2009 the UAE ranked in 81st place but it improved to 45th in 2013 as, according to WEF, some rules and regulations were adjusted to better support the sector's development.

[3] Other MENA countries located among the top 50 in the world are Bahrain (40th), Qatar (42nd), Israel (46th), and Tunisia (47th).

7.4.6 Regional Competition

The Middle East has significantly contributed to the increasing importance of tourism in emerging economies. The number of international tourist arrivals in the Middle East increased from around 10 million in 1990 to 60 million in 2010 but declined slightly afterwards to 52 million in 2012 as a result of political turmoil. Table 7.2 provides a comparative overview of the UAE versus other economies in the Middle East region.

In 2010 the UAE received one in every eight international tourists visiting the Middle East. This represented an annual increase of 6 per cent from 2000, a significant expansion but well below the average increase experienced by the region (11 per cent) suggesting that, despite its well-publicized success as a tourist destination, Dubai did not benefit much from the noteworthy expansion of regional tourism prior to the global recession and Arab Spring. The increase in tourism in the Middle East in the period 2000/10 was driven by the inflow of tourists to Egypt, Jordan, and Saudi Arabia which have ample offers in terms of historical heritage and religious sites. The UAE on the other hand, does not have such heritage sights and must rely on man-made attractions and general business climate to lure visitors. Prior to the Arab Spring and despite the lack of historical and religious sites, the UAE managed to attract one-half of the tourists visiting Egypt or Saudi Arabia and twice as many as Jordan. The UAE avoided political turmoil in the early 2010s altogether and, while hard-hit by the global slowdown, it was able to attract a significant proportion of regional tourism, increasing its share from 12 per cent to 17 per cent in 2012. Table 7.2 also shows that, while the number of tourists visiting Dubai is not as high as in Egypt or Saudi Arabia, its total receipts per passenger are much higher. This naturally reflects Dubai's strategy of concentrating on the

Table 7.2. Middle East tourism indicators, 2008–12

	International tourist arrivals				International tourists receipts in 2012	
	millions					
	2000	2008	**2010**	2012	US$ billions	share of regional total
Egypt	5.1	12.3	14.1	11.1	9.9	21.1
Jordan	1.6	3.8	4.5	4.1	3.6	7.7
Saudi Arabia	6.6	14.8	10.9	13.6	7.4	15.7
Qatar	0.3	1.4	1.5	2.0[1]	2.9	6.2
Others[2]	6.9	15.8	21.4	12.2	12.8	27.2
UAE	**4.0**	**7.1**	**7.4**	**9.0**	**10.4**	**22.1**
Total Middle East	20.5	55.2	59.8	52.0	47.0	100.0

[1] Authors own projection based on data from national authorities.

[2] Others include Lebanon, Oman, Palestine, Syrian Arab Republic, and Yemen.

Source: UNWTO *Tourism Highlights 2013 Edition*

high-end of the tourism industry but, while receipts per tourist are much higher in the emirate, this does not indicate that the profitability of the Emirati tourism industry is higher than in the rest of the region as the costs of servicing this segment of the market are also much higher. Unfortunately we do not have information on actual cost per tourist either for the UAE or for any of the countries included in the table.

7.5 INSTITUTIONAL ISSUES

Arguably, all emirates in the UAE share similar tourism conditions in terms of location, weather, historical landmarks, and the like. Furthermore, other regions in the Gulf of Arabia share very similar conditions (e.g. Qatar, Bahrain). Yet Dubai has managed to become the focal point of tourism in the region. This is largely the result of early pro-tourism policies on the part of the government and an aggressive investment strategy on the part of the private sector. Underneath there is institutional fabric that makes it possible for this strategy to be successful. However, there are institutional reforms that could improve markedly the economic performance of the industry.

The government can significantly affect tourism in, at least, two dimensions. First, the entry, stay, and exit of visitors are usually highly regulated by governments; the UAE is not an exception and could be classified as quite restrictive. Second, governments provide institutional arrangements that can foster or impede the development of the industry. The UAE has implemented a peculiar institutional fabric that greatly affects tourism, both positively and negatively. Most of the regulations operate at the federal level and cannot be easily modified at the emirate level.

Regarding the institutional mechanisms governing the entry and permanence of tourists in Dubai, one key issue is that of visa requirements. The UAE prides itself as a refuge of safety and security in a rather unstable neighbourhood; unfortunately, entry safety comes at a potential cost for tourism. On one hand, there are significant asymmetries and arbitrariness in terms of the entry mechanisms for different nationalities: while some citizens of some countries are exempt of any requirements (e.g. Europeans, North Americans) and obtain de facto multiple-entry visas, others need to secure a company or individual to act as sponsor or, more awkwardly, book a ticket on Emirates Airlines to obtain a fourteen-day, single-entry visa. On the other hand, when required, visas are unjustifiably expensive (US$180) except as a pure tax, have anti-touristic features (single entry and reapplication within 30 days is forbidden), and go through a slow and cumbersome system to be delivered.

All these elements act as obvious deterrents to tourism, most of all for a country that, lacking natural attractions, must base its tourism strategy in providing a good ratio of cost to quality. In particular, single-entry visas and high fees impede passengers' use of Dubai as a centre for travel within the region, thus hampering the vision of Dubai as a tourism hub. The number of nationalities that require a visa is too large and, most importantly, include countries with large populations and significant purchasing power that could contribute significantly to boost demand. For example, the 600 million Latin American citizens are restricted even though most of them do not require visas to travel to other places such as Europe (e.g. Argentina, Brazil, Mexico, and Venezuela). Furthermore, the list of countries exempted from visa requirements has not changed significantly since 1971 (except for the inclusion of Canada). However, the purchasing power of many economies has changed significantly since then (e.g. Russia, China) and not accounting for these dynamic changes can lead to competitiveness losses for the tourist industry in Dubai.

The second area of government influence relates to the formal and informal institutional arrangements that affect the attractiveness and profitability of tourism in Dubai. The government of Dubai has been very active in positioning the city worldwide as a tourist destination; most certainly, it has boosted the number of tourist arrivals. Since 1997, there is a dedicated authority—the DTCM—mandated to promote Dubai as a destination for both tourists and tourism investors and which operates both within and beyond the UAE. The DTCM has a second mandate, so far less successful than its promoting role, as the agency in charge of collecting and analysing data on tourism activities. As mentioned, the lack of information is pervasive and policymaking proceeds blindly. In contrast, countries where tourism is an important sector also provide timely, trustworthy, and publicly available statistics covering the different segments of the industry. Lack of information is a severe limitation to tourism development.

Promotion in the past has invariably been skewed towards portraying Dubai as a luxury destination, although the rationale behind it is questionable. For example, a DTCM promotion in the UK entitled 'Affordable Luxury: Discover Dubai' concentrated only in the newspaper 'Daily Express' which targets low- to middle-class readers with low to average educational background. However, such a specifically targeted campaign might have missed a significant fraction of the UK population and the response would have not been very significant. According to estimates by Fernandes and Karnik (2010), the income elasticity of the demand of British travellers to Dubai is very low (0.14) so that spending money to lure low-to-middle income families may not be very profitable. Targeting South Africa, on the other hand, was spurred by the observation that South African visitors are very few (80,000 on average per year) despite its large population and income level. After the campaign the number of visitors increased by 4,000. A quick calculation suggests that, at best, the promotion has generated US$1.6 million in gross revenue for the H&R sector and, eventually, some US$5 million in total extra revenues for tourism (based on an average room rate of US$100 and a stay of 4 nights). Whether this has been a cost-effective tourism investment depends on the actual cost of the promotion which is unknown. However, hosting a promotion to get 4,000 extra visitors seems to be not very relevant when compared to the 10 million visitors Dubai receives every year. The soundness of this type of project may be debatable but the main issue is that, as with many other interventions, there has not been an *ex post* evaluation of the use of public resources.

7.6 CONCLUSIONS AND POLICY RECOMMENDATIONS

Tourism in Dubai is largely a man-made project, built as a response to its lack of historical, natural, or heritage attractions and based upon a clever combination of top-notch public infrastructure, an ample supply of hotel accommodation and a myriad of selected events to lure the visitors. This mix has been quite successful and, until the recent global crisis, made tourism an engine for sustained growth; Dubai is nowadays the regional hub for tourism and, particularly, for businessmen operating between Asia and the Middle East.

Despite its success, several elements indicate the need to reappraise the evolution and strategy of the tourism industry, in particular vis-à-vis the future development of tourism worldwide and the emergence of regional contenders (e.g. Qatar). The global crisis of the late 2000s revealed some weaknesses in the industry vis-à-vis economic fluctuations. Perhaps, after two decades of sustained growth the business strategy of the sector might have grown into maturity and offers limited expansion in the future.

Identifying the weaknesses and strengths of the tourism industry in Dubai and evaluating alternative policies to foster the development of the tourism industry is severely limited by the pervasive lack of timely, reliable, and public data. There are sufficient financial and human means in Dubai to be able to develop a statistical and informational system that can provide tourism data beyond the number of passengers in hotels.

Much of the tourism in Dubai is associated with the luxury segment of the market (from luxury hotels to luxury events) or to low-income travellers while the middle-income segment of tourism (e.g. budget holidays) has been largely neglected. This has adverse consequences. First, the tourism industry in Dubai is riskier than that in economies that have better diversified tourism markets and, as result, is more susceptible to downturns as shown in the global financial crisis of 2008–10. Secondly, by focusing excessively on the luxury segment, the tourist industry in Dubai is losing out to potential visitors from emerging economies that are increasing their demand for tourism (Russia, China, India) but might not be willing to pay for exclusively luxury holidays. Diversification of the market could bring about an increase in the demand for tourism not just from economies classically associated with high disposable incomes but from other economies with a growing number of wealthier individuals. There are rising top spenders that could be considered for tourism growth in Dubai. In particular, the first four ranked in terms of tourism spenders are the UK (ranked fourth) spending US$49 billion in 2010; China (ranked third) with US$55 billion; Germany (ranked second) with US$78 billion, and the US (ranked first) with US$76 billion. Among the ten bigger spenders Russia and China are the ones that have showed stronger growth in 2010, increasing by 27 per cent and 26 per cent respectively over the past five years. This should be taken into consideration by the authorities (DCTM) when promoting Dubai to the rest of the world (e.g. when promoting Dubai with highly expensive information campaigns that target country by country).

The competitive edge of tourism in Dubai could be enhanced by developing those areas in which international comparison suggests there are obvious limitations. One such example is the backwardation in terms of the environmental costs of tourism-related activities. As mentioned, Dubai and the UAE rank very low for international standards and, in a world of increasing environmental awareness, this may become a severe limitation for future development. Past initiatives aimed at the conservation of natural resources and a sensible use of energy, water, and gas are to be heightened and supported by far-reaching policies aimed at encouraging better environmental practices in the hospitality industry. Increasing awareness and social responsibility is important to develop native capacities to identify and implement best practices to improve the service standards and excellence in the tourism industry.

REFERENCES

Barros, C. P. and Machado, L. P., 2010. 'The Length of Stay in Tourism'. *Annuals of Tourism Research,* 37(3): 692–706.

De Roos, J. A., 1999. 'Natural Occupancy Rates and Development Gaps: A Look at the U.S. Lodging Industry'. *Cornell Hospitality Quarterly,* 40(02): 14–22.

DTCM, 2013. *Online Database Department of Tourism and Commerce Marketing.* [Online] Available at: http://www.visitdubai.com/en/department-of-tourism_new, accessed 2 September 2015.

Dubai Statistics Center, 2013. *Dubai National Accounts.* [Online] Available at: https://www.dsc.gov.ae/en-us/Themes/Pages/National-Accounts.aspx?Theme=24, accessed 2 September 2015.

Elgonemy, A. R., 2002. 'Debt-financing Alternatives—Refinancing and Restructuring in the Lodging Industry'. *The Cornell Hotel and Restaurant Administration Quarterly*, 43(3): 7–21.

ESCAP, 2011. *Statistical Yearbook for Asia and the Pacific*, Bangkok: United Nations Publications.

Eurostat, 2011. *Eurostat Yearbook: Europe in Figures*, Luxembourg: Eurostat.

Fernandes, C., and Karnik, A., 2010. 'Estimating Elasticity of Demand for Tourism in Dubai?' *Tourism Analysis*, 15(1): 57–69.

Mak, J., 2004. *Tourism and the Economy: Understanding the Economics of Tourism*, Hawaii: University of Hawaii Press.

Mammoser, K. (2009, 5-March). 'Hotel Loan Performance in a Rapidly Deteriorating Market'. *Global CMBS Newsletter*, 5 March. [Online] Available at: http://www.dbrs.com/research/227125/global-cmbs-newsletter/hotelloan-performance-in-a-rapidly-deteriorating-market.pdf, accessed 2 September 2015.

Milburn, R., 2011. *UK Hospitality and Leisure Review 2011*, London, UK: PwC.

Saidi, N., Scacciavillani, F., and Ali, F., 2008. *DIFC Economic Note 8: Forecasting Tourism in Dubai*, Dubai: Dubai International Financial Center.

Singapore Tourism Board, 2010. *Annual Report on Tourism Statistics*, Singapore: Singapore Tourism Board.

Singstat, 2011. *Yearbook of Statistics*, Singapore: Singapore Statistics.

UNWTO, 2013. *Tourism Highlights, 2013 Edition*, Madrid, Spain: United Nations World Tourism Organization.

VisitBritain, 2010. *Overseas Visitors to Britain: Understanding Trends, Attitudes and Characteristics*, London: VisitBritain.

VisitBritain, 2012. *Inbound Tourism Facts*, London: VisitBritain.

WEF, 2013. *The Global Competitiveness Report 2013–2014: Full Data Edition*, World Economic Forum, Geneva, Switzerland.

World Bank, 2013. *World Development Indicators*. [Online] Available at: http://databank.worldbank.org/data/download/WDI-2013-ebook.pdf, accessed 2 September 2015.

8

The Financial Sector: Performance and Issues

Mohamed Trabelsi and Dhuha Fadhel

8.1 INTRODUCTION

In all countries, the key mission of the financial system is the promotion of economic growth by providing funds to the entrepreneurial sector. An extensive literature on finance and growth highlights the role of efficient financial systems in easing the exchange of goods and services, mobilizing savings, and diversifying risks. Efficient financial markets also play a chief role in processing information about investment opportunities and in exerting corporate governance after providing funds.

The initial objective of Dubai's authorities was to develop a sound financial sector capable of funding local as well as foreign enterprises and enhance the competitiveness of the different sectors of the economy. In time, Dubai authorities saw the opportunity to strengthen further its financial industry and transform it into a leading engine of growth. This led to an ambitious plan of developing a world class regional financial centre, which has been implemented in the form of an off-shore facility—the Dubai International Financial Centre (DIFC)—composed of banks, insurance companies, financial entities, and consulting firms and regulated by its own legal and judiciary system.

While the DIFC has been quite successful, the domestic financial sector has also flourished despite being more constrained in its operations and more susceptible to domestic and external shocks. The last decade has witnessed Dubai becoming the business capital of the UAE. This performance has been largely the result of deliberate policies aimed at integrating Dubai into the world economy and transforming the emirate into an attractive regional financial hub, dynamic and highly integrated with the global financial system.

The aim of this chapter is to provide a critical analysis of these efforts to develop the financial sector in Dubai and their contribution to the development of the entrepreneurial and business environment in the emirate. More specifically, the chapter focuses on evaluating the soundness of the banking sector (by assessing capital adequacy ratios, asset quality, and liquidity and profitability indicators), describing the performance of the different entities during and after the financial turmoil of 2008–9, and identifying the challenges imposed by the Basel III requirements. In addition to revising the performance of the financial sector, this chapter also reviews two pending issues that need to be tackled by the authorities. First, the massive debt overhang accumulated by government-related entities (GREs) and its effect on the banking sector. Second, the causes of the limited access to bank financing in Dubai and the preference of the business sector to use internal resources to fund investment operations.

Regarding the debt overhang, it is worth noting that Dubai's economic model has historically relied on leverage to finance massive development projects both by the private sector and the government. The global economic crisis of 2008 and 2009, nevertheless, hit the economy hard and put its domestic financial sector under stress. While the private sector suffered from the downturn, Dubai's financial stress was largely the result of the massive debt overhang accumulated by GREs which had invested heavily in real estate. Mirroring, to some extent, the situation in the main financial centres of the world, the crisis unveiled the importance of a properly functioning financial sector for the stability of the economy in a fully integrated world. It also made financial authorities aware that without proper regulations and adequate prudential measures, financial development and globalization may simply be a blueprint for instability and inefficient growth.

Regarding access to lending, and despite the leverage policy that has supported the economic development of Dubai, recent empirical studies and based on the analysis provided in this chapter, we show that access to bank finance is still rather limited: more than 80 per cent of the 700 firms surveyed by the 'Business Environment and Enterprise Performance Survey 2010' (Dubai Economic Council, 2010) in Main Dubai and the free zones indicated that they rely on internal resources or retained earnings to fund their investment or working capital. Improving the access of the private sector to the services offered by the financial system—particularly the banking sector—is of capital importance for Dubai's development both to foster much needed productivity gains in local enterprises and to maintain the attractiveness of the emirate for multinational corporations.

A systematic assessment of the performance of the financial sector and its capacity to finance the investment needs of the business sector is crucial for policymakers in any modern economy. In the case of Dubai there is the additional task of dealing with the above-mentioned pending issues that need resolution in the years to come.

8.2 THE STRUCTURE OF THE FINANCIAL SECTOR

The financial sector has played a major role in transforming the emirate into an attractive regional site of financial services. As mentioned, this sector is divided between Main Dubai and the Dubai International Financial Center (DIFC) which actually operates as a free zone of financial services. The internal banking activity is concentrated in Main Dubai where twenty-eight national and foreign banks are operating and providing trade, project, and consumer financing. Three banks also offer a full range of Sharia-compliant banking services. The capital market in main Dubai is represented by the Dubai Financial Market (DFM) which serves as a stock exchange trading in bonds and equities. The DFM commenced operations in March 2000 as a public institution where the activity includes mainly trading of securities issued by public shareholding companies and units of investment funds.

The DIFC is an offshore financial centre where the main areas of focus are capital markets, banking and brokerage, Islamic securities, and re-insurance. The Dubai International Financial Exchange (DIFX) (also called Nasdaq Dubai) is the stock market of the free zone, open to foreign investment and providing a comprehensive framework for trading of bonds, equities, and derivatives. It is also considered as one of the most important and liquid exchange of Islamic securities (*Sukuks*) worldwide.

8.2.1 The Banking Sector

The banking sector makes up the core of the financial activity in the UAE (and therefore of Dubai) and it operates under the rules and regulations of the Central Bank of the UAE (hereafter CBUAE). By 2012, the total number of licensed banks operating in UAE was fifty-one, of which twenty-three were national banks and twenty-eight were foreign owned. The sector is quite concentrated, with ten of the banks accounting for about 75 per cent of the total banking assets in 2012 while for the remaining forty-four banks the total share was below 25 per cent (see Figure 8.1).

The size of UAE banking assets experienced a substantial increase in 2007 and 2008 (see Table 8.2), largely driven by strong growth performance in most of the economic sectors, led by construction and services. The increase in the size of assets before the 2008 crisis also reflects the high global oil prices and strong domestic demand fuelled by growing population and large infrastructure projects in Dubai and Abu Dhabi (Chailloux and Hakura, 2009). Total banking assets continued to increase in 2009 and 2010 though at a decelerating pace due to the impact of the global financial turmoil on the banking sector and the economy as a whole. In 2012, banking assets increased at a

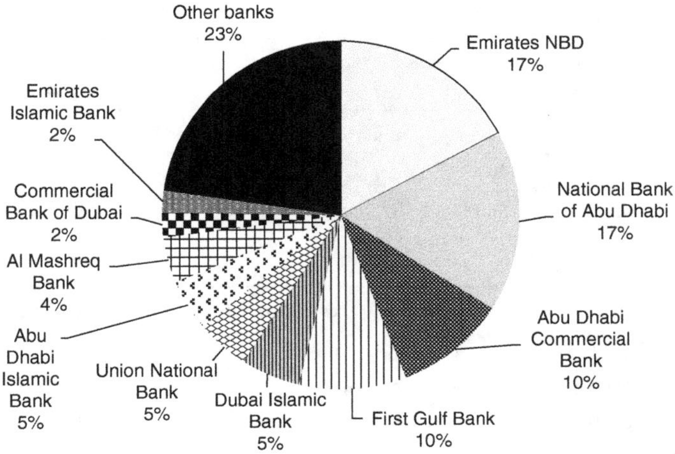

Figure 8.1. Market shares of banks in UAE in terms of assets in 2012
Source: Central Bank of the UAE (2013) and Securities and Commodities Authority (2013)

higher pace in line with the recovery of real activity and the driving sectors of the economy.

The number of banks operating in Dubai reached twenty-eight, both national and foreign-owned, and they provide corporate as well as consumer financing. However, in the aftermath of the financial turmoil in 2008–10, banks have been more reluctant to finance real estate and construction activities.[1] In 2009, the Emirates Bank and National Bank of Dubai merged into a single entity called the Emirates National Bank of Dubai (Emirates NBD) which became the largest bank in Dubai and UAE in terms of assets (see Figure 8.1) with total assets of about $US84 billion in 2012 (almost 22 per cent of UAE nominal GDP). Emirates NBD bank is considered to be one of the largest banks in the Middle East region by total assets. However, when measured relative to the size of the economy, Emirates NBD is smaller than Hong Kong and Shanghai Banking Corporation Limited that makes up to 298 per cent of Hong Kong nominal GDP, DBS Bank Ltd whose size is equal to 100 per cent of Singapore nominal GDP and Qatar National Bank that makes up to 52 per cent of Qatar nominal GDP. But it is still larger than Saudi's National Commercial Bank whose size is close to 13 per cent of Saudi Arabia's nominal GDP (see Table 8.1).

The number of banks has remained quite stable for a number of years largely due to the ban on new foreign-bank entrants. Local banks have substantially high market shares vis-à-vis foreign banks which, despite their profusion, face restrictions on the number of branches that they can operate

[1] See more details in section 8.4.

Table 8.1. The size of the largest banks in UAE and benchmark economies in 2012

Country	Largest bank by total assets	Total assets ($bn)	Nominal GDP ($bn)	Assets to GDP (%)
Saudi Arabia	National Commercial Bank	92	711	13
Qatar	Qatar National Bank	100	192	52
Singapore	DBS Bank Ltd	284	277	100
Hong Kong	Hong Kong and Shanghai Banking Corporation Limited	783	263	298
UAE	Emirates NBD	84	384	22

Source: Securities and Commodities Authority (2013) and International Monetary Fund (2013)

domestically. The majority of these foreign entities have established offices in Dubai. The ownership of local banks is mainly by UAE nationals as foreign participation is limited to 15 per cent even from GCC countries. Moreover, foreign banks are also subject to a 20 per cent tax on profits, which is not applied to local banks (International Monetary Fund, 2007).

The largest foreign banks in terms of assets operating in UAE are HSBC which reported $US26 billion of total assets in 2010 and Standard Chartered Bank posting $US21 billion. Although foreign banks outnumber national banks, their share in the total assets of the banking sector did not exceed 19 per cent in 2012; slightly below its highest level of 22.6 per cent in 2007 (see Table 8.2). In contrast, the share of state-owned banks witnessed a steady increase since 2007 reaching a peak in 2012 at around 66 per cent.

All these constraints imposed on the entry and operations of foreign banks certainly have not favoured market discipline or the emergence of a competitive banking sector in Dubai and the UAE. As in other sectors of the economy, fully effective competition in the banking sector helps enhance efficiency, encourages innovative financial services, provides better products to final consumers, and lowers prices in addition to enabling efficient banks to enter the market and replace the inefficient banks. For these reasons, opening up the UAE banking sector to foreign banks and relaxing the constraints imposed on their operations might be a critical issue to move forward and contribute to the growth and well-functioning of the economy.

Dubai-based Islamic banks are developing rapidly alongside the conventional system and provide important services that are compliant with the Muslim faith. The four institutions based and operating in Dubai (Dubai Islamic Bank (DIB), Emirates Islamic Bank (EIB), Dubai Bank (DB), and Noor Islamic Bank (NIB)) are among the important banks in the region.[2] In 2012, these banks had combined assets of around US$41 billion, which was

[2] In December 2012 Emirates Islamic Bank (EIB) and Dubai Bank (DB) announced their merger to create one of the leading Sharia-compliant banking units in the UAE.

Table 8.2. UAE banking system structure

	2006	2007	2008	2009	2010	2011	2012
Number of banks	46	49	52	52	51	51	51
National banks	21	22	24	24	23	23	23
Foreign Banks	25	27	28	28	28	28	28
Islamic	4	6	8	8	8	8	8
Non-Islamic	42	42	44	44	43	43	43
Private	31	33	35	35	35	35	35
National	6	6	7	7	7	7	7
Foreign owned	25	27	28	28	28	28	28
State-owned	15	16	17	17	16	16	16
Concentration[1]	11	11	11	10	10	10	10
Assets share (%)							
Private	36.4	38.2	36.8	35.5	34.6	35.9	34.1
Local	14.5	15.6	16.3	16.6	15.9	15.6	14.9
Foreign owned	21.9	22.6	20.6	18.9	18.6	20.3	19.2
State-owned	63.6	61.8	63.2	64.5	65.4	64.1	65.9
Islamic	14.0	14.2	15.7	16.0	16.8	15.6	16.0
Non-Islamic	86.0	85.8	84.3	84.0	83.2	84.4	84.0
Deposits share (%)							
Private	40.1	39.9	37.7	37.2	35.0	36.2	33.1
Local	15.6	16.7	16.6	17.2	16.2	16.0	15.2
Foreign	24.5	23.2	21.1	20.0	18.7	20.2	17.9
State-owned	59.9	60.1	62.3	62.8	65.0	63.8	66.9
Islamic	16.0	17.1	18.1	18.7	18.8	18.0	18.0
Non-Islamic	84.0	82.9	81.9	81.3	81.2	82.0	82.0
Total assets (Bill AED)	826	1,202	1,448	1,521	1,610	1,662	1,791

[1] Number of banks with 75 per cent of total assets.
Source: Central Bank of the UAE (2013), International Monetary Fund (2011), and DEC staff estimates

almost 8 per cent of the whole banking sector in UAE. Other Islamic banks also operate in the UAE such as the Abu Dhabi Islamic Bank (ADIB) that reported total assets of about $US23 billion in 2012, being of a similar size to Dubai Islamic Bank (DIB) which also reported around $US26 billion the same year.

The substantial development of Islamic banking services has encouraged many conventional national and foreign banks to create operating windows working in accordance with Islamic principles to meet the growing demand in the market. Islamic banking is also expected to be enhanced in Dubai after the strategic decision in early 2013 to transform the emirate into a global centre of Islamic economy and finance. However, Islamic banks in Dubai/UAE are still smaller and less diversified when compared to conventional banks. This is expected since, given the nature of their activities, they do not benefit from the various available funding facilities such as money markets and hedging instruments.

8.2.2 The Capital Market

The chief objective of the capital market is to channel funds to the most profitable companies, provide capital for investment, and subsequently promote economic growth. Since its creation, this sector has played a substantial role in transforming Dubai into a regional and undisputed financial hub. The sector features two stock exchanges trading primarily bonds and equities, Dubai Financial Market (DFM) and Dubai Financial Exchange (DIFX), also known as Nasdaq Dubai.

The DFM commenced operations in 2000 as a market for trading securities and bonds issued by public joint-stock companies as well as federal or local governments and public entities. Access to property by foreigners in the DFM is limited and their ownership stake cannot exceed 49 per cent. The DFM became the first stock exchange to be privatized in the region after offering 20 per cent of its shares for public subscription in 2005. However, while activity in this market centres on local and regional trading of securities generally issued by public shareholding companies, the market for fixed-income securities is still not developed as the value of traded debt instruments with respect to the exchanges' total market capitalization is less than 1 per cent. In fact, with the exception of *Sukuk* bonds which are compliant with Sharia, the listings in traditional corporate bonds are really thin.

During 2007, the market witnessed strong trading activity that was supported by low interest rates, the performance of listed companies, and positive economic conditions where oil revenues played an important role. The performance of the DFM was severely affected by the financial crisis as the General Index experienced a sharp decline during most of 2008 (Figure 8.2)

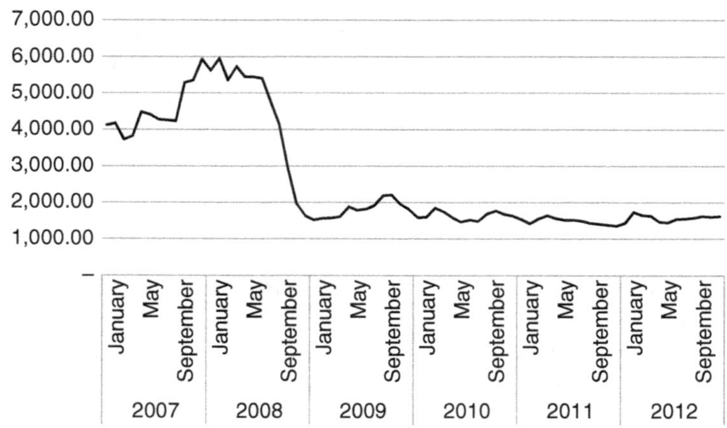

Figure 8.2. The DFM Index

Source: Dubai Financial Market (DFM) monthly bulletins

and reached its lowest level on 25 December. In the post-crisis period the market performance reversed the trend, crossing the 2,000-point mark in late 2009. However, in 2010, the overall performance decreased by 9.6 per cent to reach 1,630.5 points at the end of the year and it seemed that the recovery was very slow as the mood remained circumspect. The market showed, however, an upward trend during the years 2011 and 2012 as the general index increased substantially from 1,353.4 at end of 2011 to 1,622.5 at end of December 2012. With such a performance, the DFM seemed to be following the recovery of the Dubai economy and especially in the sectors considered the drivers of economic growth in the emirate. The market was also expected to continue its recovery in the foreseeable future that would bring it back to a bullish mode.

Regarding Dubai's status as an offshore financial sector, all activities are done inside the Dubai International Financial Center (DIFC) that was created in 2004. It is a self-regulating financial free zone that is governed by its own independent regulator and supervisory body called Dubai Financial Services Authority (DFSA). To enhance trading of Islamic securities or *Sukuks*, the DIFC established in 2005 a second stock market that provides a comprehensive framework for dealing with such financial products: the Dubai International Financial Exchange (DIFX) also called NASDAQ Dubai. This market is fully open to foreign investment and is deemed as one of the most active and liquid exchanges for Islamic bonds worldwide.[3] In July 2010, a first step was taken in the consolidation of the equity market in Dubai with the merger of NASDAQ Dubai and DFM. This creation of a single trading platform through the merger has been seen as a reasonable enhancement for investors and has led to a substantial promotion of new listings in the market.

Nevertheless, it has to be noted that despite all these achievements, it seems that the financial sector in Dubai still has some weaknesses due to (a) the dual structure of the market in terms of Main Dubai/DIFC operating under different rules, serving different types of consumers, and having possibly very different levels of efficiency due to the protection of internal banks, and (b) the dual nature—yet possibly complimentary—of the banking sector (traditional/Islamic banks). This suggests the need for policy reforms to improve its working and enhance its role in fostering sustained growth and development.

[3] DIFX also offers trading in equities and funds, derivatives, and bonds and it's not limited to *Sukuks*.

8.3 ASSESSING THE SOUNDNESS OF THE BANKING SECTOR IN DUBAI RELATIVE TO ABU DHABI AND UAE

The Dubai and UAE banking sectors performed well during the 2003–8 oil boom, but it was also during this period when the risks started to build up on banks' balance sheets. Flourishing economic activity and abundant liquidity resulting from higher oil prices promoted excessive credit growth, inflation, and asset price increases especially in the real estate sector. During the same period, banks increased their exposure to real estate and the construction sector as well as the equity markets which led to a build-up of vulnerabilities on their balance sheets that materialized when the global crisis took hold in 2008 (Khamis and Senhadji, 2010).

The global financial crisis affected the UAE economy through trade and financial channels. The decline in oil prices had a direct impact on government finances and external positions. Also, the sharp falls in Dubai and Abu Dhabi stock markets, tightened global liquidity conditions, and widening credit default swaps (CDSs) spreads on sovereign debt have exacerbated the impact of the crisis. Moreover, the reversal of capital inflows that entered the country earlier in 2007 and 2008 speculating on a revaluation of dirham further intensified liquidity pressures since banks used a substantial part of these inflows to finance long-term projects which exacerbated maturity mismatches on their balance sheets (Chailloux and Hakura, 2009).

These developments triggered a sharp decline in assets and real estate prices, weakened the balance sheets of banks, and led to a slowdown in economic activity. This, together with wide global deleveraging, increasing international liquidity pressures, and higher funding costs, led banks to draw down their reserves with the Central Bank. Short-term interest rates significantly jumped, though temporarily. Eventually, banks became more reluctant to lend and some were forced to deleverage (Khamis and Senhadji, 2010).

To counter the shocks brought on by the global crisis, the UAE government and Central Bank took decisive actions that comprised an expansionary fiscal policy, capital and liquidity injections, interest rate cuts, and a blanket guarantee of deposits for three years. The intervention measures are summarized in Table 8.3.

The set of measures that were adopted by the federal government helped moderate the impact of the financial crisis on the banking sector. This is evident through the results of the assessment conducted on a sample of five local banks in Dubai and five others in Abu Dhabi, altogether making up about 75 per cent of total assets in the UAE banking sector. The assessment shows that, except for the non-performing loans (NPLs) ratio, Dubai and UAE

Table 8.3. Government intervention measures to counteract the financial crisis of 2008–10

Month	Type	Description
March 2008	Liquidity support	• A US dollar swap facility was introduced by the Central Bank intended to mitigate the impact of the reversal of speculative capital flows that entered the market in late 2007 and 2008. US $8 billion were provided to banks through this facility.
April–June 2008		• An additional net flow of US$1.2 billion was injected by the central bank.
September 2008		• Banks were allowed to borrow against their reserve requirements.
September 2008		• The liquidity support facility was introduced by the central bank. Under this facility, banks could obtain dirham liquidity against certificates of deposits (CDs) with maturities of up to fourteen days.
October 2008		• The Central Bank of UAE transferred $US19.1 bn (AED 70 bn) to the Ministry of Finance (MOF) in return for the purchase of a five-year Treasury bond to help support banks that meet certain conditions. Borrowing banks had to issue a promissory note.
October 2008	Interest rate cut	• Reductions on repo rate and rates on liquidity support facility (LSF).
October 2008	Deposits insurance	• A blanket guarantee on deposits and inter-bank lending for three years was announced by the Ministry of Finance.
February 2009	Capital injection	• Banks were allowed to convert the MOF liquidity facility into Tier 2 capital. • Abu Dhabi government injected $US4.4 bn to recapitalize five of its banks.

Source: Chailloux and Hakura (2009) and Khamis and Senhadji (2010)

banking sectors have weathered the storm and managed to strengthen capital adequacy bases and improve liquidity profiles. However, the NPLs ratio sharply increased in 2009 and 2010 as the full impact of the crisis worked through banks' balance sheets, especially assets related to the real estate sector which endured a sharp correction during the financial crisis of 2009–10.

Following the 2009 crisis, UAE banks started to consolidate their balance sheets, strengthen their capital bases, and improve their liquidity positions. As of 2012, the banking system looked sounder and better capitalized, despite the high levels of NPLs that peaked in 2011 at about 14 per cent. However, the potential restructuring of GRE debt could possibly lead to a further increase in the NPLs ratios.

8.3.1 Capital Adequacy Ratio (CAR)

The CAR is the main indicator measuring banking soundness.[4] It refers to the amount of capital a bank should set aside as a proportion of its assets risk-weighted for credit, market, and operational risks of the bank on- and off-balance sheet items. It is calculated as the ratio of total capital (Tier 1 + Tier 2) to risk-weighted assets:

$$\text{The bank's capital ratio} = \frac{\text{Total capital}}{\text{Risk Weighted Assets}} = \frac{\text{Tier 1} + \text{Tier 2}}{\text{Risk Weighted Assets}}$$

Where Tier 1 capital consists of paid up capital and reserves and Tier 2 capital comprises long-term loans (Bank for International Settlement (BIS), 2010).

According to data in Figure 8.3, UAE banks have successfully managed to maintain their capital adequacy ratios above the minimum requirement set by Basel III Accords as well as the CBUAE. During the years that preceded the global financial crisis, Dubai banks were well capitalized but showed lower ratios compared to Abu Dhabi banks. However, when the financial crisis hit

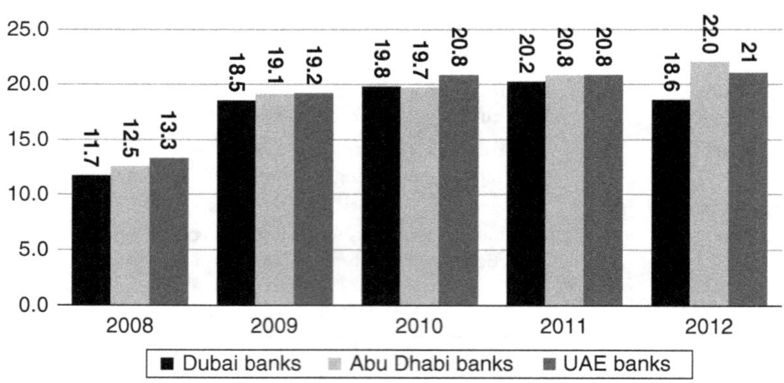

Figure 8.3. Average capital adequacy ratios in (%) for Dubai- and Abu Dhabi-based banks

Source: Securities and Commodities Authority (2013)

[4] In the aftermath of the financial crisis, the Basel Committee on banking supervision has set the minimum capital ratio at 8 per cent (as under Basel II accords) but has been strengthened by adding capital buffers that would increase the capital adequacy ratio in total to 10.5 per cent (under Basel III). The main objective behind the increase of the capital requirements is to enhance banking sector resilience to unexpected shocks and to promote financial stability. However, the CBUAE is currently requiring all operating banks in the country to achieve a minimum regulatory CAR of no less than 12 per cent effective from 30 June, 2010. Until the end of 2008, the ratio in the UAE was set at 10 per cent and was revised to 11 per cent in June 2009 and finally revised again to the current 12 per cent CAR ratio.

the global markets in 2008, capital adequacy ratios had declined significantly although they remained above the regulatory requirement of 10 per cent in place at that time. Dubai Banks maintained an average CAR of 11.7 per cent against 12.5 per cent in Abu Dhabi banks.

During the years 2009 and 2010, Dubai banks witnessed a significant improvement on their average capital adequacy ratio following the government intervention to provide financial support to troubled banks. Those banks have utilized the rescue package to strengthen their capital positions. Besides the government financial support, banks took some individual measures to help strengthen their capital base such as reducing their cash dividends and slowing their loan growth. These steps have helped banks to achieve average capital adequacy ratios of 18.9 per cent and 19.8 per cent in Dubai banks in 2009 and 2010, respectively. These high ratios are far above the minimum regulatory ratios of the CBUAE and seem to be costly.

Through 2011–12, Dubai banks continued to strengthen their capital bases so as to be ready to absorb potential losses following the surge in the level of NPLs and further restructuring of GRE debt. Average CAR ratio maintained high levels in 2011 and 2012 of 20.2 per cent and 18.6 per cent, respectively.

8.3.2 Tier 1 Capital Adequacy Ratios

Tier 1 capital ratio or core equity capital ratio provides another important indicator on bank capitalization since common equity makes up the main component of this ratio. Similar to the CAR ratio, it is calculated as the percentage of risk-weighted assets that should not get below the minima set by regulatory authorities.

According to Figure 8.4, before the crisis of 2008, Dubai banks showed high Tier 1 capitalization levels that exceeded the minimum requirements of

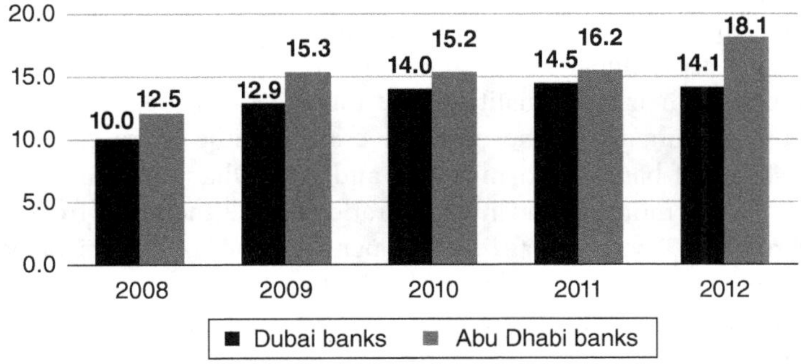

Figure 8.4. Average Tier 1 capital ratio for Dubai and Abu Dhabi banks
Source: Annual Financial Reports of UAE banks

8 per cent set by CBUAE and 6 per cent set by Basel III although they were below the average reported by Abu Dhabi banks. Even during the years of crisis in 2008 and 2009, Dubai banks maintained their capital well above these minimum requirements. The official intervention through capital injections and other instruments helped these banks minimize their losses and keep their capital above the regulatory minima. By 2010, Dubai banks—as well as Abu Dhabi banks—were in a better capitalization position. However, it is worth noting that CBUAE allows banks to hold hybrid instruments as part of their Tier 1 capital along with common equities which will not be allowed under Basel III. This suggests that UAE banks should revise their capital bases so as to include quality components that are better able to absorb shocks (i.e. common equity).

While increasing capital adequacy ratios is widely believed to provide an extra cushion to absorb potential losses for banks, it is also likely to increase borrowing costs for end users and reduce banks' profitability (Buehler et al., 2009). That is why regulators and policymakers should carefully examine 'how high is high enough' for minimum capital ratios.

In 2011 and 2012, Tier 1 ratios improved further to provide adequate buffers for any potential losses related to the further restructuring of the GRE debt and the rise in already high levels of NPLs that might happen as a result of the restructuring. Average Tier 1 capital ratios registered comfortable levels of 14.5 per cent and 14.1 per cent in 2011 and 2012.

8.3.3 Quality of Assets

Banks in Dubai and Abu Dhabi witnessed an improvement in the quality of their assets during the period that preceded the financial crisis when the ratio of NPLs to total gross loans (NPL) dropped from about 2.3 per cent in Dubai and 1.8 per cent in Abu Dhabi in 2005 to around 1.6 per cent and 1 per cent respectively in 2007. In 2008, UAE banks started to feel the heat of the financial turmoil as the ratio of NPLs increased in Abu Dhabi Banks to about 1.5 per cent. Dubai banks, on the other hand, did not see a significant deterioration in their asset quality at that time (see Figure 8.5).

In 2009, the impact of the financial crisis became more visible on the balance sheets of banks both in Dubai and Abu Dhabi. Yet the impact on Dubai banks was more significant as the ratio of NPLs increased from its 2008 level to reach 4.5 per cent against 3.5 per cent in Abu Dhabi banks. The deterioration in the asset quality of banks had been largely caused by the collapse in the real estate market and the associated impact on growth and employment.

During 2010, the NPLs ratio had almost doubled achieving an average of 9.2 per cent in Dubai banks against almost 6 per cent in Abu Dhabi. This was

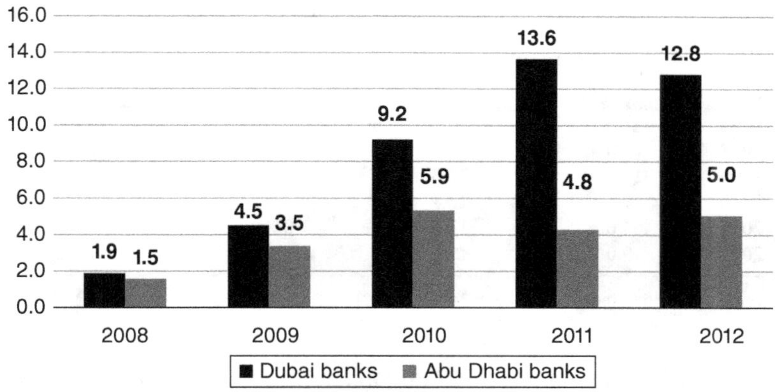

Figure 8.5. Average ratio of non-performing loans to total gross loans in Dubai- and Abu Dhabi-based banks

Source: Securities and Commodities Authority (2013)

largely the result of a continuing fall in property prices. The NPL ratio in Dubai banks would be higher if the GRE debt is classified—as it should be—among NPLs, especially if Dubai World (DW) and Dubai Holding (DH) are taken into consideration. Another reason that could explain the high levels of NPLs is the introduction of more tightening of the regulatory standards by the CBUAE by which the classification period of NPLs was reduced from 180 to 90 days. Generally, Abu Dhabi banks maintained a relatively better asset quality than Dubai banks but the gap between the two widened further after the financial crisis.

In 2011–12, the quality of asset portfolios continued to deteriorate with the average ratio of NPLs reaching unprecedented levels of 13.6 per cent and 12.8 per cent in 2011 and 2012, respectively. The NPL ratio is expected to increase further following the potential restructuring of GRE debt, including the already restricted debt. Joint CBU/IMF stress tests in 2013 revealed that the UAE banking system is resilient enough to absorb further increases in NPLs levels. However, a few banks fell somewhat below the minimum regulatory capital adequacy ratios when stress-tested for the event of extreme shock (International Monetary Fund, 2013).

8.3.4 Profitability Indicators

Despite the decreasing trend in profitability indicators, UAE banks remained profitable throughout the period 2005–10 and, somewhat surprisingly, also during the years of the crisis 2008–10 (see Table 8.4). Starting from their peak in 2005 when the average return over equity (ROE) ratio reached 23.8 per cent

Table 8.4. Profitability indicators in UAE banks

	Return on equity		Return on assets	
Year	Dubai banks	Abu Dhabi banks	Dubai banks	Abu Dhabi banks
2008	18.0	19.3	1.9	2.1
2009	11.4	10.3	1.3	1.2
2010	8.1	15.1	1.0	1.6
2011	4.6	17.6	0.72	1.8
2012	9.0	13.0	1.27	1.8

Source: Securities and Commodities Authority (2013)

in Dubai against 28.5 per cent in Abu Dhabi, benefiting from substantial fees and margin interest income they made in that year. In 2006, a sharp correction in equity markets impacted the profitability of the banking sector in UAE. However, strong retail banking, credit growth, and diversification helped mitigate the impact on bank profits.

In the following years, UAE banks continued to witness a declining trend in profitability which reached its lowest level in 2010, reporting an average ROE of 8.1 per cent in Dubai banks against 15.1 per cent in Abu Dhabi banks as a result of the increasing NPL ratios and the associated provisioning as well as the banks' willingness to improve their liquidity profile.

In 2011, banks' profitability has almost halved to 4.6 per cent due to balance sheets losses resulting from high NPL levels and increased provisioning. However, banks regained momentum in 2012 against the backdrop of a continued recovery in construction and real estate sectors, registering an average of 9 per cent compared to 13 per cent in Abu Dhabi banks.

8.3.5 Liquidity Issues

The financial crisis of 2008–10 highlighted the importance of liquidity to the adequate functioning of the banking sector and the financial system in general. To this end, the Basel committee on banking supervision (BCBS) introduced a consultative document providing detailed guidance for a better liquidity risk-management framework. In that document, the Basel Committee developed two minimum standards for funding liquidity, namely: a liquidity coverage ratio (LCR) to help promote the short-term resilience of banks' liquidity and a net stable funding ratio (NSFR) which aims at promoting banks' liquidity over a longer time horizon.

The UAE's financial system was no exception to the liquidity crisis associated with the global financial turmoil which in 2008 put all financial systems in the world under significant liquidity pressures. In fact, shortly before the crisis,

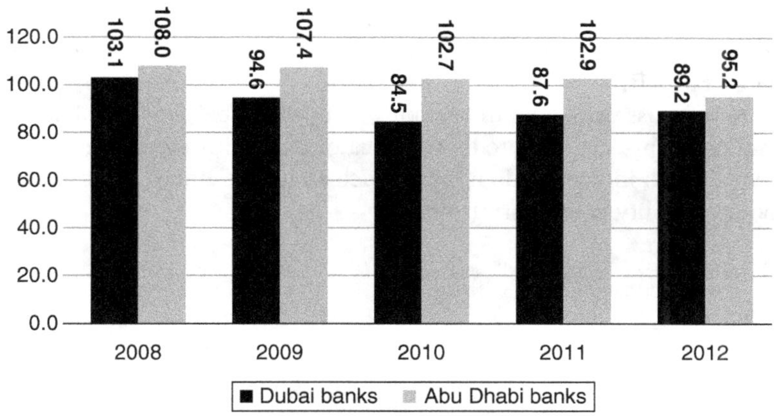

Figure 8.6. Loans-to-deposits ratio in Dubai and Abu Dhabi
Source: Securities and Commodities Authority (2013)

markets had witnessed the arrival of large amounts of capital inflows, mostly short term in nature and for speculative purposes. Nevertheless, after governmental assurances that the hard peg of the UAE dirham to the US$ would not be changed in 2008, foreign investors started to excessively withdraw their money from the UAE because of the deterioration of their financial positions and credit standings in their respective countries. This created a liquidity shortage as short-term deposits were used by Dubai-/UAE-based banks to finance long-term projects, which eventually led to a direct intervention by the federal government and the CBUAE to inject liquidity into banks at favourable interest rates.

Figure 8.6 illustrates the changes in loans-to-deposits ratios—the only liquidity indicator currently observed by the CBUAE—both in Dubai and Abu Dhabi. The figure shows a downward trend of these ratios in Dubai banks throughout the post-crisis period reflecting better liquidity management during the period 2009–12 that allowed the ratio to be kept below the regulatory limit set by CBUAE at 100 per cent. However, for Abu Dhabi banks the data show evidence of liquidity pressures with an average loans-to-deposits ratio ranging between 108 per cent in 2008 and 102.9 per cent in 2011.

Several factors have contributed to the increases in liquidity levels in Dubai banks. Most important of which is the broadening recovery of economic activity that helped attract more deposits to the banks which remain in a circumspect mood of lending. Also, the increasing capital inflows from the region following the social unrest that swept many Arab countries have helped strengthen liquidity in the UAE banking system. Moreover, banks have taken some measures to improve their liquidity profiles in order to comply with the new set of rules and regulations introduced by the CBUAE which require banks to adhere to some qualitative, quantitative, and reporting requirements on liquidity risk management following the new banking requirements introduced by Basel III.

Overall, the assessment of the banking sector in Dubai shows that banks are on a solid footing according to these indicators, but with a warning that, being prudential, such indicators do not say much about the efficiency of the system or about its ability to support growth.

8.4 THE PERSISTING ISSUES IN DUBAI'S FINANCIAL SECTOR

As discussed, the banking sector in Dubai/UAE weathered the 2008–10 crisis thanks to a combination of favourable initial conditions, forceful government intervention, and adequate regulation and supervision. However, the crisis revealed some other persisting, unresolved issues that should be addressed to maintain the positive prospects for banks. These problems are related to banks' exposures to GREs, the pressure of the amortization of the financial public support, and the limited access of the business sector to bank finance.

8.4.1 The Problem of Government-related Entities (GREs)

The growth performance achieved by Dubai during the pre-crisis period witnessed the emergence of some GREs as important players especially in the real estate sector. Elbadawi (2014) provides a description of recent developments in the land and real estate markets and highlights the role of GREs. However, such developments did not happen without taking significant risks and accumulating massive debts. The global financial crisis of 2008 forced the emirate to undertake a severe correction in the overvalued real estate sector (a drop in prices and rents of around 50 per cent) and the ensuing domestic financial crisis was centred on the debt-restructuring of Dubai World (DW) and other public companies.

The high exposure of some banks to GREs largely affected the banking sector in the post-crisis period as 16 per cent of the Dubai banks' loans and 9 per cent of the whole banking system's lending were directed towards these public entities. For example, in the case of Dubai World (DW), local banks were owed 40 per cent of the debt subject to restructuring (US$14.4 billion), of which 60 per cent was concentrated in Dubai banks (International Monetary Fund, 2011). In this context, banks with higher proportions of restructured loans on their books should be better prepared to absorb contingent liabilities from falling property values and the announced decline in federal government support to banks starting from 2012. The DW debt standstill also caused a significant increase in the sovereign debt and closed access to international capital markets; the government of Dubai (GD) regained financial markets' access only in September 2010 but with a higher cost compared to similar sovereign issuers. The first GRE that was allowed to regain access to international markets was Dubai Electricity and Water Authority (DEWA) which issued a US$1 billion bond in April 2010.

The year 2013 witnessed the completion of a large part of the GRE debt-restructurings related to the last crisis. However, several major maturities are falling due in 2014[5] and the restructured debt of Dubai World and Nakheel is also drawing closer (2015–16) which imposes a clear and timely communication about these maturities (International Monetary Fund, 2013).

8.4.2 The Banking Sector in Dubai Is Sound but Has to Withstand Further Pressure

The analysis in this section shows that the post-crisis period witnessed a significant improvement in regulatory ratios in the aggregate banking system making it compliant with Basel III requirements and able to withstand further pressure. The stress tests[6] carried out by the International Monetary Fund (2011) for aggregate banks in UAE and Dubai using end-of-2010 data and two scenarios where NPLs are equal to 10 per cent and 15 per cent, respectively, show that the banking system in Dubai/UAE could withstand the stress as they would still be compliant with minimum requirements on the aggregate.[7] More specifically, for banks operating in Dubai, the regulatory capital ratio was predicted to fall to 15.3 per cent and 19.2 per cent in 2011 with NPLs equal to 15 per cent and 10 per cent, respectively (see Table 8.5). Nevertheless, it is worth noting that although Dubai banks would meet the regulatory minima in the aggregate, it is possible that some of them would not be able to meet such targets especially those with higher risk of exposure to GREs. The International Monetary Fund (IMF) simulations display also low Tier 1 ratios in Dubai

[5] The year 2013 witnessed the completion of a large part of the GRE debt-restructurings related to the last crisis. Several major maturities due in 2014 were also restructured when the government of Abu Dhabi and the Central Bank of the UAE agreed to roll over the debt for five years at a 1 per cent annual interest rate. Still, the restructuring of the debt of Dubai World and Nakheel is also drawing closer (2015–16) which imposes a clear and timely communication about these maturities (International Monetary Fund, 2013).

[6] The bank stress tests received a great deal of attention in the aftermath of the latest financial crisis. They are designed to determine if a bank has enough capital to withstand the impact of crisis situations, so that necessary actions can be taken by the regulatory oversight of the banks.

[7] Simulations assume that provisioning is maintained at a high 90 per cent according to IFRS regulations and that half of 2010 profits are retained by banks.

Table 8.5. Stress tests for aggregate local and Dubai banks

	Aggregate Dubai banks		Local banks in UAE		
	Regulatory capital	Tier 1 capital	Regulatory capital	Tier 1 capital	Comments
2009 capital ratios	19.7%	13.8%	19.9%	16.0%	Tier 2 capital provided by government
2010 pre-provision earnings	11,000	—	32,000	—	—
2010 profits (AED m)	4,500	—	18,000	—	—
2010 CAR	20.2%	14.3%	20.8%	16.9%	Assuming 50% of profits retained[1]
NPL ratio (end of 2010)	8%	—	5.9%	—	—
Provision rate (end 2010)	87%	—	89%	—	IFRS general and specific
Provisions if NPLs rise to 10% in 2010	10,000	—	38,000	—	Assuming provision rate of 90% on new NPLs[2,3]
2011 CAR with NPLs of 10%	19.2%	13.3%	18.7%	14.8%	Assuming 50% lower pre-provisions earnings
2011 CAR with NPLs of 15%	15.3%	9.4%	14.8%	10.9%	—
Minimum regulatory capital	12%	8.0%	12.0%	8.0%	—
Total assets (AED bn)	550	—	1,352	—	—
Risk weighted assets (AED bn)	411	—	1,055	—	—

[1] In line with Central Bank Instructions that limit distribution of 2010 profits.
[2] Including Dubai Holding provisions of 20 per cent of original principal.
[3] Assuming local banks exposure to Dubai holding is 90 per cent with Dubai banks 50 per cent.
Source: International Monetary Fund (IMF) (2011)

banks compared to UAE banks in 2011, especially with the severe scenario test of (NPLs = 15 per cent). This ratio (9.4 per cent) means a greater pressure on Dubai banks, especially with the provisioning commitment.

However, it has to be noted that banks operating in Dubai will still have to deal with the decline in capital support by the federal government over the medium term. In fact, the banks have to deal with the amortization of such support in the form of capital notes ending in 2012. According to the International Monetary Fund (2011), the capital notes' amortization would imply a decline in the bank's regulatory ratio by 1 per cent each year during the period 2013–17 which would need more retained earnings for the replacement of maturing notes with Tier 1 equity.

8.4.3 The Business Sector Has Limited Access to Bank Finance

Despite the relatively developed financial sector in Dubai,[8] firms have little access to bank finance and seem to prefer internal funds for financing business operations. In fact, according to the Business Environment and Enterprise Performance Survey 2010 (Dubai Economic Council, 2010) conducted with a sample of 709 firms located in Main Dubai and free zones, the percentage of firms that have either a line of credit or a loan from different financial institutions constituted 16.6 per cent from the total number of firms[9] (see Figure 8.7). By firm size, the group of large firms had the highest percentage of firms with a line of credit or loan (35.8 per cent) given their high capacity to meet collateral requirements, while the group of small and medium enterprises (SMEs)[10] had only 14.6 per cent (see Figure 8.7). This result is consistent with the findings of many other studies (e.g. Schiffer and Weder, 2001; Beck et al., 2005; Beck et al., 2008; and Rocha et al., 2011) which show that SMEs are traditionally more constrained by financial obstacles compared to large firms.

In a recent survey and research paper (Rocha et al., 2011) jointly conducted by the World Bank and the Union of Arab banks on a sample of MENA banks, the share of lending to SMEs was only 2 per cent of banks' total lending in GCC countries (in UAE, the share was only 4 per cent, still the highest among all GCC countries) as opposed to 15 per cent in non-GCC MENA countries (see Figure 8.8).

This lack of adequate access to finance can be accounted for by many reasons.

First, banks abstained from extending credit and attempted to augment their deposits as a result of the requirements of Basel III vis-à-vis the quantity and quality of capital and liquidity buffers (see Figure 8.9).

Second, the cost of credit was perceived as high in the post-crisis period which contributed significantly to reducing the demand for bank loans. In fact, given the incapacity of monetary policy to work properly in the UAE as a result of the fixed exchange rate, the repo (policy) rate was not effective in influencing market rates used by banks especially in the post crisis period (Maratheftis, 2009). When the CBUAE reduced the repo rate to as low as 1 per cent in July 2008, the deposit rate witnessed a decrease in the following years, however, given the will of banking institutions to achieve minimum net

[8] See Boughrara (2010) for a comprehensive analysis of the financial sector in Dubai.

[9] Despite the importance of the result, the Business Environment and Enterprise Performance Survey 2010, seems to underestimate the access to finance as firms are only asked if they currently have a loan from a financial institution or if they applied for a loan in the past.

[10] SMEs are defined as enterprises with up to 99 employees.

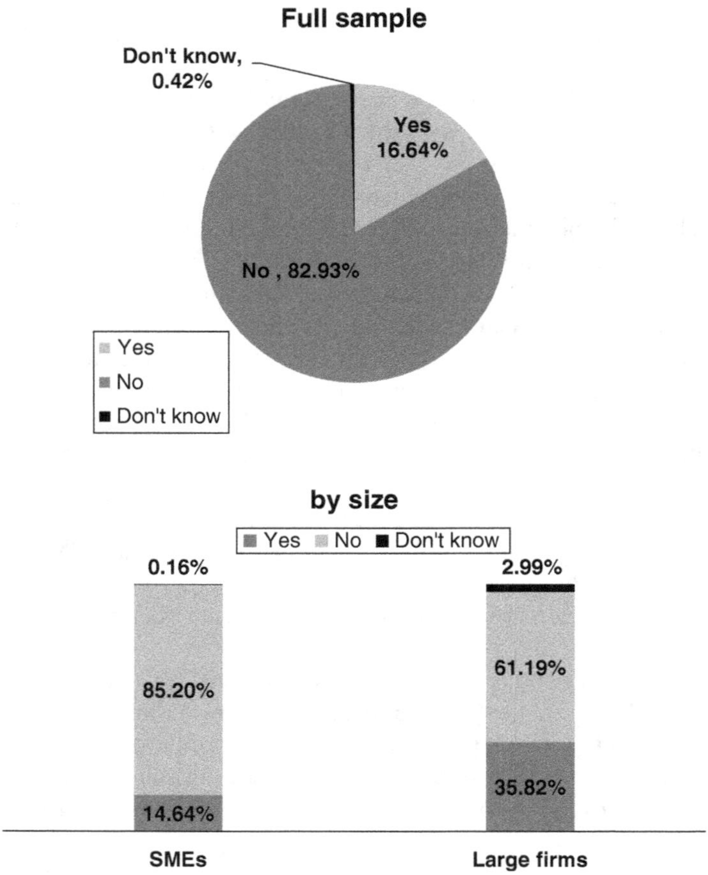

Figure 8.7. Percentage of firms that have a line of credit or a loan from a financial institution

Source: Dubai Economic Council (2010)

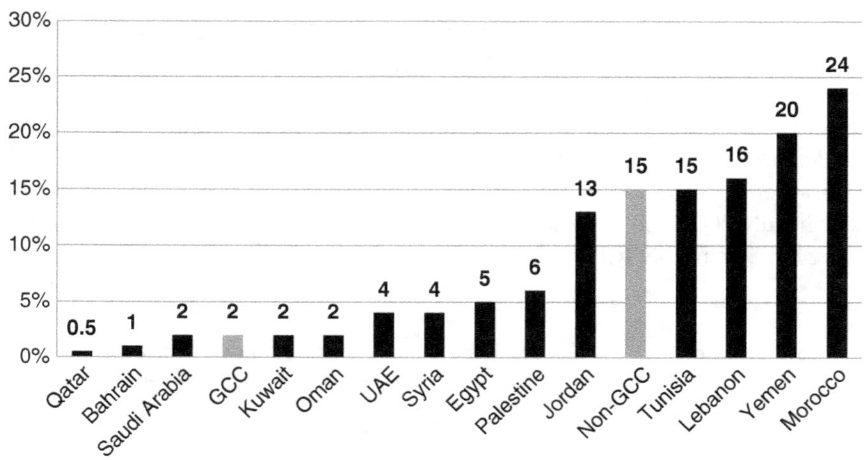

Figure 8.8. SMEs loans/total loans (%), MENA countries

Source: Rocha et al. (2011) and authors own elaboration

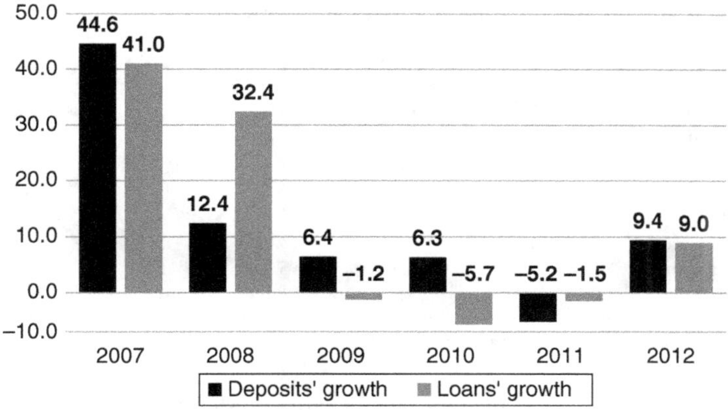

Figure 8.9. Growth rate of loans and deposits in Dubai banks
Source: Securities and Commodities Authority (2013)

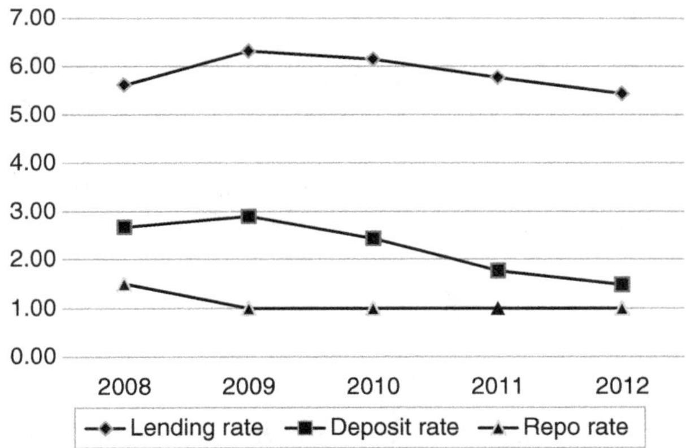

Figure 8.10. The net interest margin and the repo rate
Source: Central Bank of the UAE (2013) and Securities and Commodities Authority (2013)

interest margin income, the resulting lending rates were high enough to discourage firms' demand for bank loans from 2008 (see Figure 8.10).

Additionally, the interest rate spread in UAE, equal to the difference between the lending and deposit rates, is not substantially high compared to its peers in the region and even to Singapore and Hong Kong, but it is still far from the average in developed countries which is revolving around 1 per cent (Table 8.6). This may be accounted for by the absence of competition in the banking sector as the top five banks dominate the sector with roughly 60 per cent of the banking sector's assets and in most of them the government is a majority shareholder. Moreover, the sector is not yet fully open to foreign

Table 8.6. Interest rate spread in selected countries

Country	2008	2009	2010	2011	2012
Bahrain	6.6	6.4	6.0	5.8	5.0
Kuwait	2.8	3.3	2.6	3.0	2.9
Qatar	3.9	2.8	4.4	3.7	3.7
UAE	2.94	3.41	3.71	4.00	3.96
MENA	3.6	3.7	4.4	4.4	3.9
Hong Kong	4.6	5.0	5.0	5.0	5.0
Singapore	5.0	5.1	5.2	5.2	5.2
Japan	1.3	1.3	1.1	1.0	0.9

Source: World Bank (2013) and Securities and Commodities Authority (2013)

competition since entry barriers remain in place, including that foreign banks are not allowed to acquire majority ownership and face higher taxes on their profits.

Finally, the insufficient access to credit may be accounted for by unsuitable collateral especially in the case of SMEs. In fact, since SMEs' capital stock is composed to a large extent of movable assets (i.e. machinery, equipment, and receivables), banks are usually reluctant to accept such assets as collateral and have a greater preference for land, buildings, and real estate. Moreover, the lack of reliable financial statements and poor information about firms' managerial quality, especially SMEs, are also cited as important factors that account for the perceived low creditworthiness of SMEs.

8.5 CONCLUSIONS

As in all countries, the financial system has been instrumental in the promotion of economic growth in Dubai and the UAE by providing funds to the entrepreneurial sector, easing the exchange of goods and services, mobilizing savings, and diversifying risks. Furthermore, the authorities have ambitiously aimed at transforming Dubai into a regional financial hub capable of serving business in the Gulf and the Middle East in a similar form to how Singapore and Hong Kong operate in Asia. To a large extent, this latter mandate has been developed successfully within the confines of an off-shore facility, the DIFC, which operates in isolation from the internal financial sector comprising national and foreign banks located primarily in Dubai and Abu Dhabi.

The internal financial sector, which is the subject of this chapter, has also developed gradually but in a far more conservative manner. Its main feature is the presence of institutional limitations and restrictions that prevent healthy competition between domestic and foreign institutions. Protection has benefited domestic banks and allowed for sustained expansion (largely by extending credit to GREs) but as shown during the 2008–10 crisis it has reduced competition, softened prudential policies, and allowed excessive risk-taking. The timely and decisive reactions by the local authorities—which provided liquidity and restored confidence in financial institutions—avoided higher adjustment costs after the real estate market collapsed.

As expected, the crisis made clear the need to enhance regulations and, particularly, improve risk assessment tools, but it also unveiled two areas where substantial reforms are urgently needed. First, the solution to the GREs debt overhang, which include rescheduling and repayment of debts, and the expansion and deepening of the internal financial sector, in particular in order to improve access to the financing of new investment.

In this chapter we analysed the financial sector in Dubai through the assessment of its soundness indicators as well as the persisiting issues that the sector should tackle in the years to come. Overall, the banking sector in Dubai has shown comfortable levels of capitalization. However Dubai-based banks still present significant exposure to GREs, deeply involved in real estate and construction activities. Following the 2008 crisis, the NPLs ratio, as a measure of assets quality, witnessed a significant increase achieving an average of 8 per cent in 2010 due mainly to falling property prices. This ratio would be even higher if GREs' loans and in particular Dubai World (DW) and Dubai Holding Group (DH) were systematically classified as NPLs.

As for profitability, a close inspection of individual banks' balance sheets reveals a declining trend in profitability as measured by average returns on equities (ROAE) and assets (ROAA) since 2008. The ROAE in Dubai banks witnessed a sharp decline from 23.8 per cent in 2005 to 8.1 per cent in 2010 reflecting to a large extent banks' efforts to increase their provisioning and their willingness to improve their liquidity profile. The second indicator, the ROAA, displays the same declining pattern in profitability. However, despite the decreasing trend in profitability indicators, profits remained positive in banks even during the post-crisis period.

On the liquidity side, the banking sector in Dubai/UAE depicted an upward trend in the loan-to-deposit ratio during the pre-crisis period, reflecting a low liquidity level and a potential stress on the sector. The ratio increased far above the regulatory threshold set by the CBUAE at 100 per cent with an average reaching 103.1 per cent and 108 per cent in Dubai and Abu Dhabi banks respectively in 2008. The sovereign risk spread, declining asset prices, and large capital outflows intensified the liquidity shortage of banks already suffering from the global financial turmoil. The government intervention after the crisis seems to have eased the strains on UAE banks as many of them succeeded in reducing significantly the loan-to-deposit ratio even below the CBUAE limit.

The chapter also points out that the aggregate banking sector seems able to withstand further pressure thanks to its high capitalization base. The stress tests carried out by the International Monetary Fund (2011) on UAE and Dubai banks, with two different scenarios where NPLs are set at 10 per cent and 15 per cent respectively; show that they could withstand the stress as they would still be compliant with minimum requirements at the aggregate level. However, Dubai banks still have to deal with restructured real estate and construction credits with maturities starting after 2014 and the amortization of the government financial support in the form of capital notes ending in 2012.

Another finding that has been highlighted based on the 'Business Environment and Enterprise Performance Survey 2010' is that firms in Dubai have low access to bank finance and seem to prefer internal funds for financing business operations. This might be attributed to (i) the bulk of proposals under Basel III that forced the banks to abstain from extending their lending; (ii) the high cost of credit in the banking sector; and (iii) the lack of suitable collateral, especially in the case of SMEs.

It is also worth noting that although the banking sector has been closely monitored by financial and monetary authorities in UAE in the aftermath of the financial crisis of 2008–10 through effectively taken actions, it seems that more is still needed to keep up the momentum of development. This could be done through the implementation of the following policy measures.

First, there is a need to improve risk management practices in Dubai-based banks. In this context, banks need also to invest more in risk management through acquiring additional infrastructure to improve data, reporting systems, and validation capacity, particularly those using the more advanced approaches in measuring credit risk. Likewise, the banks need to strengthen the role of the chief risk officer and to establish an internal risk monitoring committee that oversees on a regular basis the implementation of its risk management policy. Better credit risk management in banks also implies the revision of collateral policies adopted so far, as well as the diversification of their loans' portfolios in a way that allows them to reduce their high level of exposure to the real estate and construction sectors.

Second, the role of the Central Bank is very important through the supervision and the surveillance of risk management practices. Specifically, the CBUAE should adopt more sophisticated instruments to deal with credit risk in the banking system which is likely to target institutions that might impact systemic risk. The underlying idea is that even with more stringent safety measures laid down by new Basel requirements, the likelihood of future periods of stress would not be reduced significantly without strengthened surveillance over bank risk management practices by financial authorities.

Third, the financial sector needs the development of a local bond market that would allow the issuing of federal government securities along with the recapitalization of the banking sector. It would also provide an alternative to public as well as private infrastructure spending that is expected to resume in the years to come, and this would help avoid issuing foreign currency-denominated sovereign bonds in international markets.

Fourth, there is a pressing need to set more elaborate corporate governance standards in the banking sector. In this context, it is strongly advisable that banks define a permanent corporate governance structure that improves policy implementation and internal control procedures as well as standard operations. Better governance implies also an improvement in the board's capability for independent decision-making along with increased checks and balances and accountability.

Fifth, it is also strongly recommended to have risk management frameworks for GREs to avoid extended borrowing from local banks or international markets as well as frequent demands for bailouts. For that there should be regular assessments and monitoring of contingent liabilities and their maturity profiles arising from GREs activities.

REFERENCES

Bank for International Settlement (BIS), 2010. *Basel III: A Global Regulatory Framework for More Resilient Banks and Banking Systems,* Basel: Basel Committee on Banking Supervision.

Beck, T., Demirgüç-Kunt, A., and Maksimovic, V., 2005. 'Financial and Legal Constraints to Firm Growth: Does Firm Size Matter?' *Journal of Finance,* 60(1): 137–77.

Beck, T., Demirguc-Kunt, A., and Martinez Peria, M., 2008. 'Bank Financing for SMEs around the World: Drivers, Obstacles, Business Models and Lending Practices'. World Bank Policy Research Working Paper No. 4785.

Boughrara, A., 2010. *Dubai Financial Sector: Development and Performance,* Dubai: Dubai Economic Council, Dubai Government.

Buehler, K., Samandari, H., and Mazingo, C., 2009. Capital Ratios and Financial Distress: Lessons from the Crisis. *McKinsey Working Papers on Risk.*

Central Bank of the UAE, 2013. *Monthly Statistical Bulletin.* [Online] Available at: http://www.centralbank.ae/en/index.php?option=com_content&view=article&id=73&Itemid=114, accessed 2 September 2015.

Chailloux, A. and Hakura, D., 2009. 'Systemic Liquidity Management in the UAE: Issues and Options'. IMF Working Paper Series, September, No. WP/09/261.

Dubai Economic Council, 2010. *Business Environment and Enterprise Performance Survey.* Dubai: Dubai Economic Council, Dubai Government.

International Monetary Fund, 2007. *Country Report No 07/357: United Arab Emirates: Financial System Stability Assessment,* Washington, DC: International Monetary Fund.

International Monetary Fund, 2011. *IMF Country Report No. 11/12: United Arab Emirates: Selected Issues and Statistical Appendix,* Washington, DC: International Monetary Fund.

International Monetary Fund, 2013. *World Economic Outlook,* Washington, DC: International Monetary Fund.

Khamis, M. and Senhadji, A., 2010. *Impact of the Global Financial Crisis on the Gulf Cooperation Council Countries and Challenges Ahead,* Washington, DC: International Monetary Fund.

Maratheftis, M., 2009. 'Monetary Policy: Constraints and Measures'. Dubai Economic Council Working Paper (June) No. 05.

Rocha, R., Farazi, S., Khouri, R., and Pearce, D., 2011. 'The Status of Bank Lending to SMEs in the Middle East and North Africa Region: The Results of a Joint Survey of the Union of Arab Bank and the World Bank'. World Bank Policy Research Working Paper No. 5607.

Schiffer, M., and Weder, B., 2001. 'Firm Size and the Business Environment: Worldwide Survey Results'. International Finance Corporation Discussion Paper 43.

Securities and Commodities Authority, 2013. *Financial Reports.* [Online] Available at: http://esm.sca.ae/English/Securities/shares/Pages/FinancialReports.aspx, accessed December 2013.

World Bank, 2013. *World Development Indicators,* Washington, DC: World Bank Group.

9

The Retail Sector: Prospects and Potential

Boaz Nandwa and Hessa Al Ameemi

9.1 INTRODUCTION

In a matter of two decades retail activities in Dubai have become one of its major industries and a source of sustained economic growth. As of 2012, retail activities represented around 15 per cent of Dubai's GDP (Dubai Statistics Center, 2013). Broadly speaking, retail activities comprise 'the sale of goods or commodities in small quantities directly to consumers or final end users'. However, this is a rather limited vision of what retail markets with regional scope actually do and ramifications of what they do. While selling at retail can be succinctly defined as above, the retail industry involves not only the producers, the consumers, and the sellers, but also comprise other linked activities that, in a complex and advanced economy such as Dubai, frequently interact with retailers to provide its characteristic shape to the business. The definition of retail business, therefore, encompasses a myriad of transactions and activities directed to consumers or end users, and this tends to differ given the country-specific or regional structural characteristics.

The retail sector can be identified along different criteria or dimensions. In principle, the standard classification of the retail sector is according to the type of goods and services offered, as outlined by the North American Product Classification System (NAPCS). The NAPCS identifies fifty-two separate retail segments, each selling its own type of merchandise.[1] Further, the market segment can also be classified according to the quality of goods and the type of customers. These would include, for example, luxury goods (expensive and well-known brands), middle-end products (neither pricey nor inexpensive), and the lower-end products (easily affordable and used daily). The different types of goods and services are placed in the market with very diverse retail strategies aimed at households that vary widely in terms of taste and income.

[1] US Census Bureau (2011).

This kind of classification might be helpful but, compared to regional and global retail industry, it would be limited in the case of Dubai. This is because the salient characteristics of retailing in Dubai have been developed according to different business models. In Dubai, retail is distinctively associated with large-sized thematic malls where shopping is provided along with entertainment, hostelling, supermarkets, and a large variety of customer services. In addition, Dubai's retailing encompasses off-mall single shops and community shopping centres.

In Dubai, retail activities have grown to maturity: its shopping malls are among the largest and most sophisticated in the world, luxury brands thrive, and the population benefits from access to a wide variety of goods and services in all qualities. The traditional form of retail—individual shops alongside the street—has also successfully consolidated and transformed in different areas of the city (from Deira to Bur Dubai), benefiting from their ability to sell in market niches such as textiles, gold, and perfumes.

9.2 SALIENT FEATURES OF THE RETAIL SECTOR

Dubai is based on a long-standing tradition of free-trade initiatives and policies, under which the retail activities have today grown to maturity.[2] Almost all of the categories outlined in NAPCS are present in Dubai, indicating the presence of a wide variety of goods and services. Furthermore, Dubai retailers offer an ample range of qualities for these goods and services. While the classification according to the nature and quality of goods and services is helpful, it would be limited in the case of Dubai. The salient characteristic of retailing in Dubai is that it has been provided basically along two types of business models: shopping malls and off-mall, single-shop retailing. Dubai's shopping malls are among the largest and most sophisticated in the world. Moreover, traditional single-shop retail has successfully consolidated in market niches such as gold, computers, and perfumes. The retail sector in Dubai followed different business models which have evolved over the years. The initial business model was the off-mall single retail shop that was developed along the creek and whose activities were the initial driver of the retail industry since they helped establish Dubai as the major trade centre on the Gulf coast and the regional centre for foreign trade and financing. The single shop offers customers competitive prices for non-branded goods and allows people to

[2] See Dubai Economic Council (2011) for a comprehensive review of the history and transformation of the retail sector in Dubai. The Appendix provides a timeline history of Dubai's retail industry between 1950 and 2013.

Table 9.1. Sales in mass grocery retail in the UAE (in AED bn)

	2002	2003	2004	2005	2006	2007	2008	2009	2010
Supermarkets	1.58	1.84	2.06	2.46	2.97	3.60	4.40	4.71	5.09
Hypermarkets	4.99	5.47	6.13	6.97	7.96	9.18	10.72	11.32	12.17
Convenience stores	0.26	0.29	0.33	0.40	0.44	0.55	0.62	0.69	0.78
Total	6.83	7.60	8.51	9.84	11.38	13.32	15.74	16.72	18.04

Source: BMI UAE Retail Report, 2010 and UAE Ministry of Planning

bargain to obtain good prices for their purchased items. In addition, they are known to be specialized in certain market niches (e.g. the Gold Souk, Spice Souk, and Textile Market) that offer unique products. Therefore, those traditional shops retain a significant portion of the core activities.

However, in the last twenty years, the traditional shopping areas of Dubai have lost space to the dynamic explosion of shopping malls as seen in Table 9.1. Shopping-mall retail is the result of massive, organized investments by real estate developers who were largely anticipating the future growth of Dubai and the shopping needs of the population. These shopping malls offer customers a variety of products, a better shopping experience (e.g. air conditioned facilities, parking), and family entertainment (e.g. Ski Dubai in the Mall of the Emirates). The shopping mall concentrates on the largest share of the market for the high-end users and luxury goods. They also retail to a substantial part of the middle-income segment of the market for entertainment, groceries, and clothing.

In the last decade, community centres were founded in the UAE as a new alternative to the urbanites living in housing developments relatively distant from major shopping centres. These centres resemble the strip-malls in the US and Canada, but without the gas station. They are typically in-between shopping malls and off-mall retail shops in terms of size and product variety. They are service oriented and host a supermarket and a few other shops to attract people within the residential area. They offer a reduced menu of products but still provide for the daily shopping needs of their targeted customers. A new form of retail in this core component is the Aswaaq (cooperative), which is a government agency that provides a retail approach deeply rooted in the needs of the community it serves whereby customers benefit from both an attractive price–quality ratio for goods and a return on purchases through loyalty programmes.

Finally, the Dubai Duty Free, the fourth key activity which forms part of the core industry, is the single largest airport retailer in the world. In 2010, its turnover reached a record of AED4.66 bn (US$1.27 bn) representing a 14 per cent increase over 2009 figures, making it comparable to sales by supermarkets in Dubai. Dubai Duty Free, which is an integral part of the retail industry, caters to a very specific market segment of international travellers and connecting passengers at the Dubai International Airport.

9.2.1 Related Industries and Activities Supporting the Retail Sector in Dubai

Related industries refers to other industries that shape the form in which activities in Dubai have developed (e.g. real estate) or which are expected to play a significant role in the future (e.g. tourism). The core of the retail industry is connected to four other related industries: tourism, construction and real estate, transport and logistics, and finance.[3] The demand for retail goods and services by tourists has shaped the appearance and the expansion of the shopping malls in Dubai. Available data show that the total number of Dubai tourists and population has been increasing substantially. Also, according to the statistics, the city hotel guests increased from 2 million in 1998 to over 7.5 million in 2009 and the population grew from fewer than 600,000 inhabitants in 1990 to almost two million in 2010. This increase in the number of tourists and in the population has reshaped the city to fulfil the needs of its population. For example, massive investments in housing and infrastructure occurred; more shopping malls and community centres were built. Hence, the providence of the retail services to that of the construction and real estate industries is directly linked to tourism.

Since its formation in the early twentieth century, transport and logistics has been closely linked to retail trading activities. Initially, Dubai creek waterway played a major role in the movements of commodities into and out of Dubai. Through the creek, Dubai became the chief partner for Southern Iran and the supplier for the rest of the Trucial coast through warehousing goods that were transported down the coast. Later, seaports, airports, and a high-quality road network have played the integral task of supporting retail and enhancing its activities in Dubai. Dubai airport's duty free store provides a vivid example of the connectivity of both activities. The retail sector has benefited from the top-notch capacities of the logistics sector in Dubai—among the top-five in the world—to provide the low-cost, in-time services that increase the retail industry's competitiveness.

The financial services industry is instrumental in providing credit and liquidity to retail operations. The recent crunch in domestic credit as a result of the global recession attests to the importance of the financial sector for retail activities, both by financing the purchasing of durable goods by consumers

[3] For an insight on Dubai industries, see Dubai Economic Council (2009).

as well as by providing working capital and long-term operating capital for retailers.

Further, there is a significant number of suppliers who provide various goods and services that directly support the core of the retail industry, ranging from promotion to packaging. For example, the Dubai shopping promotion campaigns such as Dubai Shopping Festival (DSF) and Dubai Summer Surprises (DSS) are scheduled annually to boost demand for the retail industry and involve a large number of retailers. Marketing activities undertaken by specialized agencies and the shops themselves are an essential component of retailing that raise awareness and provide consumers with information about the availability of the wide range of goods in shopping malls and other shops.

Moreover, wholesale activities are the backbone of the retail industry as they provide the necessary intermediation of goods from the producers to the retailers. Product design deals with the efficient and effective idea of development through a process that leads to new products in the market. Packaging can be described as a coordinated system of preparing goods for transport, warehousing, logistics, sales, and end use. These services are frequently used by the retailers—especially small- and medium-scale firms that outsource their needs to providers—in designing and delivering their goods to increasingly demanding markets.

9.2.2 Dubai Government Agencies and the Retail Sector

Government regulations and trade supporting agencies are an essential component of the retail industry in Dubai. The government agencies that have a direct relation to the retail sector are: the UAE Ministry of Economy which provides the federal laws and regulation for establishing businesses in the UAE; the Dubai Economic Department which is responsible for licensing and approving economic activities in Dubai; the Dubai Events and Promotions Establishment that is responsible for the shopping events and promotions. Finally, the UAE Ministry of Labour covers aspects related to labour policy issues.

9.3 OUTLOOK OF THE RETAIL SECTOR

The retail activities affect much of the economic activities in Dubai and, at the same time, are affected by the related activities of the other sectors, such as real estate, finance, transport and logistics, and tourism. Official statistics in the national accounts of Dubai refer generally to internal trade, that is, they refer

Table 9.2. Relative size of the retail industry (in % of total GDP)

Contribution to total value added	2002	2006	2007	2008	2009	2010	Average 2006/10
Retail[e]	20.5	13.2	13.1	12.7	12.6	13.0	12.9
Wholesale[e]	26.7	16.3	14.7	14.3	14.2	17.3	14.9
Real estate	5.3	16.2	17.9	17.6	14.4	13.7	16.5
Construction	9.8	11.4	11.9	13.6	11.2	9.4	12.0
Financial sector	9.4	9.7	10.6	11.0	11.7	11.3	10.8

[e] estimated. Data for 2010 is not available.
Source: Own elaboration based on data from Dubai Statistics Center

to an aggregate of wholesale and retail activities as well as repairing services.[4] Individual components are not publicly available and this study has, therefore, been constrained to devise a methodology to account for the fraction that corresponds to retail activities in Dubai's national accounts.[5] From the available microeconomic data, the proportion of economic activities accrued by retail is estimated. Real values are used to take into account the significant impact of inflation in the 2008–9 period. The results, which are presented in Table 9.2, are indicative of the main trends in the activity of the retail industry.

It can be seen that the retail industry accounted for 13 per cent of total economic activity in the last four years and, consequently, it is one of the most important sectors in Dubai's economy. As a point of reference, it is about the same size as the other most important sectors in the economy, namely the wholesale trade, the financial sector, the real estate, and the construction sector. The relative size of the retail industry is slightly higher than that of highly developed economies: in the UK the retail sector accounted for around 8 per cent of GDP in 2010, while in the US it represented almost 10 per cent. This is not surprising given that Dubai's economy has been historically based on trading activities: in 2002, for instance, internal trade accounted for around 50 per cent of GDP. The subsequent growth in other sectors of the economy, a result of the natural development of the economy, reduced its share to 30 per cent.

Beyond its relative importance in the economy of Dubai, the recent evolution of the retail industry is marked by the significant adverse effects of the recent global economic recession. As shown in Table 9.3, where we have collected the main indicators available for the industry, retail did not escape the downturn of Dubai's economy and in 2009 its value added—that is, the gross profit it generated—declined by a similar rate to the rest of the economy.

[4] See Dubai Statistical Center, *Annual Yearbook 2010*.

[5] *Business Environment, Enterprise Performance, and Economic Development in Dubai*, DEC Policy Report, May 2011.

Table 9.3. Main economic indicators of the Dubai economy and retail industry

	2002	2006	2007	2008	2009
GDP (value added) of Dubai (in millions AED of 2006)	161,069	241,014	284,577	293,572	286,617
Value added in wholesale, retail, and repairing services (in millions AED of 2006)	76,947	77,301	86,410	86,423	83,714
Estimated value added in retail activities (*) (in millions AED of 2006)	33,087	33,239	37,156	37,162	35,997
Employment in wholesale, retail and repairing services	165,232	225,878	299,817	217,924	208,415
Estimated employment in retail activities (*)	62,788	85,834	113,930	82,811	79,198

Source: Dubai Statistics Center, except (*) own elaboration based on data from Dubai Statistics Center

This contraction occurred even though the demand by foreigners—largely the result of tourism—did not change significantly between 2008 and 2009.

According to data from Department of Tourism and Commerce Marketing (DTCM), there was a marginal increase in hotel guests and guest nights of around 1 per cent in 2009, although tourist expenditures in hostelling in real terms declined somewhat. Further, Table 9.3 also indicates that, while sensitive to downturns, the sector has also benefited from the sustained economic growth of the past at a similar pace as the rest of the economy. This came as no surprise since most of the retail activities are also largely linked to the income of the families living in Dubai—and to some extent for those living in other emirates that use Dubai as their preferred shopping venue—which, in turn, depend significantly on the economic cycle. In periods of boom, employment and incomes rise, thus giving a boost to retail activities. In periods of decline, employment and income shrink and lead to more depressed retail activities.

9.4 PERFORMANCE OF THE RETAIL SECTOR

A core assessment of performance of any sector in the economy is how well it responds to both endogenous and exogenous shocks. The following econometric model is estimated to distinguish three features of the working of the internal trade sector in Dubai; (a) the short-run response of the retail industry to an increase in global economic activity; (b) the long-run response of the wholesale and retail trade to such an increase in economic activity, and (c) the time it takes for a shock to the sector to dissipate. The specification is a very simple one, given the lack of data and because the interest is in modelling the dynamics of adjustments in the sector. The specification is also consistent with a dynamic error-correction model, which describes the short-run dynamics of value added in wholesale and retail activities as a result of transitory shocks to GDP, permanent shocks to GDP, as well as a result of the self-correcting mechanism that adjusts the previous period disequilibrium:

$$\Delta RS_{t+1} = -\gamma(RS_t - \alpha - \beta GDP_t) + \sum_{i=1}^{p} \delta_i \Delta GDP_{t-i} + \varepsilon_{t+1}$$

where Δ indicates per cent change, RS represents value-added in retail and wholesale, GDP is the gross domestic product, and the disturbance ε_{t+1} is a stationary random variable composed of the one-step-ahead forecast error in value added in retail and wholesale. All variables are in log form.

The model indicates that the future growth of RS is determined by three elements: (1) the adjustment of previous disequilibrium in the market, that is, the difference between what RS is today and what is determined by GDP, that is adjusted by a fraction φ every period, (2) the lagged effect of economic growth, which can take several periods to fully adjust, and (3) the presence of unpredictable random shocks. The model clearly incorporates the dynamics of adjustment. Suppose, for example, that we start from an initial condition of low activity in RS (i.e. the error-correction term is negative), then the self-correcting mechanism immediately calls for a future expansion of the RS specification.

The results of the estimation are presented in the appendix. The results show that the long-term elasticity is around 0.8, the speed of adjustments indicate that 95 per cent of a shock dissipates in around five years, and that the main parameters of the estimation are statistically significant and with the appropriate signs. The best way to represent these three features of the dynamics in the wholesale and retail industry is illustrated in Figure 9.1.

Figure 9.1 shows the evolution of the activity in the industry after a shock is given to economic growth: this is the dynamic response of retail to a shock in economic growth of typical size (i.e. which occurs around 65 per cent of the time). The response from the secular or long-run trend of the economic activity is isolated so that the response corresponds only to the economic cycle. It can be seen in Figure 9.1 that, immediately after the positive increase in GDP, the retail and wholesale sector responds with a positive expansion of approximately three-quarters of the original shock size. This indicates that, as in most countries, in Dubai the economy operates with a lag. That is, once the expansion in economic activity sets in, it is the expansion in employment and rising incomes of the family that sets the retail sector in motion. The maximum response of the industry to shock would be between the second and third year. This is a quite rapid response, indicating that there are few constraints to the expansion in economic activity in the industry. Other sectors of the economy (e.g. aluminium smelting) are characterized by investments with long gestation lags that induce very slow adjustment patterns. On

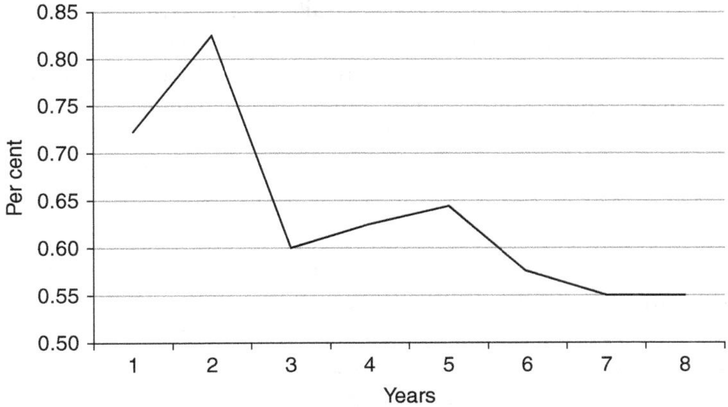

Figure 9.1. Cyclical dynamics of the retail industry in Dubai

Note: The curve shows the response of economic activity in wholesale and retail GDP to a 1 per cent shock in total GDP.

the contrary, the retail and wholesale sector adjusts promptly. Further, Figure 9.1 also indicates that the response of the industry to aggregate shocks reaches quite rapidly its long-term impact: the complete response takes a matter of three to four years. An alternative view of this dynamic is to note that, according to the model, the negative effects of the shock in 2008 should have reached its main effect by 2011 and that fast recovery should ensue. The subsequent vigorous expansion of retail activities observed after 2011 is, thus, congruent with model predictions suggesting that, while retail can be affected by economic downturns, it has a significant ability to make the most of an economic upswing.

The second indicator used to assess performance of the retail industry is employment. There are no official data available for the retail industry and the study relies on the data of the aggregate wholesale, retail, and repairing services. Furthermore, different publications from the Dubai Statistics Center produce widely dissimilar estimates for employment in the years 2007 to 2009, perhaps as a result of unreported methodological changes. Based on the data collected for the *Business Environment, Enterprise Performance, and Economic Development in Dubai* report, it is estimated that the retail industry employs around 38 per cent of the wholesale, retail, and repairing services sector in Dubai. Employment in free zones is added as part of wholesale, retail, and repairing services, as obtained from the workforce survey. As can be seen from Table 9.3, employment in wholesale, retail, and repairing services sector in Dubai grew steadily since 2002 to reach a peak of around 300,000 workers in 2007 (this latter figure may overestimate the actual employment level), before dissipating in 2008 and 2009, according to the official statistics. Employment in retail, which as earlier mentioned accounts for around 38 per cent of the sector total, might have followed a very similar trend. While undoubtedly the global crisis must have induced a significant decline in employment—most of all in small and medium enterprises, SMEs—part of the decline could also be the result of changes in the way the statistics are computed. If employment effectively declined to the levels in Table 9.3, that is, by around 30 per cent between 2007 and 2009, then the adjustment largely exceeded the drop in value added of 2.4 per cent observed in this period, indicating a high level of sensitivity of employment in the retail sector to the business cycle. This also suggests that, most likely, employment in retail will rebound strongly with the recovery of the Dubai economy in the future.

A third measure of the retail industry performance is the average productivity of the labour force, defined as total value added per worker, this is depicted in Figure 9.2. The average productivity of the labour force in Figure 9.2 is directly derived from Table 9.3, but when compared to other sectors in the economy, it adds a useful perspective to the analysis. Because labour productivity measures the value added by each worker in the

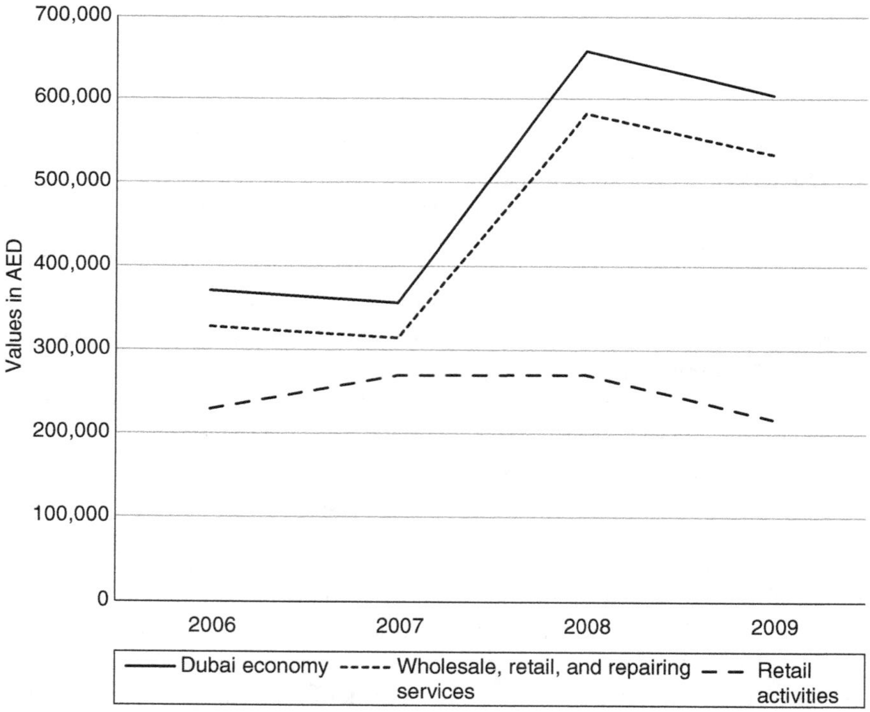

Figure 9.2. Average labour productivity in retail and Dubai's economy (in thousand AED of 2006)

Source: Own elaboration based on data from Dubai Statistical Center and Dubai Economic Council

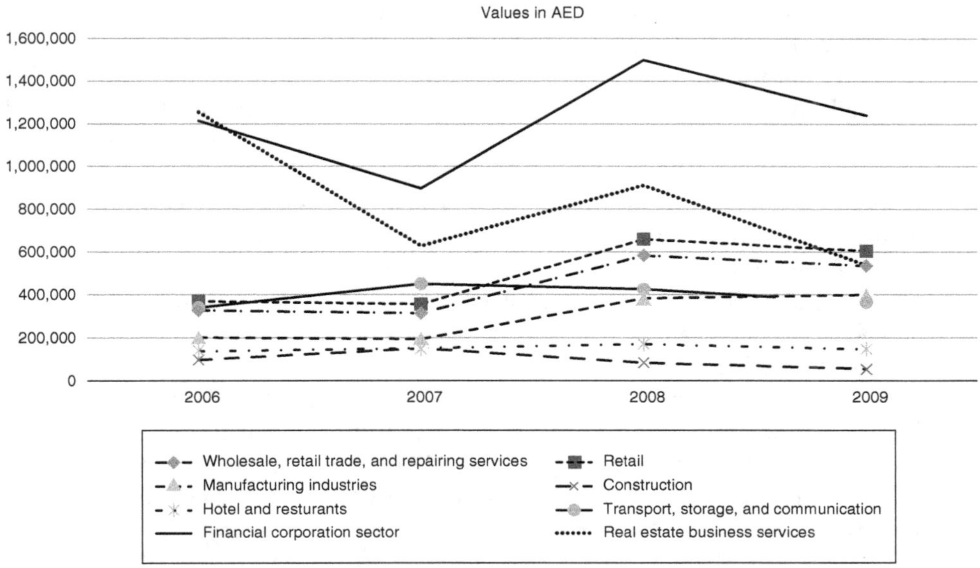

Figure 9.3. Average labour productivity in different sectors (in thousand AED of 2006)
Source: Own elaboration based on data from Dubai Statistical Center and Dubai Economic Council

production of goods and services, it actually reflects the efficiency in the use of resources. Figure 9.2 displays estimates of average labour productivity in the retail industry as compared to the productivity of an employee in the whole economy of Dubai. Notably, productivity of an employee in the retail industry is higher than that of the whole economy (above 50 per cent higher). Evidently, this is expected since the rest of the economy includes sizeable sectors with traditionally low productivity such as construction, hotels and restaurants, as well as the government.

Similarly, productivity is also higher in retail activities than in the entire wholesale, retail, and repairing services sector. This is partially due to the fact that the repairing services sector is of low productivity and very labour-intensive. There was a remarkable increase in labour productivity in the retail industry between 2006 and 2008, following the consumption boom spurred by the real estate bubble. However, contrary to the rest of the economy, productivity did not decline in 2009 when the adverse results of the financial crisis were being felt by Dubai. This is largely the result of the significant reduction in employment in the sector. Labour productivity in the retail industry is relatively high by Dubai standards and second only to that in the financial sector and the real estate business services (see Figure 9.3). But contrary to the latter, average productivity in retail seems to be improving over time, while in real estate it declined as a result of the bursting of the real estate bubble. Productivity is also higher than in manufacturing industries and the closely related tourism industry (including hotel, entertainment, and restaurants sectors).

Finally, it is important to illuminate the investment levels in the retail sector for two reasons. First, investment—which largely determines the long-term evolution of retail activities—is a forward-looking indicator of the future outcome of the industry. Private firms anticipate the future demand in retail activities and invest today to be ready to profit when such demand materializes in the future. Second, and as discussed later in the chapter, the most likely driver of future developments in retail will be investment in tourism instead of real estate. In the recent past, a significant fraction of investment in retail was the result of real estate firms undertaking massive housing and office projects, which had a component of retail services included in the form of supermarkets, malls, community centres, and the like. With the collapse of the real estate sector, and considering the substantial idle capacity existing, real estate is likely to play a lesser role and the engine of growth in the retail sector—and indeed in the whole economy—will be the external sector, including prominently tourism and trade. In the case of retail activities the main driver of growth will be tourism.

The first indicator of investment in the retail industry in Dubai can be considered as the expansion in retail space over time. The development of malls and shopping centres started in 1978 and continued until the recent crisis at a remarkable rate. As of 2010, Dubai has 65 per cent of the total 'gross leasable area' (GLA) of the UAE (around 4,000,000 m^2 in total).[6] Figure 9.4 shows the development in the GLA in Dubai shopping malls, that is, excluding off-mall properties for which data are not available. As expressed earlier, the first mall to open, the Al Mulla Plaza, was built in 1978 and it totalled only 7,000 m^2 GLA. The construction of new shopping malls proceeded at a steady yet moderate pace over the years until the late 1990s when investment entered a second phase of massive development. While by 2000, GLA had reached around 500,000 m^2, from 2001 onwards around 250,000m^2 entered the market every year. GLA in shopping malls reached above 2,600,000 m^2 by the end of 2009 as shown by Figure 9.4.

The evidence in Figure 9.4 indicates a phenomenal growth in GLA for retail in the last forty years. In fact, on average in that period, the GLA doubled every five years. While impressive, this high growth rate is the result of the small base from which shopping malls and retail in general started in the late 1970s. If one concentrates on the last twenty years only, the growth rate in GLA is still quite high (around 10 per cent per year) but more in line with other economies where retail has developed massively.

[6] Retail International (2010).

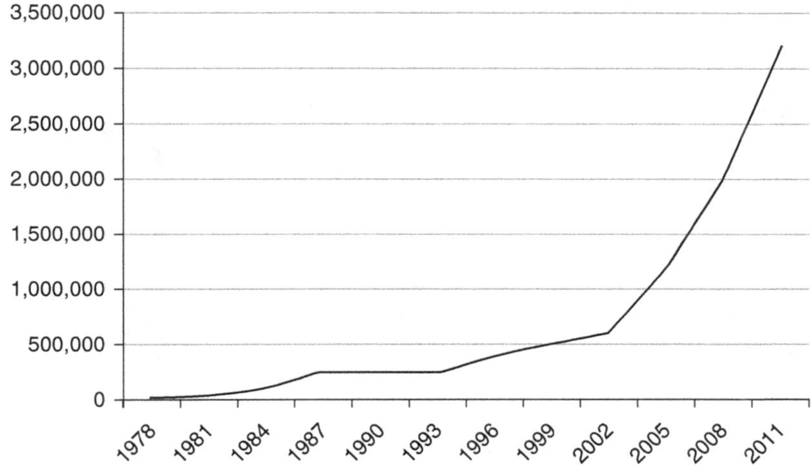

Figure 9.4. Gross leasable area in shopping malls (in ft^2)
Source: Jones Lang-LaSalle *UAE Retail Reports*

Consider the significant investment effort on the part of the government and domestic companies into positioning Dubai as a regional hub for retailing. Since the mid 1990s, the Dubai Events and Promotions Establishment authority has engaged in promoting large-scale retail events, including the Dubai Shopping Festival (DSF) or the Dubai Summer Surprises (DSS). Although no official statistics are available, an estimate by Colliers International in 2008 indicated that tourism accounts for 21 per cent of Dubai's retail spending, increasing to over 40 per cent in the new generation 'destination' shopping malls.[7] As shown in Figures 9.5 and 9.6, these events have had a significant impact in boosting retailing in periods of seasonal low demand.

It can be seen that the number of visitors and their total spending in the DSF is significant and has been increasing rapidly over the years since the inception of the first festival in 1996. By 2008, the DSF had increased visitors to around 3.2 million and associated sales had reached AED10 billion. However, and understandably, there was a slight decrease in the total spending of the last two years as a result of the global crisis. The results of the DSS event are equally auspicious yet less impressive. In the decade before the global crisis visitors expanded from around 1.5 million to slightly over 2.2 million. Associated sales doubled to AED3.5 million in the same period, as depicted in Figure 9.6.

The global economic crisis severely affected the economy of Dubai and precipitated the collapse of the real estate boom. Naturally, the retail sector

[7] Colliers International (2008).

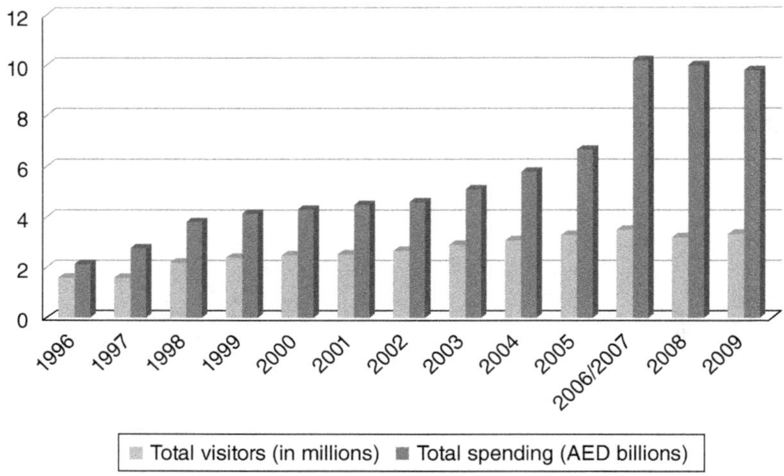

Figure 9.5. Main indicators of Dubai Shopping Festival
Source: Dubai Events and Promotions Establishment

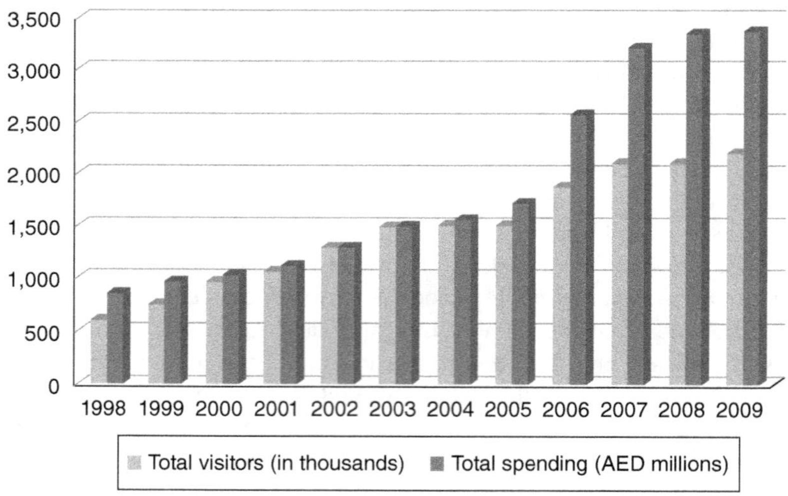

Figure 9.6. Main indicators of Dubai Summer Surprises
Source: Dubai Events and Promotions Establishment

was also affected since, as in other affected countries, consumer spending had been excessive during the pre-recession era and largely financed by debt. From the perspective of the cost of retail space: in periods of boom, the demand for retail space pushes costs up for retailers, while in recessions costs tend to fall. Figure 9.7 shows the estimated inflation-unadjusted rental value of retail space

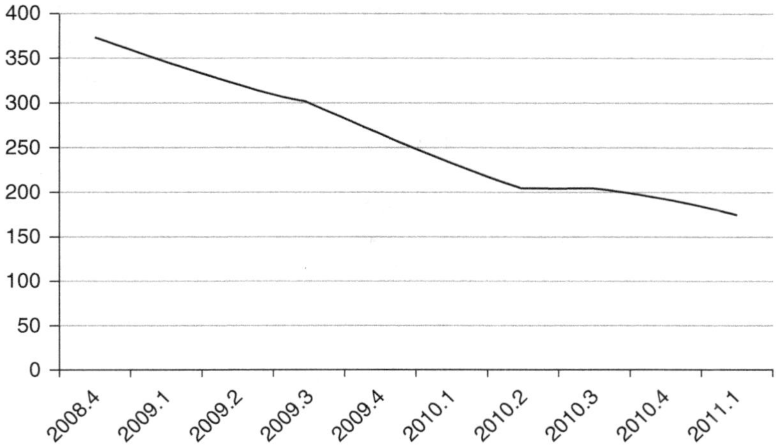

Figure 9.7. Annual rental value of retail space (in AED per ft^2)
Source: Jones Lang-LaSalle *UAE Real Estate Market Overview* (various issues)

as estimated by Jones Lang-LaSalle in several issues of their quarterly *Real Estate Market Overview*. The impact of the crisis is apparent: rental prices have declined steadily to a cumulative value of –53 per cent between the last quarter of 2008, that is at the peak of the retail market, and the latest available information for the first quarter of 2011.

Benchmark economies were less affected by the crisis: for example, annual retail rental values declined by around 20 per cent in the trough of the crisis in Hong Kong, but by the end of 2010 had recovered to pre-crisis maxima. In Singapore rental prices actually increased in 2009 and 2010, though by a small amount. Despite the substantial price decline, there are no signs of it bottoming out: vacancies in retail malls continued to be between 15 per cent and 30 per cent in the first quarter of 2011, according to the same source, indicating the need for further adjustment. The expected marginal expansion in retail area in 2011, nevertheless, will not have an effect in rental prices. In fact, by 2010 Dubai's average rental value was comparatively low. New York ranked at the top in annual retail rents with \$1,725 per ft^2 while Singapore ranked seventeen with annual values of \$436 per ft^2.

These general indicators, therefore, portray a clear picture of the retail sector in Dubai as being dynamic and of relatively high productivity, as well as capable of weathering the negative effects of the economic downturn initiated in 2008. Nevertheless, the indicators are centred only on the recent events in the retail industry, while additional long-term indicators are indeed needed in order to gain a more accurate perspective on the development of this industry. Data limitations precluded analysis using other indicators. This confined the focus mainly on employment, productivity, investment, and the long-term promotional programmes of the DSF and DSS. The lack of reliable, public, and timely information is a major limitation not only for this analysis but, more importantly, for the design and implementation of adequate policies and for the efficient operation of the retail sector itself. It is a serious limitation for policymakers because good policy proposals require empirical support and this in turn depends on reliable and timely information. It is also a limitation for doing business, because reliable information allows for easier identification and development of profitable market opportunities, enhances competitive market practices, reduces corruption, and eases the understanding of government policies.

9.4.1 Benchmarking Performance of the Retail Sector in Dubai

Benchmarking retail activities in Dubai is of paramount importance in understanding the current standing of the industry as well as for projecting its future development relative to its peers and the frontier economies. Benchmarking requires first that we determine a suitable set of countries to compare Dubai's current position and, second, that we select a proper set of indicators for such benchmarking. It would be natural to use regional economies—such as Qatar, Baḥrain, or the Kingdom of Saudi Arabia—or the other emirates (e.g. Abu Dhabi) to perform as benchmarks for Dubai. After all, they share a similar location, history, and level of social and economic development. Nevertheless, that would put too low a reference point for Dubai's retail sector which is considered more advanced in terms of maturity and sophistication. Dubai's performance is therefore benchmarked against two stronger candidates—Hong Kong and Singapore—which share with Dubai unique aspects such as size, strategic location, lack of natural resources, substantial immigration, and a relatively short independent life. It should be pointed out that, potential threats of other regional economies (e.g. Qatar) or emirates within the UAE (e.g. Abu Dhabi) should not be dismissed, but the study deemed it more illuminating to focus on small, open, non-resource-based, city-states which are highly integrated into the global economy than to focus on oil-based economies.

Table 9.4 presents the latest available data on sales in the 250 largest retail companies in the world, as identified by Deloitte, grouped by country of origin of the headquarters and then by continent. Middle East retailers are not ranked in the top 250 companies in the world and, therefore, they are still not part of the major league. The eight companies listed under the Africa and Middle East label are from South Africa and Turkey. Furthermore these companies, as well as Latin American companies, are still relatively small in terms of sales, internationalization, and investment.

Table 9.4. Worldwide sales of the largest 250 retail companies in 2009

	Number of companies	Average retail sales (in US$ million)	Retail sales from foreign operations (%)	Average number of countries served
Africa and Middle East	8	4,858	8.7	8.5
Asia Pacific	46	10,267	10.5	3.5
Japan	32	9,254	6.9	2.9
Europe	92	16,507	36.5	13.0
France	13	28,620	41.3	29.1
Germany	19	23,046	41.6	13.7
UK	15	17,287	21.9	10.7
Latin America	10	5,868	12.0	1.9
North America	94	17,820	13.3	5.1
US	84	18,851	13.3	5.5

Source: Deloitte (2011)

Compared to Dubai, economic recovery in benchmark economies started in early 2010: Singaporean authorities expect retail to grow around 5 per cent in 2011 and in Hong Kong sales are expected to increase by almost 6 per cent in 2011. Benchmark economies have been able to profit from the sustained post-crisis expansion in economic activity in China, India, Indonesia, and other Asian economies. In 2010 the Asia Pacific region grew at 8.8 per cent; moreover, a UN report expects economic growth in the Asia Pacific region to continue at a vigorous 7.3 per cent in 2011. Several Middle Eastern and African economies have also experienced a much faster recovery from the crisis than Dubai and, consequently, retail flourishes. Dubai, nevertheless, seems to have a good footing for prompt recovery in terms of the variety of goods and services made available by retailers to customers. An ample variety of goods indicates the maturity of the industry. Research conducted by CB Richard Ellis (CBRE, 2011) in 2011 revealed that the emirate was on a par with London as the world's premier retail city: 56 per cent of all the top international retail brands have a presence in Dubai as depicted in Table 9.5.[8]

Dubai's position of pre-eminence in the ranking reflects, most likely, the combination of a long-run policy of franchising luxury brands initiated very early in the development of the industry and the short-term effects of the global recession which have limited the ability of retailers in developed countries to expand domestically. CBRE (2011) also speculates that the growth of the emirate as a shopping destination has been fuelled by the emergence of a wealthy, well-educated, and well-travelled population in the region. Accordingly, a number of Middle Eastern cities have made significant progress in the

[8] CBRE's methodology considers surveying 323 international retailers across 73 countries. One half of such retailers have a presence in at least three continents.

Table 9.5. 2011 Global Retail Ranking: most targeted retail destination

Ranking	Country	Index
1	Dubai, UAE	56.0%
1	London	56.0%
3	New York	44.3%
4	Paris	43.6%
5	Madrid	41.6%
6	Hong Kong	40.9%
7	Moscow	39.9%
8	Los Angeles	38.6%
9	Singapore	38.3%
9	Barcelona	38.3%
11	Beijing	37.9%
11	Shanghai	37.9%
13	Berlin	37.2%
13	Kuwait City	37.2%
13	Istanbul	37.2%
16	Riyadh	36.6%
17	Milano	36.2%
18	Munich	35.6%
19	Tokyo	35.2%
20	Las Vegas	34.6%
20	Miami	34.6%
20	Hamburg	34.6%

Source: *How Global Is the Business of Retail?* CBRE 2011

global hierarchy, moving sharply up the ranking and entering the top twenty positions (Riyadh and Kuwait City). The recent entry of other regional cities to the high-quality retail market could be a source of concern for Dubai which, as mentioned, has enjoyed a leading position in regional terms. Nevertheless, investment figures suggest the contrary, as shown in Table 9.6.

On one hand, UAE retailers and in particular Dubai-based companies enjoy a considerable advantage in terms of existing retail capacity. With around 2.6 million m^2 of shopping centres built as of early 2010, Dubai has around 1.3 m^2 per capita of shopping mall facilities and largely outweighs all other emirates and the rest of the GCC countries in terms of investment. Despite its relatively large investment, the Kingdom of Saudi Arabia has only 0.16 m^2 per capita of shopping centres and thus lags considerably, even in regional terms. And despite its recent entry into the premier retail city rankings, investment in Kuwait City is only a mere 0.2 m^2 per capita. On the other hand, according to the information by Retail International also presented in Table 9.6, retailers and investors in the GCC countries plan to expand shopping capacity in the next five years by around 50 per cent, totalling around 15 million m^2. While impressive, this expansion is largely the result of investments in Dubai: out of the additional 5 million m^2 planned, around one-third would be added to

Table 9.6. Completed and planned investment in shopping centres in the GCC (estimated floor area, gross leasable area in m^2)

	Completed as of start of 2010	Planned investments to 2015
United Arab Emirates		
Abu Dhabi	667,700	1,159,930
Ajman	169,000	75,000
Al Ain	201,000	131,000
Ras Al Khaimah	93,000	n.a.
Dubai	2,655,100	1,427,100
Sharjah	259,000	167,500
Fujeira	n.a.	76,000
Total	4,044,800	3,036,530
Bahrain		
Manama	639,000	100,750
Kuwait		
Kuwait City	570,900	348,000
Kingdom of Saudi Arabia		
Al Khobar	655,500	299,000
Riyadh	1,402,200	212,400
Jeddah	1,909,700	463,400
Makkah/Medina	266,300	237,000
Total	4,233,700	1,211,800
Oman		
Muscat	311,400	35,000
Qatar		
Doha	521,000	648,300
Total GCC countries	10,320,800	5,380,380

Source: Retail International (2010)

expand retail in Dubai. Furthermore, these estimates were made before the Arab countries entered the current wave of political turmoil and, consequently, it would not be surprising if such investments are postponed or fail to materialize altogether.

In 2010, consulting firm A. T. Kearny issued a new version of its Global Retail Development Index (GRDI), an index it has been publishing since 2002. The GRDI ranks the retail expansion attractiveness of emerging countries based on a set of twenty-five variables including economic and political risk, retail market attractiveness, retail saturation levels, and modern retailing sales area and sales growth. As such, the index focuses on opportunities for mass merchant and food retailers, which are typically the bellwether for modern retailing concepts in a country. The GRDI considers Dubai as representative of the whole UAE but provides data only for the years 2004–10. Table 9.7 presents the top ten emerging economies in terms of retail development. Dubai shows important improvements in recent years: from being in second-tier positions until 2008 to seventh place in 2010. The utility of this

Table 9.7. Global Retail Development Index 2010

Ranking	2004	2007	2008	2010
1	Russia	India	Vietnam	China
2	India	Russia	India	Kuwait
3	China	China	Russia	India
4	Slovenia	Vietnam	China	Saudi Arabia
4	Croatia	Ukraine	Egypt	Brazil
6	Latvia	Chile	Morocco	Chile
7	Vietnam	Latvia	Saudi Arabia	UAE
8	Turkey	Malaysia	Chile	Uruguay
9	Slovakia	Mexico	Brazil	Peru
10	Thailand	Saudi Arabia	Turkey	Russia
	UAE not rated	UAE ranked 18	UAE ranked 20	UAE ranked 7

Source: A. T. Kearny *Global Retail Development Index* (several issues)

index is not in the ranking itself but rather the reasons for changes in a country's position as given by the experts: the report indicates that the drop is largely due to the contraction of the market after the crisis and the closure of emblematic stores and, contrary to other emerging economies, the tardiness in the recovery of the entire economy and the luxury segment of the retail sector. This lag in response provides space for profitable opportunities should Dubai return to fast growth.

9.5 CONCLUSION AND POLICY ISSUES

Retail activities involve not only the producers, consumers, and sellers of retail goods but a myriad of linked activities. Consequently, the performance of retail affects many economic activities in Dubai, most notably, private investment and employment. At the same time, the industry is largely affected by these related activities, in particular tourism and real estate. Retail is one of the most important sectors in Dubai's economy and accounts for around 13 per cent of total GDP. In terms of value, it is about the same size as the financial sector, the real estate, and the construction sector. As witnessed in the aftermath of the global economic crisis, activities in the retail industry are quite sensitive to economic cycles. Industry estimates suggest retail sales could have dropped by as much as 25 per cent as a result of the global economic crisis that affected Dubai and the world in 2008. Casual evidence suggests that luxury and higher-end goods suffered the most, but mass grocery weathered the downturn better and their sales dissipated only slightly. Retail activities, nevertheless, respond fast to economic cycles and, according to the econometric estimates presented, the negative effects of the global crisis should be over by the end of 2011 and fast recovery should be at hand. Anecdotal evidence provided by newspapers and consulting firms tends to confirm the forecast. Nevertheless, there remain significant challenges ahead.

Worldwide, retail is becoming a global business, with retailers expanding quite rapidly into other countries and continents. Increasing global competition for resources, market shares, and spheres of influence make competitiveness a decisive element for survival in the global economy. While initially retailers of developed economies penetrated emerging countries, the new wave is for retailers in emerging countries to enter markets in Europe, North America, and Japan. The internationalization of Dubai-based retail activities is in its initial stages, with a few companies entering neighbouring GCC countries. Globalization could bring profitable opportunities to Dubai-based companies. Higher international exposure also brings the challenge of weathering periods of economic turbulence as amply demonstrated during the recent global crisis. It is on this premise that it is imperative for the Dubai government to address some of the key issues that are affecting the competitiveness of the retail sector.

First, access to finance is identified as one of the most problematic factors for doing business in Dubai. Credit has been quite tight since the unravelling of the economic crisis in 2008, in spite of the generous rescue package provided by the government to banks. Second, one out of three companies in Dubai indicates that the labour force is the most problematic factor for doing business. Government regulations reduce the flexibility of the labour market and are marred by arbitrary labour fees. More importantly, retailers cannot hire part-time workers to cope with seasonal fluctuations. Third, public bureaucracy is also identified by the CEOs of the retail companies as a main limitation when doing business. Bureaucracy, red tape, and the lack of consistency in government rules and regulations further exacerbates inefficiency.

Furthermore, there is a perceived lack of transparency in the operation of both the retail sector (and its associate, the real estate sector) and the government. Dubai ranks low in retail and real estate transparency, far below Hong Kong and Singapore and other emerging economies. Transparency becomes a decisive aspect when it comes to attracting foreign direct investment, improving the operation of the different segments of the markets, and fostering innovation and technological upgrades. To the extent that retail operates largely in an international context, partnership with foreign retail companies is the cornerstone to further development of the retail industry in Dubai, in particular for entering markets in other countries (e.g. India). For these, the current high sovereign risk of Dubai is a serious obstacle. The latter stems largely from the perceived lack of transparency in government operations, in particular, in debt-restructuring.

Finally, worldwide changes in retail will also present challenges for retail in Dubai. Most analysts indicate that the current recession will induce permanent changes in consumer behaviour like becoming more value conscious, more attracted to private labels, and less likely to purchase large discretionary items. Retail in Dubai will, therefore, face a compression in its luxury segment of the market because consumers aspiring for luxury brands face a severe drop in their disposable wealth and, thus, reduces their willingness to engage in luxury spending. Private-label retailing, on the other hand, is gaining prominence worldwide and in some European economies it has reached up to 50 per cent of market share. Finally, technological changes will also re-shape retail activities. On one hand, consumer's information and awareness is improving as a result of rising social networking. New forms of communication and access to information make consumers demand greater access to information about retailers, their products, and their pricing. On the other hand, technology changes and market pressures will force Dubai retailers to improve on IT and product management. As of 2012, Dubai lags behind benchmark economies when it comes to online retailing, local logistics, and IT capabilities.

Appendix

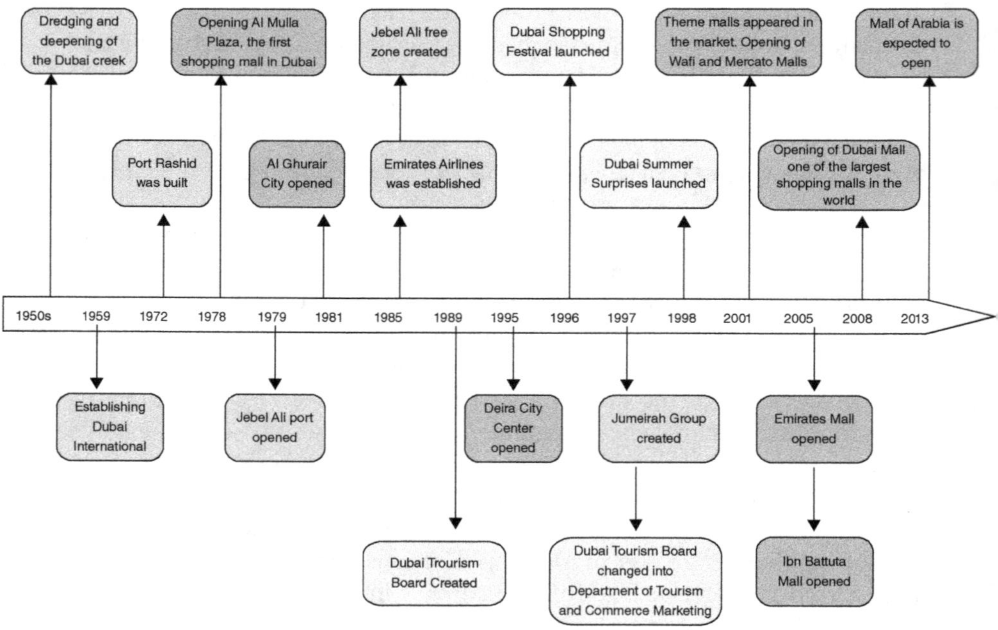

Figure 9A.1. Timeline history of Dubai
Source: Dubai Retail Industry Report, 2011

Table 9A.1. Estimation results for the wholesale and retail cyclical activity model

Vector Error Correction Estimates

Sample (adjusted): 1978 2009
Included observations: 32 after adjustments
Standard errors in ( ) and t-statistics in [ ]

Cointegrating Eq:	CointEq1	
CYCLE_D_WRR(-1)	1.000000	
CYCLE_D_GDP(-1)	-0.829171 (0.20341) [-4.07644]	
C	-0.007029	
Error Correction:	**D(CYCLE_D_WRR)**	**D(CYCLE_D_GDP)**
CointEq1	-0.506203 [-1.73843]	0.403351 [1.61706]
D(CYCLE_D_WRR(-1))	0.336182 [1.18743]	-0.082227 [-0.33904]
D(CYCLE_D_WRR(-2))	0.219448 [0.85646]	-0.174541 [-0.79521]
D(CYCLE_D_GDP(-1))	-0.181284 [-0.66975]	0.026520 [0.11438]
D(CYCLE_D_GDP(-2))	-0.370363 [-1.52303]	-0.163105 [-0.78299]
C	-0.012654 [-0.63234]	0.001476 [0.08609]
R-squared	0.155795	0.167549
Adj. R-squared	-0.006552	0.007463
Sum sq. residuals	0.323597	0.237458
S.E. equation	0.111562	0.095567
F-statistic	0.959640	1.046616
Log likelihood	28.09783	33.05000
Akaike AIC	-1.381114	-1.690625
Schwarz SC	-1.106289	-1.415800
Mean dependent	-0.012354	-0.002998
S.D. dependent	0.111198	0.095925
Determinant residual covariance (dof adj.)		6.72E-05
Determinant residual covariance		4.43E-05
Log likelihood		69.56772
Akaike information criterion		-3.472983
Schwarz criterion		-2.831723

Table 9A.2. Estimation results for the long-run retail and wholesale model

Dependent Variable: L_GDP_WRR

Sample (adjusted): 1976 2009
Included observations: 34 after adjustments
Convergence achieved after 11 iterations

Variable	Coefficient	Std. Error	t-Statistic	Prob.
L_GDP	1.498709	0.157348	9.524806	0
C	−7.14598	1.761156	−4.057552	0.0003
AR(1)	0.807754	0.068816	11.73793	0
R-squared	0.976812	Mean dependent variable		9.194161
Adjusted R-squared	0.975316	S.D. dependent variable		0.836277
S.E. of regression	0.131388	Akaike info criterion		−1.13722
Sum squared residuals	0.53515	Schwarz criterion		−1.00254
Log likelihood	22.33276	F-statistic		652.9526
Durbin-Watson stat	1.6216	Prob(F-statistic)		0
Inverted AR Roots	0.81			

REFERENCES

CB Richard Ellis, 2011. 'How Global Is the Business of Retail?' *Global Major Report.* [Online] Available at: http://www.cbre.com/EN/Research/pages/globalreports.aspx, accessed 2 September 2015.

Colliers International, 2008. *Dubai Retail Snapshot: Second Quarter*, Dubai: Colliers International.

Deloitte, 2011. *Emerging from the Downturn: Global Powers of Retailing*, New York: Deloitte.

Dubai Economic Council, 2009. *Clusters and Dubai's Competitiveness*, Dubai: Dubai Economic Council.

Dubai Economic Council, 2011. *Dubai Retail Industry Report*, Dubai: Dubai Economic Council.

Dubai Statistics Center, 2013. *Dubai National Accounts.* [Online] Available at: https://www.dsc.gov.ae/en-us/Themes/Pages/National-Accounts.aspx?Theme=24, accessed April 2013.

Retail International, 2010. 'The Annual Report', *Retail International*, 18:1.

US Census Bureau, 2011. *Monthly Retail Trade and Food Services.* [Online] Available at: http://www.census.gov/retail/index.html, accessed 2 September 2015.

10

Education in Dubai: From Quantity to Quality

Raimundo Soto

10.1 INTRODUCTION

Education in Dubai has developed at a very fast pace in the four decades since independence. Access to basic education—be it primary or secondary—has extended to the entire population regardless of their nationality. Enrolment into tertiary education grew dramatically in the 2000s, although it is still much lower than in developed economies. This is a remarkable achievement that speaks highly of government commitment to human capital formation. In less than forty years, Dubai transformed its education sector from a group of weak schools without even its own curriculum into a modern, dynamic education system.

The task is, nevertheless, only half completed. Although access to education has increased markedly, the quality of such education has not progressed at a similar pace. While primary education is of average quality by international standards, secondary education is quite limited and does not match either the skills demanded by the labour market or the minimum abilities required at university level. Remedial courses are a norm at university entry and substantial on-the-job training is required for debutant workers in the labour market. The quality of education is also highly unequal, with private schools outperforming public schools by a substantial margin. Inequality is also pervasive in terms of gender, with boys in public schools and universities performing worse than girls and dropping out at a much higher rate. Access to education is also highly uneven as Emirati nationals enjoy the benefit of accessing education at virtually no cost, while expatriates are restricted to private providers at a sometimes very high cost.

The mediocre quality of the education system is a serious limitation to long-run development. The government of Dubai has identified the need to change its investment-led growth strategy towards the development of a knowledge-based economy in the medium to long run. In this transformation the education sector plays a crucial role: knowledge-based economies rise from the basis of their education systems; their success depends largely on their capacity to educate and train the labour force as required by increasingly demanding markets; and their productivity and competitiveness is mostly determined by the clever articulation of formal education entities, labour markets, and on-the-job training in firms and businesses. Thriving knowledge-based economies, such as Hong Kong, Singapore, and Taiwan, pride themselves on their high-quality education systems.

The mediocre quality of education in Dubai is a concern for society and its authorities. In 2010, the government started to implement measures to improve on quality, yet these measures are timid and/or in their initial stages, too early to be properly evaluated. The federal government has also started to address the serious limitations of public schools and national universities. This chapter reviews Dubai's education sector, identifies its strengths and weaknesses, and discusses areas in which policy action is needed and possible. Our conclusion is that, to improve quality, the government ought to change the industrial organization of education, modify the incentives given to the different actors so that they operate under more efficient frameworks, implement new policies where existing ones are insufficient or incomplete, and inject accountability where none is currently in place.

10.2 ACCESS TO EDUCATION IN DUBAI

When the UAE Federation was established in 1971, educational services were immature and inaccessible to many cities and villages and enrolment in primary and secondary education was around 28,000 students. In the subsequent years, enrolment in primary and secondary schools doubled roughly every ten years. Such a significant expansion in coverage has been accompanied by the development of pre-primary education and, more recently, of preschool services such as nurseries. At the other end of the education chain, universities and higher education have also gone through a phase of rapid growth as shown in Table 10.1.

10.2.1 Primary and Secondary Schools

Some 220,000 students were enrolled in 227 schools in the school year 2010/11 in Dubai (KHDA, 2011). Most schools offer the full range of courses from grade 1 to grade 12, while a few concentrate exclusively on either primary or

Table 10.1. Providers, enrolment, and teachers in academic year 2010–11

	Number of providers		Student enrolment		Teachers	
	Private	Public	Private	Public	Private	Public
Nurseries	82	2	7,551	43	726	6
Kindergartens	123	11	34,558	1,832	1,799	149
Primary education	148	79	130,075	17,940	7,471	1,529
Secondary education	135	79	28,690	6,877	2,980	635
Higher education	43	9	35,612	7,300[e]	1,531	430[e]
Total	534	177	236,486	33,416	14,507	2,749

Note: [e] own estimation based on information provided by the institutions.
Source: own elaboration based on data from KHDA and UAE Ministry of Social Affairs and Ministry of Education

secondary education. The entry of private-sector providers has been substantial: according to data from the Knowledge and Human Development Authority (KHDA), the number of private schools doubled between 1990 and 2010, despite the fact that the size of schools also expanded markedly (from an average of 750 students per school in 2000 to around 1,100 in 2010). On the contrary, public schools have suffered a protracted contraction in enrolment: in 2010, public schools served less than two-thirds of the students enrolled in 1995. A significant number of students originally attending public schools switched to the private sector, most likely in search of higher-quality education as discussed later in this chapter.

Naturally, such a significant expansion in schools has been accompanied by a similar expansion in teachers. In 1990, there were around 2,000 teachers in the private sector; by 2010 they had increased to over 12,000. Of these, less than fifty are Emirati locals. On the other hand, teachers in the public sector have remained stable in the last twenty years, hovering around 2,200 in total of which 55 per cent are Emirati nationals and 45 per cent are foreigners. As in most countries, the share of female teachers is much larger than that of males in the private sector (80 per cent are females) and in the public sector (71 per cent).

10.2.2 Nurseries and Kindergartens

Nurseries are relatively new in Dubai, when compared to primary and secondary schools and also by international standards. In 2010 there were only two public nurseries catering for only forty-three Emirati children. In contrast, in the same year a total of eighty-two private nurseries catered for around 7,600 children, of which Emirati nationals accounted for less than 10 per cent (Bennett, 2009). Enrolment in nurseries is arguably very low, particularly among the local population: less than 5 per cent of eligible Emirati children are enrolled in nurseries, the rest being raised at home (Karaman, 2011). In developed countries pre-school enrolment surpasses 60 per cent while in middle-income developing countries, such as Chile, it reaches 40 per cent. Other related services that usually support nurseries (e.g. family day-care homes, drop-in services, play groups, and family centres) are yet to be developed in Dubai.

In contrast to the low enrolment rates in nurseries, the number of students attending kindergarten classes is fairly high. Around 7,000 Emirati students and almost 29,000 expatriates were enrolled in both public and private sector kindergartens in 2011. These figures would indicate that around 90 per cent of children aged four and five attend kindergarten. Most Emirati families prefer to send their children to private kindergartens even if they have to pay tuition as they provide better English instruction. Because private kindergartens are expensive, public kindergartens are increasingly serving low- and middle-income Emirati families, creating a gap in choices of access to quality education. The emphasis on learning English at a young age is becoming the deciding factor for Emirati families when selecting a pre-school education.

10.2.3 Higher Education

As of 2011, there were fifty-two higher education providers in Dubai. The three federal entities that operate in Dubai cater almost exclusively for UAE nationals (99.1 per cent of total students), offer tuition-free education, and are segregated by gender. These universities—serving around 7,000 students in total—typically offer undergraduate courses leading to bachelor degrees and diplomas, as well as postgraduate programmes leading to professional and master degrees. The full-time faculty is small in these universities (around 400 teachers) when compared to equal-size counterparts in developed economies, which indicates an excess reliance on part-time teachers. In addition to these entities, there are six tertiary institutions established and financed by the Government of Dubai (Dubai Police Academy, Dubai School of Government, Hamdan Bin Mohammed e-University, Islamic and Arab Studies College, Imam Malik College, and the National Institute of Vocational Education).

There are forty-three private universities located both in Main Dubai and in dedicated free zones (most of them in Dubai Knowledge City and Dubai International Academic City). The latter comprise mostly international branches of American and European universities offering international degrees. Figures on enrolment, faculty, and programmes offered, as well as endowment and investment are typically unavailable or out of date. Based on partial data, we estimate that around 38,000 students are enrolled in around 400 programmes in private sector universities. Their expansion, nevertheless, has been substantial, particularly in free zones and after 2000.

10.2.4 Regulators and Policymakers

As in most countries, the government is heavily involved in the education industry. On one hand, it is the promoter of educational initiatives, including educational free-trade zones, public schools, and universities. On the other hand, it issues guidelines and regulations for the operation of the private and public schools, as well as providing for long-run and strategic planning. Finally, it also provides guidelines to improve the quality of education.

The institutional structure of education in Dubai is somewhat complicated by the overlapping of responsibilities between local and federal authorities. The Ministry of Education is responsible for planning, executing, following, and supervising the educational system in the UAE. The KHDA is responsible for the growth, direction, and quality of education and learning in Dubai. Having federal and emirate-level education authorities with similar mandates, however, does not necessarily ensure better quality of education. According to Lane (2010), this setup 'has resulted in dual quality assurance mechanisms at the federal and local levels, as well as a lack of coordination throughout the sector. This has created an environment where there is significant duplication of degree offerings, confusion over regulation, and concern about the quality of some programs.'

The responsibility for pre-school education in the UAE lies with the Ministry of Social Affairs. It is somewhat surprising that nurseries and pre-school education are not considered an integral part of the education process; by being part of the Ministry of Social Affairs, they are relegated to the status of an assistance programme. In Dubai, where early childhood education is primarily provided by the private sector, other local government institutions are also involved, resulting in a fragmented regulatory environment. KHDA supplies licensing, quality assurance, policy development, and support; the Department of Economic Development (DED) issues the required commercial licenses to all nurseries and kindergartens in the private sector; Dubai Women's Establishment (DWE) monitors early childcare standards; and the Community Development Authority (CDA) provides parenting services and support for children with special needs.

The Ministry of Higher Education and Scientific Research is responsible for the general planning of higher education and scientific research. Among other faculties, it authorizes the establishment of private higher education institutions and the adoption of academic programmes, and it aims at ensuring quality levels for higher education. The Commission for Academic Accreditation, as its name indicates, is a federal agency in charge of quality assurance and of promoting educational excellence across diverse institutions of higher education in the UAE. It licenses post-secondary educational institutions and accredits individual programmes according to international standards and aims at assuring high-quality education, consistent with international standards, for the MOHESR. The University Quality Assurance International Board (UQAIB) was established by the KHDA in 2008 to assess and license universities operating in the education free zones in Dubai like Academic City and Knowledge Village.

This fragmented structure is relatively unique: in most countries—either federal or unitary—the majority if not all educational matters are dealt with by a single ministry. Whether this fractional arrangement is better for Dubai and the UAE is beyond the scope of this chapter but it ought to be recognized that coordination among ministries and emirate-level authorities is an increasingly important issue.

10.3 THE QUALITY OF EDUCATION IN PRIMARY AND SECONDARY SCHOOLS

Access to primary and secondary education in the UAE, and particularly in Dubai, has expanded remarkably in the last three decades. This is an important achievement: as of 2011, coverage was similar to that of OECD countries in primary school education and with advanced emerging economies in secondary school education (UNESCO, 2009). Likewise, efforts have been made more recently by the authorities to generate the conditions for tertiary as well as pre-primary education to be provided by the private sector, but the results are yet to be properly assessed.

However, there are worrisome indicators that the quality of primary and secondary education has not followed the trend. For example, local universities require incoming students to take one or two years of remedial courses (called 'foundations') to reach the level required by university programmes.[1] This is a prima facie indication of the weak education received in secondary schools. Likewise, there is a relatively widespread use of private tutors to support the education received by children at school, in particular in families that have enough income to afford private classes for up to around US$50 per hour.[2] While in principle tutoring provides support to lagging children, when widespread it also indicates the inability of schools to educate students to the right level. In addition, because tutoring is costly and can only be afforded by

[1] Marshall Drummond, then Provost of the Higher Colleges of Technology (HCT), revealed to Gulf News that around 90 per cent of public and private secondary school graduates in the UAE who apply to federal universities are not qualified for undergraduate studies. Gulf News, 2 October 2010.

[2] According to *The Khaleej Times* of 24 August 2010 as many as 60 per cent of senior students in some schools are taking on some private tuition. The article also mentions that the Abu Dhabi Department for Economic Development estimates that 27 per cent of Emirati families spend almost US$400 per month on private tuition.

some families, it tends to generate large inequalities in access to education. Finally, the significant drop-out of male students in the last years of secondary school also indicates that many individuals consider it not worth investing in an additional year of education, perhaps as the result of a very low market return of that education in terms of income (KHDA, 2012).

A more decisive indicator of the quality of education in Dubai is the behaviour of the Emirati population. In the last decade the number of students in public schools nearly halved; while in the late 1990s there were around 38,000 students in public schools by 2010/11 enrolment was less than 25,000 students. This decline occurred in spite of the continuous growth in the local population and corresponds to a voluntary decision by Emirati families to enrol their children in private schools to escape the progressive deterioration in the quality of public education. In fact, currently public schools educate fewer Emirati children than the private sector: around 29,000 in private schools versus 20,000 in public schools. Figure 10.1 displays the participation of public schools in the education of Emirati children. It can be seen that in the early 1990s over 80 per cent of Emirati students attended public schools, while by 2010/11 this figure had declined to 40 per cent. Not only are Emirati families withdrawing from public schools, the few expatriates that are allowed to enrol their children in public schools have also followed the trend: in 1998

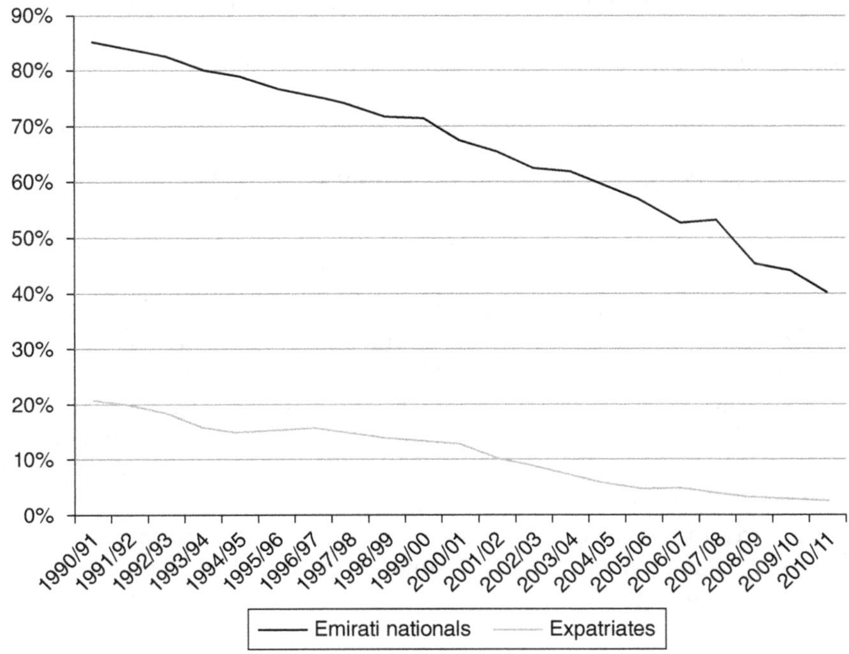

Figure 10.1. Students attending public schools (% of total students)

there were around 12,000 students of expatriates in public schools (15 per cent of the total), but by 2010/11 they had reduced in number to 4,700 (less than 3 per cent of total non-Emirati students).

Assessing the quality of education is difficult because the educational process is quite complex and involves both schools and parents, it depends on personal innate abilities and attitudes towards education, and is largely determined by the incentives provided by the labour market. In principle there are two forms of measuring education quality. The first is to assess the quality of the components used in the education process (teachers, curricula, access to libraries, and supporting material). Accordingly, better quality of inputs ought to produce better quality of education. The alternative way is to study the performance of students in school and, later, in the labour market. This second way of looking at quality focuses on the outcomes of the education process as opposed to the above-mentioned method that focuses on components. Both ways provide complementary views of the education process: poor outcomes in performance for a group of individuals most likely are the result of a bad mix in the inputs of the education process.

Given the lack of school-level data, we focus on the performance of the students in international tests of knowledge and reasoning as a measure of the quality of education in Dubai. Since these tests are exactly the same in all countries (except for being translated into local languages) the results can be compared across nations which provides a very useful benchmark for the analysis. Likewise, because of their design and size the results of these tests are representative of the entire educational system of Dubai.

10.3.1 Using International Benchmarks to Measure Quality

We use two international tests to benchmark the quality of education in Dubai vis-à-vis other economies. The first test is called TIMSS, an acronym for Trends in International Mathematics and Sciences Study, and is taken by primary education students (of years 4 and 8) in around fifty countries and cities in the world.[3] Dubai participated for the first time in 2007: around 3,000 students from ninety-six schools (25 public and 71 private) were examined in Grade 4, while almost 3,200 students from eighty-eight schools (28 public and 60 private) took the year-8 test. The second test is called PISA, an acronym for the Programme for International Student Assessment of the OECD, and it is administered to 15-year-olds in secondary schools. Dubai participated in 2009 for the first time, when over 5,600 students from both public and private schools took the test.

[3] The TIMSS test is administered by International Association for the Evaluation of Educational Achievement in Amsterdam, the Netherlands.

Table 10.2. 2007 TIMSS results: Dubai and selected economies

	Students in Grade 4				Students in Grade 8			
	Average scores		Not achieving minimal skills (%)		Average scores		Not achieving minimal skills (%)	
	Maths	Science	Maths	Science	Maths	Science	Maths	Science
Average of all countries	500	500	10	7	500	500	25	22
Dubai	***444***	***460***	***31***	***28***	***461***	***489***	***26***	***18***
Average OECD countries	*512*	*524*	7	7	*505*	*519*	10	8
USA	529	539	5	6	508	520	8	8
England	541	542	6	5	513	542	10	6
Average East Asian countries	*594*	*566*	1	3	*536*	*520*	13	14
Singapore	597	587	4	4	593	567	3	7
Hong Kong	607	554	0	2	572	530	6	8
Taiwan	576	557	1	3	598	561	5	5
Average Arab countries	*323*	*309*	77	73	*383*	*418*	59	45
Algeria	378	354	59	67	387	408	59	45
Egypt	n.a.	n.a.	n.a.	n.a.	391	408	53	45
Kuwait	316	348	79	63	354	418	71	40
Lebanon	n.a.	n.a.	n.a.	n.a.	449	414	26	45
Qatar	296	294	87	77	307	319	84	71
Tunisia	n.a.	n.a.	72	68	n.a.	n.a.	39	23
Yemen	224	197	94	92	n.a.	n.a.	n.a.	n.a.

Notes: Students of 38 countries took the Grade 4 tests (3 East Asian economies, 17 countries from the OECD, 7 Arab countries, and 12 economies from Africa, East Europe, and Latin America). Students of 49 countries were tested in Grade 4 (6 countries from East Asia, 13 OECD economies, 14 Arab countries, and 18 countries from other regions).
Source: Own elaboration based on data from TIMMS (2008)

The results of the TIMSS are presented in Table 10.2.[4] It can be seen that East Asian countries are the highest achievers in science and mathematics both at year 4 or year 8 of primary education. Dubai's students rank below the test average by a significant measure in mathematics at both education levels, whereas they lag substantially in science in year 4 but approach the average in year 8. On average, OECD economies perform above the 500 points mark, with England and United States ranking relatively high in the scale in both mathematics and science. Nevertheless the top performers are the East Asian economies, in particular those to be seen as potential competitors to Dubai in its ambitions of becoming a hub for world trade and finances (Singapore, Taiwan, and Hong Kong). In regional terms, Dubai scored significantly higher than all Arab countries, including the GCC countries and countries such as Algeria, Egypt, and Lebanon. This is poor consolation as the latter are clearly not adequate benchmarks for Dubai.

[4] A thorough description of TIMSS results for Dubai in 2007 can be found in Helal (2009).

The use of averages hides an important feature of the school system in Dubai: the significant disparities in the quality of education provided by public and private schools. TIMMS tests identify the number of students that do not achieve *minimal skills* in mathematics and science. In mathematics at Grade 4 the standard for minimal skills only requires students to demonstrate an understanding of adding and subtracting with whole numbers, familiarity with triangles, and ability to read information from simple bar graphs and tables. For Grade 8 students, it considers in addition calculations using decimals (e.g. percentages). Because these requirements are not very demanding, students who fail to achieve basic skills indicate the extent of the weaknesses in school systems.

Information in Table 10.2 also indicates that around 10 per cent of the students do not achieve the minimum skills in mathematics or science at Grade 4 in a typical country. This number increases to around 25 per cent at Grade 8 in both disciplines. Dubai shows much higher levels of non-achievement at Grade 4: one in every three students did not achieve minimum skills in maths or science in 2007. The gap reduces somewhat by Grade 8. Nevertheless, these levels are much higher than those in East Asian countries where only 1 or 2 per cent of students do not attain minimum levels of competency. On the other hand, Dubai compares very favourably with other Arab countries such as Kuwait or Qatar where over 75 per cent of students did not acquire minimal skills. Consequently, the mediocre quality of primary education in Dubai is significant: a poor academic achievement in primary school hampers the student's performance and self-confidence at advanced education levels and even in the labour market.[5]

The most worrying feature of the educational system in Dubai, nevertheless, is the significant differences in student achievement—and educational quality—between public and private schools. As shown in Table 10.3, students in Grade 4 in private schools scored about 40 points higher in mathematics than those in public schools. In Grade 8 the score differential widens to more than one hundred points. A similar pattern occurs in science: while the gap is around 70 score points in favour of private schools in Grade 4, it widens to 80 score points at Grade 8.

The weak performance of public schools also shows in the number of students who do not achieve the minimum competencies at their respective level. At Grade 4, almost one half of the students in public schools do not achieve the low benchmark in mathematics or science compared to less than

[5] Dubai's educational system does not provide education evenly by gender. Although there are no differences in average scores for boys and girls at Grade 4, the number of boys that failed to acquire minimal skills is much larger than that of girls in both mathematics and science (35 per cent vs 25 per cent). At Grade 8, boys and girls failed equally in mathematics but in science girls outperform boys.

Table 10.3. TIMSS 2007: Students not achieving basic skills by type of school

	Mathematics		Science	
	Score	Students not achieving basic skills	Score	Students not achieving basic skills
Grade 4: public schools	409	45%	404	46%
Grade 4: private schools	452	29%	471	25%
Grade 8: public schools	378	61%	427	37%
Grade 8: private schools	483	17%	506	13%

Source: Own elaboration based on TIMSS (2008)

30 per cent of students in private schools. These numbers contrast with the median figure for all countries in the TIMSS of 10 per cent. Moreover, while in private schools performance improves markedly at Grade 8 by halving the number of non-performing students, in the public schools there is a dramatic decline in performance in mathematics: two out of every three students do not possess the minimum abilities required. In science there is some improvement, yet non-performance is three times higher than in private schools.

PISA tests are taken by children at 15 years of age (10th and 11th grades) and reflect the quality of secondary education. In many countries students at that age would be just entering secondary education, so these exams 'assess how far students near the end of compulsory education have acquired some of the knowledge and skills that are essential for full participation in society. In all cycles, the domains of reading, mathematical and scientific literacy are covered not merely in terms of mastery of the school curriculum, but in terms of important knowledge and skills needed in adult life' (OECD, 2010). Approximately two-thirds of Dubai's 15-year-olds were tested for PISA in April and May 2009; 5,620 students from 134 public and private schools took part, and they were chosen by the OECD's scientific sampling to reflect accurately Dubai's diversity of language, nationalities, and school curricula. They were tested in their language of instruction, either Arabic or English. This test provides us with the opportunity to check, in addition to mathematics and sciences, the language skills of the students. Language has been traditionally the focus of public education in Dubai and the UAE.

Of the 65 countries assessed in 2009, Dubai came 42nd in reading proficiency with a score of 459, 41st in mathematics with a score of 453, and 41st in science with a score of 466 (see Table 10.4). These scores are well below the 500 points mark set by the Organization for Economic Co-operation and Development (OECD) as a long-term target. Again East Asian economies such as Hong Kong and Singapore are top scorers. Dubai was placed higher than Arab countries like Jordan, Tunisia, and Qatar. In reading and science, Dubai's female students outperformed male students. In mathematics, there was no significant difference between the average scores for males and females.

Table 10.4. 2009 PISA results: Dubai and selected economies

	Reading	Mathematics	Science
OECD intended target	500	500	500
Dubai	**459**	**453**	**466**
Average OECD countries	*493*	*496*	*501*
USA	500	487	502
England	495	503	499
Average East Asian countries	*489*	*489*	*488*
Hong Kong	533	555	549
Singapore	526	562	542
Taiwan	495	543	520
Average Arab countries	*410*	*400*	*410*
Jordan	405	387	415
Tunisia	404	371	401
Qatar	372	368	379

Notes: Students of 65 countries took the PISA tests (34 countries from the OECD, 4 Arab economies, 7 East Asian countries, and 20 economies from East Europe and Latin America).
Source: Own elaboration based on OECD (2010)

Language skills do not appear to be better developed than mathematics or science.

In summary, both TIMMS and PISA tests indicate that the average quality of education in Dubai is mediocre and that public schools lag substantially behind private schools. Current quality levels are below what would be consistent with the country's socioeconomic development and, more importantly, they provide a weak foundation for switching the development strategy towards the much-publicized knowledge-based economy. The reasons for the quality differences between private and public schools are numerous and include the low quality of the national curricula, the poor working conditions given to teachers, and the weak incentives given to school managers to perform adequately. We review these issues in what follows.

There are several curricula in Dubai including the National Curriculum designed by the government, the British, American, and Indian curricula, and the International Baccalaureate among others. The results in the TIMSS indicate that the performance of students in schools using the National Curriculum is far worse than any other curricula. Average scores are significantly low (one hundred points below average): one in every two students does not acquire minimal skills in Grade 4 in either mathematics or science.[6] On the other hand, students using the British curriculum perform

[6] The weaknesses of the national curriculum in public schools have not gone unnoticed by the government, which launched in 2007 the Madares Al Ghad (Schools of Tomorrow) programme aimed at revamping the content and teaching methods in mathematics and science. No ex-post evaluation is yet available.

overwhelmingly better than other students and reach the international average in mathematics and science in Grade 8 and in science in Grade 4.

The performance of students depends largely on the motivation and working conditions of the teachers (workload, hours worked, salaries, training, etc.). In Dubai, there are significant differences between teachers in public and private schools but such differences cannot explain the differences in performance. First, teachers in public schools are not overloaded and schools are not understaffed. In 2010, there were roughly nine students per teacher while in private schools there were 15 students per teacher (equivalent to the average ratio of students/teachers in the US the same year).[7] Thus, teachers in public schools in Dubai have, on average, much lower teaching loads. After inspecting 228 schools in Dubai, the School Inspection Board concluded that in public schools 'the teaching loads of individual teachers are very light compared to international norms' (Dubai Schools Inspection Bureau, 2009: 26). Moreover, it concludes that 'the light teaching load in public schools represents a poor return on the investment in teachers' remuneration and their professional development. There is considerable scope for reviewing the size of the teaching workforce and conditions of service to raise teachers' status, maximize their deployment and improve their contribution to students' progress and attainment' (p. 95). Moreover, public schools do not seem to show signs of being understaffed in terms of administrative and support personnel. The ratio of administrative staff per teacher in private schools is, and has historically been, lower than in public schools; considering that there are comparatively more teachers in public schools, this indicates that there is no shortage of personnel in public schools.

With regards to salaries, many influential reports advocate paying high salaries as a means of attracting and retaining more talented teachers in public schools and of encouraging harder work by current teachers (Hanushek et al., 1999). In the UAE, the Ministry of Education sets the minimum salary for teachers, which differs between Emirati and expatriate teachers. Emirati teacher salaries in the public sector start from around US$3,000 per month while for expatriates the monthly salary starts at around US$2,200 (these are net values since there are no income taxes in the UAE). In the private sector wages are, on average, substantially lower: the median range is between US $1,500 and US$2,300, according to a sample of 125 private schools collected for this chapter. So in comparative terms, teachers in public schools are being paid equally or more than teachers in private schools and, therefore, wage gaps are unlikely to justify the weaker performance of government schools.

Finally, the most obvious explanation for the poor performance of children in public schools that follow the National Curriculum could be that they are

[7] US Department of Education, National Center for Education Statistics, Table 33.

being taught less intensively than children in schools following the UK, US, or Indian curricula. Farah and Ridge (2009) conclude otherwise: in the UAE children in grades 7 to 9 have 33 per cent more hours of language (Arabic), 35 per cent more hours in mathematics, 33 per cent more hours in science, and 300 per cent more hours of religion than in OECD economies. Despite the heavy time allocation to these subjects in the UAE, student's performance remains weak indicating that simply having more hours in a subject is not enough to see test score gains (Farah and Ridge, 2009).

One more promising area to understand the reasons for the relative weakness of public schools lies in the ability of managers to set up incentives by which teachers and administrative personnel are adequately rewarded for their efforts. On one hand, public servants cannot be easily held accountable for their actions and their wages are totally disconnected from their effort. Second, as recognized by the DSIB 2009 annual report, 'The lack of local discretion for the deployment of resources, including teachers, in public schools substantially reduces their efficiency and effectiveness. All public schools have essentially flat management structures, with the only paid responsibilities at principal and vice or assistant principal level' (p. 26). The reason for this is that the Ministry of Education actually makes most of the decisions that ought to be made at the school level: school principals have little responsibility in selecting, managing, and evaluating the performance of their workforce. This, consequently, limits the ability to challenge weaker teachers to improve their professional practice and, at the same time, does not allow good teachers to be adequately rewarded for their effort and be recognized for their contribution to human capital formation.

The reasons for the substantial differences in test performance among private and public schools in Dubai are still largely unexplored. Additional research is urgently needed to provide meaningful and actionable reform policies; such research should attempt to identify the main determinants of academic performance, acknowledging for the particular characteristics of Dubai in terms of the diversity of students, teachers, cultures, and languages. Moreover, there is a significant lack of public data on important issues that hamper the choice of schools by Emirati and expatriate families, including the quality of education (e.g. the TIMSS and PISA test results should be made available to families), the cost of public education, the qualifications and evaluation of teachers, and so on. These are the elements that the families should have at hand in order to decide on the education of their children.

10.4 THE QUALITY OF HIGHER EDUCATION

Dubai and UAE universities are quite young and yet they have been assigned a prominent role by the government as a backbone of the knowledge-based economy that is to emerge in the following years to replace the current investment-led growth strategy. The World Bank considers that the foundations of a knowledge-based economy are based on an educated and skilled population that can create and use knowledge and an innovation network composed of firms, research centres, universities, consultants, and other organizations that can tap into the growing stock of global knowledge, adapt it to local needs, and transform it into products valued by markets. It is thus convenient to assess the quality of education and, more importantly, the depth, scope, and quality of the research and innovation that Dubai universities currently produce and that is supposed to become a central component in developing the new high value-added industries that would eventually replace the current industrial base of the economy.

As discussed in Chapter 2, access to higher education has expanded noticeably in the last decades in Dubai. In 2011, there were around 38,000 students enrolled in public and private universities, indicating a significant effort of society to expand human capital formation. Enrolment rates, however, are below international standards and the requirements of a knowledge-based economy: according to UNDP (2009) enrolment rates have grown from around 17 per cent in 1999 to 25 per cent in 2008. These figures are not very impressive: developed economies have enrolment rates above 50 per cent and a significant group of emerging countries (e.g. Latin American countries) have enrolment rates above 35 per cent. Nevertheless, it must be remembered that the population in Dubai has more than doubled in the same period of time; consequently, there has been a significant growth in the group of potential higher education students. Most of this notable expansion in coverage is the result of the entry of private universities. National universities have taken a back seat in this process, perhaps because they are restricted to enrolling only Emirati nationals. Enrolment in UAE University, Zayed University, and HCT has remained stagnant or grown very slowly since 2000. Enrolment among nationals is very heterogeneous: in 2010 around 70 per cent of women enrolled in universities, while only around 25 per cent of men attended higher education.

Although the expansion in access has been significant, quality has not improved at a similar pace as we discuss in detail in this section. In international terms, Dubai universities lag behind universities in other Arab countries, such as the Kingdom of Saudi Arabia, Egypt, or Tunisia. They also lag considerably when compared to countries with similar level of income per capita and, most significantly, when compared to the economies that Dubai would like to emulate, such as Singapore, Hong Kong, or Taiwan.

As in the case of primary and secondary education, evaluating the quality of education in universities is cumbersome. Universities play a key role in contributing to innovation, advancing knowledge, and enhancing the competitive advantages of any economy. However, the form and quantity of their contribution vary notably; advanced economies devote significant private and public resources to ensuring the quality of teaching, research, and dissemination of applied technology. The scope and depth of these activities, however, are to be assessed in relative terms, that is, against the abilities of universities in other countries chosen to be used as benchmarks. Several organizations have developed indicators of higher education performance across a wide spectrum of countries. Among the most popular are the Academic Ranking of World Universities (ARWU), the World University Rankings, and the QS World University Rankings. All rankings employ indicators of the quality of different aspects of higher education (including teaching and research), their financial endowment, the awards won by faculty and alumni, and reputation and impact of the university in terms of innovation and knowledge creation.

According to all indices, the top universities in the world are in the US (e.g. Harvard, Stanford, or MIT) and the UK (Cambridge, Oxford, or Imperial College). No university in Dubai ranks among the top 500 universities in the world. In the Middle East, only Israeli universities rank consistently among the top 150 universities and outperform similar institutions in the Kingdom of Saudi Arabia (King Saud University and King Fahd University), Turkey (Bilkent), and Egypt (Alexandria University). Only UAE University in Al Ain has been ranked with an entry of 372 among 400 universities surveyed by QS World University Rankings in 2012.

A complementary view of these issues consists in evaluating the impact of research activities within fields of knowledge (engineering, medicine, economics, etc.). Data on research outcomes and impacts for Dubai are not available and thus we refer to UAE data. According to SRI International, an independent, non-profit research institute, the UAE ranked 66th in the world as a producer of scientific publications and 87th in publication impact in 2006. This is a relatively backward position considering the high income per capita and the level of development. In fact, the UAE ranks relatively low even in regional terms (7th), behind Egypt and Iran among others. An alternative measurement of research quality is provided by the number of publications in scientific journals. The Arab Knowledge Report 2009 issued by the UNDP indicates that, as of 2005, the UAE lagged significantly behind most countries in the MENA region. However, it exhibited a positive trend: annual publication of scientific documents by UAE researchers was around 500 articles in the period 1996–2002 and it has grown to nearly 2,000 articles in the period 2008–9. When compared to the natural benchmarks of Dubai, that is, Hong Kong and Singapore, the scientific research of the UAE is in its infant stage: East Asian economies produce around six times more research articles than the UAE and their growth rates are markedly higher. These figures refer mostly to the UAE and largely reflect the production of national universities. Indeed, the quantity and quality of research in universities in Dubai is insignificant: according to the most prestigious survey of economic research—the ISI Science Citation Index—the vast majority of the scientific research published by UAE researchers is actually being done outside Dubai, mainly in the UAE University, American University of Sharjah, or the University of Sharjah.

In summary, judging by these performance indicators, Dubai's higher education system does not appear to be truly competitive in international terms. There are several reasons for the backwardness of Dubai's universities and we do not expect to cover all the issues here. One important consideration is the relative youth of the universities, in particular the branches of international universities that have only recently started operations in Dubai. Evidently, in time these universities should progress in coverage and quality and, consequently, would improve their reputation. The majority of these universities had focused mostly on undergraduate teaching, relegating research and links to industry to a minor—and usually insignificant—role.

Another reason why Dubai universities fail to make an impression in these indices is because few of them are fully fledged institutions. These institutions, to a large extent, offer a very limited number of programmes, use mostly part-time teachers and cater for a small student body. On average, enrolment in private universities in free zones does not reach 500 students; as a reference point, universities in the US granting 4-year degrees enrol on average 4,500 students.[8] The vast majority of universities in Dubai actually offer one or two academic programmes (typically masters in Business Administration or in IT) for which the content and material has been produced abroad in the university home country. Consequently, it is not surprising that research and innovation is non-existent. The few larger private institutions—such as AUD or Wollongong—offer a wider range of programmes and have achieved critical mass in terms of faculty and resources in areas such as engineering or technology.

A third reason for the relative weaknesses of universities in Dubai relates to the requirements and regulations that affect universities. Universities in Dubai have only minimal, formal requirements to open; it is to some extent surprising that no development plan is actually required. The KHDA has the responsibility for overseeing private universities in Dubai and a mandate to care for the quality of education. It has enacted the policy that branches of international universities in Dubai must offer education at the same quality of that offered in their home country. This is a relatively inexpensive approach to ensure the quality of education, yet it has two main drawbacks. First, while equalizing domestic and foreign teaching levels avoids universities simply profiting from their reputation, there is no assurance that home quality is as desirable: a mediocre university overseas can set up an equally mediocre

[8] See US Department of Education, National Center for Education Statistics, Integrated Postsecondary Education Data System (IPEDS); US Department of Education (2012).

branch in Dubai. Second, and more importantly, this only requires universities to care for quality in education; other important dimensions of academic life such as research and dissemination can be neglected. Furthermore, foreign universities currently installed in Dubai do not rank among the top 500 universities according to the international rankings mentioned above, either in general or in field rankings.

One additional worrisome issue regarding the performance of the universities in Dubai (and also the UAE) is the almost exclusive focus on business administration, religion, and information technology, both at the undergraduate and graduate levels. According to KHDA (2012), 55 per cent of all Dubai graduates are in business administration, while another 25 per cent split equally between religious studies and information technology. Less than 2 per cent of students are engaged in natural and physical sciences or education, two areas where Dubai is lagging behind most emerging economies. Emirati students follow exactly the same pattern.

While preferences play a role, the actual supply of academic programmes is very relevant to determine the skill composition of the students. Dubai's open-door policy to new universities allows institutions to determine the programmes that they offer, based on student demand and willingness to pay. Moreover, because start-up costs are not low, incoming universities tend to concentrate on low-cost programmes and avoid disciplines that would require heavy investments (such as hospitals for medical schools or laboratories for natural sciences). Not surprisingly, the majority of undergraduate programmes are in business and IT-related subjects and the MBAs are the most common graduate programme. Most of the scientific disciplines occupy a marginal role in academic life. In fact, Dubai has very few research programmes that will provide a supply of skilled researchers and scientists needed to make the switch to the knowledge-based economy, and it is unlikely that newly established for-profit institutions will provide these degrees in the future. Therefore, for a foreseeable future, Dubai will continue to rely on imported professionals to support its R&D capacity.

An additional feature of higher education that impinges on higher quality is its gender inequality. As noted by Ridge (2009), while at the preparatory and secondary education levels enrolment rates are slightly higher for girls than boys, only 12 per cent of males have an education at the tertiary level compared with nearly 40 per cent of females. The gap between men and women is even more pronounced among Emirati nationals: according to the Ministry of Higher Education only 27 per cent of Emirati males are attending higher education, compared with over 70 per cent of Emirati females. Among the reasons for this phenomenon, Ridge indicates that 'in societies where the quality of education is low and public sector employment is high, individuals often make distorted educational choices, as they perceive that there are no real gains to further education'. The higher education system in Dubai, nevertheless, shows a more balanced gender structure of Emirati nationals: according to KHDA (2011), around 52 per cent of the students in universities in Dubai are male while females only reach around 48 per cent. To some extent, and considering the high cost of private universities, this challenges the notion that Emirati males are not interested in higher education.

The relative backwardness of UAE and Dubai tertiary education, more than any other factor, is a key limiting factor in the development of a knowledge-based economy. The World Bank Institute has developed a set of indices to help countries identify the challenges and opportunities they face in making the transition to a knowledge-based economy. The Knowledge Index measures the performance of countries in economic incentives and institutional regime; education; innovation; and information and communications technologies (ICT). As shown in Table 10.5, in 2009 the UAE ranked 45 among 146 countries (no data are available for Dubai, but one can rest assured that the emirate would not perform worse than the UAE average). While the UAE significantly outperformed the average economy in ICT and economic incentives, it only has a marginal superiority in education and falls very short in innovation. These results are most likely the result of the effort on the part of the government in providing an adequate business environment and

Table 10.5. Knowledge Index in 2009

Country	Knowledge Index	Economic Incentive Index	Innovation Index	Education Index	ICT Index
All countries	6.19	5.21	8.11	4.24	6.22
Taiwan, China	8.79	7.42	9.27	7.97	9.13
Singapore	8.03	9.68	9.58	5.29	9.22
United Arab Emirates	*6.72*	*6.75*	*6.69*	*4.90*	*8.59*
Middle East and North Africa	5.68	4.86	7.57	3.75	5.71
Qatar	6.63	7.05	6.45	5.37	8.06
Bahrain	5.80	6.75	4.29	5.82	7.30
Kuwait	5.63	6.50	4.98	4.93	6.96
Jordan	5.39	5.99	5.59	5.62	4.95
Saudi Arabia	5.10	5.94	3.97	4.89	6.43
Turkey	5.07	6.98	5.83	4.46	4.92
Lebanon	4.93	4.42	4.53	4.92	5.35
Oman	4.77	7.15	4.94	4.47	4.90
Iran, Islamic Rep.	4.67	0.99	4.56	3.80	5.65
Tunisia	4.54	4.04	4.65	4.08	4.88
Egypt, Arab Rep.	4.24	3.59	4.44	4.35	3.92
Algeria	3.57	2.18	3.59	3.66	3.46
Syrian Arab Republic	3.57	1.65	3.17	3.10	4.43
Yemen, Rep.	2.04	2.66	2.67	1.79	1.67

Source: Knowledge for Development Program, World Bank

improving the infrastructure in information and communications. The relative weakness of the education and innovation indexes is congruent with the low quality of universities and suggests the need to revise educational policies.

In relative terms, UAE and Dubai outperform all GCC and other Arab countries although not for a significant margin in the case of Qatar or Bahrain. While in regional terms Dubai outranks all other economies, when compared to the leading countries it would like to emulate, it falls very short. Only in ICT does Dubai approach the levels of Hong Kong, Singapore, or Taiwan. In the rest, and particularly in education, it lags significantly behind.

The backwardness of the educational system not only negatively affects the long-run switch towards a knowledge-based economy but it also affects current economic growth. Research concludes that there is a statistically significant causal relationship running from the level of knowledge accumulation as measured by the knowledge index to future economic growth (World Bank, 2009). Researchers have also concluded that to move to a knowledge-based economy, countries must give priority to branches of science (natural, exact, and applied) in tertiary education programmes.

10.5 THE COST OF EDUCATION

As described, education in Dubai is widespread and accessible but of mediocre quality. An important consideration is the cost at which such education levels are obtained. Mediocre quality could be the result of allocating too few resources to education, as is the case of most developing economies, or as a result of low productivity in the use of available resources. Developed economies allocate significant resources to education maintaining, at the same time, a balance in terms of the costs and benefits among the different segments of the education chain. These countries are thus good benchmarks for expenditures in education, performance, and costs.

The direct cost for the families of education in Dubai depends on nationality. Public schools are free for Emirati nationals, while a very few expatriate children are allowed to attend for a fee of around US$2,000 and subject to space availability (the fee is justified as the cost of uniforms, books, and other materials). On the contrary, private education is very expensive. Annual school fees for primary and secondary education ranged between US$1,400 at a crowded and poorly resourced school and US$25,000 per year at the more reputable schools. The median annual fee in 2009/10 in a sample of 125 private schools collected for this chapter was slightly above US$4,500. The same study estimated that the median annual fee charged by private universities in Dubai was around US$13,500. National universities, on the other hand, are free for Emiratis and banned for expatriates but other public institutions allow non-Emiratis at a substantial fee for enrolment (up to US $21,800).

The direct costs of private education are quite high by international standards: as a reference, the average tuition in US universities granting 4-year degrees was US$9,000 in 2010.[9] Needless to say, the quality of university education in the US is substantially higher, indicating a very low quality/price ratio in Dubai. With regards to primary and secondary private education, the quality/price ratio is slightly better but well below international standards. When comparing Dubai to Chile, a country exhibiting similar TIMMS results, the annual costs of private education in the latter would be around one fifth of those in Dubai.

But the direct costs to families of private education does not take into account the significant effort made by the government to build human capital. We use this information on expenditures and UNESCO data on enrolment to estimate the cost of public education in the UAE. The results are in Table 10.6, where we have also added our previous estimates on tuition fees in private schools as a reference point. It can be seen that the government spends around US$8,500 per year for each student enrolled in public pre-primary, primary, and secondary schools and over US$20,000 for tertiary students. Presumably, the costs of public education in Dubai are similar to the national average costs and we, thus, use them for comparison.

It can be seen that public education in Dubai is, on average, far more expensive than private education in early childhood, primary, and secondary education, even if one considers public expenditures to be inflated by

Table 10.6. Estimated costs of education in the public and private sectors (school year 2009/10)

	Estimated enrolment	Annual government expenditures (US$ m)	Estimated annual cost per student (US$)
UAE (public sector)			
Pre-primary	6,360	207	8,880
Primary	24,020	813	9,230
Secondary	39,900	1,190	8,120
Tertiary	9,800	740	20,550
Dubai (private sector)			
Pre-primary	10,850	217	5,450
Primary	36,000	612	4,660
Secondary	4,530	77	4,660
Tertiary	8,750	557	17,900

Source: Own estimates based on data from UNESCO and KHDA

[9] US Department of Education, National Center for Education Statistics, Integrated Post-secondary Education Data System (IPEDS).

administrative costs and other ministry expenditures. This, of course, is the reflection of the above-mentioned overstaffing of public schools and the fact that Emirati nationals are paid substantially more than expatriate teachers and staff. UNESCO data indicate that around 80 per cent of all public expenditures in education in the period 1999–2009 in the UAE corresponded to salaries. In contrast, in the OECD economies salaries amounted to 75 per cent in the same period and in benchmark economies (Hong Kong, Singapore, and Taiwan) it did not reach 65 per cent. The high cost per student of public education is also the result of the protracted decline in enrolment in public schools that has led to very small size of classes. On the other hand, government expenditures at the tertiary education level are slightly higher than those in the private sector. Consider, however, that private universities are largely for profit.

An alternative way to understand how costly education is in Dubai and the UAE is to use as benchmark economies with a similar performance in international academic tests such as TIMSS and PISA and for which data on costs is available. Chile is a useful point of reference. It performed only marginally worse than Dubai in PISA, but the annual cost per student in public schools is around US$1,400 per student and private schools charge pupils tuition fees in the range of US$1,400 to US$8,200 per year.

10.6 CONCLUSIONS

Education in Dubai has developed at a fast pace in the last three decades yet it is far from being consolidated. Access to primary and secondary education has been extended to the whole population, regardless of nationality. Tertiary and early-childhood education, however, lag significantly behind.

Although access to education has expanded markedly, the quality of education has not progressed at a similar pace. Primary education is at best mediocre by international standards and the quality of secondary and tertiary education is poor. The quality of primary and secondary education is highly unequal: private schools outperform public schools in international performance tests by a substantial margin. Quality is unequal in terms of gender, with boys in public schools and universities performing worse than girls and dropping out at a much higher rate. Quality is also highly heterogeneous in tertiary education, with national universities taking the lead over private universities but underperforming by international standards.

A mediocre and unequal quality of education is a serious limitation to Dubai's long-run development and its aspiration of becoming a knowledge-based society. Knowledge-based economies rely on the quality of their education system and on their capacity to educate the labour force as required by increasingly demanding global markets. Productivity and competitiveness are mostly determined by a clever articulation of formal education entities, labour markets, and on-the-job training in firms and businesses. The low quality of education in Dubai is a source of concern for both society and its authorities. The government of Dubai has started to implement measures to improve on quality, yet these measures are timid and/or still in their initial stages to be properly evaluated. The UAE government has also launched initiatives to improve teaching and school management.

This chapter concludes that to improve quality, it is necessary to change the organization of the education cluster, modifying the incentives given to the participants so that they operate under more efficient frameworks, implementing new policies where existing ones are insufficient or incomplete and injecting accountability where none is currently in place. The path towards higher quality builds upon the existing structure of policies and regulations. Policies and regulations have long-lasting effects on the fate of the education cluster and on the quality of human capital formation. Undertaking remedial policies at this stage will ensure future success.

REFERENCES

Bennett, J., 2009. *Early Childhood and Education Services in Dubai,* Dubai: Knowledge and Human Development Authority, Dubai.

Dubai Schools Inspection Bureau, 2009. *Annual Report,* Dubai: Knowledge and Human Development Authority.

Farah, S. and Ridge, N., 2009. *Challenges to Curriculum Development in the UAE,* Dubai: Dubai School of Government.

Hanushek, E. A., Kain, J. F., and Rivkin, S. G., 1999. 'Do Higher Salaries Buy Better Teachers?' NBER Working Paper (April) No. 7082.

Helal, M., 2009. *Benchmarking Education: Dubai and the Trends in Mathematics and Science Study 2007,* Dubai: Dubai School of Government.

Karaman, J., 2011. *Policy Brief No 23: Early Childhood Education in Dubai,* Dubai: Dubai School of Government.

KHDA, 2011. *The Higher Education Landscape in Dubai 2010,* Dubai: Knowledge and Human Development Authority of Dubai.

KHDA, 2012. *Key Education Statistics for Dubai: 2010/11 Academic Year,* Dubai: Knowledge and Human Development Authority of Dubai.

Lane, J., 2010. *Policy Brief No 20: Campuses, Free Zones, and Quality Assurance: Policy Issues for Dubai and the UAE,* Dubai: Dubai School of Government.

OECD, 2010. *PISA 2009 Results: What Students Know and Can Do: Student Performance in Reading,* Paris: Organization of Economic Co-operation and Development.

OECD, 2011. *National Accounts.* [Online] Available at: http://www.oecd.org/std/na/, accessed 14 September 2011.

Ridge, N., 2009. *Policy Brief No 12: The Hidden Gender Gap in Education in the UAE,* Dubai: Dubai School of Government.

TIMSS, 2008. *TIMSS 2007 Encyclopedia: A Guide to Mathematics and Science Education around the World.* Chestnut Hill, MA: Lynch School of Education, Boston College.

UNDP, 2009. *Arab Knowledge Report 2009: Towards Productive Intercommunication for Knowledge,* Dubai: Al Ghurair Printing & Publishing House.

UNESCO, 2009. 'Education (full dataset)'. [Online] Available at: http://data.uis.unesco.org/Index.aspx?DataSetCode=EDULIT_DS, accessed 2 September 2015.

US Department of Education, 2012. *National Center for Education Statistics*, available at nces.ed.gov/ipeds/, accessed 4 April 2015.

World Bank, 2009. *Measuring Knowledge in the World's Economies,* Washington, DC: World Bank Knowledge for Development Program.

11

Labour Markets in Transition

Raimundo Soto and Yousif Rashid

11.1 INTRODUCTION

This chapter describes and analyses the working of the labour market in Dubai and its impacts on the economy of the Emirate. As is the case with other countries in the Gulf Cooperating Council (GCC), Dubai's workforce relies heavily on foreign expatriates: according to the 2009 UAE Labour Force Survey (hereafter, LFS-2009), 91 per cent of the economically active population are foreigners of which 78.6 per cent participate in the labour market.[1] These participants are mostly male (87 per cent), fairly young (50 per cent are between 25 and 35 years of age), and with low educational attainment (62 per cent have secondary schooling or below).

The high participation of expatriate workers is the result of the sponsorship system (*Kafala* in Arabic), an idiosyncratic scheme that has shaped the development of GCC economies. It requires each migrant to be sponsored by an Emirati national or Emirati-controlled firm that becomes his/her legal representative (illegally, some employers even retain the worker's passport). The migrant becomes tied to the sponsor for the duration of his/her contract—from one to three years—and cannot change sponsor unless they obtain written consent (no objection certificate). In principle, workers should leave the UAE immediately upon termination of the contract but renewals are frequently observed. The elimination of the no objection certificate has been a recurrent issue but as of 2013 no reforms had been implemented.

[1] Estimates in this chapter draw from the 2009 Labour Force Survey and the 2008 Employment, Hours and Wage survey. The former is representative at the household level (excluding labour camps), and it provides information on both labour market participants and non-participants. The latter collects information at the firm level and provides information on employers and employees (both in the public and the private sector). Consequently, it includes labour camps.

In addition to the expatriate workforce, the Emirati also participate in the labour market but without the restrictions implied by the sponsorship system. Emirati workers are free to move between available vacancies in accordance with their preferences and, at the same time, they are protected by the rules and regulations emanating from the Emiratization programme that shelters them from openly competing with expatriates in the labour market. As discussed below, the participation rate of Emirati in Dubai's labour market has increased from 22 per cent in 1975 to 44 per cent in 2009; the change is mostly due to the increase in the participation of females from about 2 per cent in 1975 to 25 per cent in 2009. Nationals are largely employed in the public sector; among the Emirati that participate in the labour market, around 79 per cent are employees of either the local or federal administration. They also tend to occupy high-level positions (both in the private and public sectors) sometimes uncorrelated to their educational attainment.

The fact that Emirati nationals and expatriate workers operate under different labour laws results in a dual labour market along nationality lines. As discussed later in the chapter, this duality contributes to distorting labour market incentives for Emirati and expatriate workers alike, reducing businesses' efficiency and technology adoption. Distortions disconnect efforts from salaries, induce non-accountability, and hamper human capital accumulation. Such distortions are further exacerbated by public employment policies that often use the labour market to distribute oil-based wealth among Emirati nationals. The sponsorship system does not produce the labour market incentives needed to motivate expatriate and Emirati workers to exercise the effort levels that are usually associated with the efficiency and productivity of labour markets in modern economies.

Although the sponsorship system and the existing public employment policies are largely responsible for current labour market distortions, historical reasons justify its initial implementation. At the take-off stage in the 1970s, Dubai had to overcome the shortage of native workers in order to develop its physical and industrial infrastructure. At that point attracting large volumes of low-cost workers with low human-capital levels might have been the optimal policy. But Dubai can no longer be considered an economy at the take-off stage and, consequently, the *Kafala* system is no longer an efficient development instrument. The authorities have expressed a desire to move toward a productive model relying significantly more on high-skilled workers operating in technology-based industries and less on the low-cost labour-intensive productive methods currently in use. Furthermore, they aim at seeing Emirati workers playing an increasing role in the private sector. However, the success of this strategic plan requires knowledge on how current policies affect the working of the labour market and how they limit the emirate from adopting more productive technologies. In this section we discuss what direction policy reforms should take in order to be congruent with long-run development.

11.2 POPULATION AND DEMOGRAPHICS

In economies with traditional labour markets the structure of the workforce depends mainly on the characteristics of the population: the size of the different age-cohorts, the participation rates by gender, and the education levels all determine the labour supply and the evolution of the stock of human capital of the economy. In Dubai the dynamics are quite the opposite: the structure of the workforce is largely demand driven. Worker's characteristics (skill distribution, gender, age structure, etc.) are determined by the aggregate requirements of the different economic sectors. Thus, inward migration flows principally determine both the characteristics and the structure of the workforce and, consequently, the demographic structure of the population. In fact, only the native Emirati display demographic characteristics resembling traditional societies and, consequently, they conform closer to the typical workforce in a modern labour market. However, even in the case of the Emirati, as discussed later in the chapter, there are several constraints in place for them to be treated as a standard case.

The population of Dubai as of 2010 was estimated by the Dubai Statistics Center to be close to two million, up by 44 per cent from the 1.3 million recorded in the census of 2005 (see Table 11.1). The figures reveal that during the last two decades there was an extremely fast expansion in population as a result of the massive inflows of migrants. The annual growth rate between 2005 and 2010 was 7.6 per cent, around seven times the average annual growth of the population in the world (1.1 per cent, according to the US Bureau of the Census). Dubai accounts for roughly 30 per cent of the population of the UAE, making it the second most populated emirate after Abu Dhabi.

A second feature of the population is the notoriously small number of Emirati vis-à-vis the massive population of expatriates. Estimates by the UAE National Bureau of Statistics in Table 11.1 indicate that as of 2010 the local population was around 170,000; this is equivalent to 9 per cent of the total population of Dubai. According to these estimates, the native population also grows at a high rate (4.4 per cent annually). While this rate is much higher than the world average in the same period, it is nevertheless much lower than the net annual immigration growth of 8 per cent per year. Not surprisingly, relative to expatriates the local population has declined systematically since the Census in 2005.

Table 11.1. Population by origin and gender, 2005 and 2010

	Males 2005	Females 2005	Total 2005	Males 2010	Females 2010	Total 2010
Total*	989,305	332,148	1,321,453	1,485,046	420,430	1,905,476
Emirati**	68,995	68,578	135,735	84,245	83,784	168,029
Expatriates	920,310	263,570	1,183,880	1,400,801	336,646	1,737,447

Notes: (*) data from the Dubai Statistics Center, (**) data from the UAE Bureau of Statistics.

A third feature of the population is its gender imbalance. As shown in Table 11.1, while the local population abides by the world standard of having a similar share of women vis-à-vis men, the expatriate population is highly skewed in favour of men. In 2010, the ratio of males to females in the expatriate population was over four, reflecting largely two factors. First, expatriates are not allowed to bring their families to the UAE unless they earn a monthly salary of US$2,725 or more. According to the 2008 UAE Employment, Hours and Wage Survey (hereafter, EHWS-2008) only 15 per cent of expatriates fulfil such condition.[2] A second reason for the gender imbalance among expatriates is that the demand for workers comes mainly from industries that are traditionally associated with male employment (such as construction). Data suggest that the gender imbalance among the expatriates increased over the years: the ratio of males to females was 3.5 in 2005 but increased to about 4.1 in 2010.

The dual nature of the population along nationality lines, together with the relatively high fertility rate of the Emirati,[3] shapes the age structure of the population in a peculiar way. First, the age structure is unevenly distributed by gender, being largely dominated by males. Second, the population is relatively young with a very high concentration in the segment of 25 to 35 years of age. Figure 11.1 shows that such an age segment accounts for about 40 per cent of

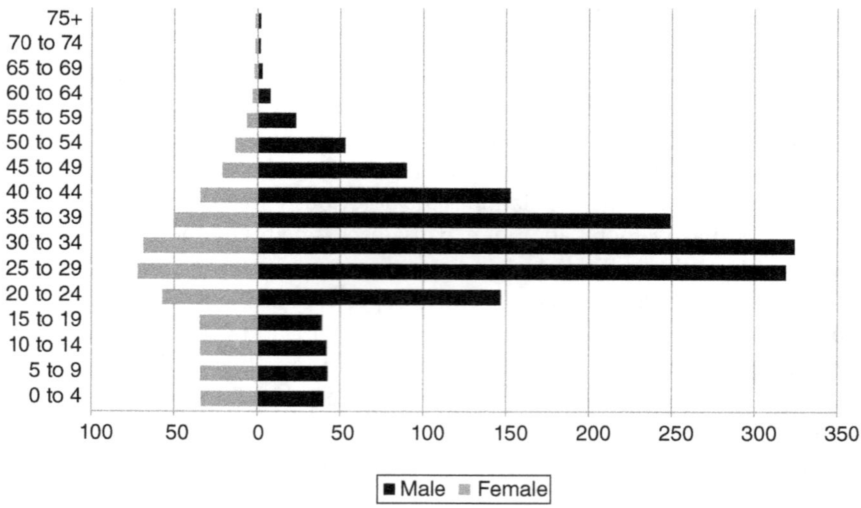

Figure 11.1. Dubai's age pyramid
Source: Dubai Statistics Center

[2] In January 2010 the minimum monthly requirement for family reunification set by the government was raised from AED6,000 (US$1,635) to AED10,000 (US$2,675).

[3] According to the World Bank (2011), the UAE average fertility rate between 1990 and 2010 was 3 births per female whereas the world average over the same period was 2.5.

the population (50 per cent in terms of labour force) whereas the world share for the same age group is estimated at around 17 per cent (UN, 2011). Likewise, the share of elderly people (above 65 years) is much smaller than world standards: in Dubai it reaches only 0.6 per cent of total population in contrast with the world average of 7.5 per cent. The evidence from Table 11.1 and Figure 11.1 confirms that the structure of the population has been largely determined by the demand for labour in the labour market and not vice-versa.

11.3 THE CHARACTERISTICS OF THE LABOUR FORCE

The total labour force in Dubai—defined as individuals over fifteen years of age working or seeking an occupation—was estimated by the Dubai Statistics Center to be 1.4 million in 2009 (LFS-2009). This is significantly greater than the labour force of around one million estimated by the Census in 2005. Of the total labour force, around 46,000 are UAE nationals and the rest are expatriates.

The striking differences between the local Emirati and the expatriates in terms of gender and population size reflect the dynamic effects induced by the different regulations under which each type of worker operates. In fact, Dubai organizes as a highly segmented dual labour market and, accordingly, we start by providing stylized facts for each group, Emirati and expatriates, and follow with an analysis of how such facts and the interaction among both groups affect the performance of the labour market.

11.3.1 The Emirati Workforce

Between 1975 and 2009 the participation rate of Emirati in the labour force grew at an average 0.65 per cent per year, increasing from 22 per cent in 1975 to 44 per cent in 2009. Figure 11.2 shows that the greatest change happened between 2005 and 2009 when the participation of Emirati grew at an average rate of 3.1 per cent per year. One factor that could explain the secular increase in participation is the change in the educational system; in 1975 education in the UAE became compulsory for individuals aged five to fifteen (see Chapter 10, this volume). Subsequently and gradually the number of individuals entering higher education grew, thereby effectively increasing the labour participation rate of Emirati nationals in the years to come. Figure 11.2 shows that much of the growth in the participation rate of Emirati is due to the increasing participation of women, especially between 1995 and 2009 when

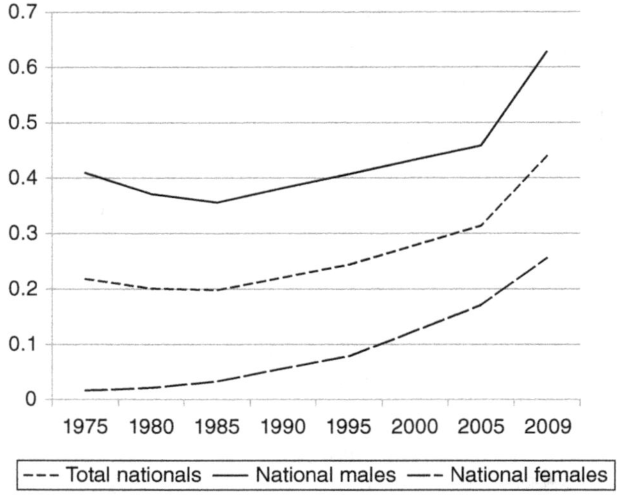

Figure 11.2. Participation rates of Emirati nationals in the labour market
Source: Own elaboration based on data from UAE Censuses and 2009 Labour Force Survey

the rate grew on average by two percentage points per year. The increase in educational attainment is likely to have contributed to higher participation, particularly among females; likewise, greater social acceptance of working mothers has also contributed.

Despite the sustained increase, participation rates of Emirati still remain well below those of OECD economies. As of 2010, about 45 per cent of Emirati—males and females—are active in the labour market: the percentage is well below that of OECD economies where 73 per cent of prime age individuals participate, 83 per cent for males and 64 per cent for females (OECD, 2010). This indicates a substantial reserve of manpower in Dubai that could enter the labour market and contribute to economic development. The increase in participation rates in the period 2005–10 could be due to the high demand for labour in the years preceding the crisis, as well as the result of undisclosed methodological changes in the statistics.

Table 11.2 shows the status of prime-age Emirati that do not participate in the labour market. Around 20 per cent of males classify themselves as 'not willing to work'; clearly, this marks the difference between male participation in Dubai and the OECD economies. In the latter, males not willing to work are typically below 1.5 per cent (Eurostat, 2011 and Weir, 2003). And it also reflects the Emirati society as one with a very high reservation wage.[4] In the

[4] A reservation wage corresponds to the minimum salary a person would demand to become active in the labour market. If offered a salary below the reservation wage, the individual would prefer to stay home.

Table 11.2. Characteristics of prime-age Emirati population, 2009

	% of all non-participants	Average age	Education level			Average household size[1]
			Primary or less	High school education	Above high school	
Male non-participants						
Early retired	13.3	55	58%	32%	10%	8
Full-time students	61.2	18	42%	56%	2%	8
Disabled	5.0	39	92%	0%	8%	7
Not willing to work	20.5	46	58%	25%	17%	7
House-husbands	0.0	—	—	—	—	—
Male participants	—	35	23%	45%	32%	8
Female non-participants						
Early retired	3.0	62	91%	0%	9%	6
Full-time students	32.2	18	39%	56%	5%	8
Disabled	2.2	54	85%	15%	—	6
Not willing to work	7.1	36	36%	64%	—	7
Housewives	55.5	37	50%	39%	11%	8
Female participants	—	30	4%	45%	51%	7

[1] Excludes maidservants in the household.
Source: UAE Labour Force Survey, 2009

case of females, housewife status explains their low participation rates relative to OECD estimates. Table 11.2 also shows that compared to non-participants (excluding full-time students), participating Emirati are younger and have attained higher educational levels. Especially in the case of females, education is a determining factor in their labour market behaviour: 51 per cent of those who participate are university graduates compared to only 8.1 per cent of non-participating females. Figure 11.3 further confirms that the participation of females increases substantially for increasing educational sub-groups. In contrast the participation of males spans across all educational levels.

Among the Emirati that participate in the labour market, 5 per cent are self-employed, 10 per cent are unemployed, and the rest are employed. The proportion of self-employed is significantly below that of OECD economies where around 17 per cent of the actively employed are registered as self-employed (OECD, 2010). On the other hand, the 10 per cent classified as involuntary unemployed in Dubai in 2009 are characterized as quite young (on average 25 years old), more likely to be females (54 per cent), mostly first time job-seekers (82 per cent), and relatively uneducated: 28 per cent have at most up to primary school and only 53 per cent have completed secondary education. Only 19 per cent of the unemployed have university education or above; among first time job-seekers 20 per cent are university graduates of which 56 per cent are females.

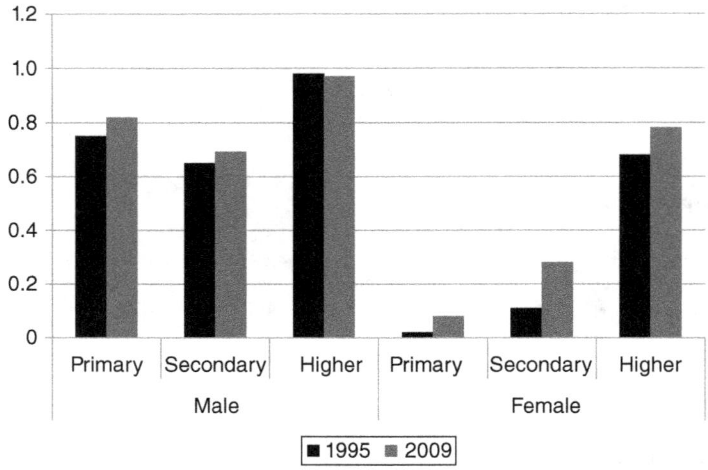

Figure 11.3. Participation rates of Emirati by education levels
Source: UAE Labour Force Survey, 2009

It is important to point out that the term of involuntary unemployment in the UAE has to be taken with caution. The LFS-2009 asked first-time job-seekers for their preferences in terms of public versus private sector employment: 100 per cent declared a preference for the public sector (62 per cent preferred local government employment and 38 per cent preferred to work for the federal administration). These figures could well indicate that a status of involuntary unemployment among Emirati reflects labour market preferences rather than frictional problems or a labour market mismatch: some UAE citizens would thus be waiting for an opening in the government instead of actively searching for a job in the labour market.[5] If this is the case some of the involuntary unemployed in Dubai ought to be classified as inactive by international standards. This caveat does not belittle the importance of unemployment among the Emirati. As shown in Figure 11.4, in 1997 the Emirati unemployment rate was 8.3 per cent; by 2009 it had dropped somewhat to 6.5 per cent. However, the same figure shows that unemployment is concentrated in young Emirati and, especially, among females. One reason that might explain the rise in unemployment among females is their increasing participation in the labour market: in fact, the share of females among first time job-seekers increased from 49 per cent in 1997 to 54 per cent in 2009. In addition, the relative absence of part-time occupations in the UAE labour market, itself the result of government regulations, would make it difficult for women

[5] The strategy of waiting for an opening in the public sector is akin to the 'neither in the labour force nor in education or training' phenomenon in the UK and other developed countries (Roberts, 2011).

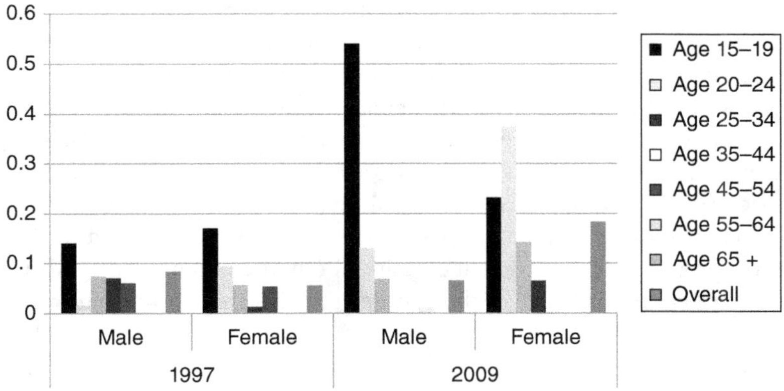

Figure 11.4. Unemployment rate of resident Emirati

Source: Own elaboration based on data from 1997 UAE Household Budget Survey and 2009 UAE Labour Force Survey

to work during their fertile years. More worrisome, however, is the evidence compiled in Chapter 10 regarding the perceived inability of the educational system to produce graduates that have the competencies demanded by prospective employers.

Among Emirati, 85 per cent are classified as employees of which a staggering 83.4 per cent work for the public sector (26.4 per cent in the local administration, 56.7 per cent work for the federal government, and 0.2 per cent work for public–private partnerships, i.e. private firms with a substantial degree of government ownership). There are several reasons for such preference. First, historically there was a need to develop most government institutions (the country was founded in 1971) which led to a sustained growth in public sector jobs that, for a long time, rivalled the job creation of the private sector; it is likely that this trend contributed to form expectations of a birthright to public employment among subsequent Emirati generations. At the same time, the authorities had often used the labour market to distribute resource-based wealth, resulting in a significant earning's gap in favour of Emirati employees in the public sector vis-à-vis equivalent positions in the private sector.[6] According to the LFS-2009 the average differential in monthly earnings between Emirati in the public sector and those working in the private sector is US$890. Besides higher earnings, other public sector employment

[6] These are generalized features of labour markets in GCC countries. WEF (2014) provides a comprehensive analysis of how these elements shape the working of the labour market, account for low productivity, and determine unemployment rates of the nationals, particularly the youth. Policy recommendations from the report call for bold leadership in fundamentally rebuilding the employment system to create a new, more sustainable form of social stability.

benefits include shorter working hours (three less per week), very generous direct transfers (allowances), and more opportunities for training. Working for the government is also associated with greater job security through clauses by which laying-off an Emirati public servant becomes very difficult. Altogether, these are sufficient reasons to make public sector employment more appealing than the private sector for Emirati at equal salaries.

As described, historical reasons led Emirati to focus almost exclusively on the public sector for employment. In 1995 the authorities put forward the 'Emiratization programme' aimed at increasing the participation of Emirati in the labour market, in particular in the private sector. Although the Emiratization programme has gone through various amendments, as of 2011 it embodied three main pillars: (1) a 4 per cent mandatory quota of Emirati employees for firms that have fifty employees or more; (2) active labour market policies applicable to unemployed Emirati that wish to work (e.g. training courses, search assistance, and wage subsidies); and (3) nationalization of particular occupations for firms outside free zones (in particular, staff in human resource departments, public representation officers, secretarial positions, and teaching positions for primary schools). In practice the Emiratization programme is a protectionist measure that forces employers to hire Emirati thus reducing the demand for foreign workers at the semi-skilled and entry-level professional categories. At the same time the Emiratization programme increases the total wage bill of firms because it establishes a minimum wage applicable only to Emirati.[7] However, fifteen years after the process was first implemented, existing data suggest that it has not been very successful: in 1997 the proportion of Emirati employed in Dubai's private sector was around 7 per cent and it increased to only 11 per cent in 2009 (LFS-2009).

11.3.2 The Expatriate Workforce

Expatriates account for 91 per cent of the population of the emirate and 87 per cent of its workforce. According to the LFS-2009, 77 per cent of expatriates are employed, 15 per cent are housewives and the rest are out of the labour force (mainly full-time students). The gender distribution of expatriates is highly skewed—70 per cent are male and 30 per cent are females—but among the employed the gender imbalance is even higher: 86 per cent are males and 14 per cent are female. On average, expatriate workers are relatively young (50 per cent are between the age of 25 and 35) and work mainly in low-skilled

[7] The minimum wage for Emirati was fixed in 2007 at US$1,160 per month irrespective of the educational background of individuals. Previously it was established according to educational attainment: US$820 for employees with primary education or less, US$1,100 for high-school graduates, and US$1,360 for those with education above high school.

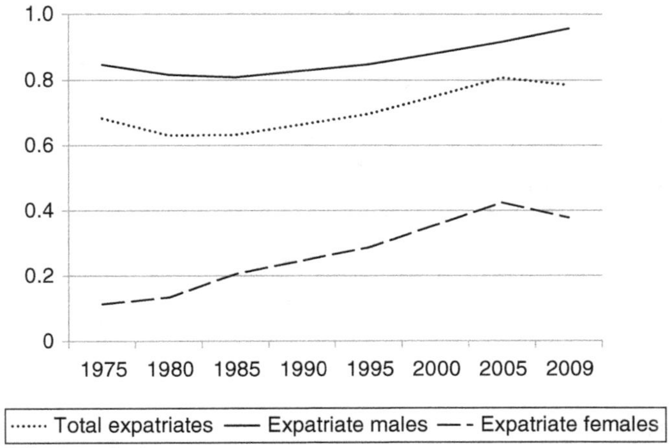

Figure 11.5. Participation rates of expatriates

Source: Own elaboration based on data from UAE Census and 2009 Labour Force Survey

occupations: 39 per cent in semi-skilled jobs (clerks, customer services, and crafts) and 17 per cent fall in the non-skilled elementary occupations (machinery operators, basic transportation, etc.).

Figure 11.5 shows that the participation rate of expatriates is consistently above that of Emirati (compare with Figure 11.2), which is not surprising because by law expatriates can only remain in the UAE if they are employed, so that neither voluntary nor involuntary unemployment is an option. Participation of expatriate females has grown at a higher rate than that of expatriate males or Emirati females: starting from 11 per cent in 1975 their participation rate has grown at almost one percentage point per year on average. Despite this, female participation remains well below the average of OECD economies of 64 per cent (OECD, 2010). The reason is that most expatriate females in Dubai arrive to accompany their male spouses and not as labour market participants, finding it difficult to access an occupation once in the country. The drop in participation observed between 2005 and 2009 likely reflects the adverse effects of the financial crisis.

In section 11.2 we argued that Dubai's population (and therefore its workforce) is largely demand driven by sponsors that use migrants to make up for the shortage of native workers. As in the other oil-endowed GCC economies, the first waves of migrants arrived in the 1960s from poorer neighbouring Arab economies. Nowadays they arrive mostly from the Indian sub-continent. Table 11.3 shows that between 1997 and 2009 the representation of Arabs (MENA and GCC) dropped from 20.6 per cent to 7.7 per cent in favour of Asia migrants (Euro-Asia, Russia, or China).

Table 11.3. Origins and education of expatriate participants

	Percentage of total	Illiterate %	Primary %	Secondary %	University %
1997					
GCC excluding UAE	0.8	16.7	22.2	50.0	11.1
Arab MENA excluding GCC	19.8	0.9	8.5	35.7	54.9
BIPP+	65.9	7.9	19.7	25.7	46.7
Asia	3.6	5.1	33.3	29.5	32.1
Westerners	9.7	0.5	7.6	25.7	66.2
Rest of the World	0.1	—	—	66.7	33.3
Emirati nationals		14.2	34.7	37.3	13.8
Emirati and expatriate participants		9.4	24.5	32.1	34.0
2009					
GCC excluding UAE	0.2	1.5	—	33.7	64.8
MENA excluding GCC	7.5	0.2	8.4	29.3	62.1
BIPP+	53.5	19.0	14.9	26.5	39.7
Asia	32.6	14.4	21.5	32.8	31.4
Westerners	4.7	—	—	12.2	87.8
Rest of the World	1.5	4.6	3.6	54.4	37.5
Emirati nationals		2.6	14.3	45.3	37.8
Emirati and expatriate participants		14.0	15.5	29.9	40.7

Notes: All estimates based on active participants only. BIPP includes Bangladesh, India, Philippines, Pakistan, Nepal, and Bhutan. Asia includes Iran, Euro-Asian economies, and China, but excludes the Asian Tigers. Westerners include Europe, North and South America, Oceania, and Asian Tigers.
Sources: 1997 UAE Household Budget Survey and 2009 UAE Labour Force Survey

Concurrently with Dubai's development, there has also been an increase in the demand for higher educational levels among expatriates: in 1997 only 11 per cent of GCC, 54 per cent of MENA Arabs, and 66 per cent of Westerners were university graduates; in 2009 these had increased to 65 per cent, 62 per cent, and 88 per cent respectively. The observed increase in university graduates to 41 per cent of the workforce means that Dubai compares equally to economies such as Japan and the USA where the proportion of graduates in the workforce is around 40 per cent (OECD, 2010). In fact, in 2010 the proportion of Emirati nationals with university studies (37.8 per cent) was also in line with international standards. However, as we shall see later, this figure hides the fact that the nature of university degrees does not necessarily match the skills demanded by private sector employers in Dubai.

An important feature in Dubai's labour market is the weak correlation between educational attainment and occupational positions for Emirati and expatriates. Table 11.4 shows that 76.3 per cent of Emirati occupy high-skilled and managerial positions although 16.9 per cent have (at most) primary education and 45.3 per cent are only high school graduates. In contrast, only 15 per cent of migrants from the BIPP economies occupy high-skilled and

Table 11.4. Sector and occupation of participants by nationality in 2008 (%)

	Works in the public sector	Unskilled	Low skills	Semi and technical skills	High skills, managerial
GCC excluding UAE	94.3	2.7	15.6	33.1	48.6
Arab (MENA) excluding GCC	73.2	2.3	15.1	13.2	69.4
BIPP	28.4	16.5	54.2	14.3	15.0
Asia	37.5	5.5	37.9	29.8	26.8
Westerners	25.5	3.8	15.4	12.3	68.5
Rest of the World	17.9	12.0	29.2	37.9	21.0
Emirati	94.9	1.4	4.1	18.2	76.3

Notes: All estimates based on active participants only. BIPP includes Bangladesh, India, Philippines, Pakistan, Nepal, and Bhutan. Asia includes Iran, Euro-Asian economies, and China, but excludes the Asian Tigers. Westerners include Europe, North and South America, Oceania, and Asian Tigers.
Source: Own elaboration based on 2008 UAE Employment, Hours and Wage Survey in Dubai

managerial positions although 26.5 per cent are high school graduates and around 40 per cent have at least a university degree. Table 11.4 also shows that the three groups of expatriates with the greatest share of graduates (GCC nationals, Arabs from MENA economies, and Westerners) are those with the greatest proportions of individuals in high-skilled and managerial positions. However, whereas Westerners at the top scale of the educational distribution are more likely to be hired by the private sector (only 25.5 per cent works for the public administration), Arabs from GCC and MENA economies are clearly employed by the public sector (94 per cent and 73 per cent, respectively) probably as a consequence of their comparative advantage as Arab speakers.

Three additional features characterize the labour dynamics of expatriate workers in Dubai, namely, significant wage differentials among nationalities; falling real earnings; and a very high turnover rate. The latter is largely the outcome of visa restrictions that lead to a labour market characterized by very-short contracts (two to three years). In turn, these short contracts induce a high frequency of entry and exits among the expatriate workers. According to the LFS-2009 the length of stay of Westerners in Dubai is the shortest (five years on average) compared to other nationalities that claim an average stay of eight to ten years.[8] In practice, the law impedes expatriates settling in Dubai; they and their families can remain as legal aliens for as long as they are sponsored. In this sense, although the authorities do not apply numeric

[8] Surveyed households provide a biased estimate of the length of stay because these are only the survivors and do not account for those that have already left. No other data source on workers' permanence is available.

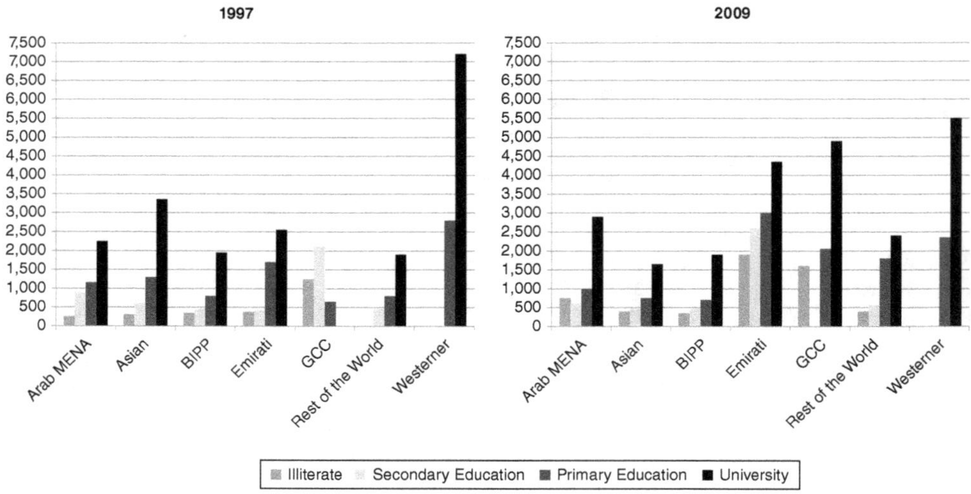

Figure 11.6. Real earnings by nationality and education level

Note: BIPP includes Bangladesh, India, Philippines, Pakistan, Nepal, and Bhutan. Asia includes Iran, Euro-Asian economies, and China, but excludes the Asian Tigers. Westerners include Europe, North and South America, Oceania, and Asian Tigers.

Source: UAE 1997 Household Budget Surveys for 1997 and UAE 2009 Labour Force Survey, Dubai only. CPI for 2008 in base year 1997 is 151.39

caps, these short-term contracts naturally restrict the settling of migrants. The high turnover rate, however, is likely to affect the investment decisions of individuals, including that of human capital formation, capital investment, and social investment, as discussed in section 11.4.

As shown in Figure 11.6, there have been significant wage differentials among nationals of different countries even for similar levels of formal education. It is clear that, both in 1997 and in 2009, earnings have significant variability for most education levels, except the illiterate. Such differences seem to be more pronounced in higher education levels and tend to benefit Westerners the most. One reason for such differences could be that the quality of the education received by expatriate workers is also quite heterogeneous, thus leading to wage differentials. Likewise, work habits and command of English could also be an important factor. However, and as discussed in section 11.4, these differentials could also be the result of different degrees of market power exerted by Dubai firms when hiring workers. For the same skills level, the negotiating capacity of workers from the labour-abundant economies of the Indian subcontinent is substantially lower than their counterparts in American or European countries. This would indicate that average earnings in Dubai are determined not only by skill differentials but also by reservation wages at the country of origin of expatriate workers. Thus, on average, expatriates from economies characterized by very low opportunity costs, informality and, in some cases, high unemployment are those whose average earnings in Dubai are at the lowest.

The evolution of earnings is also revealing. At all educational categories, the earnings of GCC nationals and Emirati have increased in real terms between 1997 and 2009. The trend could be the result of the increase in higher education levels of Emirati over the years. The Emiratization programme coupled with higher minimum and public wages could also explain the trend. For other nationalities, and somewhat surprisingly for an economy that has tripled GDP in the same period, real earnings have remained constant or fallen, especially for expatriates from labour-abundant economies. For example, in 1997 the average earnings of a university graduate with an Asian nationality was $3,250; by 2009 it had dropped by more than 50 per cent in real terms relative to 1997. Likewise, the average earnings of Westerners with university studies had also fallen in real terms by 21 per cent in the same period.

Vazquez-Alvarez (2010) shows, that in most cases, the time-profile of the earnings of expatriate workers remains flat throughout the contractual period—typically at the initial contractual nominal value—for all skill levels. Figure 11.6 seems to further suggest that given the difficulties in changing sponsors, it is likely that subsequent contracts are renewed at the nominal value of the initial one; this gives rise to earnings' profiles that either decrease or remain constant in real terms. Clearly, the opportunity cost of changing sponsors for the vast majority of expatriate workers is too high, for example, as measured by the loss in earning they would incur in the event of having to exit and wait outside the UAE before being allowed to re-enter with a new contract. The same figure is also a reflection of the falling labour productivity detected by Elbadawi and Soto (2012).

11.4 LABOUR MARKET OUTCOMES: ISSUES AND POLICIES

The stylized description above indicates that Dubai's labour market is highly idiosyncratic even for the standards of oil-rich Gulf economies. Historic reasons and labour market regulations, such as the sponsorship system and the Emiratization programme, have created a largely non-competitive labour market riddled with distortions that hamper its performance. Such distortions are likely to retard the development of a much-needed modern labour market in Dubai.

In what follows we review key issues that need addressing at the policy level before the labour market can become the dynamic and efficient tool that is the pillar of the technologically advanced economies Dubai aims to emulate. We focus on three topics, namely (a) the lack of flexibility of the labour market for both expatriates and Emirati, (b) the age, skills, and gender imbalances resulting from the labour structure, and (c) the existence of abnormal profits and significant inefficiencies arising from current regulations.

11.4.1 Duality and Immobility

As mentioned, Emirati and expatriates operate under different labour regulations which results in a dual labour market along nationality lines. Table 11.5 illustrates the importance of such duality for individuals with characteristics that are representative of an average Emirati worker (i.e. males with education equal to secondary or above). Compared to migrants, Emirati earn on average 118 per cent more per hour in basic wages, 177 per cent more per hour in allowances, work 3.5 hours less per week, and are 33 per cent more likely to be placed in the higher occupational categories (higher-skilled or managerial). On average, however, their educational attainment (years of education) is not above that of expatriates and, consequently, cannot be the main explanation for the gaps. Likewise, quality differentials in the education received by Emirati cannot, on average, explain the wage gaps since secondary and tertiary education in Dubai and the UAE falls below world standards (see Soto, 2014).

This duality in outcomes would not exist if the labour market were competitive for both Emirati and expatriates. First, the difference of almost US$15 in hourly wages in favour of Emirati should give rise to arbitrage: observing such a significant gap indicates the existence of market barriers that preclude the free movement of workers between potentially available vacancies. Second, other things being equal, there is no reason to believe that Emirati are significantly more productive than migrants: the statistics in Table 11.5 compares two samples homogeneous in gender, working status, and education levels. Observing higher average earnings—basic wages and allowances—together with lower working hours for Emirati most likely reflect institutional differentials rather than productivity differentials between sub-groups. It also reflects public employment policies that induce Emirati away from the private sector by paying them significantly higher wages not necessarily related to productivity levels. Such policies, however, exacerbate the problem of employability and mobility among Emirati workers: it is unlikely that public servants will receive an equalizing offer from the private sector if expatriates can be employed by a private firm at a fraction of the cost. Finally, although both groups in Table 11.5 are selected so that all individuals are alike, Emirati workers occupy positions with significantly higher skill requirements than migrants and, by the same token, a significant fraction of migrants with

Table 11.5. Labour market outcomes and labour market duality in 2009

	Migrant workers	Emirati workers	Difference
Basic labour market outcomes:			
Hourly basic wage rate (US$)	12.4	27.0	−14.6**
Hourly allowances (US$)	2.7	7.5	−4.8**
Hours worked per week	47.2	43.7	+3.5**
Occupational distribution:			
Managerial	21%	27%	−6.0%**
High skilled	25%	52%	−27.0%**
High semi-skilled	24%	18%	+6.0%**
Semi-skilled	15%	1%	+14.0%**
Low skilled	9%	1%	+8.0%**
Unskilled	6%	1%	+5.0%**
Average years in education	13.2	12.9	+0.3

Note: Estimates based on male employees, with secondary education or above. ** signals statistical significance at least at the 5% level.
Source: Own elaboration based on data from 2009 Labour Force Survey

secondary or tertiary education occupy unskilled or low skilled positions (in the case of Emirati these are only 3 per cent).

Naturally, the significant benefits in favour of Emirati reflect the government's desire to transfer part of the oil wealth to the citizens. Ironically, in setting up a segmented labour market whereby the expatriate workers have limited mobility and the native population is highly protected, the *Kafala* has also limited the labour opportunities for Emirati, as evidenced in unemployment rates—particularly for the young—which are much higher than expected for an economy that has grown at almost 10 per cent for twenty years. As an indication of the degree of labour market limitation of the Emirati recall that, as mentioned, 100 per cent of first-time job-seekers in 2009 declared a preference for the public sector.

On the other hand, and contrary to popular belief, the expatriate segment of the labour market is only partially flexible: while there is significant international mobility (i.e. for hiring and firing international migrants) there is virtually no internal mobility (to relocate workers among firms and sectors). Such internal rigidity stems from the restrictions imposed by the *Kafala* system and additional restrictions on temporary and part-time employment. In fact, casual evidence indicates the inexistence of an active internal labour market. Furthermore, international mobility attains at a possibly high cost: while hiring and firing low-skilled and unskilled workers may be easy and costless, the same cannot be said of high-skilled workers and professionals, as wage differentials in Figure 11.6 clearly suggest.

Overall, the observed differences in skills-based occupational distribution and wages between different nationality groups, coupled with the institutional rigidities already identified, suggest that labour-allocating mechanisms in

Dubai do not perform properly and that they allocate workers according to factors other than their economically most-efficient use. In turn, this hampers productivity growth and economic development. Estimates by Soto and Vazquez-Alvarez (2011) show that gross labour productivity in 2010 has dropped by 45 per cent in Dubai compared to peak rates in the early 1980s. It has long been recognized that labour mobility is a desirable characteristic of modern, efficient labour markets. Mortensen (1994) and Pissarides (1985) identify several channels by which labour market rigidities lead to poor labour market outcomes. For example, low mobility—which usually results in fixed wages—leads workers to exercise low effort levels and induces low productivity growth: if workers do not benefit from higher productivity they have no incentive to be more efficient. Furthermore, immobile workers are discouraged from accumulating human capital because they cannot profit from switching to alternative vacancies with greater potential for economic gains. Likewise, employers face a thin pool of workers from where to choose potential substitutes for their current workforce. Moreover, low mobility reduces employment creation at the higher skills levels because these workers are more expensive to acquire and costlier to replace.

11.4.2 Human Capital Formation

Firms in modern labour markets often invest in training their workers and enhancing their human capital so as to profit from higher productivity. Whereas firm-specific training directly increases worker's productivity within the firm, general training can be used in any firm. Consequently, firms are less willing to invest in general education unless it can be offered as a strategy to retain the most able workers. There is ample evidence of how profitable training can be. For example, in a study by Bassi et al. (2000) 500 firms were surveyed in the US and asked about their training strategies. Controlling for all possible complimentary effects, the study found that investing US$1,500 per employee per year in training compared to those that spend the minimum in the sample (US$125) led to a 24 per cent higher gross profit margin and 218 per cent higher revenue per employee.

According to the EHWS-2008, the number of firms that offer training to their workers is only 12 per cent, which falls short of the 40 per cent of firms offering training in eurozone economies (OECD, 2010). This is unsurprising given that about 67 per cent of the workforce in Dubai is allocated to semi, low, or unskilled positions and most likely remain in the firm for a relatively short period of time (two to three years). Nevertheless, while predictable, it is also damaging for the economy.

Investing in training, as any other investment, depends on the expected return and the direct costs. The expected return, in turn, depends on how much would productivity increase after training and for how long it is expected that the worker will provide additional profits to the firm. It seems, therefore, that the low levels of investment in human capital formation among firms in Dubai are a consequence of the conditions imposed by the sponsorship system: workers arrive with a very short expected stay (due to short-term contracts) and, consequently, receive little or no training. Over time, they are replaced by new waves of incoming workers that only eventually may provide an upgrade in human capital relative to previous waves. Workers have little incentive to invest in firm-specific training since their contracts are short and there is no guarantee that they can be renewed in better conditions. However, this is a very inefficient scheme as whatever firms invest in on-the-job training for workers is lost when they migrate back to their countries. Furthermore, this prevents the economy from developing in-house institutional capabilities for the development of human capital in the workforce.

Human capital formation of Emirati is also distorted but for different reasons. Emirati endogenously decide on their education levels but, as noted, they hold high expectations of becoming public sector employees. Their choice of university degrees, therefore, seems to be very much guided by the skill needs of the government (i.e. law and business degrees) to the detriment of careers in science and technology that might be more in tune with the demands of the private sector and the needs for sustained development.

A study by the RAND Qatar Policy Institute (Gonzalez et al., 2008) revealed that 77 per cent of Emirati graduating from secondary education in 2007 choose subjects related to the arts and humanities rather than science and technology. Later, these individuals find it difficult to gain a position and often require more training to adjust their skills in the labour market. At post-secondary education—that is, vocational schools or first degrees—the gap between what is demanded by industry and what is supplied by the UAE educational system is also acute (see Chapter 10). For example, enrolment data published by the UAE University—the national university exclusively for Emirati—shows that for the academic year 2010/11 around 30 per cent of those who enrolled chose scientific and technical degrees (see Table 11.6). In contrast, 65 per cent of students enrolled at the National University of Singapore 2010/11 chose science and technology.[9] Furthermore, these imbalances in skills deepen the dependency of Dubai on foreign human capital in technical areas and impede the development of local capabilities.

[9] See the following link: https://share.nus.edu.sg/registrar/info/statistics/ug-enrol-20102011.pdf.

Table 11.6. Enrolment, Emirati students at UAE University, academic year 2010/11

	Male	Female	Total	% of total
Humanities and social sciences	259	2,629	2,888	24.7
Sciences	276	752	1,028	8.8
Education	0	750	750	6.4
Business studies	884	1,926	2,810	24.0
Law	366	436	802	6.8
Food and agriculture	96	477	573	4.9
Engineering	756	1,098	1,854	15.8
Medicine and health sciences	105	247	352	3.0
Information and technology	105	454	559	4.8
Teaching diploma	0	96	96	0.8
Total in science and technology	1,137	2,304	3,441	29.4

Source: Own elaboration based on data from the UAE University Facts and Figures webpage

11.4.3 Economic Rents, Productivity Growth, and Inefficiencies

Labour market rigidities, as noted, induce inefficiency and misuse of economic resources. Nevertheless, they also generate benefits for those in a position to profit from such rigidities. When workers' mobility is severely limited as in Dubai this results in market power for employers whereby they have the ability to extract abnormal benefits or 'economic rents' from the manpower (Manning, 2003). The fact that economic rents are being collected by firms—and ultimately by some individuals—also explains the traditional resistance to policy changes vis-à-vis labour conditions. Furthermore, unions and other labour organizations, that could counterbalance the market power of employers, are prohibited by the UAE constitution.

In Dubai there is suggestive evidence of economic rents. In Chapter 14, Elbadawi compares salaries and productivity in free zones (FZ) and in the rest of the economy (called Main Dubai or MD) for the same type of industry. The main difference between FZ and MD is that within the former there is substantially less labour inflexibility and workers can switch positions among firms if they are offered better conditions. As a result of increased competition, wages in FZ are higher for equivalent occupations and firms are forced to generate profits from a more efficient use of resources.[10]

[10] In 2007, the UAE Ministry of Labour launched a programme called Wage Protection System (WPS) whereby companies are required to use an electronic, centralized system to pay workers. This, according to the Ministry, was necessary to avoid abuses and ensure that the salary payment records sent to banks are accurate and fair. The type of abuse most likely refers to unscrupulous entrepreneurs that, for a fee, provide work visas to unskilled workers and leave them to work unprotected in the informal sector (e.g. domestic services).

The main long-run outcome of labour immobility and rent-extraction is abnormally low productivity growth and a massive expansion in the expatriate labour force. As discussed in Chapter 2 total output per worker—GDP per working age person—and estimated total factor productivity (TFP) stagnated during most of the period 1985–2005 (see Figure 2.8). Therefore, there have been no significant changes in the efficiency of use of economic factors in Dubai and the spectacular growth in economic output has been the result of accumulating physical capital via investment and importing low-skilled expatriate workers from neighbouring countries or the Indian subcontinent.

The mechanics of this phenomenon are simple but their effects sizeable. Absence of horizontal mobility allows employers to extract economic rents, even if the worker is better paid than in his/her country of origin. When choosing production technologies, therefore, employers would tend to focus on labour-intensive techniques that, in addition to the normal profit obtained from selling goods and services, would allow them to extract the highest rents from the worker. Naturally, this skews production towards labour-intensive technologies. Moreover, it biases employment towards low-skilled workers that have less ability to negotiate their salaries. High-skilled workers are relatively scarcer and better educated than low-skilled workers and, consequently, they are better equipped to counterbalance the market power of employers. As discussed above, wage differentials in the UAE between locals and migrants for identical job-characteristics reduce markedly as employees have more education and tend to disappear altogether at the postgraduate level.

In a competitive environment with high mobility, an increase in the demand for labour would allow workers to command higher wages. In the *Kafala* system, wages are kept flat for the duration of the contract. In the short run, the lack of mobility provided by the sponsorship prevents rising labour costs and keeps profits high for investors.

In the long-run, however, the *Kafala* destroys incentives to increase efficiency and the ability of firms to be profitable on the basis of their efficiency to compete, for two reasons. First, resources do not freely adjust to their most efficient use and therefore there are no incentives to correct an inefficient allocation of workers. Second, labour-saving technical improvements would be disregarded by entrepreneurs as they lower rent-extraction. Labour-saving technological changes will be implemented only when the cost reduction is such that it increases market profits significantly more than the sacrifice in rent extraction derived from lower employment.

In keeping sponsorship as a centrepiece of economic policy in the UAE, the authorities might have considered that increases in labour costs would reduce the profitability of firms and, therefore, the incentives to invest in new, more efficient technologies. An alternative view is that, historically, whenever labour becomes scarce and wages soar, entrepreneurs implement new technologies to replace workers by more efficient technologies based on machines (Acemoglu, 2010). The empirical evidence indicates that in Dubai the former view is incorrect: private sector profits and riches have grown significantly since the 1990s and employment has expanded massively, but labour productivity has stagnated. Therefore, the *Kafala* has inhibited technological change because in keeping wages low it has not given entrepreneurs incentives to acquire more advanced technologies.

11.5 CONCLUSIONS AND NEW DIRECTIONS IN DUBAI'S LABOUR MARKET

In the past forty years, Dubai has managed to grow exceptionally fast and transform itself from a backward territory in the Arabian Gulf into a regional hub for economic activity. To a large extent, this economic transformation has been fuelled by the disappearance in the 1980s of its natural resources and a necessary opening to global markets. More decisively, it has been the result of the implementation of sound macroeconomic policies and a substantial accumulation of physical capital in the form of infrastructure and social capital in the form of institutions (rule of law, absence of corruption, etc.).

The labour market has played an important role in the economic development of Dubai, in spite of the severe limitations within which it operates. The current regulation, which stems from the sponsorship system, has effectively created a dual labour market—one for Emirati and another for expatriates—with little overlap or interaction. As a result, the following elements define its working. First, while there is significant mobility for Emirati, there is no mobility for expatriate workers in the internal labour market (international mobility is high for expatriates). Second, lack of internal mobility allows employers to exert market power and collect rents from expatriates. This induces acquiring labour-intensive technologies and a massive hiring of expatriate workers. Third, the public sector has preference for Emirati workers and hires at wages substantially above earnings in the private sector. Fourth, Emirati enjoy significant protection vis-à-vis expatriate workers in terms of lay-off conditions, lower working hours, minimum wages, and so on. These two elements lower the employability of Emirati in the private sector. The problem is compounded by the weak education received by Emirati that does not prepare them for private sector employment.

Job creation for Emirati has faltered in Dubai in the last fifteen years. In our view, this is largely the result of the combined effects of the *Kafala* system, public sector recruitment, and salary policies. This is a worrying feature since the Emirati comprise a very young population and a large number of young people are expected to enter the labour market every year for the foreseeable future. Using the LFS-2009 we estimate that (on average) Dubai has to create around 2,500 jobs per year just to cover the supply of labour of Emirati in the population: these estimates are a lower bound because they assume that current female participation rates remain fixed and there is no reason why they shouldn't continue to grow in the future. Clearly, job creation in the public sector cannot cover the expected additional supply. In fact, in response to the economic downturn and the increase in unemployment among Emirati, between 2009 and 2010 the government created about 7,000 new jobs in the public sector (at the Emirate local and federal level) of which only about 1,000 were located in Dubai. At this rate, it is clear that public administration cannot be assigned the task of creating jobs for all new entrants. Nor is it desirable: as discussed in Soto and Haouas (2012), labour productivity in the government sector has declined steadily since the mid 1990s when the government started to hire Emirati to reduce unemployment and public overemployment is extensive.

Therefore, in the long run the main source of employment for the incoming Emirati workers will necessarily be the private sector. In this respect, nationals will have to upgrade their education to match the skills demanded by private firms and adjust their occupational expectations. However, under the straightjacket of the sponsorship system and without a change in government employment policies this is unlikely to happen. The rigidities of the labour market are not unknown nor can the damaging effects be ignored. Yet, there is little evidence of far reaching labour market reforms in the near future.

The empirical evidence, on the other hand, points to the beneficial results of deregulating the *Kafala*. Dubai was the first to realize the costs of the limitations implied by the sponsorship system when it ran out of oil reserves in the 1980s and the massive flows of foreign direct investment required to diversify its economy away from oil failed to materialize. To bypass the system, Dubai opened free zones where labour and investment regulations are much less restrictive. In particular, workers can opt for alternative occupations within the free zone according to their preferences and the available vacancies, yet they cannot opt for firms outside the free zone. Employers can freely hire and fire from the pool of workers within the free zone. This creates a degree of mobility within the free zones that is lacking in the non-free zone of Dubai. A study by Soto and Vazquez-Alvarez (2011) employs stochastic frontier models to compare the degree of technical inefficiency between firms inside and outside the free zones. The results suggest that much of the technical inefficiency in Dubai results from the sponsorship system.

Dubai is not the only authority realizing the inefficiencies of the sponsorship system. Starting in August 2009, Bahrain has been the first GCC economy to announce a progressive dismantling of the *Kafala*: workers arriving to work for an employer are effectively sponsored by the government—instead of a local firm or individual—and are allowed to switch between employers without restrictions and to stay in the country at most four weeks after finishing their contracts. After two years, the outcome of the reform has been mixed although no proper study has been issued. However, business—in particular small- and medium-sized businesses—claim that it is no longer cost-effective to bring migrants to Bahrain (precisely the intended goal of the policy). Kuwait has timidly followed suit.

The UAE has also shown intentions of a gradual move away from sponsorship; this being the case, the labour market in Dubai would move closer to its 2015 Strategic Plan. A new set of regulations informally announced in January 2011 would allow workers that have spent two or more years in the UAE to change jobs without the written permission of their employer and without the need to leave and return to the country. Also, expatriates already in the UAE working in a professional category would be allowed to change employers at will if they could prove that change implies an upgrade to his or her occupational category and earnings. At the time of writing this article, the measures were announced but the new policies have yet to be regulated into labour laws by the Ministry of Labour. The fact that they were announced indicates that the authorities realize the constraints imposed by the current system and the need for such to change towards a more efficient and modern labour market. Its lack of implementation indicates that they are not a priority.

REFERENCES

Acemoglu, D., 2010. 'When Does Labor Scarcity Encourage Innovation?' *Journal of Political Economy*, 118(6): 1037–78.

Bassi, L., Ludwig, J., McMurrer, D. and van Buren, M., 2000. 'Profiting from Learning: Do Firms' Investment in Education and Training Pay Off?' *Singapore Management Review*, 24(3): 61–76.

Elbadawi, I. and Soto, R., 2012. 'Sources of Economic Growth and Development Strategy in Dubai'. In A. Sadik and I. Elbadawi (eds) *The Global Economic Crisis and Consequences for Development Strategy in Dubai.* New York: Palgrave Macmillan, pp. 121–53.

Eurostat, 2011. *Eurostat Yearbook: Europe in Figures,* Luxembourg: Eurostat.

Gonzalez, G., Karoly, L. A., Constant, L., Salem, H., and Goldman, C. A., 2008. *Facing Human Capital Challenges of the 21st Century: Education and Labor Market Initiatives in Lebanon, Oman, Qatar, and the United Arab Emirates*. Rand-Qatar Policy Institute, Doha, Qatar.

Manning, A., 2003. 'The Real Thin Theory: Monopsony in Modern Labour Markets'. *Labour Economics,* 10: 105–31.

Mortensen, D. T., 1994. 'Reducing Supply Side Disincentives to Job Creation', in *Reducing Unemployment: Current Issues and Policy Options*. Kansas City: Federal Reserve Bank of Kansas City, pp. 189–219.

OECD, 2010. *National Accounts*. [Online] Available at: http://www.oecd.org/std/na/, accessed 2 September 2011.

Pissarides, C., 1985. 'Short Run Equilibrium Dynamics of Unemployment, Vacancies, and Real Wages'. *American Economic Review*, 75(4): 676–90.

Roberts, S., 2011. 'Beyond "NEET" and "Tidy" Pathways: Considering the "Missing Middle" of Youth Transition Studies', *Journal of Youth Studies*, 14(1): 21–39.

Soto, R. and Haouas, I., 2012. 'Has the UAE Escaped the Oil Curse?' Economic Research Forum Working Paper No. 728.

Soto, R. and Vazquez-Alvarez, R., 2011. 'The Efficiency Costs of the Kafala in Dubai: A Stochastic Frontier Analysis'. Documento de Trabajo 399, Instituto de Economia. Pontificia Universidad Católica de Chile.

UN, 2011. *World Population Prospect: The 2010 Revision*, Washington, DC: Population Division of the Department of Economic and Social Affairs of the United Nations.

Vazquez-Alvarez, R., 2010. 'The Micro-Structure of Wages and Wage Determination in the UAE'. Dubai Economic Council Working Paper, 12 October.

Weir, G., 2003. 'Economic Inactivity in Selected Countries'. *Labour Market Trends*, 111(6): 299–309.

World Bank, 2011. *World Development Indicators*. [Online] Available at: http://data.worldbank.org/products/wdi, accessed 2 September 2015.

12

A Primer on Dubai's Energy Sector

Mahmoud Al Iriani and Eshrak Al Maamari

12.1 INTRODUCTION

With a population of 2.1 million and an area of 4,100 square kilometres, the emirate of Dubai is the second largest of seven emirates comprising the United Arab Emirates (UAE). Hydrocarbon resources in Dubai are limited to 4 billion barrels of oil and 4,000 billion cubic feet of natural gas. Therefore, its economy is less oil-dependent than the neighbouring emirate of Abu Dhabi. In 2012 oil contributed less than 3 per cent to the emirate's GDP (Figure 12.1) compared to more than 56 per cent in Abu Dhabi.

Dwindling oil reserves incentivized the government of Dubai to adopt rigorous diversification policies that have been instrumental in transforming the emirate from a traditional nomadic to a modern dynamic and urban economy in a period of less than four decades. Today, Dubai boosts an investor-friendly, diverse, and innovative economy, highly visible within the Gulf Cooperation Council (GCC). It has become the trading, financial, and tourist centre of the UAE and the region. Liberal economic policies and a strong economic infrastructure in Dubai helped in achieving exceptional economic growth during the last three decades. Thanks to such favourable conditions, Dubai's real GDP reached about $87 billion in 2012, with a per capita GDP of US $43,000 (DSC, 2013).

As a result of its stable business environment, location, high quality infrastructure, and liberal economic system, Dubai has become a favourite destination for major multinational companies. Substantial volumes of foreign direct investments (FDI) have relocated to Dubai and have been instrumental in boosting Dubai's economy. Despite the recent international financial crisis, reports have concluded that Dubai remains the most attractive FDI destination in the Middle East. The recent FDI confidence index ranks Dubai 1st in the Middle East and 11th among the world's preferred FDI destinations (A. T. Kearney, 2013).

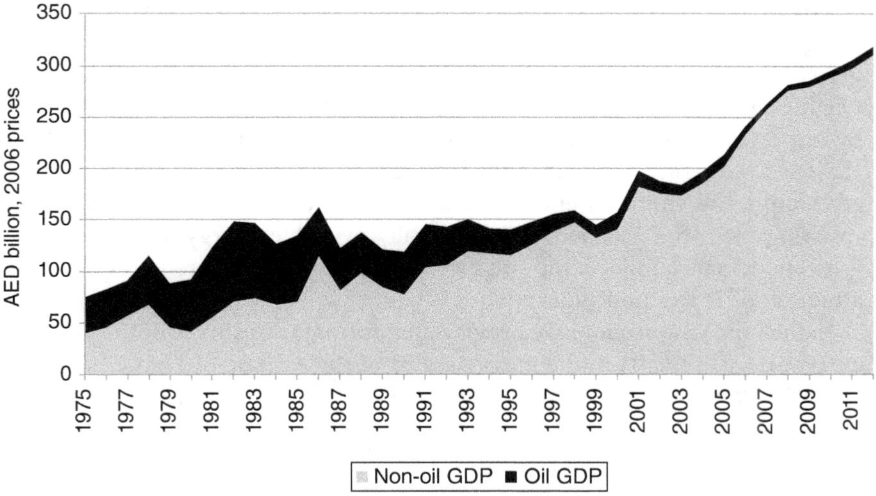

Figure 12.1. Dubai real GDP composition

Source: DSC (2006–10) and Dubai Municipality (1975–2005)

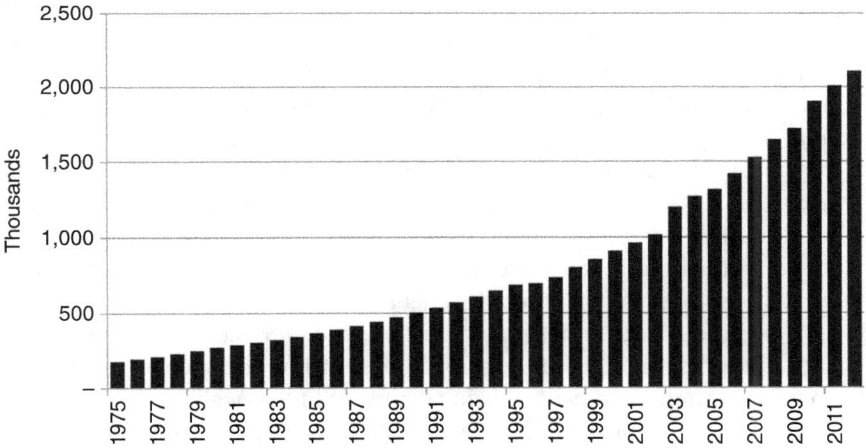

Figure 12.2. Dubai population

Source: DEC, based on DSC (2006–10) and Dubai Municipality data (1975–2005)

Robust economic development and the increased FDI activities have in turn attracted hundreds of thousands of foreign workers into Dubai. The population of Dubai has therefore more than tripled within the past seventeen years (Figure 12.2).

The growing population, the booming construction sector, and the expanding energy-intensive industries have been the main drivers for an unprecedented growth in energy demand in recent years. Certainly Dubai recognized the importance of energy as a necessary engine for economic growth and therefore made available to its growing economy sufficient and reliable energy sources. It has complemented its local limited energy resources by imported fuels from other emirates and from the international markets. However, to sustain growth and development there is a pressing need to restructure the emirate's energy sector in order to cope with the challenges resulting from the gap between the locally available energy supply and the growing demand. Indeed, the situation in the energy sector requires the close attention of Dubai policymakers.

In the following sections we provide an informational survey of the past and current developments in the energy sector of the emirate of Dubai as well as reviewing key strategies for energy security and efficiency in the emirate.

12.2 AN OVERVIEW OF DUBAI'S ENERGY SECTOR

Unlike the emirate of Abu Dhabi which is a major oil producer and exporter, Dubai owns less than 4 per cent of the UAE's total oil reserves and 2 per cent of its natural gas reserves. It produces a marginal amount of oil that has dropped from a peak of 410,000 barrels per day in 1991 (Butt and Al Abed, 2001) to less than 80,000 in 2012. As a result, Dubai is a net energy importer. In addition, the current developments in the local, regional, and global energy markets have led Dubai to face both an energy demand boom and supply constraints that require a thorough analysis of the sustainability of the emirate's energy sector at a time when its economy is becoming increasingly energy-dependent.

The structure and performance of Dubai's energy sector is affected by five main factors, three factors affect its energy supply and the other two affect energy demand. The first factor pertains to Dubai's limited local conventional energy resources. Second are the possibilities for importing energy resources from other emirates and neighbouring countries in the Arabian Gulf. Third is the availability of non-conventional alternative energy resources including opportunities for the development of renewable energy. Fourth is the overall high economic activity in the emirate and its growth over time. Finally, the Dubai energy sector is also affected by the government's policies promoting efficiency in managing available energy resources.

12.2.1 Oil

Although the UAE is rich in crude oil resources, Dubai sits on only 4 billion barrels, about 4 per cent of the UAE's 97 billion barrels of oil reserves (see

Table 12.1. Energy reserves, production, and consumption in Dubai, 2012

Crude Oil	
Proved reserves (billion barrels)	4
Production (thousand barrels per day)	less than 80
Refinery capacity (thousand barrels per day)	120
Natural Gas	
Proved reserves (billion cubic feet)	4,000
Consumption (billion cubic feet/day)	2.5*
Electricity	
Net consumption (thousand GWh)	36.3
Installed capacity (GW)	9.65

Note: * 2012 gas consumption was estimated using a projected 3.5 per cent growth rate from 2009 level.
Source: DEWA (1990–2012), US EIA (2013), British Petroleum (2012), and DEC estimates

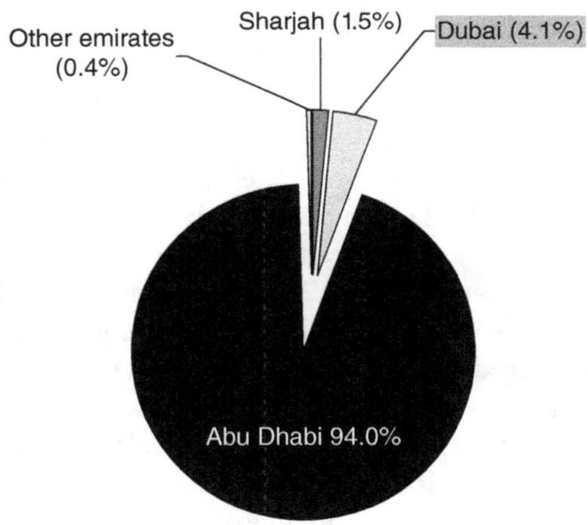

Figure 12.3. Share of Dubai and other emirates in UAE oil reserves, 2012
Source: Oxford Business Group, 2009

Table 12.1 and Figure 12.3). The UAE federation arrangements allow each individual emirate to keep full control of its own natural resources and hence Dubai currently claims an estimated production of only 80,000 barrels/d. Therefore, a significant portion of Dubai's oil needs is imported.

12.2.1.1 A Brief History of Crude Oil in Dubai

Dubai's experience with crude oil production dates back to as early as 1937 when a concession was granted to the Iraq Petroleum Company (IPC) and extended to 1961. The concession was later acquired by the Continental Oil

Company which formed the Dubai Petroleum Establishment (DPE) in 1963. Another company, Spanish Petroleum Company (HISPANOIL), obtained an onshore concession in 1954 and formed later the Dubai Marine Areas (DUMA), 50 per cent of DUMA's shares were acquired by DPC in the same year.[1] In 1975, the government of Dubai made a decision to acquire 60 per cent of DUMA-DPC and in 2007 the government took complete control of DPC and Dubai's oil fields.

It took these concessions until 1966 to make the first offshore oil discovery at the Fateh field. Production and export however did not begin until late 1969. More oil was discovered in 1970 at South West Fateh field and Rashid field, both of which are offshore locations. The only onshore discovery was at Margham field in 1982. No new oil and gas discoveries were made until February 2010 when the Dubai government announced a new oil discovery, Al Jalila Field, the size of which is yet to be determined.

Although Dubai is not a major oil producer, the important location of Dubai as a trade hub and its advanced infrastructure allowed the emirate to play the role of a trade centre for crude oil. In June 2007, the emirate established the Dubai Mercantile Exchange (DME) which lists the Oman Crude Oil Futures Contract (DME Oman) as its leading contract. In addition, DME contracts include the Brent Crude Oil Financial Contract and Oman Crude Oil Financial Contract. DME has become the premier energy-focused commodities exchange and home to the world's third crude benchmark.[2] The DME is regulated by the Dubai Financial Services Authority and all trades executed on the DME are cleared through and guaranteed by NYMEX (a member of CME Group), which is regulated by the US Commodity Futures Trading Commission (CFTC). Dubai has also introduced liquefied natural gas (LNG) future contracts through Dubai Multi Commodities Centre (DMCC) and established a petroleum training centre as a joint venture between the Dubai Petroleum Establishment (DPE) and PETROFAC. The centre is designed to provide technical and safety training for the oil and gas industry in the Middle East.

12.2.1.2 Production and Distribution of Oil Products

Up until the late 1970s, the distribution of oil products in Dubai was entirely provided by the federal Emirates General Petroleum Company (EMARAT). In 1980 however Dubai ENOC and Caltex established a joint venture called the Emirates Petroleum Products Company (EPPCO). In 1998 EPPCO began distributing products in Dubai therefore ending the EMARAT monopoly. Currently, EPPCO operate a network of over 170 service stations in Dubai and the northern emirates jointly with the Dubai government-owned 'Emirates

[1] The details of crude oil history in Dubai appeared in Metz (1993) and DPE website.

[2] The other two being Brent and West Texas benchmarks.

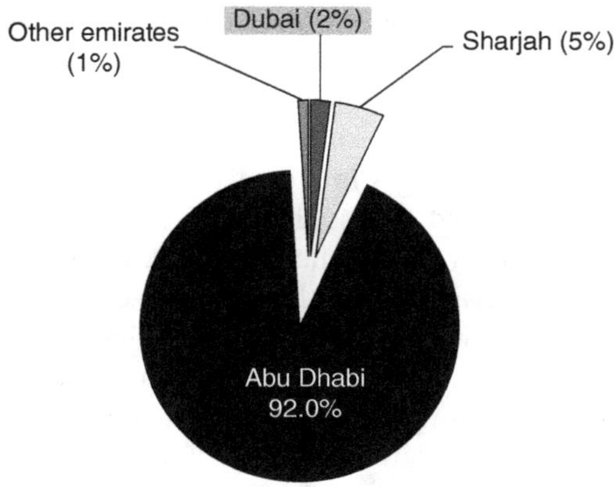

Figure 12.4. Share of Dubai and other emirates in UAE's gas reserves, 2012
Source: Oxford Business Group, 2009

National Oil Company' (ENOC), which is the sole producer of oil products in the emirate. The company produces and distributes oil products in Dubai and all other emirates (except Abu Dhabi) and has upstream operations outside the UAE.[3] ENOC operates a 120,000 bbd refinery in Jebel Ali and has a number of shipping and storage facilities including a company called Dubai Shipping.

12.2.2 Natural Gas

Natural gas production in Dubai comes associated with the oil extracted from its oil fields. Reserves currently stand at 4 trillion cubic feet, which is only about 2 per cent of the UAE's total reserves (Figure 12.4). Natural gas processing from both offshore and onshore oil fields is assigned to the Dubai Natural Gas Company (DUGAS), a company established in 1975. The government of Dubai owns 80 per cent of DUGAS, the remaining 20 per cent being owned by Scimitar Oils, a subsidiary of Sunningdale Oils of Canada. DUGAS began processing natural gas at the Jebel Ali free zone in 1980. In 2000, ENOC took DUGAS over in an effort by the government of Dubai to consolidate its oil and gas production and distribution services.

Natural gas in Dubai is mainly used as feedstock for power plants, water desalination, and for enhanced oil recovery (EOR) systems based on natural gas injections for mature oilfields. After years of producing power by traditional diesel-powered generators, Dubai has switched to natural gas-fired

[3] Among ENOC's international assets is 69.4% stake in Dragon Oil, which operates in Turkmenistan, and a number of terminals and bulk storage facilities in various parts of the world.

power plants as a cleaner option to satisfy its power needs.[4] Other major consumers of natural gas are the rapidly growing Dubai Aluminum Company (DUBAL)[5] and a number of petrochemical plants at Jebel Ali (including the LPG/NGL plant of DUGAS).

Dubai's demand for natural gas in 2012 was estimated at 2.5 billion cubic feet per day (bcfd) compared to less than 0.45 bcfd in 1995. Although the global economic crisis has reduced the need for gas in most countries, the demand for natural gas in Dubai for the purposes of power generation and industrial use has been growing steadily. Estimates indicate that demand will rise to more than 3 bcfd by 2015 (HighBeam Business, 2010).

Local production of natural gas is rather limited and does not satisfy the emirate's rising demand. As a result, Dubai imports a large portion of its natural gas requirements. Up until mid 2001 Sharjah was the sole supplier of imported natural gas but the increasing demand for natural gas in Dubai and the need of Shrajah to satisfy its own soaring demand, led to Dubai starting to look for additional sources of natural gas. The emirate had to supplement its Sharjah imports by additional imports from Abu Dhabi and lately from the state of Qatar. In May 2001, Dubai started to import 200 mcfd of natural gas from Abu Dhabi through a pipeline from the Maqta area. By 2004, Abu Dhabi National Oil Company (ADNOC) had completed a project that raised the capacity of the pipeline to 800 mcfd.

The limitations on the quantities that can be supplied to Dubai from neighbouring emirates and the growth in demand forced the emirate recently to import gas from Qatar through the Dolphin Pipeline, which became operational in the second quarter of 2007. The UAE is currently importing around 1,600 mcfd from Qatar using the pipeline. According to a 25-year contract between Qatar and the UAE, the Dubai Supply Authority (DUSUP) is supplied with 730 mcfd and the Abu Dhabi Water and Electricity Company (ADWEC) is supplied with an average of 929 mcfd of natural gas (Dolphin Energy, 2010). Starting in 2010, Dubai is also planning to import additional LNG from Qatar during the peak months of the summer when power needs are highest. The delivery of LNG from Qatar's fields to Dubai was commissioned by the DUSUP to the United Kingdom's Golar LNG in 2008 as part of a US$450 million, 10-year, contract (IHS, 2008). In 2011, Dubai imported an additional 298 bcf of natural gas, mostly from the neighbouring Qatar, to complement its local production. The natural gas shortage in the UAE in general and Dubai in particular is expected to continue and grow in the

[4] Because of a rise in diesel prices in recent years, Dubai Electricity and Water Authority estimated that the average cost of one kWh from fuel oil in 2004–7 was six times more than the cost of power from natural gas.

[5] Dubal and Abu Dhabi's Emirates Aluminum (Emal) are set to merge and form Emirates Global Aluminum (EGA).

foreseeable future unless alternative sources of energy are developed and/or demand is controlled (Dargin, 2010).

There are a number of reasons why Dubai (and the UAE with its 215 trillion cubic feet of natural gas reserves, which make it ranked seventh in the world) have become net importers of natural gas. First, power consumption in Dubai in particular and the UAE in general has been increasing at double-digit rates and almost all power generation uses natural gas as feedstock. In 2011 the UAE consumed an estimated 2,663 bcf of natural gas (US EIA, 2013). Reports indicate that gas shortages in the UAE, driven by soaring demand, may increase to 20,000 mcfd by 2025. Second, Dubai and Abu Dhabi's oil fields are depleting and in order to increase their production, EOR systems based on natural gas are being increasingly used. US EIA (2013) estimates that nearly 30 per cent of UAE's total production is re-injected within the EOR systems. Third, Dubai's industrial development created new industries like steel, aluminium, and petrochemicals, all of which require vast quantities of natural gas. Fourth, exploration and production challenges limit the ability to increase natural gas supply in the UAE and Dubai. Most of the natural gas production in the UAE comes associated with crude oil production which is governed by OPEC quotas.[6] Finally, UAE's long-term gas export commitments limit quantities available for domestic consumption.

As the natural gas shortage in Dubai will become more acute, the solution to the problem lies in taking both supply and demand measures. Securing enough gas supply can be achieved through expanding domestic gas production, increasing imports from Qatar and other neighbouring countries, and increasing the connectivity and efficiency of the national gas supply network. In addition, energy market restructuring has become necessary to deal with the energy demand issue and allow Dubai to continue fulfilling its role as a major business hub in the region. Demand measures include eliminating subsidies and allowing market mechanisms to determine energy prices. This will not only reduce energy consumption, because consumers will be paying real costs, but will also attract international investments into the sector as profits increase. Finally, the use of natural gas for oil recovery purposes may in the future be gradually replaced by alternative oil-enhancement technologies such as CO_2 capture and injection.

12.2.3 Electricity and Desalinated Water

Because it is located in one of the hottest and most arid regions of the world, Dubai has an exceptionally high demand for electric energy for the purpose of air conditioning. The emirate's need for air conditioning makes its energy

[6] However, Dubai does not consider itself bound by OPEC quotas.

demand increase during the summer months, which requires additional expensive generation capacity. Exploding demand for electricity has been exacerbated by demographic, industrial, and construction growth. In addition, Dubai's water needs are exceptionally high, when compared with countries of the same income level, and because of limited ground and surface fresh water reserves, the emirate has to depend on desalinating sea water to satisfy its growing consumption. This, in turn, further increases the need for energy to operate desalination plants.

12.2.3.1 Electricity Consumption

The growing economy of Dubai has always been highly dependent on electricity consumption. The rapid growth of the economy during the last three decades resulted in consumption of electricity increasing by almost eightfold, from 4,432 gigawatt/hour (GWh) in 1990 to 35,124 GWh in 2012 (Figure 12.5). This increase represents an average annual growth rate of about 10 per cent, a rate that is more than double the international average growth of 4 per cent. Forecasts indicate that demand for utilities (electricity and water) will continue to grow by 12 per cent and 14 per cent per annum respectively, exceeding the UAE average growth rate.

Not only has the total demand for energy been increasing over time but so has the per capita energy consumption. This reflects a favourable increase in income and living standards in the emirate as well as low efficiency in energy use. As a result, Dubai has one of the highest levels of per capita electricity

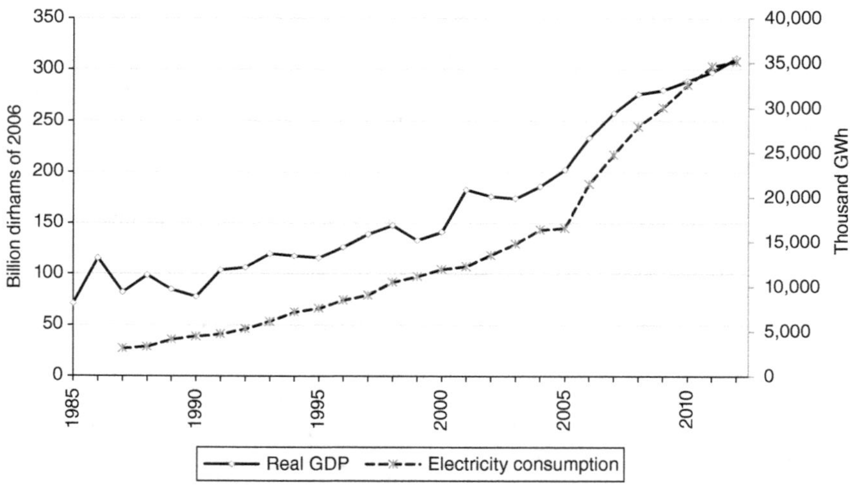

Figure 12.5. Dubai real GDP and electricity consumption

Source: DSC (2006–11), Dubai Municipality (1985–2005), and DEWA (1990–2012)

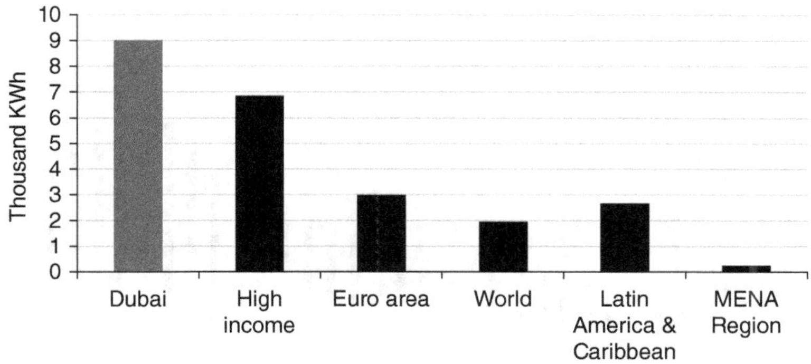

Figure 12.6. Per capita electricity consumption in Dubai and some other regions, 2012

Source: World Bank (2012) and DEWA (1990–2012)

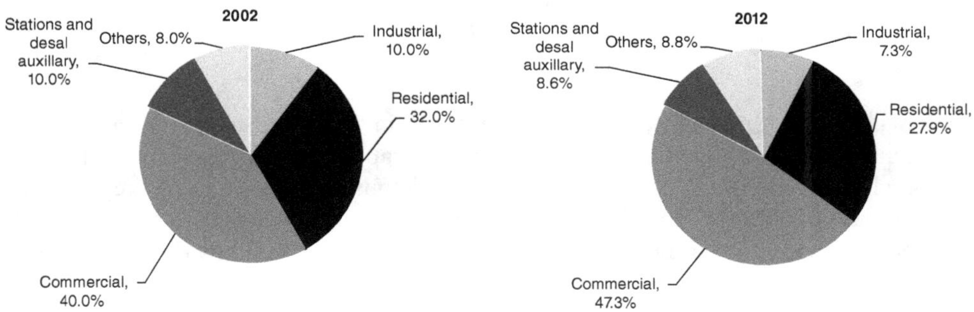

Figure 12.7. Dubai electricity consumption by sector

Source: DEWA (1990–2012)

consumption in the world. In 2012, a person in Dubai, on average, consumed more electricity than an average person in many other countries including those in either low-income or high-income groups (Figure 12.6).

It is also worth mentioning that the share of different economic sectors in electricity consumption has been changing over time. Due to the rapid developments in the trade sector between 1992 and 2012, a larger portion of electricity consumption is attributed to commercial activities and less to the residential sector (Figure 12.7). On the other hand, the share of the industrial sector in electricity consumption has been fairly stable, even though its absolute level has increased substantially over years.

12.2.3.2 Water Consumption

The location of Dubai in a very hot and arid area, and due to the exceptionally low water consumption tariffs, Dubai's water requirements are exceptionally

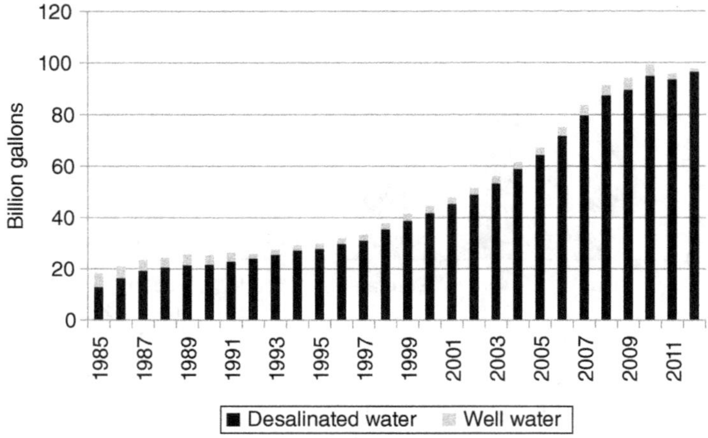

Figure 12.8. Water production in Dubai

Source: Dubai Municipality (1985–2005) and DEWA (1990–2012)

high. The emirate's total water consumption in 2012 was estimated at 97.5 billion gallons (Figure 12.8), making the per capita consumption one of the highest in the world at more than 46,300 gallons per year. Out of the total amount of water produced in 2012 to satisfy consumption, less than 1 per cent was obtained from ground reservoirs. The rest was produced by desalination plants.

12.2.3.3 Electricity Generation and Distribution

Since 1959 electricity and water in Dubai were supplied independently and respectively by the state-owned Dubai Electric Company and the Dubai Water Department. In 1992 the two entities were merged to form the current state-owned Dubai Electricity and Water Authority (DEWA). The new company has become the sole producer and distributor of water and electricity in the emirate. Additional smaller utility firms provide district cooling and desalination services but are still confined to the main real estate and industrial projects. DEWA has expanded substantially over the years and, in 2012, it is considered one of the largest state-owned companies in Dubai, employing more than 9,000 employees, and serving 624,400 electricity customers and 555,000 water customers. The company has become a cornerstone of Dubai's infrastructure, providing a reliable supply of electricity and water to all sectors of the economy.

Since its establishment, DEWA has managed to fully satisfy the increasing power needs of Dubai's residents by installing additional generation capacity and expanding its distribution system. DEWA owns a well-developed and

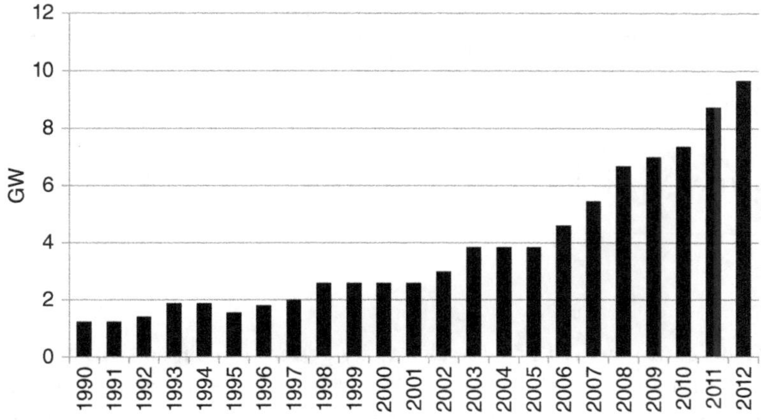

Figure 12.9. Electricity installed capacity

Source: DEWA

Table 12.2. DEWA electricity generation and water production plants, 2012

Plants	Electricity (MW/h)	Water (MG/d)
Plant 'D' -Jebel Ali	1,027	35
Plant 'E' -Jebel Ali	616	25
Plant 'G' -Jebel Ali	818	60
Plant 'K' -Jebel Ali	918	60
Plant 'L' -Jebel Ali (Phase I)	969	70
Plant 'L' -Jebel Ali (Phase II)	1,393	55
Plant 'M' -Jebel Ali	2,060	140
Reverse Osmosis Desalination Plant-Jebel Ali	—	25
Plant 'H' -Aweer (Phase I)	607	—
Plant 'H' -Aweer (Phase II)	421	—
Plant 'H' -Aweer (Phase III)	818	—
Total installed capacity, of which:	9,647	470
Gas turbines	7,105	
Steam turbines	2,542	

Source: DEWA

adequate electricity generation system that has proven to be sufficient in satisfying the soaring demand for electricity in the emirate. The installed generation capacity has increased from 1.2 gigawatt (GW) in 1990 to 9.6 GW in 2012, nearly eightfold (Figure 12.9). During 2012, DEWA produced enough power to satisfy the 35,100 GWh of electricity demand. The company also operates water desalination plants with a capacity of 470 million gallon a day, and produces 32 million gallons a day of ground water. In 2012, the company produced a total of about 96.5 billion gallons of water to satisfy the increasing demand. DEWA owns eleven electricity and water production units in both Jebel Ali and Aweer areas (Table 12.2).

Table 12.3. DEWA substations, transmission, and distribution, 2012

Voltage	No. of substations	Overhead lines (km)	Underground cables (km)
400 kV	18	876	—
132 kV	184	437	1,486
33 kV	135	113	1,992
6.6 and 11 kV	26,756	—	24,942
Total	—	1,426	28,420

Source: DEWA

The units in Jebel Ali provide electricity generation capacity in addition to water desalination, while those in Aweer produce electricity only. Almost 74 per cent of the electricity capacity comes from gas turbines; the remaining 26 per cent comes from steam turbines. Currently, only 4.5 MW of power is generated by solar energy.

Overtime, DEWA has developed quite sufficient transmission and distribution systems that extend across all the emirate's regions. The produced electricity is transmitted throughout the emirate via nearly 30,000 km of overhead lines and ground cables (Table 12.3). Furthermore, DEWA owns 1,360 km of water transmission pipelines, used to transmit water to its large number of customers.

12.2.3.4 DEWA Future Expansions

Due to limited oil and gas resources, increasing energy needs, and the current developments in the regional and global energy markets Dubai faces both high electric energy demand and supply constraints that require a thorough analysis. Dubai is connected to the UAE's Emirates National Grid (ENG) which connects the power supply of all members of the union. The ENG project was launched in 2000 under the supervision of the Federal Ministry of Energy and Water. The project was designed to be implemented in three phases. Phase I, which connects Dubai's DEWA and Abu Dhabi's Water and Electricity Authority (ADWEA) grids, was completed in May 2006. In May 2007, Phase II which connects DEWA-ADWEA grids with Sharjah's Electricity and Water Authority (SEWA) grid was completed. The unified grid of the three emirates was finally connected to the Federal Electricity and Water Authority (FEWA)'s grid in Phase III, completed in mid 2008. The UAE grid is an example of the cooperation in inter-emirates power exchange. It allows the surplus in one emirate to be channelled to other emirates therefore increasing the security of power supply to all the emirates. It also allows Dubai to benefit from the broader GCC grid by importing power from other GCC countries and countries outside the GCC, should the need arise.

The three phases of GCC power grid linking all the six GCC countries was completed by 2012 and the grid is now in operation. The UAE, Saudi Arabia, Kuwait, Qatar, and Bahrain were connected in Phase II of the grid project, Oman was connected in the final phase. The interconnection grid has the potential to provide a unified system for energy trade and exchange between the member countries. It will improve the reliability of their energy systems, lower their individual electricity investment requirements, and make building and sharing power generated from renewable energy resources more viable. DEWA can easily benefit from the GCC interconnection grid because Dubai is already connected to the UAE national grid.

12.2.3.5 Electric Energy Options for the Future

As Dubai's economy continues to grow rapidly, Dubai's power demand is likely to soar in the decades to come. With the emirate's small and dwindling oil and gas resources, satisfying the energy needs of Dubai in an efficient and environmentally friendly manner is indeed a key challenge for Dubai's authorities. As a part of the broader process of economic development, it has become necessary to formulate coherent energy policies and to coordinate actions in order to achieve Dubai's future sustainable development goals. Basically, Dubai needs to develop more sustainable ways of producing and consuming energy. The policy scope should cover two important aspects. The first is the choice of the fuel mix in order to secure reliable and sufficient supplies to power the economy, the second is restructuring the supply and demand sides of electricity in order to insure that it is efficiently produced and consumed.

12.2.4 Diversifying the Fuel Mix

In addition to its efforts to secure a sufficient supply of power and water using traditional means, Dubai has realized the importance of diversifying its fuel mix in the long run by utilizing non-conventional alternatives to generate energy. These alternatives include both renewable and non-renewable sources (Figure 12.10).

According to the Dubai Integrated Energy Strategy (DIES) 2030, the emirate is on the way to diversifying its generation mix and reduce dependency on oil and gas by introducing clean coal as a secondary fuel for electricity generation in the medium term. In addition, the latest DEWA plans also include studying the feasibility of building pilot nuclear reactors for electricity generation. These plans are consistent with the UAE's plan to use nuclear reactors to produce electricity in order to complement or even replace the existing conventional sources of power. The company is also looking into

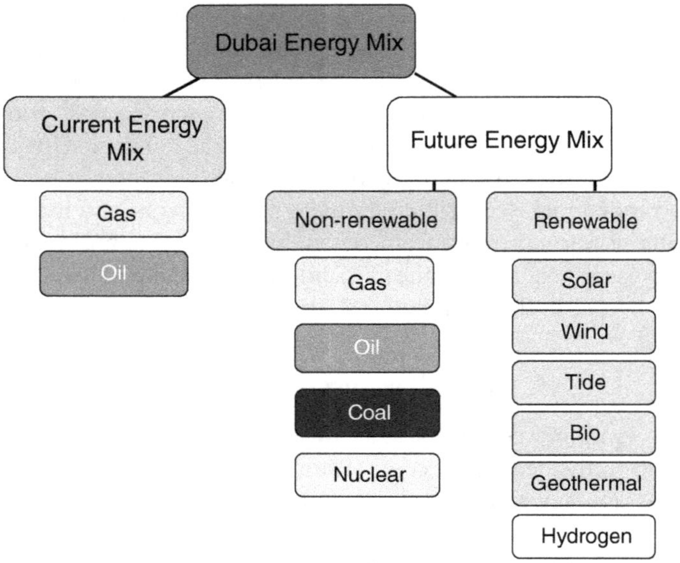

Figure 12.10. Dubai energy options

building hydrogen-fired power stations if such stations become viable in the future from a cost perspective. In addition, renewable energy is another option to obtain needed energy. Solar and wind energy are both largely accessible but still less economically viable. Once advances in renewable technologies lead to lowering costs, renewable energy may become an important part of Dubai's energy mix.

12.2.4.1 Non-renewable Sources

Dubai is considering adding other types of energy from the pool of available alternatives to its energy basket. Coal and nuclear technology are currently being weighed by the Dubai authorities as the best options to diversify Dubai's energy sources and meet near-future demand. As part of the 'Energy Strategy 2030', coal will start to be used in the electricity production mix in Dubai. DEWA announced that it is in the planning stage of its first clean coal power plant, enhancing its efforts to diversify Dubai's energy mix of traditional fuels. But, aside from the issue of supply security, the use of coal in electricity generation has its environmental costs that may not be underestimated. The use of coal will hopefully be minimal and the environment-friendlier natural gas is readily available in the region. Two major producers of natural gas, Qatar and Iran, have enough supplies to satisfy Dubai's needs, and Dubai is already connected to the Qatari gas fields through the GCC's Dolphin gas pipeline. Realizing the costs and benefits of using different fuels, the Dubai

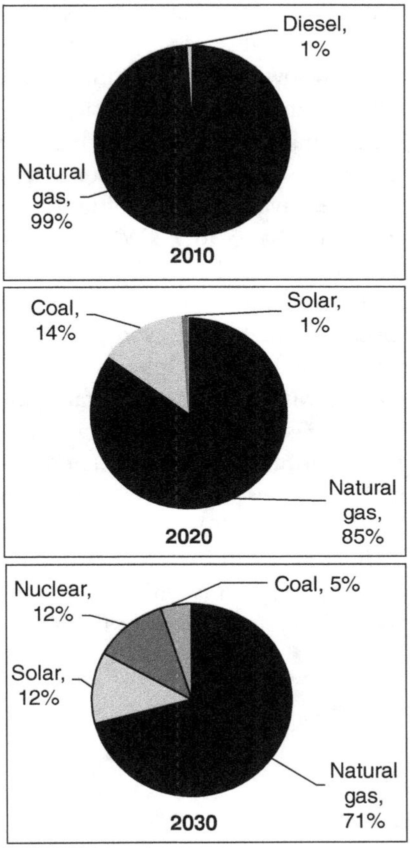

Figure 12.11. Dubai electricity fuel mix
Source: Dubai Supreme Council of Energy (2012)

Integrated Energy Strategy 2030 includes plans to achieve a mix that combines 12 per cent of electricity production from clean coal, 12 per cent from nuclear energy, 5 per cent from solar power, and 71 per cent from natural gas (Figure 12.11).

12.2.4.2 Renewable (Green) Energy Sources

While Dubai strives to diversify energy resources to meet future demand, the energy authorities are aware of the fact that there has to be increased use of non-conventional methods to generate badly needed power. In this regard, Dubai Supreme Council of Energy (SCE) has been assigned the task of overseeing the emirate's energy policy and designing an energy strategy for the next two decades.

To diversify its energy mix and reduce its carbon footprint, renewable energy is a rather obvious and preferred option for Dubai especially as technology advances lead to lower costs, making its use more feasible. The emirate can easily capitalize on its abundant renewable resources, especially solar radiation, wind, and tides. For example, it has been estimated that the average annual solar energy received on each square kilometre of the Middle East and North Africa is equivalent to burning 1.5 million barrels of oil (Climate Institute, 2009) and that 5 to 7 kWh can be generated from each square meter of surface per day in Dubai (Dobouni, 2009). In theory, this implies that less than 10 square meters of desert would be sufficient to meet the individual power needs of one human being at Dubai's current per capita consumption level. In addition, because Dubai is located in one of the hottest and most arid areas of the Middle East, solar radiation is higher than the region's average. Figure 12.12 shows the intensity of solar irradiation in the UAE as estimated by the German Aerospace Center (DLR). The figure also shows the high potential for harvesting solar energy in all the emirates within the UAE, including Dubai (DLR, 2005).

Direct solar radiation can be utilized in a number of ways; the most common are photovoltaic (PV) systems which use solar cells to convert light into electricity. Although PV systems may be theoretically used to generate

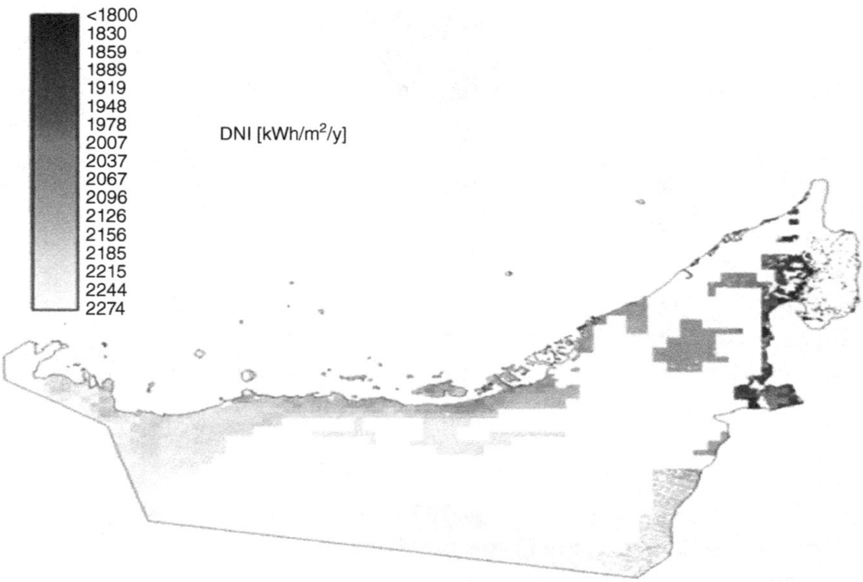

Figure 12.12. Solar electricity generation potential: direct normal irradiation (DNI) in the UAE (kWh/m^2/year)

Source: DLR (2005)

large amounts of electricity, they require expensive storage batteries to ensure continuous electricity at night. This limits their use to several megawatts making them more suitable for remote off-grid areas. However, efforts are being made globally to develop more viable, cost-effective, and larger PV systems.

Although renewable energy is being considered as an option, initiatives so far have been limited to establishing a number of 'eco-friendly buildings and communities' and encouraging the use of solar-powered tools and equipment such as parking meters and communications towers. However, in the long run, SCE has announced it is targeting renewable energy to supply 1 per cent of the emirate's energy by 2020 and 5 per cent by 2030 (see Figure 12.11). In that regard, DEWA has unveiled plans to launch the 'Mohammad Bin Rashid Al Maktoum Solar Park' at Seih Al Dahal in Dubai, an AED12 billion solar project. When completed in 2030, the project will have the capacity to generate 1,000 MW of power, using photovoltaic (PV) and concentrated solar power (CSP) technologies. Ten MW of power will be generated in the first phase of the project, which will be completed by the end of 2013 with a price tag of AED120 million. The project will be directly linked to DEWA's grid. In the following phases, the private sector will be invited to invest in the project. In addition to solar energy production facilities, the projects will include an advanced centre for studies and research, and a Renewables Academy.

Alternatively, harvested solar energy may be used in place of natural gas and oil to generate electricity using concentrated solar power (CSP) and other available technologies. CSP is a technology that allows the use of direct sunlight and mirrors to boil water and create steam that is in turn used to drive conventional turbines (Figure 12.13). CSP systems are commercially available and are more attractive than PV systems because, unlike the latter,

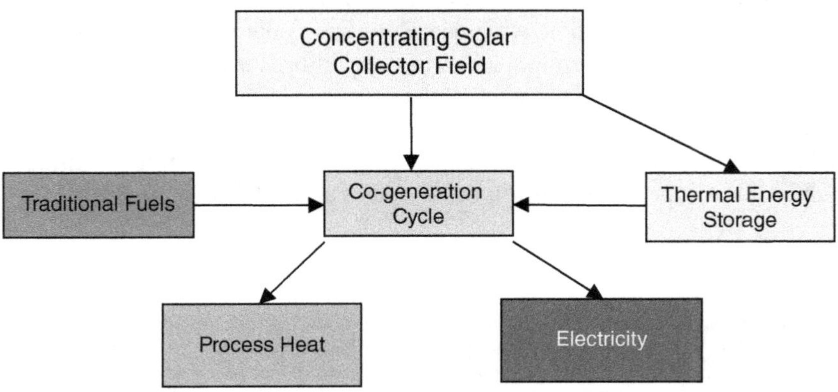

Figure 12.13. Electricity co-generation using CSP and traditional fuels

they have the capability of storing thermal energy through the use of thermal energy storage technologies. Stored thermal energy can then be used during cloudy days or at night to generate needed electricity. Using such technology, it has been indicated that the deserts of the MENA region are capable of producing enough electric energy to satisfy a major portion of Europe's electricity needs (Ummel and Wheeler, 2008).

The Union for the Mediterranean, which was initiated in 2008 and is composed of EU member states and non-EU Mediterranean nations, is exploring the possibilities of utilizing solar energy in the region. The union has adopted the Mediterranean Solar Plan (MSP) which has two complementary objectives; developing 20 GW of new renewable energy production capacity and achieving 20 per cent energy savings in the Mediterranean by 2020. Such an ambitious plan reflects the viability of CSP systems to answer much of Dubai's energy concerns. In addition to the production of electricity, waste heat from the CSP process can be used for water desalination. Furthermore, new technologies allow the storing of harvested solar energy which can be used at night. Alternatively, traditional fuels can also be used to insure continuous electricity generation at night. Although some reservations on using renewable energy might arise due to the high and uncompetitive costs of production, rapidly growing renewable energy technologies are helping push costs down. Currently, traditional sources of energy are still the most economical from a cost perspective, according to Mawdsley and Espey (2011).

Natural gas is still the cheapest source of energy and renewables are still the highest. For example, US Energy Information Administration (EIA) estimated that in 2011 the minimum levelized generation cost from solar is equivalent to \$150/barrels of oil equivalent of energy, compared to \$10 for natural gas (US EIA, 2013).[7] Due to economies of scale, mass production, and technological progress, a 50 to 70 per cent reduction in the cost of power generated from solar energy is projected within the next few decades (Ummel and Wheeler, 2008). These reductions, combined with the rising prices of fossil fuels and the high value of CO_2 reduction, will make using solar energy in power generation an increasingly feasible option. Therefore, the short-term investment costs in CSP systems in Dubai will be more than compensated for by the long-term benefits of such technologies. Once feasible from an economic perspective, using this type of renewable energy will reduce and eventually eliminate Dubai's total dependence on imported hydrocarbon fuels.

[7] US EIA defines Levelized Generation Cost, as representing 'the present value of the total cost of building and operating a generating plant over an assumed financial life and duty cycle, converted to equal annual payments and expressed in terms of real dollars to remove the impact of inflation. Levelized cost reflects overnight capital cost, fuel cost, fixed and variable O&M cost, financing costs, and an assumed utilization rate for each plant type' (US EIA, 2013).

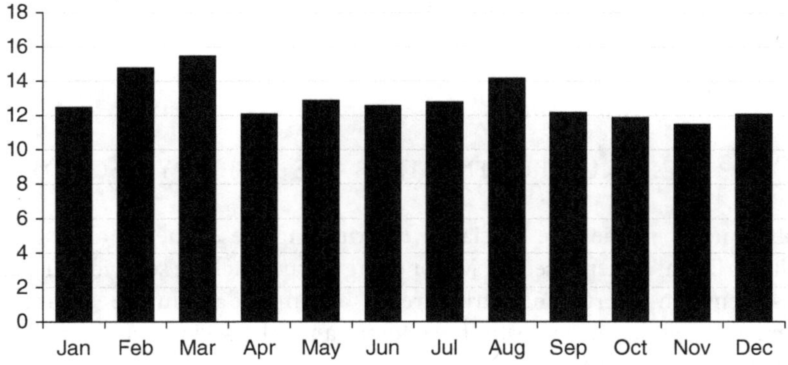

Figure 12.14. Monthly average wind speed in Dubai, 2012, km/h
Source: Dubai Airport

In addition to using solar energy, wind energy is another renewable option for Dubai. If studies conducted by DEWA show wind energy to be technically and economically feasible, this could be another alternative to hydrocarbons in power provision. Scientifically, the minimum wind speed required to harness power from wind is 3 to 12 kilometers per hour depending on the type of wind turbine used. In Dubai, the monthly average wind speed is 8 to 10 km per hour[8] (Figure 12.14), a speed that is sufficient for harnessing power by modern, efficient turbines.

Despite its location advantages, applications of renewable energy in Dubai are still limited. There is, however, a growing interest in renewable energy technologies by the private sector in Dubai, represented by a number of renewable energy companies that are involved in manufacturing and trading renewable energy products. Prior to the economic crisis of 2008–10, the private sector announced a number of green projects, but construction plans have stopped due to the global economic and financial crisis. Although, these projects are put on hold for the time being, they do, however, reflect ambitious efforts to introduce renewable energy use into Dubai. In total, it is reported that there exist seventeen environmentally friendly buildings in the UAE; all of which are located in Dubai.

Finally, another issue worth mentioning is that Dubai can attract foreign investments in renewable energy from countries which are obliged by the Kyoto Protocol to reduce their own CO_2 emissions. Dubai, as a major FDI hosting country, may encourage investments in renewable energy that will lead to reductions in CO_2 emissions and can, according to the Protocol, be

[8] This is according to readings at Dubai Airport. Speed at the coasts is expected to be higher.

used as credits against the maximum emissions requirements in the investing foreign countries.

12.3 RESTRUCTURING DUBAI'S ENERGY SECTOR

Public energy policies are crucial in determining the efficiency and sustainability of Dubai's energy sector. Major energy issues include securing sufficient investments in energy infrastructure to accommodate future expansions, reducing dependence on costly fuels to enhance the security and stability of the energy supply, and promoting end-use efficiency to reduce energy demand and hence the required supply capacity. To achieve and sustain an effective and efficient energy sector in Dubai a review of existing structure and current energy-related regulations is warranted. Policy tools needed in the restructuring process may be identified as those tools governing energy supply plus tools concerning energy demand. There is considerable space for improvement in supply and demand efficiencies and both supply and demand policies are complementary in achieving desired improvements. Carefully designing sound energy policies and effectively implementing them is essential for the energy sector to play its designated role as an engine for Dubai's growth.

As indicated earlier, Dubai's energy sector has performed well in terms of providing a sufficient supply of energy during the last four decades. The efficient and effective provision of energy necessitated expanding the supply chain to keep up with the increasing demand for energy of all types. That, in turn, required large investments in building new power stations, power transmission lines, fuel storage, and supply facilities. To continue this pattern in the future, there are mounting pressures on the public sector to provide badly needed investment. The government of Dubai is attempting to relieve some of the pressure by allowing partnership with the private sector, specifically by allowing private sector investments in electricity generation using the public–private partnership (PPP) criteria. Such a PPP would require changing the current rules and regulations to increase the private sector's willingness to invest in energy projects. Evidence from other countries, and the PPP in the power sector of the neighbouring emirate of Abu Dhabi, reveal that efficiency of energy provision may be improved by involving the private sector and opening up opportunities for foreign investment in the provision of energy.

In addition to its efforts to secure sufficient investment into its energy infrastructure, the energy authorities in Dubai are reconsidering the current energy mix and looking for policy changes that will diversify it by introducing new fuels and resources. Alternatives to traditional fossil fuels used in Dubai are being considered. These alternatives include non-renewable fuels as well as renewable sources. The emirate is planning to encourage and increase the use of renewable energy such that it constitutes 5 per cent of its energy mix by 2030. To achieve such a target, measures to discourage the use of traditional energy may be used. This includes, but is not limited to, phasing out current consumption subsidies to electricity and water.

The market structure of both supply and demand of energy determines the degree of efficiency and sustainability of the sector. Reviewing the current supply structure on one hand reveals the overwhelming control of the public sector, represented by DEWA, on production and distribution of energy fuels and electric power. Other fuels for manufacturing and transportation are provided by a small number of publicly owned companies. On the other hand, pricing is not market-determined and the energy sector is heavily subsidized. International experience shows that publicly controlled sectors may be able to satisfy the energy needs of a country but they are plagued with inefficiencies. Recognizing this fact, the authorities in Dubai may consider restructuring the energy sector and engaging the private sector in some specific activities within the sector.

12.3.1 Restructuring the Oil Products Market

Because of the primary role played by energy in any country's development, governments in many countries favour subsidizing the prices of different energy sources, including fuels. The argument typically advanced to defend subsidies is that of helping the economy by making all types of energy accessible to low-income groups and increasing the competitiveness of domestic producers in the international markets. In addition, stable domestic energy prices reduce variations in overall price levels. Furthermore, energy subsidies have been used in the oil-and-gas-rich GCC countries as means to redistribute oil income to citizens and help their economies grow rapidly. In the UAE, the most common argument for energy subsidies is that cheap energy prices ensure the citizens reap some of the benefits of their country's abundant oil and gas wealth.

On the supply side, publicly owned companies have been in charge of all activities related to production, import, and distribution of oil products in Dubai. They have been successful in securing the emirate's needs of such products and in providing decent services to the final consumers. But recently these companies are complaining about the below-cost pricing imposed by the government which they claim causes them to incur huge losses. In addition, low oil product prices have encouraged wasteful use of such precious resources. Although compared to other oil countries in the region the prices of oil products in Dubai and the UAE are considered high, the prices paid by end consumers are still largely subsidized if compared to international levels. The regular gasoline price at the pump in 2011 was AED1.72 (US$0.47) per litre

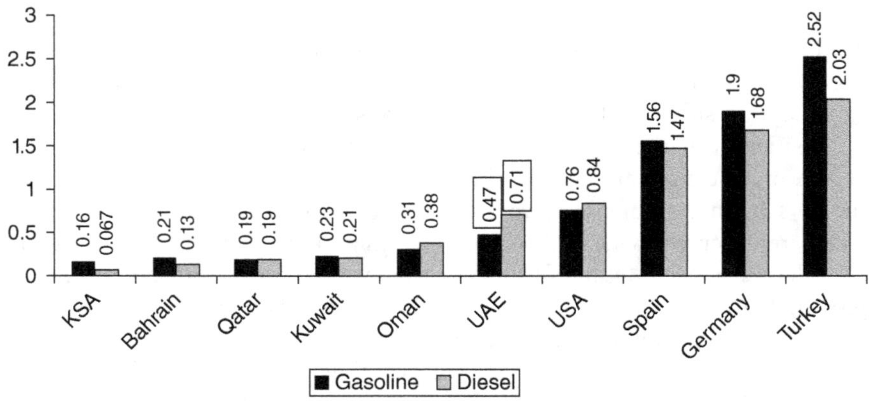

Figure 12.15. Fuel prices in selected countries (US$)
Source: GIZ (2011)

in Dubai, compared to AED1.14 (US$0.31) in neighbouring Oman, but well below that in Turkey, Germany, and Spain (Figure 12.15).

Despite their current subsidized levels, the Federal National Council (FNC) was reported in early 2012 to have asked the government to reduce fuel prices in the UAE to levels comparable with neighbouring GCC countries. If approved, this reduction will further increase consumption and widen the energy gap in Dubai. While the proposal has its political merits, its economic consequences will be overwhelming on resource-poor emirates like Dubai and the northern emirates, unless the resulting deficit is financed by the federal government.

While cheap fuel provides residents of the UAE with the opportunity to feel the blessing of their country's wealth, sustainability of such subsidies in the long run is questionable. Cheap energy resulting from subsidies will preclude any incentives to adopt technologies that are less energy-intensive and develop other forms of energy, including renewable energy. In addition, with rising international energy prices it will become more difficult for the governments in different emirates to finance the current level of subsidies. For Dubai as a net energy importer, the task of securing the required funds to subsidize cheap energy will be even more challenging. On the contrary, rational use of Dubai's limited energy resources and concerns about the environment call for phasing out subsidies and charging prices to the final consumers of oil products that are closer to the international market levels.

12.3.2 Restructuring the Electricity Sector

As indicated previously, electricity and water production and distribution in Dubai has always been handled by the public sector. Currently DEWA operates as a vertically integrated company and performs a variety activities including generation, transmission, and distribution of electricity for the entire emirate. In addition, the company is responsible for all activities related to water desalination and distribution. During the last four decades, the Dubai authorities have been successful in securing resources to match the emirate's higher power and water demand by expanding its generation and distribution capacities.

Due to the high cost of investment and concerns about the sustainability of Dubai's energy sector, the authorities are currently reconsidering the energy strategy and energy-mix choices to deal with some of the pressing issues associated with electricity provision. Recognizing the difficulties and uncertainty associated with securing the necessary funds and resources to fuel its generation plants, the emirate has announced plans to open its electricity generation sector to the private sector through PPP arrangements. It is also studying the possibility of using clean coal and nuclear energy in generating electricity. However, there seems to be a need to speed up the implementation of PPP arrangements and to introduce more competition to the sector by expanding the PPP plans to include other electricity provision activities. In addition, renewable energy, particularly that which is generated from solar irradiation, also provides an increasingly viable option for Dubai. More efforts are needed to encourage the use of renewable energy, especially by individual consumers and the private sector in general. There are some international examples of successful programmes that led to considerable increases in renewable energy use. In Germany, for example, feed-in electricity tariffs have been introduced to encourage the use of new energy technologies. The result was that in 2011, 20 per cent of electricity in Germany came from renewable sources.[9] Nevertheless, it is unlikely that a significant increase in the use of renewable energy by the private sector in Dubai is likely because of the presence of consumption subsidies for electricity and water that lead to huge cost differences in favour of traditional energy.

In addition to expanding supply capacity to cope with rising energy consumption, policy measures are needed to curb the growth of demand. Dubai's consumption levels and the resulting high energy intensity levels[10] are to some extent a consequence of high energy requirements due to Dubai's exceptionally hot and arid climate. However, these high levels are also a result of inefficiencies in energy consumption which, in turn, demonstrate the need for immediate policy actions to improve efficiency. After a long history of

[9] A feed-in tariff is a rate of money paid by the government to consumers to generate their own electricity through small-scale green energy installations such as solar panels.

[10] The term 'energy intensity' refers to the amount of energy required to produce one unit of output.

targeting its efforts to increasing the supply of electricity, the government of Dubai has recently expanded its efforts to encourage more efficient demand.

DEWA is adopting some demand-side policies including measures that increase the efficiency on the end-user side. The authority's measures are still limited to media informational campaigns that are designed to educate people about the importance and applicability of conserving electricity and water. Nevertheless, media campaigns are usually complementary to more comprehensive policies known to induce electricity end-use efficiency. They are small elements of the so-called 'demand-side management' (DSM) programmes, which became popular in oil-importing countries during the 1970s, in an effort by those countries to reduce their dependency on imported oil. A typical DSM programme includes a set of customer-focused measures that are intended to influence the amount and timing of energy use by consumers therefore increasing energy efficiency. Such programmes involve the design and implementation of various measures that aim to manage energy use especially electricity loads (load management programmes, or peak-clipping and load shifting). According to some estimates, the potential for electricity efficiency in high-income countries which have high per capita energy consumption, such as the UAE, may reach 30 per cent (Al-Iriani, 2005).

If Dubai adopts a more comprehensive DSM programme, it will achieve higher allocation efficiency of resources by reallocating these resources from the energy sector to other sectors of the economy. End-use efficiency improvements provide multiple benefits such as financial benefits to consumers and environmental benefits to the society at large. In particular, DSM reduces the investments required for additional generation capacity and the cost of providing energy to end users. Furthermore, DSM benefits the society by reducing energy-related CO_2 emissions.

In addition to increasing the awareness of consumers about the importance of energy conservation through educational and media campaigns, Dubai may need to use more tools for DSM including setting efficiency standards for buildings, vehicles, appliances, and other energy-consuming equipment. Another DSM tool is providing public funds in the form of energy efficiency assistance to end users in order to encourage them to replace their old inefficient equipment with new more efficient models and improve insulation as well as encouraging investors to invest in developing energy-efficient equipment. Among all the prescribed DSM elements, there is evidence that providing economic incentives is the most powerful tool in terms of its favourable effect of efficiency. For instance, consumers in general react to tariff changes that bring utility prices to free market levels more than to informational campaigns. To achieve a higher degree of end-use efficiency, tariffs should reflect the supply and externality costs of energy. With the exception of some minor tariff increases during recent years, triggered by the increasing cost of production rather than efficiency considerations, the

Table 12.4. Electricity tariffs in Dubai (UAE fils)

Slab(kWh)	2008			2012		
	Residential and commercial		Industrial and others	Residential and commercial		Industrial and others
	Non-citizen	Citizen		Non-citizen	Citizen	
1–2,000	20	7.5	20	23	7.5	23
2,001–4,000	24	9.0	20	28	9.0	23
4,001–6,000	28	10.5	20	32	10.5	23
Over 6,000	33	12.5	20	38	12.5	23
Over 10,000	33	12.5	23	38	12.5	38

Note: 1 fils = US $0.00272.
Source: DEWA (1990–2012)

Table 12.5. Water tariffs in Dubai (UAE fils)

Slab(IG)	2008			2012		
	Residential		Industrial and others	Residential		Industrial and others
	Non-citizen	Citizen		Non-citizen	Citizen	
1–6,000	3.0	0.0	3.0	3.5	0	3.5
6,001–10,000	3.5	0.0	3.0	4.0	0	3.5
10,001–12,000	3.5	1.5	3.5	4.0	0	4.0
12,001–20,000	4.0	1.5	3.5	4.6	0	4.0
Over 20,000	4.0	1.5	4.0	4.6	1.5	4.6

Note: 1 fils = US $0.00272.
Source: DEWA (1990–2012)

nominal prices of all types of energy in Dubai are regulated and largely fixed (implying that real prices are actually declining).

In an effort to curb electricity demand growth and increase end-user efficiency, the government of Dubai through DEWA has recently implemented a new slab system of tariffs for electricity and water. The slab system is designed to charge higher rates when usage of electricity and water by a consumer increases above certain blocks (Tables 12.4 and 12.5). In addition, in January 2011 the company announced a new pricing scheme which includes a 15 per cent price increase on electricity and water consumed by expatriates. But current tariffs still do not reflect the total opportunity cost to the society, including environmental cost, and they are still substantially below international levels (Figure 12.16). A further tariff adjustment according to the DSM principle is needed. It will, of course, result in higher energy and water

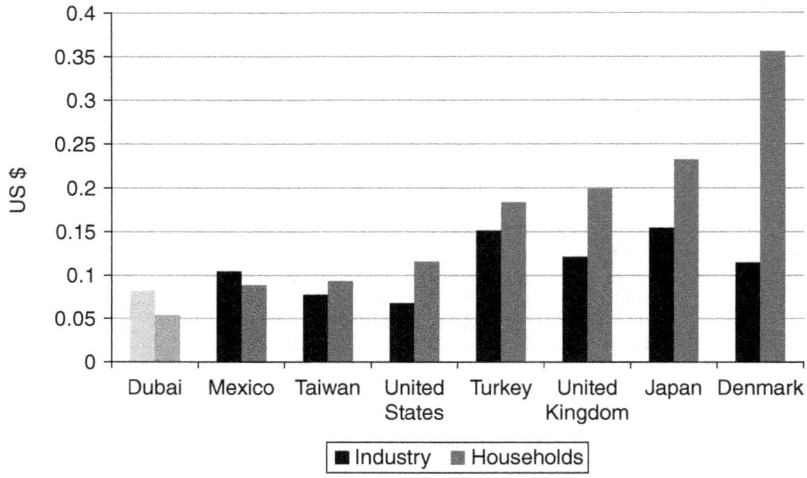

Figure 12.16. Electricity tariffs in Dubai and some other selected countries
Source: IEA (2011) and DEWA (1990–2012)

prices to consumers but this cost increase will constitute an incentive for consumers to use energy more rationally.

Before deciding on the appropriate tariff levels, the effects of any further increases on Dubai's population and the economy should be studied. Should higher tariffs be determined to negatively affect Dubai's competitiveness, then other simultaneous measures that offset their negative effects and reduce the cost of doing business may be used. In addition, achieving higher consumption efficiency dictates that tariffs should be equalized among utility consumers, expatriates, and citizens. The government of Dubai may continue subsidizing citizens by reverting to a cash subsidy that is financed by the extra revenues collected from higher tariffs. This will preserve citizens' welfare, and in fact may increase it because a cash subsidy gives consumers more consumption choices and at the same time increases efficiency in their consumption decisions.

12.4 CONCLUSIONS AND A LOOK INTO THE FUTURE

The energy sector in the emirate of Dubai has recently witnessed important challenges that are expected to continue in the near future. The location of Dubai in an arid and hot area makes its energy requirements exceptionally high. In addition, strong economic and demographic growth coupled with low consumption efficiency, largely due to the current energy and water subsidies, led to unprecedented growth in energy demand.

The government of Dubai has been able to match the soaring demand of all energy types by increasing its supply capacities. Oil products are secured from domestic production and imports, and provided to consumers at subsidized prices. Electricity and desalinated water are provided through investing in expanding generation and desalination capacities, keeping up with the economy's needs. The feedstock for electricity generation has traditionally been supplied from the emirate's limited resources of conventional hydrocarbon fuels, and by importing fuels from the neighbouring emirates and international markets.

Additional investments in the energy infrastructure have, however, become costlier and progressively more difficult to obtain. This fact is changing Dubai's determination to keep the public sector's exclusive control on energy supply, and therefore is making a case for private sector participation through PPP. However, additional steps may be needed to liberalize the energy sector in order to make it more sustainable.

Furthermore, some energy resources in the UAE as a whole are falling short of satisfying the country's exploding need for fuels, let alone Dubai's. Therefore, Dubai has resorted to importing natural gas from neighbouring countries in the region. Given Dubai's increasing energy bill, the current energy situation has become increasingly difficult to sustain, calling for policy measures to seek alternative energy sources and to curb the chronic increase in demand. Dubai's energy supply options include, in addition to conventional oil and natural gas, importing coal, building nuclear reactors, and using renewable energy. Due to cost, security and environmental concerns, the most appealing of those three options is the development and use of renewable energy. Dubai's location allows the emirate to take advantage of its abundant solar, thermal, and wind resources. Recent technological advances in harvesting energy from renewable sources, and the resulting decrease in costs, will make it easier for Dubai to adopt the renewable energy option in the near future.

Equally important in dealing with the energy issue in Dubai is adopting proper energy demand policies leading to a comprehensive programme of energy demand-side management (DSM). The energy sector is plagued with subsidies that result in inefficiencies and waste. A comprehensive DSM programme should include, in addition to the current informational campaigns, regulatory measures plus economic incentives. Regulations governing the use of energy-efficient appliances and tools, and that set other efficiency standards should be considered. Economic incentives that help encourage the rational use of energy by consumers should include subsidizing a more efficient use of energy and water on one hand, and eliminating current consumption subsidies on the other.

REFERENCES

Al-Iriani, M., 2005. 'Climate-related Electricity Demand-side Management in Oil-exporting Countries: The Case of the United Arab Emirates'. *Energy Policy*, 33: 2350–60.

A. T. Kearney, 2013. *Foreign Direct Investment (FDI) Confidence Index 2013.* [Online] Available at: http://www.atkearney.com, accessed 6 August 2015.

British Petroleum, 2012. *Statistical Review of World Energy,* London: British Petroleum.

Butt, G., and Al Abed, I., 2001. 'Oil and Gas in the UAE'. In I. Abed and P. Hellyer (eds) *United Arab Emirates: A New Perspective*, London: Trident Press, pp. 231–48.

Climate Institute, 2009. 'Sustainable Solutions for Energy and Water Security in the United Arab Emirates'. *Climate Alert,* 19(1): 1–12.

Dargin, J., 2010. 'Addressing the UAE Natural Gas Crisis: Strategies for a Rational Energy Policy', Policy Briefs of The Dubai Initiative, Better Center for Science and International Affairs, Harvard University, August.

DEWA, 1990–2012. *DEWA Statistics,* Dubai, UAE: Dubai Electricity and Water Authority.

DLR, 2005. *Concentrating Solar Power for the Mediterranean Region.* Stuttgart: Institute of Technical Thermodynamics Section Systems Analysis and Technology Assessment.

Dobouni, M., 2009. 'Organic Photovoltaic Module Application in MENA Region: Feasibility Study'. Doctorate Program/Environmental Management–Sustainable Development, Houston University.

Dolphin Energy, 2010. *Natural Gas Core Customers and Volumes.* [Online] Available at: http://www.dolphinenergy.com/Public/marketing-distribution/marketing-natural-gas-customers-volumes.htm, accessed 10 November 2011.

DSC, 2013. *Real GDP Statistics,* Dubai, UAE: Dubai Statistics Center.

Dubai Supreme Council of Energy, 2012. *DIES 2030: Dubai Projected Fuel Mix Scenario.* [Online] Available at: http://www.dubaisce.gov.ae/dubai_projected.aspx, accessed 26 August 2015.

GIZ, 2011. *International Fuel Prices Database*, Deutsche Gesellschaft für Internationale Zusammenarbeit, Bonn, Germany.

HighBeam Business, 2010. 'UAE Gas Shortages to Triple by 2025'. *APS Review Gas Market Trends*, 31 May 2010.

IHS, 2008. *IHS Global Insight: Country & Industry Forecasting.* [Online] Available at: http://www.ihs.com/products/global-insight/industry-economic-report.aspx?ID=106596896&pu=1&rd=globalinsight_com, accessed 10 November 2010.

Mawdsley, J., and Espey, C., 2011. *Renewables vs. Hydrocarbons: The Energy Reality,* Calgary, Alberta: AltaCorp Capital Inc.

Metz, H. C. (ed.) 1993. *Persian Gulf States: A Country Study.* Washington, DC: GPO for the Library of Congress.

Ummel, K., and Wheeler, D., 2008. 'Desert Power: The Economics of Solar Thermal Electricity for Europe, North Africa, and the Middle East', Working paper 156, Center for Global Development. [Online] Available at: http://www.cgdev.org/publication/desert-power-economics-solar-thermal-electricity-europe-north-africa-and-middle-east, accessed 2 September 2015.

US EIA, 2011. *Annual Energy Outlook 2015,* Washington, DC: US DOE.

US EIA, 2013. 'Levelized Cost of New Generation Resources'. In *Annual Energy Outlook 2013.* Washington, DC: US DOE.

13

Access to Land and the Investment Behaviour of Firms

Ibrahim Elbadawi

13.1 INTRODUCTION

Land—or its equivalent in the form of built-up space for commercial use—is a fundamental input among the factors required to start and operate a business. Commercial land ownership serves at least three purposes. First, it provides the physical facilities for production. Second, it provides a reserve of wealth that can be used as collateral for loans or to hedge against risks. Third, it provides a return on investment in the form of rental flows and capital gains. Constraints on access to land, including constrains to land ownership, therefore, could become a major obstacle for economic development, as they are likely to have an adverse impact on the potential to create new enterprises or expand existing ones. In this context the evidence from the 2010 Enterprise Level Survey—where 51.3 per cent of surveyed firms find 'lack of access to land' to be the major obstacle to their business operation in Dubai—should merit careful consideration.[1]

In mature economies with established infrastructures and possibly high population density there might be problems of land scarcity and high cost. However, the existence of robust institutions and efficient regulatory systems will likely ensure that the problem of urban and commercial land allocation can be solved through the market mechanism. The population density in Dubai—and that of the UAE in general—is low despite the huge entry of expatriate workers since the late 1950s. In 2012, density in Dubai was around 400 inhabitants/km^2 vis-à-vis other city-states such as Hong Kong or

[1] This survey collected information in 2010 from a representative sample of 709 establishments in Dubai (free zones and non-free zones). Among the questions, firms are asked to declare which problem—among 15 possible categories—was the biggest obstacle to their operations. These categories include access to finance, crime rate, or public administration among others.

Singapore which were above 5,000 inhabitants/km^2. Likewise, the development of Dubai's physical infrastructure has not yet reached a steady state. Moreover, the huge surge of real estate development that has accounted for much of GDP growth in the past two decades would lead one to think that the physical availability of land and/or built-up space for industrial and commercial use is not scarce.

It seems, therefore, that the problem of land access in Dubai, as reflected in the above-mentioned survey, is likely to be associated with institutional and regulatory problems. This chapter therefore, asks two fundamental questions: what are the regulatory and institutional factors that might have complicated firms' access to land in Dubai? And equally importantly, what are the consequences of such declared constraint for the future economic development of the emirate?

There are three key aspects that underlie a study of 'land' as an obstacle for business operations in Dubai. First, the vast majority of entrepreneurs opening and running business in the emirate are foreigners: in fact, our evidence indicates that in 2010 only 10 per cent of the population was local and only about 2.5 per cent of enterprises in Dubai were solely owned by locals. The second aspect is the asymmetric treatment of firms based on foreign participation: firms wishing to set up a business in the free zones are not allowed to buy land for their operations and can only rent land or land with built-up premises. In Main Dubai, foreigners continue to be restricted but nationals are allowed to own land. Therefore it is important to understand that for the vast majority of entrepreneurs in the free zones 'access to land' problems could imply 'limited access to buying land'; while in Main Dubai it is likely to be associated with 'limited access to rental land and/or property for commercial use'. The third important aspect is not directly linked to the land market but it indirectly affects the ways in which entrepreneurs do business and approach land markets. It refers to the sponsorship system that applies to firms operating outside free zones and ties each foreigner willing to invest in Dubai with a sponsor (the 'local' partner). In the case of public and limited shareholdings, the local sponsor automatically owns at least 51 per cent of the shares and, at the same time, has to receive an annuity for his services as legal representative.[2]

[2] An Emirati local-business sponsor is a UAE national or a corporate body where all board members are UAE nationals. The sponsor represents the company in all legal matters. For limited liability companies, the foreign investor must allocate at least 51% of the shares to the sponsor, although the sponsor is not expected to invest money in the business. The sponsor, nevertheless, does not have the right to share profits proportionally, frequently agreeing with the foreign investor to receive an annual fee. In the case of a sole proprietor or civil companies ownership is 100% for the foreign investor. However, it is compulsory to appoint a UAE national sponsor as 'the local service agent'. This local service agent is not involved in business operations and is paid an annual fixed fee or a share of profits.

To bypass the rules implied by the sponsorship system foreigners can set up their business inside free zones where they are still unable to buy land but are allowed full ownership of their business, that is, the physical installations, full share ownership, and in full command of the profits generated by the firm. An advantage of setting up a business in free zones is that the rules and regulations that underlie the operations of the firm (regulations for the leasing of commercial property, the cost of leasing, or even the fees attached to the leasing permit, among others) are well established and monitored by the Free Zone Authority (see Appendix I).[3]

Such certainty is not necessarily a characteristic of the land market in Main Dubai, where the lack of transparency and predictability of the land regulatory system (especially with regards to adjudication of disputes), adds risk and uncertainty to the operations of firms. Over the years there has been a tendency for the local government to reduce commercial land uncertainty: on 31 July 2007, the Real Estate Regulatory Agency (RERA) was launched as an agency under the Dubai Land Department with autonomy to monitor and regulate the real estate market (including rental price increases) and resolve disputes between leasers and landlords. However, in the case of rental prices and despite the fact that rental increases are legally established and regulated, the implementation of these remains fairly ambiguous, which gives rise to potential abuses by both renters and local landowners.[4]

The fact that business (and especially foreign investors who accounted for 97.5 per cent of businesses in Dubai in 2010) can opt to establish themselves in free zones implies that Dubai operates under two sets of rules and regulations for land-related issues. While it is clear that the lack of predictability and certainty of the land market in Main Dubai might be directly associated with the problem of 'lack of land access', the same cannot be said about free zones where no such uncertainty exists. Instead, it seems that in

[3] Though not related to the issue of land access, it is perhaps pertinent to note that a disadvantage for firms that decide to settle in the free zones is that they are treated as 'foreign firms', i.e. their goods are sold as exported goods to GCC markets and this includes Dubai and the other emirates in the union. Thus, for firms in Dubai's free zones the custom-tariff cost is the price paid to avoid the costs, risks, and uncertainties associated with the influence of a local sponsor. This cost translates to an increase of 5% of the finished good, paid in the form of import duty.

[4] There have been attempts to establish the rules to determine the rental price of a commercial property. Decree No. 2, issued in January 2011, establishes maximum rent increases according to the difference between the actual rental price and the average rental prices of similar properties. However, there are no legally established rules to define what is a 'similar property' thereby inducing uncertainty and arbitrariness. At the same time, the rental price of properties is established by an alleged 'Rent Index of the Emirate of Dubai' that should have been produced by RERA but remains unpublished and unknown to the business community.

the case of firms in the free zones 'lack of access to land' corresponds to lack of access to land ownership, which is an option available for some firms in Main Dubai but not for those firms located in the free zones. Focus-group discussions with firms located in JAFZA, the largest free-zone authority in Dubai, confirmed that this is the main reason for identifying 'lack of land access' to be the most serious constraint they face. In comparison to their counterparts in Main Dubai, firms in the free zone consider themselves deprived of owning commercial land and eventually using it as collateral to finance their operations.

This chapter undertakes an econometric analysis using the Dubai 2010 Firms Survey database. We model the determinants of the probability that a firm will declare 'lack of access to land' as a major constraint, controlling for firm characteristics, sector, and economic zone, and nationality of ownership. We find that access to land problems appear to be more severe for firms located in free zones than in Main Dubai. However, Main Dubai firms that are de facto owned by foreigners—as opposed to those where they are minority partners—tend to be more severely constrained.

Finally, in addition to studying the severity of the problem of being restricted in the access to land, this chapter also analyses the potential impacts that this obstacle might have on physical and human capital investments by firms. Our estimates suggest that investing in assets would increase by 22 per cent if lack of access to land were not an obstacle to firms while investment in human capital—proxied by training provision—would increase by 35 per cent if firms could expand their operations as result of an improvement in accessing land. The policy implications of these results is straightforward. There is an apparent need to revise and amend the laws and regulations concerning the 'access to land' for commercial purposes, particularly to reduce asymmetries between locally owned and foreign-based companies in order to reduce the detrimental effects of uncertainty on investment, increase capital and human investment, and potentially allow for greater employment creation in the emirate of Dubai.

The chapter is organized as follows: section 13.2 provides an overview and comparison of the laws that govern real estate use (for buyers and renters) as background for our discussion of the empirical estimates. Section 13.3 reviews the preliminary evidence in the 2010 Dubai Enterprise Level Survey to assess the relative importance of market uncertainty in explaining problems of access to land in Main Dubai and its interaction with the sponsorship system, on one hand, and the prohibition of commercial land ownership in the free zone, on the other. Section 13.4 provides estimates of an econometric model for analysing the problem of access to land from the firms' perspective. Moreover, this section also assesses the implications of the constraints on access to land for firms' physical and human capital investment decisions. Section 13.5 concludes.

13.2 THE COMMERCIAL LAND MARKET REGULATIONS IN DUBAI

The market for commercial land (i.e. excluding land used for residential purposes) in Dubai is dual. One segment of the market, covering the majority of land and commonly labelled Main Dubai, allows for ownership by Emirati companies or nationals for commercial purposes but it only allows for surrogate property by firms where there is foreign participation. The other segment comprises free zones—isolated areas devoted to the development of specific businesses for foreign trade—where the nationality regulations of Main Dubai do not apply and land is allocated using long-term tradable leases.

Free zones in Dubai—in the UAE in general—are industrial parks created by the local government to attract companies using a set of incentives that facilitate firms getting closer to their objectives. Besides the benefits offered by free zones in most developed countries—that is, tax breaks and lower operational fees—free zones in Dubai are tailored to the economy, that is, they allow firms to jump the rules associated with the 'sponsorship system' that applies in full in Main Dubai. Thus, firms inside free zones are sponsored by the corresponding free-zone authority and do not have to find a local partner to act as their legal representative. The implication is that foreign investors are allowed to own 100 per cent of the business although in common with Main Dubai, foreigners are not allowed to own land in free zone areas. Another advantage for firms in the free zones is their ability to tap into the zone's mobile labour market to find employees, that is, firms inside the free zone are not subject to the labour code that operates in Main Dubai where workers are tied to the sponsor for the duration of their contract. Instead, the labour markets inside a free zone operate in ways that are far similar to modern labour markets so that the behaviour, the motivation, the work effort, and the productivity of workers inside free zones is considerably greater than that in Main Dubai (see for example, Vazquez-Alvarez, 2010 and Elbadawi and Vazquez-Alvarez, 2011).

In general, the government establishes free zones by allocating a landmark to be developed for industrial and commercial purposes. The free zone is broken into plots that are leased to the client(s), that is, firms wanting to set up their business there. The free-zone authority constructs warehouses, factory plants, and office spaces so that the client does not need to heavily invest in construction. However, all free zones offer the possibility to rent out plots of land if the client wishes to construct their own plants and office facilities. Once the client is set in the free zone, they become a separate legal entity with limited liability single-shareholding under the rules and regulations of each free-zone authority. Each client wishing to obtain such a legal status within a free zone has to go through the following steps:

1. *Apply to the Free Zone Sales and Marketing Department* that will approve the application and allocate the client to a plot with facilities—or transfer the responsibility of approval to the Property Department if the client wishes to build their own facilities.
2. *Apply to the Property Development Department* to get approval on a proposal to build a particular plant, factory, or premises of the client and allocate accommodation to the client's potential employees if required.
3. *Apply to the Civil Engineering Department* to get approval on the building, expansion, or setting-up of the business in the allocated plot/land/building.
4. *Apply to the Group Environmental, Health and Safety Division* to obtain an operation fitness certificate that proves the health fitness of the client, employees, and premises.
5. *Register with the Free Zone Customer Service Department* who will issue the leases contract, entry permit, visa and work contracts, vehicle registration, and all the paper work associated with the establishment of the firm as a full member of the free zone.
6. *Connect the utilities—telecommunications, electricity, water, and postal services*—which are usually provided by sole suppliers to the zones—for example, in the case of Jebel Ali Free Zone, the sole providers are ETISALAT, DEWA, and Emirates Post, respectively.

Once a client has followed the steps and has set up operations in the free zone, the type of 'license' issued to the entity determines the rules and regulations with which to operate.[5] Appendix I details the basic rules and regulations that apply almost identically to any type of industrial/commercial licence issued in the free zones. What becomes clear from such rules and regulations is that firms in the free zones start and continue to operate under a climate where the rules of the game are clear and known. This implies that the uncertainty and risk attached to the cost of leasing land and building is fully removed from the onset. Thus, firms in the free zone know their legal status; they know the rental cost and how this will change in the future; they know all required fees and permits in advance; they know fees and permits will not vary on an ad hoc basis; they know their obligations and rights, and they know that each free-zone authority acts as the guardian of such rights and obligations.

On the other hand, in Main Dubai the rules of the game underlying the operation of firms are not necessarily as clear as in the free zones.

[5] All licences operate under the same rules and regulations and vary in name according to the nature of their activity. Thus, there are four possible types of licence: trading licence, industrial licence, service licence and national industrial licence. The latter are issued to companies that operate in and out of the free zone and therefore are subject to the 51% GCC ownership status, but forgo the other rules attached to the sponsorship system.

To resolve or at least contain the consequences of the ensuing uncertainty, the sponsorship system, we would argue, plays an important role. Firms that are de facto owned by foreigners, where the Emirati sponsorship share is exactly at 51 per cent—the minimum required by the sponsorship law—are likely to face the brunt of the land market imperfections. It is widely believed that these are firms actually owned by foreigners that require the backing of a local in order to set up a business in Dubai, but the locals are not likely to be true business partners. Instead, those that are sponsored through genuine Emirati partnership (more than 51 per cent sponsorship share) or are fully owned by Emirati are likely to avoid the consequences because the Emirati business partner should be able to 'informally' resolve land access problems through the strong social network that is not likely to be available to foreign businessmen.

However, although foreign investors in the free zone come with almost no uncertainty compared to land-leasing problems in Main Dubai, unlike their counterpart in the latter, they cannot own commercial land and hence they are unable to use land as collateral for business loans.

It is therefore important to explain the extent to which the uncertain land market environment in Main Dubai might have caused problems of 'land access' to be more severe than in the free zones; or that this only applies to Main Dubai firms that are fully owned by foreigners (i.e. with Emirati sponsorship share of exactly 51 per cent). This is the subject of our two next sections that provide the empirical evidence from the 2010 Dubai Enterprise Level Survey on land issues for firms operating in Dubai.

13.3 EVIDENCE ON LAND ACCESS ISSUES

The 2010 Dubai Enterprise Level Survey asked survey respondents to declare which item (among thirteen) implied the greatest obstacle to the operations of the firm. Figure 13.1 shows the percentage distribution of all firms according to the obstacle they think is having the worst effect on their operations. Clearly, 'access to land problems' is the most significant item with 51.3 per cent of firms declaring this as the major obstacle. In fact, the second and third problem areas—'access to finance' and 'permits issues'—follow with 9.2 per cent and 8.9 per cent of firms—respectively—declaring these two as major obstacles, that is, either one of them is significantly below the 51.3 per cent of firms declaring that 'access to land problems' is the greatest obstacle.

We have previously suggested that 'access to land' would be a problem for firms either in Main Dubai or firms in the free zones although for different reasons in each case. Figures 13.2 (Main Dubai) and Figure 13.3 (free zones) are analogous to Figure 13.1 but distinguish between the two economic areas:

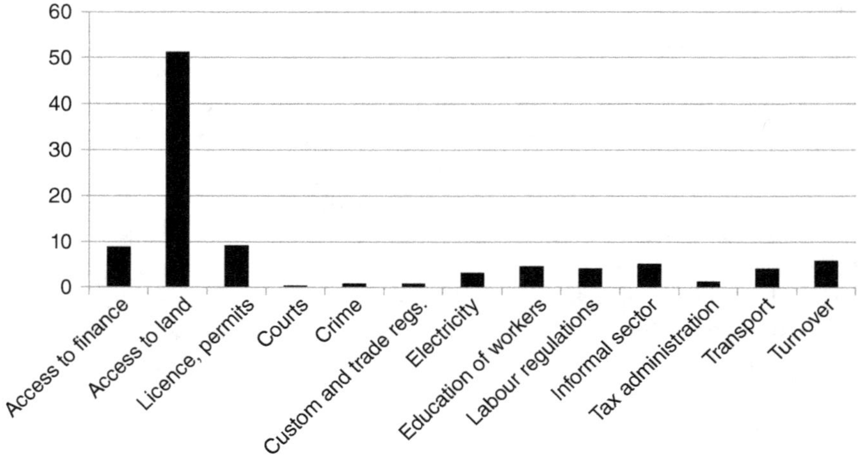

Figure 13.1. What element represents the biggest obstacle to operations?
Source: Own elaboration based on 2010 Enterprise Level Survey

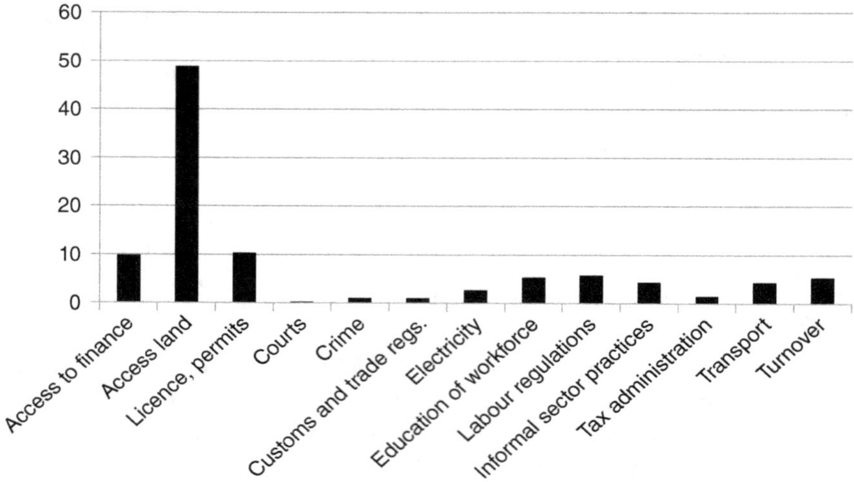

Figure 13.2. Main obstacle to firms' operations in Main Dubai
Source: Own elaboration based on 2010 Enterprise Level Survey

together they show that the issue of 'access to land' as an obstacle applies to both economic zones. In Main Dubai 48.8 per cent of firms claim 'access to land' to be the major obstacle; 57 per cent of firms in free zones make the same claim. The 8.2 per cent difference is statistically significant with a p-value of 0, that is, the problem of 'lack of access to land' is significantly larger for firms in the free zone.

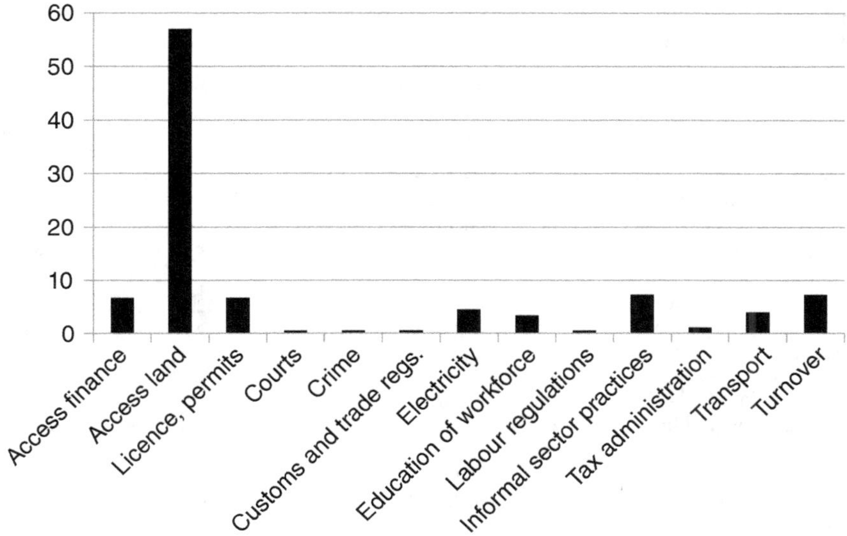

Figure 13.3. Main obstacle to firms' operations in free zones
Source: Own elaboration based on 2010 Enterprise Level Survey

Table 13.1 shows the ownership breakdown by economic region—that is, either in Main Dubai or the free zone—and by industrial activity—light or heavy manufacturing, construction, sales, non-financial and financial services. The table clearly shows the dominance of de facto foreign ownership of firms in Main Dubai, which accounts for 68 per cent of firms in this economic region of Dubai; and 53 per cent of all firms in Main Dubai and the free zones combined. In contrast only 2.5 per cent of firms are fully owned by locals, that is, entrepreneurial activity among local Emirati is weak. The sponsorship effect is greater among firms in the construction sector and, as expected, it is significant in Main Dubai relative to the effect it has in the free zones.

13.4 EMPIRICAL RESULTS

As discussed above, Table 13.1 does not identify a clear correlation between the status of firms according to degree of sponsorship and the outcome 'access to land' as a major obstacle. However, the evidence does not provide causal interpretation between outcome and co-variates. Our next step is to set up a model that might elicit such causal relation between the economic zone—Main Dubai vs free zone—and the sponsorship status, controlling for variability associated with the characteristics of the firm—industrial sector, export behaviour, and size of the enterprise among others. The key issue is that other

Table 13.1. Ownership status in reference to local ownership, by economic region and economic sector in 2010

	Full sample	Manufacturing		Construction	Sales	Services	
		Light	Heavy			Non-financial	Financial
All firms in Main Dubai and the free zones							
Average ownership by locals	56.4	66.2	53.2	63.3	37.4	52.8	62.0
Locals own exactly 0%	15.4	8.7	17.5	0.0	36.7	23.2	9.9
Locals own 1% to 50%	2.0	0.0	1.0	0.0	6.4	1.9	2.2
Locals own exactly 51%	53.0	51.3	57.1	74.1	42.2	46.3	49.7
Locals own 52%–99%	5.0	2.0	2.0	1.9	2.8	1.0	7.0
Locals own exactly 100%	2.5	38.1	22.5	24.1	11.9	27.8	31.3
Firms in Main Dubai							
Average ownership by locals	66.1	72.6	64.1	63.3	59.3	66.9	68.0
Locals own exactly 0%	0.0	0.0	0.0	0.0	0.0	0.0	0.0
Locals own 1% to 50%	0.0	0.0	0.0	0.0	0.0	0.0	0.0
Locals own exactly 51%	68.1	55.8	71.0	74.1	80.0	66.7	65.2
Locals own 52% to 99%	2.0	2.1	2.6	1.9	3.7	1.3	0.0
Locals own exactly 100%	30.1	42.1	26.3	24.1	16.4	32.0	34.8
Firms in free zones							
Average ownership by locals	32.9	5.1	15.3	—	15.2	20.9	55.7
Locals own exactly 0%	52.5	90.0	77.3	—	74.1	75.8	20.2
Locals own 1% to 50%	6.7	0.0	4.6	—	13.0	6.1	4.5
Locals own exactly 51%	16.8	10.0	9.1	—	3.7	0.0	37.7
Locals own 52% to 99%	6.3	0.0	0.0	—	1.9	0.0	13.5
Locals own exactly 100%	17.8	0.0	9.1	—	7.4	18.2	28.1

Note: Based on a variable that asks firms to declare the ownership percentage share between locals and foreigners. All percentages are with reference to local ownership such that the remaining percentage until reaching 100% is owned by foreigners. For example, free-zone ownership by locals of light manufacturing is such that 90% own 'zero percentage' of the business, i.e. 90% of light manufacturing firms in the free zone are owned by foreigners. Ownership in this context reflects ownership of the business entity and its movable assets—not land ownership. When the business is owned by locals, this might imply the ownership of land.
Source: Own elaboration based on data from 2010 Enterprise Level Survey

policies or characteristics of the firm might cause respondents to identify land as a major obstacle. Therefore, accounting for the institutional set-up in the land market in both Main Dubai and the free zone and controlling for heterogeneity within the data allows formulating and testing the following three hypotheses regarding potential causes behind the problems of land access in the two regions of the Dubai economy:

> Hypothesis 1: Controlling for firm characteristics, sectors, and other plausible attributes, firms located in Main Dubai are more likely to identify 'access to land' as a major constraint than their counterparts in the free zone.

Hypothesis 1 essentially assigns the underlining cause to the incomplete land markets in Main Dubai, due to the institutional problems discussed above.

Empirically this is tested in a probability model of the incidence of access to land being declared as a major constraint by firms, where the Main Dubai dummy is expected to be positive and significant. If instead, the dummy was found to be negative and significant, the implication would be that the lack of access to land ownership in the free zone rather than the land market uncertainty in Main Dubai was the major constraint. Furthermore, if the dummy was not found to be statistically significant, it could be interpreted that the two types of institutions/regulatory systems in the two economic regions have equivalent influence; that is identical firms in the two economic regions are equally likely to declare problems of access to land as a major constraint.

However, as discussed earlier there is anecdotal evidence that Emirati businessmen have, by and large, been able to 'informally' resolve the constraints to lands access in Main Dubai due to their access to social networks that also include key decision-makers. This suggests that businesses that are only 'nominally' sponsored by Emirati but actually fully owned and operated by foreigners are likely to bear the brunt of the constraints. We identify such businesses as those where the recorded Emirati share is exactly 51 per cent, which is the minimum requirement by law. Instead, in firms where the Emirati share is higher, it is likely that it is a genuine partnership, where the local partner has a stake in the business and is, therefore, expected to exploit the 'informal' networks for resolving any potential constraints to land access his firm might face. Hence, taking this consideration into account we state two further and more nuanced hypotheses:

> Hypothesis 2: Compared to firms located in the free zone firms with identical characteristics, those in Main Dubai with Emirati sponsorship share at exactly 51 per cent are more likely to identify 'lack of access to land' as a major constraint.
>
> Hypothesis 3: Considering firms with identical characteristics in Main Dubai only, firms with Emirati sponsorship share at exactly 51 per cent are more likely to identify 'lack of access to land' as a major constraint than firms with Emirati sponsorship higher than 51 per cent.

Appendix II contains the full econometric results of the empirical models in Table 13A.1. In what follows we summarize the main results:

a) Firms in the sales sectors are more likely to identify that 'lack of access to land' is a problem relative to firms in other sectors.
b) Firms that are fully owned by Emirati nationals (100 per cent local ownership) are less likely to claim that 'lack of access to land' is a problem for their operations.
c) Firms in free zones are more likely to declare that lack of access to land is a major constraint than their counterparts in Main Dubai, thus rejecting Hypothesis 1.

d) Foreign-owned firms in Main Dubai are more likely to declare lack of access to land as a serious constraint than any other category of firms in Main Dubai or the free zone.
e) Firms in Main Dubai with genuine Emirati ownership (above 51 per cent) are less likely to declare 'lack of access to land' as a major problem than those where ownership is exactly 51 per cent, even when controlling for firm characteristics, thus supporting Hypothesis 3.
f) Firms for which 'lack of access to land' is not a major obstacle are those that have experienced higher per-worker revenue, those that have engaged in product innovation, and those with the largest size in terms of number of employees.

Finally, we want to understand not just what determines the fact that 'lack of access to land' is a major obstacle to the firm's operations, but the effect that such restriction would have on firm's ability to operate (Table 13A.2 in Appendix I). To do this, we take 'physical capital investment' as a measure of expansion by firms and estimate the impact of 'lack of access to land' as an obstacle to physical capital investment. Likewise, we estimate the effect of 'lack of access to land' as a major obstacle to human capital investment. The variable 'capital investment' is a dummy variable that classifies firms according to whether they have or have not purchased capital assets during the last calendar year.[6] 'Human capital investment' is a dummy variable that indicates if the firm has engaged in training practices for their employees or not (controlling for the number of skilled and unskilled workers operating in the firm).

The results in Appendix II indicate that both outcomes (investment in physical capital and investment in human capital) are adversely affected by the 'lack of access to land'. Those firms that answer that 'lack of access to land' is the main obstacle to their operations are also those with no investment in physical capital or investment on human capital. The result is robust when controlling for variables that capture potential confounding effects on the outcome of interest such as the age of the firm, the number of employees by type of skill, other declared obstacles, sector, and economic zone.

Results suggest that the probability of investing in physical assets would increase by 22 per cent if lack of land access was not an obstacle

[6] Clearly, this is less than perfect as a measure of physical capital investment, not only because of the discrete nature of the outcome but also because the firm could have made capital investments in years previous to the last calendar year. However, we control for variables such as the age of the firm and the size of the firm to overcome the problems associated with the outcome measured.

to their operations. Likewise, the probability of training would increase by 35 per cent if lack of land access were not an obstacle in the operation of firms.

13.5 CONCLUSIONS

In this chapter we have examined the evidence from the 2010 Dubai Enterprise Level Survey to better understand the problems associated with 'lack of access to land' in the operation of firms in Dubai. According to the survey, about 52 per cent of firms claim that access to land is a major obstacle to their operations—when ranked against another thirteen items that would imply obstacles to their operations. Lack of access to land is often a problem for industrial and commercial operations in economies where land has become scarce due to advanced development and/or where population density leads to land scarcity even if the economy is not yet at the steady-state level of development. Dubai—and the UAE in general—does not suffer from over-population while the huge surge in real estate development during the last ten years should lead to a significant supply of land for industrial and commercial use.

The question asked by this chapter was, therefore: what drives the results observed in the 2010 Dubai Enterprise Level Survey?

Our main results are threefold. First, compared to their counterparts in the free zone, Main Dubai firms are less, not more, likely to find 'lack of access to land' as a major constraint. Second, however, firms in Main Dubai that are de facto owned by foreigners (i.e. with Emirati sponsorship share at exactly 51 per cent) are more likely to identify 'lack of access to land' as a major problem, compared to their counterparts in the free zones or to other Main Dubai firms that are more than 51 per cent owned by Emirati entrepreneurs.

This evidence suggests that, overall, problems of land access appear to be more severe for firms located in the free zones; however, Main Dubai firms effectively owned by foreigners tend to face the most extreme constraints, compared to all other firms in both economic regions.

Finally, we estimated causal models to understand if a claim of 'lack of access to land' as an obstacle to operations has adverse effects on either physical or human capital investment. The results are clear cut: firms claiming that 'lack of access to land' affects their operation invest significantly less in physical capital. Furthermore, they provide no or only limited training investment for their employees. There seems to be an association between expansion problems due to land access and the ability (or willingness) of firms to invest and expand. This has clear negative implications for the industrial development of Dubai's industrial sector.

APPENDIX I: RULES AND REGULATIONS FOR 'ACCESS TO LAND' IN FREE ZONES

Land access to foreigners in both the free zones (FZ) and Main Dubai implies 'renting land' for commercial or industrial reasons.[7] In the case of FZ, the rules and regulations apply to all firms equally irrespective of who owns the largest percentage of the firm. Thus, neither foreigners nor locals are allowed to purchase land in FZ. This means that settling down in any of the FZ, the owner or owners will be subject to identical rules and regulations. These can be summarized as follows:

a. A licence is valid for one year and can be renewed if during that last calendar year the firm has complied in accordance with the rules and regulations. The renewal conditions—rental cost, benefits, penalties, and so on—are settled at the time of drawing the lease. There is no time limit to the leasing of a plot of land or premise but the renewal of the permits to operate in the FZ have to be annual. The costs of renewing permits are established by each FZ authority and apply to firms equally in accordance to the size of the rented plot.[8] In this way, the firm can plan in advance the cost of running the operations of the firm within the FZ with zero uncertainty.
b. The FZ authority approves the nature of the firm (goods produced, services supplied, etc.) and controls that illegal goods or substances are not produced and supplied from the FZ.
c. The annual movement of their physical cargo through Dubai ports has to reach at least 70 per cent of the expected movement within approximately 30 to 50 months from the commencement of the lease.
d. Sub-letting the premises to alternative uses is possible with approval from the FZ authority but it implies drawing a sub-lease contract with corresponding annual fees.
e. The firm has to submit to all building controls and accept the required amendments to allow the continuation of their operations
f. Companies cannot display or sell their goods directly into the local market (except in the case of a trade exhibition). To that extent, firms operating in the FZ are treated as 'exporters' into the local market. Each FZ customs centre publishes applicable tariffs although most overland exports are subject to the standard 5 per cent of the FOB (bill determining value of the cargo). The FZ customs centre also charges fees for the service provided. All exported cargo declared and with correct paper work must leave the FZ within 30 days of the date of export and go directly to the exit point without stopping at any intermediary point.

[7] Most of the material in Appendix I draws from the Rules & Regulations document that governs the Jebel Ali Free Zone (JAFZA) in Dubai. However, these rules and regulations apply almost identically to all free zones in Dubai since they are established by Dubai's Economic Zones Authority (EZA) that governs free zones.

[8] For example, in the case of JAFZA, the permits to be renewed and paid for annually are: the licence, sub-leasing license if any, health and safety checks, employment renewal of visas if due, traffic permits within the zone, vehicle registration within the zone, and company registration/de-registration within the zone.

g. All employees need to be registered with the FZ and comply with the FZ labour rules and regulations which are different to those that apply in Main Dubai (mostly driven by the Ministry of Labour at federal level). The FZ acts as a nominal sponsor to make sure that all employees obtain the corresponding 'visa' and related certificates. Beyond that, the FZ authority acts as the agency that monitors the vacancy match of individuals, but does not have any contractual regulations over workers. The firm, however, has to adhere to a set of safety, health, wages, and hours-worked patterns that is established by the FZ authority. Penalties for violating rules and regulations related to employees are established by the FZ. Violation of the rules and violation of penalties implies the firm is subject to having the firm's licence cancelled (see Chapter 6, this volume, for more details on the rules and regulations applied to FZ with regards to employees and employees' conditions).
h. Imported goods are exempt from import duty if these are manufactured in the GCC. This encourages the demand for local inputs among FZ firms. All other goods imported are subject to import tariffs in the same way as when entering Main Dubai.
    i. Any cargo in and out of the FZ is subject to inspection by the custom border and subject to established penalties if the cargo violates the rules and regulations of the free zone. Likewise—with regards to land—the plot provided to the firm is subject to ad hoc inspections that may lead to penalties and termination of contract if the firm violates health and safety standards associated with the use of land, or if the use of the allocated land is not as determined by the contractual conditions.
    ii When a client terminates a leasing period, termination or renewal is possible as long as the client undergoes all required inspection and settles any outstanding fees associated with the FZ. The plot will be checked for soil contamination and defects—for example, the client cannot leave the plot with built-up plants or offices that are not to be re-used for subsequent clients. All terms and conditions associated with the vacation of a plot, office, plant, or factory in the FZ are established at the commencement of the contract (leasing period) and are known even before the operation of the firm starts.

Final note: All permits, fees, violation fees, and cost associated with the use of the FZ—plots, buildings, transport, and transport infrastructure—are specified by each FZ in their 'free zone rules and regulations'. The last note on rules and regulations was issued in 2005 and supersedes the laws established in 2001 for 'Dubai's Ports and Free Zones'. The latest set of rules has been established and approved by Sultan Ahmed Bin Sulayem, the Executive Chairman of the Ports and Free Zones.

APPENDIX II: ECONOMETRIC RESULTS

This Appendix presents the econometric methodology and describes the main empirical results of this study. When modelling the determinants of the access to land, the dependent variable is a binary outcome that equals 1 if the firm answers that 'access to land' is a major obstacle, and zero otherwise.

Models 1, 2, and 3 in Table 13A.1 show the estimates using the full sample, but allowing for a dummy variable to capture the effect of being located in Main Dubai—relative to the free zones—in a causal framework: the difference between the three models is that we allow for a gradual increase of control variables with Model 3 representing the most complete specification. The last two columns show the estimates of a specification similar to that in Model 3 but adjusted so that it allows us to separate the sample between firms in Main Dubai and firms in the free zone areas.

Estimation of Model 1 suggests that firms in the 'sales' sectors are more likely to answer that 'access to land' is a problem relative to firms in other sectors. At the same time, firms that are fully owned by locals (100 per cent local ownership) are less likely to be associated with firms that claim that 'access to land' is a problem for their operations. Model 2 is similar to Model 1 but allows interactions between the Economic Zone dummy (that equals 1 if the firm is in Main Dubai) and the degree of ownership status. This more general model generates important findings. First, the coefficient of Main Dubai dummy was negative and moderately significant (at 10 per cent significance level). Hence we reject Hypothesis 1 and conclude that an overall Main Dubai–free zone comparison suggests that free zone firms are more, not less, likely to declare access to land as a major constraint than their counterparts in Main Dubai. This finding survives the further more encompassing Model 3, which controls for firm-level heterogeneity. The implication of this finding is that the problems of access to commercial land in Dubai appear to be better explained by the prohibition of commercial land ownership in the free zone than by the land market uncertainty in Main Dubai.

However, focusing on foreign-owned firms in Main Dubai (i.e. those with exactly 51 per cent 'nominal' Emirati sponsorship share), we find that this category of firms is more likely to declare access to land as a serious constraint than any other category of firms in Main Dubai or the free zone (Models 2 and 3). First, compared to firms located in the free zone, the foreign owned Main Dubai firms have a net marginal elasticity of 0.28 (=1.35 – 1.07). This suggests that the number of times a median firm in the latter group characterizes the problems of access to land as a major constraint will be 28 per cent more than the number of times for an identical firm in the free zone. Thus our evidence accepts Hypothesis 2, even when we control for firm heterogeneity (Model 3).

Second, compared to other Main Dubai firms, for which there is a genuine Emirati business partnership (i.e. sponsorship share more than 51 per cent) or total Emirati ownership, we find that the frequency that a median firm in the Main Dubai foreign-owned group identifies problems of access to land as a major constraint will be 70 per cent (= (1.35 – 0.65)100 per cent) higher than for an identical Main Dubai firm with a different ownership structure. Again our evidence accepts Hypothesis 3, while controlling for firm heterogeneity (Model 3).

Moreover, estimates from Model 3 suggest that firms' heterogeneity variables also matter as determinants. We find that firms that do not pick 'access to land' as a major obstacle are those that have experienced higher per-worker revenue, those that have engaged in product innovation, and those with the largest size in terms of number of employees. Thus, it seems that indicators of success and innovation are associated with those firms that find 'access to land' not to be an issue in their operations. The last two columns in Table 13A.2 separate the samples between economic zones. The results for Main Dubai seem to be rather weak, probably as a result of lower variability in the

Table 13A.1. Determinants of 'lack of access to land' as a hurdle to the operations of the firm (dependent variable: dummy = 1 if firm declared that 'access to land' is a problem)

	Model 1	Model 2	Model 3	Model 3	Model 3
				Main Dubai	Free zones
Sample size	709	709	709	501	208
Average dependent variable	51.30%	51.30%	51.30%	48.80%	57.00%
Covariates					
Constant	−0.004 (0.18)	−0.008 (0.18)	***1.99***** (0.61)	1.25 (0.92)	**1.69*** (1.10)
Dummy MAIN DUBAI=1	0.014 (0.18)	**−1.01*** (0.60)	**−1.07*** (0.63)	—	—
Light manufacturing	0.064 (0.18)	0.08 (0.177)	−0.08 (0.19)	−0.14 (0.196)	—
Heavy manufacturing	0.047 (0.18)	0.06 (0.18)	−0.02 (0.19)	0.007 (0.20)	**−0.3136**
Sales	***0.37***** (0.18)	***0.38***** (0.18)	0.21 (0.20)	0.28 (0.23)	−0.31 (050)
Non-financial services	0.15 (0.18)	0.14 (0.18)	−0.033 (0.19)	−0.25 (0.20)	0.05 (0.53)
Financial services	−0.04 (0.17)	−0.04 (0.17)	−0.16 (0.18)	−0.043 (0.19)	−0.90 (0.53)
Dummy EXACTLY 51% local ownership	−0.30 (0.21)	***−0.56***** (0.3)	***−0.65***** (0.3)	0.533 (0.52)	−0.41 (0.32)
Dummy 52%–99% local ownership	−0.28 (0.31)	0.10 (0.38)	0.17 (0.39)	—	0.45 (0.42)
Dummy: 100% local ownership	***−0.38***** (0.2)	−0.28 (0.25)	−0.23 (0.26)	−0.0003 (0.5)	−0.03 (0.29)
Dummy EXACTLY 51% x DM	—	***1.31***** (0.63)	***1.35***** (0.66)	—	—
Dummy EXACTLY 100% local own. x DM	—	0.90 (0.63)	0.72 (0.67)	—	—
Age of establishment (years since funded)	—	—	−0.01 (0.01)	−0.0003 (0.0)	−0.01 (0.01)
Ln (total revenue per worker)	—	—	***−0.08***** (0.1)	−0.09 (0.1)	−0.04 (0.07)
Dummy = 1, if product innovated in LCY	—	—	***−0.53***** (0.2)	***−0.44***** (0.2)	***−0.95***** (0.4)
Dummy = 1, 'COMPETITION' is problem	—	—	−0.01 (0.14)	0.044 (0.17)	−0.08 (0.27)
Dummy =1, 'CUSTOM DUTIES' is a problem	—	—	−0.07 (0.23)	−0.29 (0.32)	0.21 (0.37)
Dummy = 1, 'FINANCE' is a problem	—	—	0.005 (0.13)	−0.05 (0.152)	0.26 (0.26)
Dummy =1, has line of credit	—	—	−0.11 (0.15)	0.054 (0.18)	***−0.60***** (0.3)
Dummy =1, firm has no branches (sole firm)	—	—	−0.18 (0.14)	**−0.0627**	0.07 (0.21)
Log (no. of employees)	—	—	***−0.17***** (0.1)	***−0.16***** (0.1)	***−0.15***** (0.1)
Manager's years of experience in sector	—	—	−0.0001 (0.0)	0.001 (0.01)	−0.002 (0.01)
Diagnostics					
F-test (P-value)	19.6 (9)	24.5 (11)	61.8 (20)	29.8 (17)	**49.2*** (17)
Adjusted R-Square	0.02	0.03	0.1	0.05	***0.2***

Note: All estimates reflect population proportions based on a representative sample. The reference groups are 'free-zone' status, construction sector, and foreign ownership (below 50% local ownership). Total revenue per worker proxies for firm's performance; the dummy for 'product innovation' is one if the firm has engaged in new product lines in order to increase market share or gain access to new markets; the dummy 'competition' equals one if the firm feels that national or international competition is an obstacle for operations Significance at a 5% level is marked with bold and **; significance at 10% level is marked with bold and one *.

Source: Own elaboration based on data from 2010 Dubai Enterprise Level Survey, Dubai Economic Council

Table 13A.2. Estimating the causal effect of 'lack of access to land' as an operational hurdle on three indicators of 'firm's performance': physical capital investment, human capital investment, and expansion in size

	Dependent variable:	Dependent variable:
	Dummy = 1 if firm has engaged in *physical capital investment* over the last calendar year	Dummy =1 if firm has engaged in *training for their employees* over the last calendar year
Sample characteristics		
Sample size	709	709
Average dependent variable	28.80%	16.90%
Model specification	Probit model	Probit model
Covariates		
Constant	−***0.68***** (0.26)	−0.31 (0.29)
Dummy 'ACCESS TO LAND' is an obstacle	−***0.22***** (0.11)	−***0.35***** (0.13)
Dummy MAIN DUBAI firm	***0.99***** (0.46)	0.30 (0.45)
Light manufacturing	−0.46 (0.20)	−0.17 (0.25)
Heavy manufacturing	−0.28 (0.20)	0.18 (0.23)
Sales	−0.30 (0.21)	−0.08 (0.25)
Non-financial services	−***0.34**** (0.20)	0.23 (0.23)
Financial services	0.20 (0.18)	−0.23 (0.23)
Dummy EXACTLY 51% local ownership	0.033 (0.27)	0.26 (0.28)
Dummy EXACTLY 100% local ownership	−***0.47**** (0.29)	0.07 (0.26)
Dummy EXACTLY 51% ownership x DM	−***0.88**** (0,520)	−***1.23***** (0.51)
Dummy EXACTLY 100% local own. x DM	−0.60 (0.54)	−***1.07***** (0.52)
Age of establishment (in years since founded)	−0.002 (0.01)	0.01 (0.01)

Dummy COMPETITION is problem	−0.13 (0.15)	−0.05 (0.17)
Dummy CUSTOM DUTIES is a problem	0.36 (0.23)	−0.25 (0.28)
Dummy FINANCE is a problem	0.20 (0.13)	0.14 (0.15)
Dummy has line of credit	***0.70***** (0.14)	***0.38***** (0.16)
Dummy firm has no branches	−0.05 (0.14)	***−0.49***** (0.15)
Manager's years of experience in sector	0.01 (0.01)	0.01 (0.01)
Number of unskilled employees	−0.001 (0.001)	−0.00004 (0.0003)
Number of skilled employees	***0.001**** (0.0004)	0.0001 (0.00009)
Diagnostics		
F-test (P-value)	***102.01 (20)***	***84.6 (20)***
Adjusted R-Square	***0.12***	***0.13***

Note: Based on a variable that asks firms to declare the ownership percentage share between locals and foreigners. All percentages are with reference to local ownership such that the remaining percentage until reaching 100% is owned by foreigners. For example, free-zone ownership by locals of light manufacturing is such that 90% own 'zero percentage' of the business, i.e. 90% of light manufacturing firms in the free zone are owned by foreigners. Ownership in this context reflects ownership of the business entity and its movable assets—not land ownership. When the business is owned by locals, this might imply the ownership of land.
Source: Own elaboration based on data from 2010 Enterprise Level Survey

right-hand side variables with respect to the outcome: from such estimates we conclude that in Main Dubai not much can be said about what might determine firms to claim that 'access to land' is an obstacle; if at all, it seems that engaging in innovation, remaining a sole business (without branches), and increasing the number of employees are all associated with the claim that 'access to land' is not a major obstacle. On the other hand, estimates for the free zone are more significant and revealing: relative to other sectors, heavy manufacturing firms in the free zones are less likely to claim that 'access to land' is a problem in their operations. Likewise, 'access to land' is statistically less likely to be the case for free zone firms that engage in product innovation, free zone firms that have a line of credit, and free zone firms that are larger in size (employees).

Finally, we want to understand not just what determines the fact that 'access to land' is a major obstacle to the firm's operations, but the underlying causal effect that this answer would have on a firm's ability to operate (Table 13A.2). To do this, we take 'physical capital investment' as a measure of expansion by firms and estimate the impact of 'access to land' as an obstacle to physical capital investment. Likewise, we estimate the effect of 'access to land' as a major obstacle on human capital investment. The outcome 'capital investment' is a dummy variable that classifies firms according to whether they have or have not purchased capital assets during the last calendar year.[9] 'Human capital investment' is a dummy variable that equals 1 if the firm has engaged in training practices for their employees and 0 otherwise (controlling for the number of skilled and unskilled workers operating in the firm).

Table 13A.2 provides the causal estimates for a given specification common to the two outcomes of interest. Both outcomes (investment in physical capital, investment in human capital) are adversely affected by 'access to land', that is, those firms that answer with 'access to land' as being the main obstacle to their operations are statistically associated with no investment in physical capital or investment on human capital—controlling for variables that capture potentially confounding effects on the outcome of interest, for example, age of the firm, size of the firm by number of employees by type of skill, other declared obstacles, sector and economic zone, among others. In terms of elasticity values, Table 13A.2 suggests that the probability of investing in physical assets would increase by 22 per cent if land access was not an obstacle to their operations; likewise, the probability of training would increase by 35 per cent if land access was not an obstacle in the operation of those firms claiming that land is—among another possible thirteen items—the major obstacle in the operations of the firm.

REFERENCES

Elbadawi, I., and Vazquez-Alvarez, R., 2011. *Migration, Labour Markets and a Long-term Development Strategy for the UAE*, Dubai: Dubai Economic Council.

Vazquez-Alvarez, R., 2010. 'Labour Markets in Dubai: An Empirical Evaluation Based on the 2010 Enterprise Level Survey'. Dubai Economic Council Working Papers.

[9] Clearly, this is less than perfect as a measure of physical capital investment, not only because of the discrete nature of the outcome but also because the firm could have made capital investments in years previous to the last calendar year. However, we control for variables such as the age of the firm and the size of the firm to overcome the problems associated with the outcome measured.

14

Productivity, Efficiency, and Sustainability of Economic Growth

Ibrahim Elbadawi

14.1 INTRODUCTION

Dubai's economy multiplied by eleven times in real terms in the period 1975–2008. And in the last fifteen years of that period the emirate's gross domestic product grew at a spectacular pace of almost 9 per cent per year. This extraordinary and extended growth spell has earned Dubai membership in the small club of high-performing economies that managed to achieve sustainable growth transitions, most notably the leading city-state economies of Singapore and Hong-Kong (Elbadawi and Soto, 2012). However, while the expansion of aggregate economic activity in Dubai has been remarkable, labour productivity, as measured by output per working-age person, has not been equally fast-growing. In fact both average labour and total factor productivity (TFP) remained stagnant for a long period of time (1987–2004) following the substantial decline in the early 1980s. This contrasts sharply with the other city-states, where average labour productivity in these countries has grown steadily over time (see Figure 2.7).

Nonetheless, Dubai's non-oil-driven growth has been the prime force behind the rapid and deepening process of economic diversification in the largely oil-dependent economy of the UAE, which includes Dubai as the second largest economy after the oil-rich emirate of Abu Dhabi.[1] In the early 1970s Dubai's economy was built around the oil industry, albeit at a much lower scale than that of Abu Dhabi. In anticipation of the eventual depletion of the oil resource base, Dubai started to invest in diversifying its

[1] As of 2011, the UAE was the 36th largest economy in the world with a nominal per capita GDP of approximately $50,000 at market exchange rates (IMF 2011) and had a similar position in terms of the human development index (35th most developed in the world according to UNDP (2009).

economy as early as the turn of the 1980s decade. Since then Dubai has emerged as a global city and a business hub with a view to replicating the advanced city-state models of South East Asia. In 2010 Dubai obtained its main revenue from tourism (25 per cent), real estate and construction (23 per cent), financial services (11 per cent) and trade and re-exports (16 per cent and 15 per cent, respectively). In fact, revenues from oil and gas had declined to about 6 per cent of GDP by 2010 (Dubai Economic Council, 2011).

One of the key instruments for the diversification and development of Dubai has been the creation of free (economic) zones, that is, areas where companies can develop their business without the application of the sponsorship system that requires a minimum ownership share of 51 per cent by Emirati nationals and where they can operate without being subject to the labour laws established in (otherwise) Main Dubai (hereafter MD) economic area. The first free zone (hereafter, FZ) to be established in Dubai was Jebel Ali FZ (JAFZA) in 1985 with the purpose of servicing foreign companies in terms of unrestricted imports of labour and exports of goods and services. The building of JAFZA was strategic since it is located around the Jebel Ali port thus providing import–export firms with a key geographical advantage. JAFZA is currently home for more than 6,500 companies, over 150 of which are subsidiaries or branches of Fortune Top 500 companies. And even though JAFZA was originally established as a distribution/logistics hub, it has steadily grown into a major service and manufacturing base.

Building on JAFZA's success, the government of Dubai established a number of other FZ in and around Dubai that are also strategically located to take advantage of the port and the further development of Dubai as the financial and service centre of the Middle East (e.g. Dubai International Financial Center, technological parks, media parks, and health-related enterprises zones).[2]

As a consequence of the rapid expansion of FZ, the economy of Dubai has become home to three distinct economic areas: MD—that is, Dubai city with full adherence to the mercantile and labour laws of the local and federal government; Dubai International Financial Center (DIFC)—an inshore financial centre or an FZ for financial activities; and Dubai's free economic zones. Whereas the financial sector in Dubai (DIFC plus the financial sector in MD) is a sector of its own, the other sectors that operate in MD and the FZ are comparable in terms of industrial output and services.

Like other countries with sizeable FZ economies, the FZ in Dubai have been the subject of analysis from the perspective of their contribution to the overall economy. At the macroeconomic level the Dubai FZ were found to have contributed immensely to Dubai's economy through a host of channels,

[2] See Chapter 5 for more detailed discussion of the evolution of the FZ in Dubai.

including by attracting foreign direct investment (FDI); generating foreign exchange to the emirate as well as by creating backward and forward linkages. For example, it is estimated that in 2010 JAFZA and its zone companies alone have contributed, respectively, about 21 per cent and 8 per cent to the economies of Dubai and UAE (JAFZA, 2011). Moreover, in a more recent study based on Dubai enterprise-level data, Al Iriani et al., (2014) argue that, with appropriate industrial policy and other strategic interventions, there exists even greater potential for enhancing backward and forward linkages from the FZ to the rest of the economy.

This chapter contributes to this nascent debate at the Dubai/UAE level by asking a key question regarding the performance of FZ in terms of labour productivity and especially TFP. This question is of profound importance for the sustainability of growth in Dubai, given the relatively lacklustre performance of its economy with regard to these two pivotal indicators of economic growth. In view of this important research and policy question for the economy of Dubai, we assess the performance of the FZ relative to MD with regard to these two indicators: productivity and TFP. To undertake this analysis we use the data from the Dubai Economic Council's 2010 Dubai Enterprise Level Survey. This allows us to construct an indicator of labour productivity, as measured by value added per worker (VAW), and break it down into five main components: location, sector-specific externalities, physical capital and labour intensities, human capital, and TFP.

Section 14.2 briefly describes the 2010 Dubai Enterprise Level Survey and the construction of the VAW, the pivotal variable for the empirical evidence in this chapter. Section 14.3 compares the VAW and other main features of the production processes at the enterprise level across the three zones of the Dubai economy. Section 14.4 breaks down the measures of VAW into five components, where the weights for these components were directly estimated via regressions, except for TFP, which was derived as a residual. This allows analysis of the relative contributions of the above channels to the spread between the FZ and MD in terms of value added per worker. Section 14.5 concludes and articulates some policy issues associated with the main findings.

14.2 DATA AND THE 2010 DUBAI ENTERPRISE LEVEL SURVEY

Table 14.1 shows the distribution of the 709 firms in the 2010 Dubai Enterprise Level Survey (ELS) with respect to economic zone, industrial sector, and share of export revenues relative to total sales. It can be seen that there are around 500 firms operating in MD and 209 in FZ. In MD there are an ample

Table 14.1. Sample size by economic zone, industrial sector, and share of exports in sales

Industrial sector	Main Dubai	Free zone	Financial sector[2]
Light manufacturing	95 (9.0)[1]	10 (8.2)	—
Heavy manufacturing	76 (2.0)	22 (4.8)	—
Construction	108 (15.3)	—	—
Trading (retail, wholesale)	55 (45.6)	54 (47.9)	—
Non-financial services	75 (17.1)	33 (31.7)	—
Financial services	92 (11.0)	8 (7.5)	81 (100)
Total[3]	501 (88.7)	127 (10.3)	81 (0.08)
Share of exports in total sales (%)			
Less than 1%	0.760	0.430	0.740
From 1 to 20%	0.036	0.042	0.050
From 21% to 40%	0.081	0.079	0.010
From 41% to 60%	0.036	0.092	0.010
From 61% to 80%	0.043	0.140	—
From 81% to 100%	0.042	0.220	0.010
Total number of exporters with export shares larger than 1%	71	77	7

Notes: (1) Numeric values reflect sample counts; bracketed numbers represent population proportions. All proportions and percentages are estimated using survey weights. (2) These are the financial institutions in the FZ (DIFC and other FZ entities) and MD combined. (3) The percentages reflect the percentage in the full sample of 709 weighted by their representation in the population.

number of observations in each industrial sector, with a predominance of construction and manufacturing firms. However, in FZ manufacturing, trading, and non-financial services have an adequate sample size, while observations for financial services are rather few. Due to the nature of their business, construction firms are not represented in FZ so that the sampling strategy was to ignore the construction sector in the case of FZ.

We include the share of exports relative to total sales in the analysis because we need to control for the possibility of a bias arising from the self-selection of exporting firms in the FZ as a result of exports-related logistics (e.g. locating in JAFZA because of the proximity to the Jebel Ali port). The table shows that the combined financial sector (from both MD and the DIFC) has a limited participation in exports and no representation of other sectors. Nevertheless, the financial sector is represented in both MD and the FZ and, at the same time, we see that firms in the financial sector are equally represented among exporters irrespective of location. It is therefore sufficient reason to include them in our analysis because this will allow us to look at VAW and TFP in the financial sector in comparison to non-financial sectors operating in the local economy of Dubai.

Following standard practice in this literature, we estimate average labour productivity as annual value added per worker per year, where value added is

Table 14.2. Distribution of the sample, before and after dropping outliers

	Full sample (n=709)	Restricted sample (n=603)
Main Dubai		
Manufacturing light	95	94
Construction	108	101
Trading	55	45
Non-financial services	75	70
Financial services	92	87
FZ and the DIFC		
Manufacturing light	10	8
Manufacturing heavy	22	21
Trading	54	28
Non-financial services	33	28
Financial services	89	52

Note: The financial sector in the FZ includes both financial sector enterprises in FZ areas and firms in Dubai International Financial Center (DIFC).
Source: Own elaboration based on data from 2010 Dubai Enterprise Level Survey

computed as total gross annual revenue minus the cost of intermediate goods and other relevant production factors. The 2010 ELS of Dubai is informative on annual revenue for each firm. The survey also asked respondents to declare the total cost of intermediate goods as well as utility costs—that is, electricity, telecommunications, fuel, community fees, water, and other service fees. The values correspond to fiscal year 2009.

The initial data set contains 709 firms as described above. However, not all firms provided all the variables required to estimate value added per worker. To avoid throwing away information, when needed we have imputed missing values for the cost of utilities and other intermediate inputs. All firms were prompted to look at their administration files to provide accurate revenue values; the result is that all except two firms declared total gross revenue sales. For these two firms we imputed the average value according to the sector and economic zone they belong to. In the case of the missing utility and intermediate input costs we use an ad hoc procedure based on the classic Mahalanobis distance to impute the missing value.[3]

We construct the value added variables once all missing intermediate inputs are imputed. Next we remove outliers using Hadi's method (Hadi, 1992). This method is based on comparing the distance between the values of a variable for a given firm to the median of the variable weighted by the dispersion of such variable in the distribution; for the latter, the method does not impose any particular distributional shape when searching for outliers. In practice, what the method does is define an outlier as those observations with a

[3] See Appendix I for a full description of the Mahalanobis distance measure.

weighted distance that falls outside a 5 per cent confidence interval around the median. The method detected 106 outliers in the ELS survey; we dropped these outliers so that the sample size used in the econometric estimation is reduced to 603 observations.

Table 14.2 compares the distribution of the original sample—by economic zone and sector—to that of the 603 remaining firms in the sample after dropping the outliers. As the table suggests the sample distribution did not change in any significant form.

14.3 LABOUR PRODUCTIVITY ACROSS ECONOMIC ZONES

Table 14.3 provides estimates of average labour productivity using median values in fixed US$ 2010 values. The same table shows other indicators of firm performance including capacity utilization, capital per worker, labour cost per worker, unit labour cost, and the percentage share of exports in the total revenues of the median firm. Capacity utilization comes directly from a question that firms answered in the survey. Most firms reported that they tend to utilize between 75 per cent and 82 per cent of their capacity; with the DIFC being the one with the highest percentage.

The DIFC also stands out as the economic zone with the second highest cost per worker (at US$22,300) and, at the same time, with the highest returns per worker; the median value added per worker in the DIFC is US$193,839 annually. Compared to the DIFC, the median firm in the FZ has slightly higher cost per labour but generates only 58 per cent of the VAW achieved in the DIFC. Moreover, though the median firm in MD faces a much lower labour cost per worker, at only 30 per cent of that borne by the DIFC, it tends to generate an even lower VAW at only 14 per cent of the median for the latter sector.

As the evidence suggests, for all industrial sectors, the FZ obtains much higher returns per worker than firms in MD.[4] The greatest distance in value added per worker occurs in the light manufacturing sector where VAW in MD was US$6,328, compared to US$63,227 in the FZ—almost ten times that of MD. Even for the case of heavy manufacturing, for which value added is the closest between the two zones, the difference is fairly substantial. The VAW in MD equals US$16,562 while that of the FZ at US$48,732 is almost three times more. One factor behind the higher labour productivity in the FZ might be

[4] However, construction is not included in the comparative analysis being only identified for MD.

Table 14.3. Median firm productivity and other correlates by economic zone and industry (in thousands of US$ of 2010)

	Capacity utilization	Value added per worker (A)	Capital per worker	Labour cost per worker (B)	Unit labour cost (B/A)	Share of exports/ total revenue
Overall						
All economic zones	0.78	$29,700	$2,300	$7,700	0.26	0.16
Main Dubai	0.79	$27,100	$2,200	$6,800	0.26	0.13
Free zones	0.74	$108,000	$3,600	$22,700	0.25	0.41
DIFC	0.82	$193,900	$3,100	$22,300	0.15	0.02
By industrial sector						
Light manufacturing						
All economic zones	0.74	$7,600	$1,300	$4,500	0.63	0.05
Main Dubai	0.74	$6,300	$1,000	$4,400	0.68	0.04
Free zones	0.72	$63,200	$3,000	$17,300	0.28	0.19
DIFC	—	—	—	—	—	—
Heavy manufacturing						
All economic zones	0.76	$19,800	$3,900	$8,300	0.41	0.17
Main Dubai	0.77	$16,600	$3,100	$7,800	0.51	0.07
Free zones	0.75	$48,700	$13,500	$12,900	0.33	0.51
DIFC	—	—	—	—	—	—
Construction						
All economic zones	0.75	$20,600	$1,700	$6,200	0.32	0.001
Main Dubai	0.75	$20,600	$1,700	$6,200	0.32	0.001
Free zones	—	—	—	—	—	—
DIFC	—	—	—	—	—	—
Trading (retail, wholesale)						
All economic zones	0.80	$67,600	$3,100	$8,100	0.12	0.28
Main Dubai	0.81	$64,000	$3,000	$7,100	0.11	0.24
Free zones	0.79	$179,400	$4,500	$20,500	0.14	0.58
DIFC	—	—	—	—	—	—
Non-financial services						
All economic zones	0.78	$18,200	$1,600	$9,300	0.41	0.05
Main Dubai	0.80	$15,600	$1,600	$6,800	0.39	0.001
Free zones	0.66	$47,700	$1,100	$29,500	0.52	0.25
Financial sector	—	—	—	—	—	—
Financial services						
All economic zones	0.78	$13,100	$3,600	$9,500	0.59	0.11
Main Dubai	0.78	$11,400	$3,500	$8,800	0.70	0.11
Free zones	0.76	$133,700	$10,700	$16,500	0.12	0.18
DIFC	0.82	$193,900	$3,100	$22,300	0.12	0.02

Note: Numeric values reflect sample estimates using sample weights. All values are in US$ of 2010.
Source: Own elaboration based on data from 2010 Dubai Enterprise Level Survey

related to the role of 'motivation incentives'; as it is clear from the table that the cost of labour—average wage rate—is significantly higher in the FZ relative to MD. Thus, the FZ appears to be potentially able to attract higher-quality labour (ability, motivation, higher effort) for any given skill class, or a larger volume of workers with a greater aggregate stock of skills.

Relative labour competitiveness is often measured by the 'unit labour cost' (ULC), which is given by the ratio of labour cost per worker (wage) to value added per worker. A sector is more competitive if the ULC is lower because it implies lower cost per worker per every dollar of value added generated by the worker. Table 14.3 shows that for Dubai as a whole, ULC is at its lowest for the DIFC, while MD and the FZ have comparable aggregate labour competitiveness. However, the aggregation hides considerable differences between the latter two zones at the sector level. For example, the FZ are consistently more competitive than MD for light and heavy manufacturing and, especially, non-financial services. The ULC in MD was almost two and a half times the labour cost in the FZ for the case of light manufacturing and one and a half for heavy manufacturing.

Compared to MD the performance of the FZ with regard to financial services is even more impressive, where the ULC in the former was almost six times as much as the relative cost for financial services in the latter. Moreover, returning to the three-way comparison (FZ–DIFC–MD), we should point out that while the DIFC fares better compared to the FZ and MD in terms of the overall economic activities as discussed, it is by no means a better performer than the FZ if we confine the comparison to financial services, which is the only economic activity at the DIFC. Though the VAW in the DIFC is higher, it also comes at a higher cost per worker, however. Thus the ULC for both are identical at 0.12.

On the other hand, the trading sector in MD had a slight edge, with a ULC at 0.11 compared to 0.14 for the FZ; and in the non-financial services—for example, education, health, tourism—there was a much stronger advantage for the MD (with a ULC at 0.39 compared to 0.51 for the FZ). This latter finding can perhaps be explained by the fact that the experience of the FZ in such industries is relatively recent and, therefore, still on a developing path (e.g. Dubai Health City).

Finally, Table 14.3 shows that although competitiveness and level of exports are inversely correlated (the larger the share of exports, the lower the corresponding ULC) this correlation is weak (−0.32) and statistically insignificant (p-value of 0.14). Finding a negative correlation is consistent with the strand of the literature that argues that exporting activities entail some dynamic externalities, such as learning by exporting, and that manufacturing exports in particular generate increasing returns to scale (e.g. Matsuyama, 1992; Bigsten et al., 2002; Rodrik, 2007). It is also the case that export firms need a minimum level of competitiveness in order to become successful (i.e. the threshold effect as described, for example, in Johnson, 2012). Despite the non-significant correlation, the fact that it is negative might make us think of the possibility of some confounding effect between being an exporting firm and being a firm in the FZ. We take this into account in our causal estimates by separating samples to be as homogenous as possible with respect to exports (allowing for sample size to be sufficiently large for identification). We turn to this issue next in section 14.4, where we estimate the contributions to VAW and the corresponding TFP.

14.4 UNPACKING LABOUR PRODUCTIVITY

The breakdown of value added per worker is based on estimating the econometric production function (based on the standard Cobb–Douglas) which links total value added produced by the firms with their use of capital and labour, the latter augmented by the inclusion of an indicator of labour force skills. We use the end-of-year number of employees as a proxy for annual labour input. Similarly, we use the end-of-period book value of plant and equipment at constant prices to measure the capital stock, and average years of schooling of the workers to account for skills.

In order to control for the particular conditions existing in different sectors, we use a simple dummy variable—which we denote by S. Likewise, we also control for the fact that the economic regulations and business environment in FZ are markedly different to that of MD by including a dummy variable (FZ), which indicates if the firm is located within or outside an FZ. Thus the value added per worker (y_{isz}) can be expressed as follows:

$$\ln y_{isz} = \alpha + \alpha_s S + \alpha_{FZ} FZ + \beta_1 \ln k_i + \beta_2 \ln h_i + \beta_3 \ln n_i + \epsilon_i \qquad (14.1)$$

where α picks up the effects that are common to all firms; α_s is the coefficient of the sector dummy and α_{FZ} is the coefficient of the FZ dummy. The other three β parameters reflect the contribution of the factors of production (capital k, labour intensity n, and skills, h). The last term ϵ_i is the measure of TFP and corresponds to that part of the value added per worker that cannot be explained by the contribution from observable factors and common effects. If the parameters in equation (14.1) were known, computing TFP growth would be direct as the changes in value added per worker that cannot be accounted for by the expansion in the use of inputs: TFP would thus correspond to the efficiency in the use of such inputs. However, since parameters are unknown, we resort to econometric methods to obtain an estimator of each parameter. The results of the estimation and a thorough discussion of its implications are in the Appendices to this chapter.

The results can be summarized as follows. First, as expected capital stock and human capital have a positive and highly significant impact on labour productivity. This is congruent with the macroeconomic evidence presented in Chapter 2 of this volume which concludes that most of the growth in aggregate production is due to factor accumulation and not to rising levels of TFP. Second, labour intensity was not found to have statistically or economically relevant influence. It is somewhat surprising to find the stylized fact of many other economies, namely that firms employing more workers (higher labour-intensity) tend to have higher levels of productivity per worker. Third, in comparative terms physical capital contributes significantly less than human capital to average productivity (in a one-to-five proportion). Again, this is in agreement with the issues raised in Chapter 10 of this volume which unveils some weaknesses in the education and training of the labour force.

Additional important results emerge from the empirical analysis when considering the location and sector where each firm operates. In the first place, firms located in FZ are significantly more productive than equal size firms in MD. Average labour productivity in the FZ firms exceeds those of MD by as much as 90 per cent. Naturally, there are sectoral differences in productivity within the FZ and in MD so that the productivity differential does not apply to all firms in one sector. However, when we control for sector-specific effects, the productivity differential remains at a high 73 per cent. One implication of this result is that the FZ offer firms a strong network and other externalities that are not available to their counterparts in MD.

As for the sector-specific effects, the evidence indicates that, relative to financial services firms (which we use as the reference sector), labour productivity of light manufacturing firms with identical production structures tends to be lower by about 79 per cent.[5] On the other hand, labour productivity of firms specializing in trading would exceed financial services firms by 80 per cent. Finally, heavy manufacturing and non-financial services sectors do not have significant productivity effects which indicates that firms in these three sectors are likely to have similar levels of labour productivity.

Finally, when considering the combined sector–location effects the results are very interesting and suggest that, as expected, the benefits of locating in an FZ tend to differ quite substantially across sectors. First, we find no significant effects for the case of heavy manufacturing beyond the overall positive FZ location effect relative to MD. Therefore, the labour productivity of a heavy manufacturing firm located in the FZ would be almost three times that of an identical MD firm. Second, locating in an FZ would be most beneficial in the case of light manufacturing: other things equal, labour productivity of light manufacturing firms in the FZ would be more than four times that of their

[5] Due to the fact that we control for the factors of production.

counterparts in MD. Third, the positive effect of locating in an FZ is much lower for firms in the non-financial services sector: for two identical non-financial services firms labour productivity in the FZ firm will exceed that of MD by 65 per cent. Fourth, with regard to trade and somewhat surprisingly, we found that MD provides stronger location benefits than the FZ by around 13 per cent. The effect could be the result of firms in MD benefiting from the larger margins usually present in more closed environments as well as from the effects of the 5 per cent customs tariff that protects producers in MD.

To investigate the combined effects of locating in an economic zone and a specific sector we sub-divide the sample of the 502 firms into ten groups which correspond to two economic zones and five industrial sectors (since we are excluding construction). For each of these groups we compute the difference between the productivity of an average firm in the FZ and the productivity of an average firm in MD and break down the contribution of each fundamental factor (capital, skill, employment, and TFP) to this difference. The breakdown is based on the estimated econometric models presented in Appendix II.

The results of the breakdown are in Table 14.4, presented in per cent for easier analysis. The FZ effect and the differences in TFP levels shape the magnitude and sign of labour productivity differentials in all the sectors. They reinforce each other in favour of the FZ in the three sectors of light manufacturing, heavy manufacturing, and financial services. However, in the case of the trading sector the MD has a slight advantage in terms of location, but more importantly its advantage in TFP was so large to the extent that its excess over the TFP in the FZ reversed the large physical and human capital advantage for FZ firms. As for the non-financial sector the TFP advantage in favour of MD was substantial but not high enough to reverse the larger combined FZ advantage in terms of location and human capital. This latter

Table 14.4. Decomposition of difference in the per capita average annual value added per worker (difference taken between economic zones, for each of the industrial sectors)

Sector	Locating in FZ effect	Differences in physical capital	Differences in human capital	Differences in labour intensity	Differences in TFP
Light manufacturing	34.1%	8.97%	24.1%	0.32%	32.6%
Heavy manufacturing	48.9%	14.9%	9.7%	0.53%	26.0%
Trading (retail, wholesale)	64.0%	−30.39%	−32.1%	0.15%	100.0%
Non-financial services	76.3%	20.2%	55.4%	−0.044%	−51.7%
Financial services	43.2%	2.4%	25.7%	0.31%	33.2%

Note: Values are based on coefficient estimates from equation (14A.2). All estimates represent percentage contribution to total difference, except for the case of trading, where the differences are expressed as percentage of TFP.

Source: Own elaboration based on data from 2010 Dubai Enterprise Level Survey

channel was quite influential in all sectors and was uniformly in favour of the FZ. To a lesser extent the capital-intensity effect was also influential, especially for the cases of non-financial services and heavy manufacturing. On the other hand, as expected the labour-intensity effect was negligible.

14.5 CONCLUSIONS AND POLICY IMPLICATIONS

The main results of this chapter's analysis can be succinctly summarized into the following main conclusions. First, firms located in the FZ outperform their counterparts in MD with regards to productivity (VAW) in four out of five sectors: light manufacturing, heavy manufacturing, financial services, and non-financial services. Second, MD firms outperform their counterparts in FZ with regard to the trading sector. Third, firms in the FZ accumulate higher levels of physical capital, especially in heavy manufacturing and non-financial services, which contribute to their better performance in most sectors. Fourth, human capital accumulation has contributed even more than physical capital to induce a superior performance of firms in FZ when compared to those in MD. Fifth, unlike physical and human capital, labour intensity had no impact on the differences in value-added observed between the two economic regions. Sixth, the FZ–MD differences in labour productivity were largely shaped by the combined effect on location externality and TFP. The positive externality of being located in the FZ provided the largest contribution to the differential value added in favour of the FZ in all sectors, except for the trading sector. And, TFP reinforced the location advantage of the FZ in three out of five sectors (light manufacturing, heavy manufacturing, and financial services). However, MD outperformed the FZ with regard to TFP in the remaining two sectors of trading and non-financial services.

Three policy implications can be drawn from the above findings. First, workers' training is likely to be a factor behind the advantage of the FZ with regard to human capital accumulation (see Chapter 11 of this volume on labour markets). The evidence from the Dubai ELS 2010 survey suggests that provision of training is superior in FZ relative to the training given in MD firms. In fact, only 11 per cent of firms in MD offer training compared to 30 per cent of firms in the FZ. Specifically, the sector that differs less in terms of training provision is the heavy manufacturing sector where 27 per cent of firms in the FZ offer training versus 18 per cent in MD; the sector with the greatest gap is the financial sector where 39 per cent of firms in the FZ offer training compared to 9 per cent of financial sector firms in MD.

Second, location seems to determine largely the productivity differential between firms in the FZ relative to their counterparts in MD. To appreciate the strong positive location externality it would be necessary to understand how the FZ works. The Dubai FZ business model is based on a 'three-angle FZ model'[6] by which the FZ authorities provide centralized and more efficient services to firms that operate in such zones. Assets management (the development of products, such as ready-to-use plots, warehouses, offices, and all the related physical infrastructure), has implemented a one-stop-shop regulatory scheme (including registration, licensing, labour regulations, zoning, security, and building permits) complemented by other supporting services provided at the same location (such as telecommunications, postal, banking, and chamber of commerce services), and special attention devoted to the attraction of FDI (comprising marketing activities to attract and service foreign investments from within the region and internationally). However, besides the significant positive effects as a result of the three-angle FZ model, the business environment in MD is undermined by the effects of the sponsorship system that undermines the potential of firms in MD relative to their counterparts in the FZ. Thus, it is important to point out that application of the three-angle FZ model to MD might still not result in the improvement in productivity of firms—relative to counterfactual firms in FZ—if such a model is applied under the constrains implied by the *Kafala* system (see Soto and Vazquez-Alvarez, 2011).

Third, for both economic areas in Dubai (i.e. FZ and MD), one would expect that TFP will eventually be the main driver of growth and labour productivity. The reason for this is that Dubai has experienced rapid factor accumulation over the last thirty years such that the returns to capital and labour accumulation are likely to hit the point of diminishing returns in the near future. The implication is that economic growth will rely mostly on the attainment of higher TFP especially in the non-financial services in the FZ; as well as in the manufacturing and financial services in MD. The above argument is further backed up by the fact that modern growth literature strongly emphasizes the role of TFP in sustaining growth in the longer run. In a comprehensive review of the main evidence from the growth literature, Easterly and Levin (2001) conclude that 'factor accumulation does not account for the bulk of cross-cross differences in the level or growth rate of GDP per capital; something else—TFP—accounts for a substantial amount of cross-country differences'. Moreover, they argue that 'national policies that enhance the efficiency of capital and labour or alter the endogenous rate of technological change can boost productivity growth and thereby accelerate long-run economic growth'.

The policy recommendations that can be gleaned from the above three analytical discussions are fairly straightforward, though the specifics of such recommendations are beyond the scope of this chapter. First, it would be

[6] See Chapter 4.

necessary to provide the required incentive for firms in MD to invest more on developing the human capital formation of their labour force. Second, although politically it might not be feasible to turn the entire economy of Dubai into an FZ, at least not in the short or medium run, there are obvious design features from FZ areas that make firms in the FZ attain strong positive externality; a thorough study of FZ performance could be used to learn about such design features in order to apply them to firms in MD in a significantly shorter period of time. Finally, accelerated growth in TFP is likely to be the main contributor to growth sustainability in both regions of the economy of Dubai in the future. And since the received wisdom from the growth literature suggests that TFP can be influenced by public policy, public policy in Dubai should consider a variety of instruments for enhancing TFP in the two economic regions. Specifically, public policies associated with basic regulatory and service delivery issues but also the removal of constraints associated with the sponsorship system and its effects on industrial policy should be considered.

APPENDIX I. THE MAHALANOBIS DISTANCE MEASURE

The imputing of missing values is done individually for each non-response variable. Let n be the sample such that n=n(1)+n(0) where n(1) are the number of firms declaring a given variable x and n(0) are those firms with missing value for x. Let Z be a set of variables observed for all firms that reflect information on x and the response behaviour of firms. The Mahalanobis distance is defined as $\sqrt{(z_1 - \bar{z}_1)' s^{-1} (z_1 - \bar{z}_1)}$ to provide a measure of closeness in the set Z between the sub-groups n(1) and n(0); $\bar{z}$ is the mean value of the variable set Z and s is the variance covariance matrix of the set Z. Each firm in the set n(0) is compared to all firms in n(1) and each of the latter receives a ranking of closeness relative to the distance for each firm in n(0). The imputed value for missing x in n(0) is the x value of the n(1) whose Mahalanobis distance is the shortest. We select variables in Z that describes the ownership of the firm, location, industrial sector, economic zone, number of workers operating in the firm, output share of import/exports, and variables that measure use of technology in operations.

APPENDIX II. DECOMPOSING VALUE ADDED

Decomposing value added per worker is based on estimating a standard Cobb–Douglas production function specified in terms of capital and labour, the latter augmented by the inclusion of an indicator of labour force skills. We use the end-of-year number of employees as a proxy for annual labour input. Similarly, we use the end-of-period book value of plant and equipment at constant prices to measure the capital stock, and average years of schooling of the workers to account for skills.

We now introduce some notation to make the discussion easier to follow. Consequently, y_{iSZ} represents the VAW of firm i in sector S and economic zone Z; the stock of capital per worker by k_i; number of workers employed by n_i; and the human capital endowment (education) per worker by h_i. Define now the dummy S, which equals 1 if the firm belongs to sector S and zero elsewhere, and represents each of the five sectors (light and heavy manufacturing, trading, financial and non-financial services).[7] Also define a free-zone dummy FZ, which equals 1 if the firm is located in the FZ and 0 if located in other Dubai. This dummy variable is designed to capture the FZ specific features and conditions that are not available for firms located in MD. Thus the VAW can be expressed in the following linear logarithmic expression:

$$\ln y_{isz} = \alpha + \alpha_s S + \alpha_{FZ} FZ + \beta_1 \ln k_i + \beta_2 \ln h_i + \beta_3 \ln n_i + \epsilon_i \qquad (14A.1)$$

where α picks up the effects common to all firms; αs is the coefficient of the sector dummy and αFZ is the coefficient of the FZ dummy. The βs are the elasticity estimates of the corresponding standard factors of production; and ϵ_i stands for the log of firm's i TFP, that is, that part of VAW that cannot be explained by the contribution from observable factors and common effects. The implication is that TFP stands for the residual identified with an efficient use of factors of production. Note that if parameters were known, computing TFP growth would be direct as the changes in value added per worker that cannot be accounted for by the expansion in the use of inputs: TFP would thus correspond to the efficiency in the use of such inputs. Since parameters are unknown, we resort to econometric methods to obtain an estimator of each parameter.

Table 14A.1 contains the estimates of four variants of equation 14A.1. Model 1 is a benchmark regression that only accounts for the three standard factors of production: physical capital, human capital, and labour. Model 2 allows for a dummy variable that controls for an FZ effect, but abstracts from sector-specific effects. Model 3 allows for both zone and sector effects, whereas Model 4 allows for a general FZ effect as well a sector-specific zone effect, where the latter is given by interaction terms between the sector-specific and economic zone dummies. This generates eight interaction dummies {(MD, LM), (MD, HM), (MD, Trading), (MD, Non.Fin.), (FZ, LM), (FZ, HM), (FZ, Trading), (FZ, Non.Fin.)}, where LM and HM stand for light and heavy manufacturing sectors, respectively and Non.Fin. for the non-financial services sector. Finally financial services firms in both economic regions are taken as the reference categories.

The benchmark regression of Model 1 suggests that capital stock and human capital have had positive and highly significant impacts on labour productivity, while labour intensity was not found to have statistically or economically relevant influence. These broad conclusions survive the subsequent and more encompassing Models 2–4, though the quantitative influence of human capital is reduced. For example, in Model 4 the elasticity ($\hat{\beta}_1$) due to the capital stock is equal to 0.099. This suggests that, for any given firm in the economy, if we raise the capital stock per worker (k) by 1 per cent, the firm's labour productivity (i.e. VAW) will increase by about 0.1 per cent.

The physical capital effect, however, pales when compared with the much higher elasticity due to human capital ($\hat{\beta}_2$ =0.54), which is more than five times the elasticity due to the former. On the other hand, theory suggests that β_3, the estimated elasticity

[7] As described in Table 14.3, the sector 'construction' is only identified for the zone MD, hence all firms in the construction sector are not included in the regressions.

Table 14A.1. Labour productivity models (dependent variable: average value added per worker)

	Model 1	Model 2	Model 3	Model 4
VARIABLES				
Constant	***1.03******* (0.95)	***4.36**** (1.13)	***5.4**** (1.17)	***5.6**** (1.17)
Ln K (capital)	***0.098**** (0.02)	***0.093**** (0.02)	***0.095**** (0.019)	***0.099**** (0.019)
Ln h (human capital)	***0.90**** (0.09)	***0.64**** (0.10)	***0.53**** (0.10)	***0.54**** (0.11)
Ln N (intensity by labour size)	***0.025*** (0.05)	–0.016 (0.046)	0.006 (0.045)	–0.022.(0.045)
FZ=1 if firm operates in FZ	—	***0.66**** (0.13)	***0.55**** (0.13)	***0.98**** (0.19)
Sectors:				
Light manufacturing	—	—	***–0.58*** (0.14)	—
Heavy manufacturing	—	—	–0.094 (0.15)	—
Trading	—	—	***0.59**** (0.15)	—
Non-financial services	—	—	0.08 (0.14)	—
Financial services	—	—	reference category	—
Interaction terms: FZ firms				
Light manufacturing* FZ=1	—	—	—	***0.46**** (0.16)
Heavy manufacturing*FZ=1	—	—	—	–0.02 (0.17)
Trading*FZ=1	—	—	—	***–1.1**** (0.19)
Non-financial services*FZ=1	—	—	—	***–0.34****** (0.17)
Financial services*FZ=1	—	—	—	reference category
Interaction terms: MD firms				
Light manufacturing*MD=1	—	—	—	–0.36.(0.39)
Heavy manufacturing*MD=1	—	—	—	–0.12.(0.27)
Trading*MD=1	—	—	—	–0.22.(0.24)
Non-financial services*MD=1	—	—	—	***–0.48******.(0.24)
Financial services*MD=1	—	—	—	reference category
DIAGNOSTICS				
Adjusted R^2	0.21	0.25	0.31	0.34
Sample size	502	502	502	502

Notes: (1) We have to drop all firms in the construction sector from our estimation. This leads to a sample size of 502 enterprises; (2) * and ** indicate significance at least at 99% and 95% levels, respectively.

Source: Own elaboration based on data from 2010 Dubai Enterprise Level Survey

due 'labour intensity', should be negative thus showing that larger size has negative effects on productivity holding everything else constant. However, despite it not being negative it is clear that the magnitude of the coefficient—0.022—is relatively small and, moreover, the variable is not statistically significant.

The location effect, reflecting the externality internalized by firms located in the FZ, is highly significant and positive. Regression 2 controls for the overall FZ effect and finds that, compared to MD firms with similar characteristics, labour productivity in the FZ firms exceeds the former by 93 per cent $\{= (e^{0.66} - 1)100\%\}$. And though the FZ location externality is reduced when we control for sector effects (regression 3), the productivity differential is still high at 73 per cent. The economic significance of regressions 2 and 3 estimates is that, controlling for sector- and firm-level characteristics, the FZ offers firms strong network and other externalities that are not available to their counterparts in MD.

As for the sector-specific effects, regression 3 suggests that, relative to financial services firms (the reference sector), labour productivity of light manufacturing firms with identical production structures[8] tends to be lower by about 79 per cent. On the other hand, labour productivity of firms specializing in trading would exceed financial services firms by 80 per cent. Finally, relative to the reference sector, heavy manufacturing and non-financial services sectors do not have significant marginal productivity effects. This suggests that firms from the three sectors are likely to have similar levels of labour productivity.

Finally, being the most encompassing model, regression 4 allows for sector-specific location externality. The results are very interesting and suggest that, as should be expected, the FZ location externality tends to differ quite substantially across sectors.

First, we find that no significant sector-specific location effect was found for the case of heavy manufacturing (or, by construction, for financial services given that it is the reference sector) beyond the overall positive FZ location effect relative to MD, given by the estimated elasticity of 0.98. Therefore, labour productivity of a heavy manufacturing (or financial services) firm located in the FZ will be almost 2.7 times that of an identical MD firm ($2.66 = e^{0.98}$).

Second, the FZ location externality is most influential for the case of light manufacturing, where the sector-specific location externality tends to reinforce the overall positive externality (0.98+0.46=1.44). This suggests that, other things being equal, labour productivity of light manufacturing firms in the FZ will be more than four times that of their counterparts in MD ($4.22 = e^{1.44}$).

Third, on the other hand, the FZ 'net' location externality is still positive but much lower for the case of non-financial services. In this case MD presents sector-specific externality that partially ameliorates the overall FZ positive externality (0.98 – 0.34= 0.64). This suggests that for two identical non-financial services firms drawn from the two economic regions, labour productivity in the FZ firm will exceed that of MD by 90 per cent. A qualitatively similar estimate also follows if we consider the location externality from the perspective of firms located in MD, where these firms suffer from a 'net' negative externality, compared to their counterpart in the FZ. In this case labour productivity in the FZ firm will exceed that of MD by 65 per cent ($= e^{0.98-0.48} - 1$).[9]

[8] Due to the fact that we control for the factors of production.

[9] Note that this is the only statistically significant location-sectorial interaction effect from the perspective of firms located in MD.

Fourth, with regard to the trading sector MD provides stronger location externalities than do the FZ, where the former region presents sector-specific externality that trumps the overall FZ positive externality (0.98 – 1.1= –0.12). This suggests that, for identical firms operating in the trading sectors, labour productivity of those located in MD will exceed their FZ counterparts by 13 per cent.

Finally, we exploit the two-way typology of firms by economic zone and sectors to sub-divide the sample of the 502 firms into sub-groups. The sample represents two economic zones (where we combine the FZ financial sector to the DIFC) and five industrial sectors (not including construction); it implies that we can sub-divide the sample of 502 into—at most—ten sub-groups. With obvious notation the average value of $\ln y_i$ for each of these subgroups can be expressed as $\ln \bar{y}_{FZ,Sj}$ (for any of the j-sectors in the FZ) and $\ln \bar{y}_{MD,Sj}$ (for any of the j-sectors in MD). For each given sector sj, the expressions for the average difference in VAW and its decomposition can be easily derived using equation 14A.1 above, where the coefficients are given by the estimates of regression 4 (of Table 14.4):

$$\begin{aligned}\ln \bar{y}_{FZ,Sj} - \ln \bar{y}_{DM,Sj} = (0.98 + \alpha_{FZ,Sj})FZ + 0.099(\ln \bar{k}_{FZ,Sj} - \ln \bar{k}_{MD,Sj}) \\ +0.54(\ln \bar{h}_{FZ,Sj} - \ln \bar{h}_{MD,Sj}) + 0.022(\ln \bar{n}_{FZ,Sj} - \ln \bar{n}_{MD,Sj}) \\ +(\ln \bar{\epsilon}_{FZ,Sj} - \ln \bar{\epsilon}_{MD,Sj}) \qquad (14A.2)\end{aligned}$$

Where the 'net' sector-specific FZ location externality effect is $(0.98 + \alpha_{FZ,Sj})FZ$ and $(\ln \bar{\epsilon}_{FZ,Sj} - \ln \bar{\epsilon}_{MD,Sj})$ is the average TFP differential between the FZ and MD.

REFERENCES

Bigsten, A. et al., 2002. 'Do African Manufacturing Firms Learn from Exporting?' Working Paper WPS/2002-09. Centre for the Study of African Economies, Oxford.

Dubai Economic Council, 2011. *Dubai Economic Outlook—2010 Q4*, Dubai: Dubai Economic Council.

Easterly, W., and Levine, R., 2001. 'It Is not Factor Accumulation: Stylized Facts and Growth Models'. *World Bank Economic Review*, 15(2): 177–219.

Elbadawi, I., and Soto, R., 2012. 'Sources of Economic Growth and Development Strategy in Dubai'. In A. Al Sadik and I. A. Elbadawi (eds) *The Global Economic Crisis and Consequences for Development Strategy in Dubai*. New York: Palgrave Macmillan, pp. 121–53.

Hadi, A., 1992. 'Identifying Multiple Outliers in Multivariate Data'. *Journal of the Royal Statistical Society, Journal of the Royal Statistical Society, Series B (Methodological)*, 54(3): 761–71.

IMF, 2011. *World Economic Outlook*, Washington DC: IMF.

JAFZA, 2011. *Impact of Jebel Ali FZ on Dubai and the UAE Economy*, Dubai: Jebel Ali FZ Authority.

Johnson, R. C., 2012. 'Trade and Prices with Heterogeneous Firms'. *Journal of International Economics*, 886(1): 43.

Matsuyama, K., 1992. 'Agricultural Productivity, Comparative Advantage, and Economic Growth'. *Journal of Economic Theory*, 58(2): 317–34.

Rodrik, D., 2007. 'Why Does the Real Exchange Rate Matter to Growth?' Unpublished mimeo, Kennedy School of Government, Harvard University.

Soto, R., and Vazquez-Alvarez, R., 2011. 'The Efficiency Costs of the Kafala in Dubai: A Stochastic Frontier Analysis'. Documento de Trabajo 399, Instituto de Economia. Pontificia Universidad Católica de Chile.

UNDP, 2009. Arab Knowledge Report 2009: Towards Productive Intercommunication for Knowledge. Dubai: Al Ghurair Printing & Publishing House LLC.

15

Main Lessons and Policy Recommendations

Abdulrazak Al Faris and Raimundo Soto

During the last fifty years, Dubai transformed itself from a small fishing and trading village into an integrated, modern, and vibrant economy. The development process, as in most Gulf economies, was initiated by oil richness but, unlike all other GCC countries, it has successfully diversified away from hydrocarbons with the creation of world-class clusters of financial services, tourism, and trading activities. Understandably, Dubai has become a model of economic development not only for the other six emirates of the UAE but also for most regional economies. Indeed, its success in diversifying its economic base makes Dubai an interesting case study for any resource-dependent economy wishing to achieve sustainable prosperity by engaging in better-balanced growth paths than those typically induced by the mere exploitation of natural resources.

Economic prosperity in Dubai is largely the result of implementing the adequate economic policies at the right time in order to benefit from economic opportunities and avoid costly mistakes. In this, the emirate is no different from other successful economies. Its strength has been in identifying such opportunities, devising adequate policies and persevering in their implementation, and, most important, in providing the institutional environment needed for those policies to flourish. The emirate prides itself on its long-standing tradition of favouring free trade and supporting private initiative as a basic source of economic development. In this regard Dubai has performed very differently from other GCC economies and most oil-rich countries where resource rents in public hands have suffocated the private sector and led to very fragile institutional arrangements. In doing this, Dubai has largely avoided the so-called 'resource curse'.

This volume is the result of a long-term effort on the part of the Dubai Economic Council to undertake a systematic and scientific analysis of the economy of Dubai. Our purpose is to identify the sources of economic growth and the policies that have been instrumental in its success, understand the nature of its main development challenges, and identify the reforms and policies needed to secure those achievements in the future. In this, this volume fills a gap in our knowledge and understanding and provides valuable lessons for other economies. The first part of this book focuses on understanding the evolution of the economy from an aggregate or macroeconomic perspective; the second part takes a long-run view on the development of the most important sectors; while the third part studies the factors underlying economic progress in Dubai.

From a macroeconomic perspective, Dubai was one of the economies with the fastest development pace in the world between 1975 and 2010. Although the global economic crisis of 2008–10 badly hit the emirate and put a temporary halt to its expansion, its subsequent recovery was strong and the economy rapidly returned to high-growth levels. In this regard, Dubai's economy reflects the sensibility of small open economies to world economic cycles but it also attests to the fast recovery provided by high degrees of integration into global markets. While Dubai has largely maintained a solid macroeconomic stance—with the exception of the few years leading to global crisis—there are three important weaknesses in the sustainability of Dubai's development path.

First, there is evidence that *economic growth was mainly induced by the significant accumulation of physical capital and massive inflow of foreign workers and not by achieving ever-higher productivity levels.* In fact, labour productivity has grown slower in Dubai than in other economies enjoying similar characteristics (small, open, natural-resource limited) such as Hong Kong and Singapore and, in fact, remained stagnant for a long period of time between 1987 and 2004. Productivity growth is largely the result of a myriad of efficiency gains at the firm, industry, and sector level. The different chapters in this book provide perspectives on why productivity has not grown steadily and unanimously conclude that sustainable development requires policy reforms aimed at making production less resource dependent and increasingly more efficient.

Second, *Dubai also exhibits significant vulnerability to external shocks and domestic production is volatile despite its limited dependence on the hydrocarbon sector.* In part, this is the result of the lack of automatic stabilizers in the economy. The economy of the UAE is largely shaped by the absence of monetary policy resulting from fixing the exchange rate to the US dollar. This effectively eliminates monetary and exchange rate policies, leaving the authorities with fiscal policies as their main policy instrument. But fiscal policy in Dubai is limited vis-à-vis most economies in the use of taxes and other forms of government revenues since income and value-added taxes are conspicuously absent. The government, in fact, exacts taxes mainly in the form of fees for services which complement other revenues arising from its numerous business endeavours in real estate and trading. In Dubai the tax system cannot perform its countercyclical role (since it is largely based on fixed fees and not *ad valorem* levies) and government expenditures tend to be pro-cyclical (the result of the lack of consolidated, multiannual budget procedures). Implementing a medium-term expenditure framework—as opposed to the current annual cash-based budget preparations—is needed for the Dubai government to better guide its multi-year fiscal activities and help maintain long-term fiscal stability and sustainable growth.

Third, *contrary to its historical reliance on the private sector, to a large extent economic growth in Dubai in the decade leading to the global crisis was driven by massive government investment* in the hands of largely unsupervised government-related entities (GREs) operating in real estate and construction. The increasing importance of GREs in key economic sectors has become a major weakness of Dubai's economic strategy. On one hand, to maintain the soundness of fiscal policy additional efforts are needed to mitigate the risks arising from both the timing and amounts of the debt repayments and the perception of opaqueness in the performance of most GREs. On the other hand, economic incentives are needed for such GREs to perform efficiently and, most importantly, to avoid the implicit guarantee of government bailouts every time they run into trouble. GREs, which largely enjoy monopolistic power, crowd out the private sector which finds itself unable to compete with firms that have preferential treatment. The development of businesses in Dubai is not only about allowing investors to operate in good conditions but also about setting rules of the game that are clear, transparent, and conducive to an environment where only the most productive businesses survive. Producers—both private and public—must be free to fail because what matters for development is not more business, but more productive businesses. Predicting which businesses will be best for Dubai is not a task for the government but it can help in preparing and levelling the ground and it can even facilitate the development of certain sectors: ultimately competition will reveal what works and what does not.

Macroeconomic growth, naturally, reflects the performance of the different industries operating in the economy at each point in time. Some of these industries—such as those engaged in foreign trade, financial services, or tourism—have been identified by scholars and government authorities as key to future economic development. This volume collects studies on the performance of five key industries (foreign trade, free-trade zones, tourism, retail, and the financial sector) from which we derive important conclusions and recommendations for policy reforms.

Foreign trade has been historically one main source of sustained economic growth in Dubai since the mid 1850s and is envisioned to continue being a crucial sector in an increasingly integrated global economy. Small open economies cannot rely on domestic demand for sustained development and must turn to foreign markets. The latter provide sizeable demand for exported products which in turn allow domestic producers to reap scale economies, incentivize the adoption of better and advanced production techniques and reward the prudent investment and creativity of exporters. Moreover, foreign trade disciplines firms by forcing them to operate in more competitive environments. Overall, this boosts the efficiency and productivity of domestic firms thereby enhancing their competitiveness in the global markets. In this regard, Dubai has benefited from its strategic geographical location and from developing world-class transportation and logistics networks aimed at making the emirate a leading hub of international trade. However, improving its competitive capacity, building a resilient economic base, and profiting from the opportunities provided by fast-changing global markets require comprehensive trade policies. In particular, because the advantages in terms of location as a regional hub are not unique to Dubai: Qatar, Bahrain, and even the other emirates of the UAE share a similar location and could become competitors for, essentially, the same trade routes and cargo.

Several pressing issues need policy actions. First and foremost, *there is ample space for Dubai to expand exporting and re-exporting activities*. The city-state economies that Dubai would like to emulate in its role of regional trade hubs—Hong Kong or Singapore—export and re-export four or five times more than Dubai. Fostering exports and re-exports should be a priority for trade policy. Second, *Dubai's exports and re-exports appear to be dangerously concentrated both in terms of the product space and in partners*. Over one half of exports and re-exports are concentrated in one good (gold and jewellery) putting Dubai in a risky position as international commodity prices are notoriously unstable. In addition, exports and re-exports are also largely concentrated on two partners: India and Iran. While trade with India ought to increase in the future as the Indian subcontinent grows, trade with Iran is far riskier. While historically Iran has been an important trade partner, current trade volumes are largely the result of UN sanctions and they would certainly reduce significantly should the sanctions be relaxed or lifted altogether. Third, *export and re-exports are concentrated on goods with low technological content and with little linkages with the rest of the economy*: gold and jewellery contain some processing but their elaboration is not very sophisticated and does not link significantly with other industries thus hampering the growth-enhancing role of foreign trade.

Dubai's authorities, aware of the need to boost foreign trade as an engine of growth, have promoted the development of free-trade (or export-promoting) zones (FTZs). These special areas are designed to attract foreign investment, expand exports, and create employment in the host economy. JAFZA, the first of such endeavours established in 1985, has become one of the largest and fastest growing FTZs in the world. Two-dozen FTZs followed JAFZA's path with varying degrees of success. DEC's survey of 700 firms in 2010 indicate that *firms located in the FTZs outperform significantly their counterparts in Main Dubai in terms of productivity, capital investment, qualification of their manpower, and total factor productivity.* Furthermore, the evidence also indicates that only two of these FTZs (JAFZA and the Dubai International Financial Center) have been successful in building significant backward linkages with other sectors in the economy, thus fostering sustainable growth, while the rest have not benefited from its special-area status and perform in a similar fashion to firms in Main Dubai. The policy implication of these conclusions is that there is ample space to improve on the performance of FTZs and, more importantly, of firms in Main Dubai. Note that there is a need to understand the reasons for the lack of success in most FTZs—excluding the aforementioned JAFZA and DIFC—and provide for corrective measures. More importantly, the evidence indicates that *significant policy reforms are needed to boost the performance of firms in Main Dubai by increasing competition, rationalizing the tax system, and improving the institutional framework vis-à-vis land markets, access to financial markets, and labour market regulations.* It is precisely the improved treatment received by firms in JAFZA and DIFC regarding these issues that make them more competitive, more productive and, in the end, more likely to expand and boost sustainable economic prosperity.

Competition in world markets depends not only on the ability of Emirati entrepreneurs to produce and place goods in the markets at an advantageous price–quality relationship but also on the support and contribution of other sectors. One key conclusion arising from the firm-level evidence is that the largest majority of Dubai firms have very limited access to the financial market and are less-than-optimally served by domestic banks. The financial sector plays a crucial role in providing working capital for producers and trade financing for both exporters and importers, in channelling resources for investment and lending, and in developing coverage from fluctuations and business risks. A number of policy recommendations emerge to cope with these limitations. First, there is a *pressing need to improve risk management practices in Dubai-based banks,* including investing in data collection, reporting systems, and validation capacity. This will improve the assessment of risk, improve on portfolio management, and allow for lower spreads in interest rates thus expanding profitable investments. Second, *corporate governance standards in the banking sector are to be significantly improved,* in particular to instil appropriate levels of accountability and enforce good practices in checks and balances. Third, *the supervisory role of the Central Bank ought to be enhanced* to deal with institutions that might increase systemic risks and to allow for the development of domestic bonds.

One sector that seems to be less affected by economic fluctuations or the limitations in access to financial markets is tourism. As a tourist destination

Dubai is largely a man-made project. The lack of historical, natural, or heritage attractions forced the emirate to base its industry primarily on developing the offer of tourist accommodations and the physical infrastructure that determines the quality of the visit for a tourist. This mix has been quite successful and made tourism an engine for sustained growth in Dubai. Despite its success, there is a *need to reappraise the strategy of the tourism industry*, in particular vis-à-vis the emergence of regional contenders (e.g. Qatar). The weaknesses evidenced by the industry during the global crisis suggest that the business strategy of the sector might have grown into maturity and offers limited expansion in the future. Much of the tourism in Dubai is associated either with the luxury segment of the market (sensitive to income fluctuations) or to low-income travellers (sensitive to price fluctuations); the more stable middle-income segment has been largely neglected. This makes the tourism industry in Dubai riskier than that in better-diversified economies and susceptible to downturns. Furthermore, by focusing on the luxury segment, the industry loses potential visitors from fast-growing emerging economies (China, India, and Brazil). In addition to expanding the scope of visitors, *there is a role for the government to reduce the administrative cost for visitors, in particular regarding entry visas*. Visa issuing is a cumbersome, expensive, and arbitrary process by which citizens of some countries are exempt from any requirement or costs while others need to secure a sponsor and pay the exorbitant sum for a single-entry, no reapplication visa.

Closely linked to tourism, retail activities have also experienced notorious expansion in the preceding two decades. In terms of its contribution to GDP, the industry is about the same size as the financial sector, the real estate, or the construction sector. Dubai shopping malls are among the largest and most sophisticated in the world and customers benefit from access to a wide variety of goods and services in all qualities. However, some reforms would improve its performance significantly. First, *public bureaucracy, red tape, and the lack of consistency in government rules and regulations are identified by the CEOs of the retail companies as a main limitation when doing business*. Dubai ranks far below Hong Kong and Singapore and other emerging economies in retail and real estate transparency. Transparency becomes a decisive aspect when attracting foreign direct investment, improving the operation of the different segments of the markets, and fostering innovation and technological upgrades. To the extent that retail operates largely in an international context, partnership with foreign retail companies is the cornerstone to further development of the retail industry in Dubai. Second, *one out of three companies in Dubai indicates that the labour force is the most problematic factor for doing business*. Government regulations and arbitrary labour fees reduce the flexibility of the labour market and the ability of firms to adjust to economic fluctuations. For example, retailers cannot hire part-time workers to cope with seasonal fluctuations (such as Christmas or its famous Shopping Festivals).

Production in modern economies largely depends on the quality and training of its labour force, the working of the labour market, the cost of energy, access to physical capital (particularly, land) and, naturally, the efficiency and productivity in the use of such resources.

The quality of the labour force has been identified as a main limitation to economic development by retail and financial sectors as well as other economic activities. The quality of the labour force, in turn, largely depends on the formal and informal education of workers. For a long time the UAE—and particularly Dubai—has relied on other countries to provide the necessary manpower, be it in the form of highly trained expatriates from Western Europe or low-skilled immigrants from the Indian sub-continent. However, long-term development requires that Dubai develop the ability to generate domestically a well-educated, highly productive labour force to create and direct new businesses. It is therefore not surprising that the government has implemented several policies to foster domestic education of Emirati and expatriates.

In less than thirty years, Dubai has completely transformed its education sector from a group of weak schools without a national curriculum into a modern, dynamic education system. Access to primary and secondary education has been extended to the entire population regardless of their nationality, while enrolment in tertiary education has grown dramatically in the first decade of this century. This is a remarkable achievement that speaks highly of the commitment on the part of the government to human capital formation. The task, nevertheless, is only half completed. Although access to education has increased, the quality of such education has not progressed at a similar pace. While primary education is of average quality for international standards, secondary education is quite limited and does not match either the skills demanded by the labour market or the minimum abilities required at the university level. The evidence indicates that the quality of education is also highly unequal, with private schools outperforming public schools by a substantial margin, and gender biased, whereby boys in public schools and universities perform worse than girls and drop out at a much higher rate.

The mediocre quality of the education system is a serious limitation to long-run development. The government of Dubai recently started to implement measures to improve on quality, yet these measures are timid and/or still in their initial stages to be properly evaluated. The federal government has also started to address the serious limitations of public sector schools and national universities. The evidence in this volume suggest that, to improve quality, *the government ought to change the industrial organization of the education sector, modifying the incentives given to the different actors so that they operate under more efficient frameworks, implementing new policies where existing ones are insufficient or incomplete, and injecting accountability where none is currently in place.*

In most economies the desire to invest in education is largely determined by its return in the form of wages and earnings. In Dubai, the dual labour market significantly weakens these incentives and induces lower-than-optimal levels of human capital formation. As is the case with other GCC countries, Dubai's workforce is largely shaped by two concurrent phenomena: the sponsorship system (*Kafala* in Arabic) governing the participation of expatriates and the protection for nationals embedded in both the Emiratization programme and the public sector employment policies. Since workers under the *Kafala* find it nearly impossible to change sponsor, employers enjoy market power and collect sizeable economic rents. And because extracting rents is easier the less skilled the worker is, production tends to be labour-intensive and of low productivity. Emirati, on the other hand, are not subject to the sponsorship system but are protected by the rules and regulations emanating from the Emiratization programme. These shelter them from openly competing with expatriates in the labour market but they also reduce their employability, particularly that of young and inexperienced workers. Since the private sector cannot afford the relatively more expensive national workers, Emirati are mainly employed by the public sector (around 80 per cent are civil servants).

The evidence indicates that, beyond raising unemployment among Emirati, the current labour market regulations reduce businesses efficiency and hamper technology adoption. In keeping government intervention as the centrepiece of labour policies, the authorities might have been induced to believe that increases in labour costs would reduce the profitability of firms and, therefore, the incentives to invest in new, more efficient technologies. The empirical evidence indicates that this is incorrect: private sector profits and riches have grown significantly since the 1990s and employment has expanded massively, but labour productivity has stagnated because in keeping wages low it has favoured rent extraction and not given entrepreneurs incentives to acquire more advanced technologies.

The unintended yet adverse effects of government intervention manifest also in two other key areas for Dubai's development—energy and land—calling for urgent remedial polices. Historically, the UAE government has maintained energy prices at very low levels in order to favour industrial development. However, as a result of suboptimal government policies, energy demand in Dubai has grown at an explosive pace in the last two decades and energy efficiency is low by international standards. Energy efficiency, in turn, is a key determinant of productivity gains as market-driven energy prices demand that producers implement cost-saving measures and better technologies. Policies aiming at rebalancing energy markets are therefore urgently needed. The first recommendation is to *enact market incentives to guide the energy provision and use in Dubai along economically rational patterns.* Large investments in building new power stations, power transmission lines, and fuel storage and supply facilities are required to cope with expanding industrial and residential demand and there are mounting pressures on the public sector to provide such investments. But keeping energy in government hands in the past has not necessarily solved the issue efficiently as it led to prices that are not market-driven and for energy to be heavily subsidized. As an alternative, *the government ought to allow public–private partnership projects and a change in current regulations to increase the private sector's willingness to invest in energy projects.* Second, for a more rational use of the available energy *the government ought also to implement a combination of demand-side management programmes* (such as load management programmes, peak-clipping, and load-shifting in electricity) *and economic incentives to reduce consumption* (peak-load pricing, energy-saving rebates, etc.). Economic incentives, which proved to be the most powerful tool for energy-saving in most countries, have not been used in Dubai.

Likewise, the market for land has been kept in government hands and mainly developed by GREs operating, as mentioned, under rather opaque institutional arrangements. In most economies of the world, land availability is not a deterrent to economic growth. In some economies, as in Europe, land is scarce but appropriate market regulations and well-defined property rights allow the price mechanism to allocate the available land to its most efficient or socially profitable use. Arguably, land markets in these economies can fall prey to speculation and housing price bubbles, thereby suggesting that monitoring is needed in addition to market regulations and property rights.

In Dubai the commercial land market is significantly different in most dimensions and this affects the efficient use of resources, productivity growth, and economic development. The market for commercial land is based on allocating usage as opposed to rights: only Emirati individuals and companies can own land while expatriates can, at best, obtain a long-term right of usage even within the confines of free zones. The empirical evidence shows that over 50 per cent of firms surveyed in the 2010 Enterprise Level Survey claimed that 'lack of access to land' is their major obstacle to their business operation. Likewise leasing prices for retail shops show substantially more volatility than the norm in more developed economies as a result of the land supply being irresponsive to market pressures. This suggests that the institutional framework allowing rent leases to be capable of mimicking the positive outcomes of full property rights is not in place in Dubai and that, therefore, significant inefficiencies may be hampering the allocation of resources to best uses. The available evidence concludes that access to land largely depends on the ownership of the company and its location: firms in Main Dubai that are foreign owned are more likely to have problems of access to land than their counterparts in free zones or than firms in Main Dubai fully owned by Emirati entrepreneurs. Beyond inefficiencies in land allocation, reforms are required because restrictions to access land also have adverse effects on both physical and human capital investment: firms claiming that they lack access to land invest significantly less in physical capital and provide little or no training to their employees. The reason is simple: in order to recover the costs of such investments, entrepreneurs need the security that the benefits of improved operations are not going to be taxed away by the government in the form of higher land costs or prematurely terminated land leases.

Dubai has made great advances in terms of economic and social development in the last fifty years. Its experience is both a source of pride for the Emirati and its government as well as an inspiration for other economies in the region and elsewhere. There is much to learn from its successes and failures. This volume aims at providing a comprehensive and balanced view of the vision and economic policies that led to such outcomes.

Nevertheless, the ever-changing conditions of economic activity, the presence of foreign shocks, and the development of the society of Dubai will require new policies to be implemented in the short and long run to secure those achievements and foster a sustainable path of development. This book also identifies guidelines for the main reforms that ought to be implemented, sooner or later, to cope with the current and most pressing limitations of the development strategy.

Index

The manufacturer's authorised representative in the EU for product safety is Oxford University Press España S.A. of el Parque Empresarial San Fernando de Henares, Avenida de Castilla, 2 – 28830 Madrid (www.oup.es/en or product.safety@oup.com). OUP España S.A. also acts as importer into Spain of products made by the manufacturer.

www.ingramcontent.com/pod-product-compliance
Lightning Source LLC
LaVergne TN
LVHW011908200926
848484LV00002B/566
9780198758389